SOUTHERN AFRICAN
QUICK AND DELICIOUS
COOKBOOK

SOUTHERN AFRICAN
QUICK AND DELICIOUS
COOKBOOK

The Reader's Digest Association South Africa (Pty) Limited
Cape Town

First edition copyright © 1996
The Reader's Digest Association South Africa (Pty) Limited
130 Strand Street, Cape Town 8001

All rights reserved. No part of this book may be reproduced, translated
or stored in a retrieval system or transmitted in any form or by any means,
electronic, electrostatic, magnetic tape, mechanical photocopying, recording
or otherwise, without permission in writing from the publishers.
Reader's Digest and the Pegasus logo are registered trademarks of
The Reader's Digest Association Inc. of Pleasantville, New York, USA

ISBN 1-874912-44-0

QUICK AND DELICIOUS was edited at
The Reader's Digest Association South Africa (Pty) Limited, based on
an original work produced by Carroll & Brown Limited, London

PROJECT EDITOR Judy Beyer
ART EDITOR Valerie Phipps-Smith
CONSULTANT EDITOR Phillippa Cheifitz
RECIPE TESTERS Sarah Bush, Phillippa Cheifitz, Barbara Flax,
Marthajean White
PHOTOGRAPHERS Roger Bell, David Murray
FOOD FOR PHOTOGRAPHY Vo Pollard, Eric Treuillé, Mandy Wagstaff
PROP STYLISTS Elaine Charlesworth, Vo Pollard
PROJECT CO-ORDINATORS Carol Adams, Tania Johnson, Grant Moore
PROOFREADERS Josina Barnes, Pat Kramer, Gerda Martin
INDEXER Ethleen Lastovica

COVER PHOTO *Spaghetti with bacon and vegetables, page 226*
PAGE 2 *(from the top) Gingered beef kebabs, page 174; Rotelle with cheese and walnuts,
page 219; Paprika chicken, page 139*

The publishers would like to thank the following for their kind loan
of props for some of the photographs taken for this book:
Bric a Brac Lane, Claremont
China Works, Harfield Village
Peter Visser Interiors, Cape Town
Stuttafords, Claremont

FOREWORD

Everyone agrees that the best meals are home-made ones, lovingly prepared by someone who cares about good cooking. Yet our busy time schedules keep getting in the way. While we're determined to serve healthy, tasty food, we also want to make it quickly and with a minimum of fuss.

Quick and Delicious takes care of both of these needs beautifully in each of more than 500 recipes. The idea behind this book is that cooking with fresh ingredients need not mean long and complicated preparation – and that fresh foods can sometimes be combined with those that are tinned or ready-made in order to streamline the cooking process. The result is a wholesome and delicious dish served by a relaxed cook.

The recipes in *Quick and Delicious* include filling main dishes made with meat, poultry, fish, eggs, cheese, pasta and vegetables. There are also main-dish soups and salads, plus snacks that are hearty enough to be served as a light meal. Inventive side dishes include party appetizers, easy breads, lighter salads and vegetables. And, to bring your meals to a triumphant finale, we include desserts you can create in an instant – fruit desserts, fresh tarts, frozen confections and even cakes.

How quick is quick?

With the exception of a few make-ahead recipes in the first chapter, most of the recipes in this book can be made in 45 minutes or less. This includes preparation and cooking or chilling time, from the point at which the ingredients are taken from the pantry or shopping bag to the final, ready-to-eat, creation. Each recipe has been fully tested, where the preparation and cooking were timed realistically, with the average home cook in mind.

The book's first chapter shows you how a little advance planning, including organising your kitchen, can save time later. But, even if you are a spontaneous cook who decides what to prepare only at the last minute, you'll find that most of the recipes are surprisingly simple to make. Your family and friends are sure to applaud the impressive results.

Whether you want to serve an elegant dinner for guests or make a casual weeknight supper for the family, *Quick and Delicious* will provide you with all the inspiration you need to set a table that pleases you and those you love.

CONTENTS

ABOUT THIS BOOK 8

THE QUICK COOK 9

APPETIZERS AND SNACKS 35
Appetizers 36
Snacks 54

SOUPS 71
First-course soups 72
Main-course soups 82

SEAFOOD 97

POULTRY 129

MEAT 169
Beef 170
Lamb 190
Pork and sausage 194

PASTA AND GRAINS 211
Pasta 212
Grains 234

From the top:
Chunky salsa, page 48
Chicken soup, page 81
Chicken breast with honey mustard sauce, page 157

Eggs and cheese 245

Vegetables 271
Vegetable accompaniments 272
Main-course vegetables 286

Salads 293
Salad accompaniments 294
Main-course salads 310

Breads, cakes and biscuits 321
Breads 322
Cakes 334
Biscuits 342

Desserts 349
Fruit desserts 350
Frozen desserts 360
Custards and soufflés 370
Pies and tarts 378

Index 390

From the top:
Pasta with broccoli pesto sauce, page 223
Green salad with curried yoghurt dressing, page 305
Tutti-frutti sundae, page 365

ABOUT THIS BOOK

Quick and Delicious has been designed to provide a complete range of recipes that require little cooking time yet produce irresistible and satisfying dishes for your family and friends.

The quick cook
In order to make full use of this book, begin by looking at the ideas set out in THE QUICK COOK chapter. In it you will find suggestions for useful kitchen equipment, from large items like food processors and microwave ovens (which can provide substantial time-saving in the kitchen but are very rarely necessary for the recipes in this book), to small items like citrus juicers and pastry blenders. There are also some preliminary recipes for stocks, pie crusts and other basics that you can make ahead and store for later, as well as abundant entertaining tips and creative menu suggestions that allow you to spend less time working in the kitchen and more time with your guests. Perhaps the most important feature in THE QUICK COOK is a list of basic ingredients to keep on hand as they frequently appear in the recipes in this book.

Shelf magic
Certain super-quick recipes throughout the book take full advantage of the staples and convenience foods you probably have in your cupboard or freezer. Look for the SHELF MAGIC headings to find main-dish and side-dish recipes that are ready to serve in 15 minutes or less.

Time savers
Another feature you'll find throughout the book is called TIME SAVERS. These contain tips and information outlining ways to reduce preparation time. Their appeal lies in their simplicity – once done they won't be forgotten, as they are such practical suggestions.

Special variations
In every chapter of *Quick and Delicious* you'll find one or two special two-page features with creative ideas for dressing up simple dishes. One of these features, entitled START WITH ..., shows how to take ready-made foods such as soup stock, cooked chicken or pizza bases and, with just a few easy extras, turn them into delectable dishes in just a few minutes. The second type of special feature is entitled VARIATIONS ON THE BASIC..., in which we explain how to make a quick and basic recipe such as an omelette, a hamburger or a baked potato, and then suggest a number of creative variations to turn the dish into something really out of the ordinary. You'll find the range of recipe variations wide enough to inspire you to create some of your own culinary innovations.

Recipe notes
At the top of many of the recipes are introductory notes, such as COOK'S TIP, SERVING SUGGESTION, DIET NOTE or FOOD NOTE. In these introductions we offer some new ideas for shortening the preparation time even further, suggest simple accompaniments that can be made in minutes or purchased ready-made, provide useful information about an aspect of the dish that is particularly beneficial to your health or mention an interesting point about the origin or history of the dish.

Symbols
We have used the following symbols to give important information about each of the regular recipes:

 is the time it takes to prepare the ingredients before or after cooking, including any resting time.

 is the total amount of cooking time, not including the preparation of the ingredients. Where time is needed for chilling, this has been incorporated as Cooking/chilling time.

Once you start cooking, you'll see that *Quick and Delicious* has been planned first and foremost with you, the busy cook, in mind.

The Quick Cook

THE QUICK COOK'S PANTRY

A well-stocked kitchen is essential to the Quick Cook's peace of mind. If you keep a supply of staples in your pantry, refrigerator and freezer, you'll never be at a loss when putting together a last-minute recipe – all you will have to shop for are a few fresh ingredients and the rest will be ready and waiting for your creative culinary touch.

The recipes in this book rely on fresh ingredients first and foremost. But any cook will tell you that on some occasions you simply can't do 'fresh' and 'quick' at the same time. This is why we suggest using tinned goods, frozen foods or other ready-made products, combining them with fresh ingredients in such a way so as not to compromise taste. (In the special features labelled Shelf Magic, you'll find that the recipes rely almost entirely on packaged products – but the advantage is that each of the recipes is ready in 15 minutes or less.)

The list of pantry items that follows does not mention the traditional staples – flours, sugars and oils – that you already have. Instead, it consists of ingredients especially geared to the Quick Cook.

In addition, the boxes on page 13 list other dry ingredients, tinned goods and refrigerated and frozen items that you may want to keep on hand. Keep in mind that when you prepare any of the recipes in this book, you may want to save still more preparation time by using ready-made products, even when fresh ingredients are called for; it's for you to decide. Stock up your pantry, refrigerator and freezer, and find how you can make your kitchen work for you.

RECIPE SHORTCUTS

These ready-made staples help you cut out time-consuming preparation steps.

Tinned chopped tomatoes This invaluable ingredient is listed in many recipes throughout the book. The tomatoes are already peeled, seeded and chopped, and they usually have a better flavour in cooked dishes than the pretty, but sometimes tasteless, fresh tomatoes sold in the supermarket. Also available are tinned tomatoes mixed with onions and a variety of seasonings. These can pep up the simplest of meals.

Crushed garlic Packed in oil and sold in containers, crushed garlic is freely available. Half a teaspoon of pre-packed crushed garlic equals approximately one clove of freshly crushed garlic, which means, for example, using 1 teaspoon in Veal Parmigiana (page 188); you can adjust accordingly for other dishes. Dried chopped garlic is also useful. Half a teaspoon soaked in water for 10 minutes is the equivalent of 1 clove of garlic.

Grated cheeses Cheddar, Parmesan and mozzarella cheeses are sold already grated in various package sizes. You'll save lots of preparation time in making dishes such as Mozzarella Ramekins (page 265), or in filling a simple omelette.

Packaged bread crumbs Keep a box of plain bread crumbs in the pantry to use for crunchy toppings on baked dishes such as Stuffed Baby Marrows (page 283) and for crumb coatings on dishes such as Savoury Pan-Fried

Chicken Breasts (page 136) and Fish and Potato Pie (page 114). They'll save you the trouble of grinding fresh bread crumbs in the blender and, sealed in an airtight container, they'll store for a few months.

Prepared salad dressings The selection of bottled salad dressings available in the supermarket is getting more extensive all the time. Any of the salads that require dressing in this book can be tossed with the prepared dressing of your choice. If you prefer to make your own, there are many dressing recipes throughout the Salads chapter, including those in the special feature on page 305.

Cornflour This flavourless powder makes it possible to thicken sauces quickly, without having to make a roux of butter and flour. Most liquids can be thickened within two minutes after cornflour has been added. It is usually dissolved in a small amount of the cooking liquid or cold water before being added, in order to prevent lumps forming. Many of the poultry, meat and stir-fry dishes in this book make use of cornflour to thicken sauces quickly.

Quick-cooking oats Oats make a quick and warming meal when served on their own as a breakfast cereal, but you may also want to keep an extra box on the shelf for recipes like the delicious Date Muffins (page 332) and Oat-Raisin Biscuits (page 348).

Chopped nuts Packaged chopped nuts make dishes like Caramel Bananas (page 353) simple to prepare. Store a supply of a variety of nuts in your freezer to keep them fresh much longer than they would on the shelf. There's no need to thaw the nuts before adding them to a recipe.

Ready-rolled pastry Many of the recipes in this book need pie crusts. Use ready-rolled pastry to prepare these in minutes, as described in the recipe for Crusty Hot Dogs (page 70) or when preparing Nectarine Cheese Tart (page 378).

Ready whipped cream This is a real time saver when you compare it to the time spent whipping cream yourself (and cleaning up afterwards). Leftover cream stores perfectly in the freezer if it is first whipped stiffly. Store it in an airtight container. When unexpected guests drop in, remove the cream from the freezer and stir it gently with a fork. It will defrost in just a few minutes and is ideal for serving on scones.

Nonstick cooking spray This staple not only saves time by omitting the necessity of spreading butter or margarine in baking dishes, but it also saves on kilojoules since you use less of the spray than you would when using butter or oil.

EASY BASICS

These are staples of a different kind: they are a few key items that form the basis of dozens of dishes laid out in the special features throughout this book. Some you may want to make on your own and store for later, and some you will want to purchase; all of them are the building blocks for a variety of easy-to-make recipes.

Pizza base For a basic pizza dough that you can make ahead and freeze, see the recipe on page 26. There are also some delicious packaged bases available in the supermarket that you can freeze. You'll find a complete selection of pizzas to make on the special feature on page 62.

Tinned beef stock and chicken stock powder Throughout the Soups chapter, including the special feature on page 80, you will find stock in the list of ingredients. Since many people prefer to make their own, we've provided recipes for homemade stocks on pages 22 to 24. But if you prefer the simpler method, keep stock cubes or a few tins of stock powder in the cupboard as an indispensable ingredient in the majority of soups as well as many meat and poultry dishes.

Smoked ham This is one of the easiest meats to work with because it's ready-cooked when you buy it. For ideas on how to use it as the base for lunch and dinner recipes, see the special feature on page 198.

Pasta Spaghetti, penne, fusilli and linguine are just a few of the many pasta shapes you'll find at the supermarket. Keep a selection of different shapes in your pantry. For a delicious medley of sauces to accompany your pasta, refer to the special feature on page 222.

Basic butter cake See the feature on page 338 for ideas on how to turn this endlessly adaptable cake into everyday or fancy desserts. Make your own from the recipe on page 28 or substitute with a ready-made one purchased from a good bakery and stored in the freezer.

Ice cream and frozen yoghurt The special feature on page 364 offers tempting dessert ideas using ice cream or frozen yoghurt.

Crumb crusts Keep on hand as explained in the recipe on page 28. Flavoured biscuit crumb crusts are used to create the variety of pies in the special feature on page 384.

Pantry: dry ingredients

Stock cubes and powder
Tomato paste cubes
Croutons
Ramen noodles
Savoury biscuits and chips
Quick-cooking and
  flavoured rices
Raisins
Packaged pudding mixtures
Chocolate chips

Pantry: tinned goods

Chickpeas
Corn kernels
Kidney beans
Tomato and onion mixture
Tomato paste
Tomato sauce
Tuna
Shrimps
Black olives
Peaches
Pineapples
Pears

Refrigerator

Butter or margarine
Garlic butter
Low fat yoghurt
Ready-made barbecue sauce
Ready-made spaghetti sauce
Ready-made tomato salsa
Cream cheese
Grated Parmesan cheese
Fruit preserves
Pimentos
Lemon juice
Salad dressing

Freezer

Orange juice concentrate
Corn kernels
Mixed vegetables
Green beans
Peas
Spinach
Seafood mixture
Pastry
Pita breads
Pizza bases

When you're out of ...

Regardless of the number of trips to the supermarket, there always seems to be one ingredient in the recipe missing from your pantry or refrigerator. Rather than having to go out yet again, consult this list of convenient alternatives and you may find a substitute that you can use with almost the same results.

Ingredient Substitutions

If the recipe calls for:	Replace it with:	If the recipe calls for:	Replace it with:
baking powder, 1 teaspoon	= ¼ teaspoon bicarbonate of soda and ½ teaspoon cream of tartar	cottage cheese	= ricotta
		cornflour, 1 tablespoon	= 5 teaspoons flour and 2 teaspoons arrowroot = 2 teaspoons potato flour = 2 egg yolks
bread crumbs, 1 cup dry	= ¾ cup savoury biscuit crumbs = 2 cups fresh bread crumbs		
		Cream cheese	= Marscapone
		cream, 1 cup	= ⅞ cup buttermilk or yoghurt and 3 tablespoons (45g) butter = ¾ cup full cream milk and ⅓ cup (80g) melted butter
butter or margarine, 1 cup	= 1 cup vegetable shortening and ½ teaspoon salt	eggs (for thickening or baking), 1 whole	= 2 egg yolks
		fish stock	= vegetable or chicken stock
buttermilk, 1 cup	= 1 cup yoghurt = 1 cup full cream milk and 1 tablespoon vinegar	flour: plain (for thickening sauces), 1 tablespoon	= 1½ teaspoons cornflour = 1½ tablespoons arrowroot
chocolate, dark, 30g	= 3 tablespoons cocoa powder and 1 tablespoon (15g) butter or margarine	cake, 1 cup sifted	= 1 cup less 2 tablespoons plain flour

If the recipe calls for:	Replace it with:
fresh herbs, 1 tablespoon	= 1/3 to 1/2 teaspoon dried herbs
honey, 1/4 cup	= 5 tablespoons sugar and 1 tablespoon liquid
hot red pepper (Tabasco) sauce, 2 to 3 drops	= 1/8 teaspoon cayenne pepper
lemon juice, 1 teaspoon	= 1 teaspoon white wine = 1/2 teaspoon vinegar
milk, full cream, 1 cup	= 1/2 cup evaporated milk and 1/2 cup water = 1 cup skimmed milk and 2 tablespoons (30g) melted butter or cream
mushrooms, fresh, 4 cups sliced	= one 285g tin mushrooms, drained
olive oil	= sunflower oil
onion, chopped, 1 cup	= 1 tablespoon dried onion flakes
raisins	= finely chopped soft prunes or dates

If the recipe calls for:	Replace it with:
sour cream, 1 cup	= 3/4 cup milk and 2 1/2 teaspoons lemon juice and 1/3 cup (80g) melted butter: allow to stand for 10 minutes
stock powder, tinned	= 1 bouillon or stock cube dissolved in 1 cup hot water

sugar:
  granulated, 1 tablespoon
  1 cup
 	
  icing, 1 cup
	= 1 tablespoon castor sugar
	= 1 cup brown sugar
	= 1 cup molasses and 1/2 teaspoon bicarbonate of soda
	= 7/8 cup granulated sugar and 1 tablespoon cornflour processed in the blender

tomato sauce, 2 cups	= 3/4 cup tomato paste and 1 cup water

vinegar:
  balsamic
 	
  wine
	= slightly less red wine vinegar
	= cider vinegar and a dash of red wine
	= white distilled vinegar and a dash of white wine

yoghurt	= sour cream

Time-saving equipment

Considering all the time-saving gadgets available, there are only a few key items that truly reduce your time in the kitchen. To add to the standard pots, pans, bowls and spoons you already have on hand, here are a few pieces of equipment and valuable tools that will speed up the cooking process considerably. You won't need all of them, but you can decide which ones would be most helpful to you.

Kitchen shears for quickly cutting up meat, herbs and some vegetables; often faster than a knife.

Hand-held blender This new gadget is one step ahead of a conventional blender. It liquidizes food directly in the dish or saucepan you are using. The machine also makes milkshakes in an instant, directly in the glasses. You'll save preparation and cleaning time by not having to transfer the mixture to a blender container.

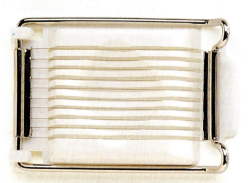

Egg slicer for slicing a hard-boiled egg evenly in one motion.

Four-sided grater for grating cheeses, chocolate and some vegetables.

Garlic press for crushing garlic quickly.

Sharp 20cm chef's knife for speeding up slicing and dicing; always keep knives well sharpened.

Sharp paring knife for cutting small items.

Pastry blender for easily cutting butter or margarine into flour.

Compact food processor The compact version of a full-size food processor is designed to handle the smaller-scale jobs of chopping and grating. The mini-processor is more economical in price and countertop space. If you tend to cook for only a few people at a time, this piece of equipment may be your best kitchen helper.

Long-handled slotted spoon for removing foods from their cooking liquids easily; prevents having to lift the pan to drain.

Citrus juicer for squeezing lemons and oranges; neat and simple using either design.

Salad spinner for drying salad leaves and fresh herbs with a few turns of the handle.

Melon-ball cutter for scooping melon into neat balls with ease.

Apple corer for coring fruit and vegetables in one motion.

Tongs for grasping hot portions of food easily during cooking.

Flexible rubber spatula for scraping out mixing bowls.

OTHER EQUIPMENT

Food processor
This is the best invention for reducing a cook's preparation time, and it's become an essential tool in many modern kitchens. It will easily slice, chop, grate and purée nearly any food in a fraction of the time it would take to do the same task by hand. With some careful reading of the instruction manual, you will be able to master all of the machine's many functions and labour-saving tricks. With a couple of additional attachments you can quickly whisk cream or egg whites, or knead dough for bread.

Blender
The blender is an old standby that is still valuable to the Quick Cook. It can be used instead of the food processor for puréeing soups, making biscuit crumbs and bread crumbs, as well as its most-used function, blending drinks.

Toaster oven
This is a wonderful standby on many kitchen counters, but it is frequently used only for small tasks like toasting bread and warming muffins. Due to its small size it takes very little time to preheat, thereby cutting down on the baking and grilling time for many other small dishes like chicken breasts and fish fillets.

Microwave oven
Without a doubt, this is the greatest modern advance for cutting cooking time. The best machines have a turntable, eliminating the need for constantly interrupting the cooking cycle to turn the dish around. Although microwave ovens are used most often for cooking frozen food and reheating leftovers, they can also be invaluable in assisting with preparing ingredients to go into a larger recipe, such as melting butter and chocolate or toasting nuts.

MICROWAVE OVEN BASICS

Although very few recipes in this book require a microwave oven, we offer microwave variations on a number of conventionally cooked recipes so that you may choose the method you prefer. By and large the best way to make use of your microwave oven in the conventional recipes throughout the book is to have it assist you with various stages of food preparation, such as melting butter and chocolate or defrosting frozen ingredients.

Some simple precautions, at right, are important to keep in mind. The list on the opposite page will help you get the most out of your oven by explaining the 10 most useful ways you can make it work for you.

TIPS AND SAFETY FACTS

■ You cannot use metal, most aluminium foil, or dishes with a metal trim in the microwave oven. In some of the newer ovens, lightweight aluminium foil can be used to shield the parts of the food that cook most quickly, such as the bony parts of chicken.

■ Uniformly-sized portions of food are best for even cooking in the microwave oven.

■ Stirring or rearranging food during the cooking process helps ensure even results. Rotating the dish in the oven performs the same function. Using the turntable built into the microwave oven is a good way to make sure that the food cooks evenly.

■ Paper towels prevent the food from splattering and they absorb grease and moisture. When using paper towels, it is best to use plain white towels without any dye in them.

■ Plastic wrap is often used in microwave cooking since it holds in both moisture and heat. To prevent chemicals in the plastic wrap from leaching into the food, don't allow the plastic to touch the food. Be sure to turn back the corner of the plastic to allow steam to escape. For long-cooking foods that should be covered, glass lids are preferred to plastic wrap. Always be careful of the steam when you lift the lid. Wax paper makes a good, loose covering when you simply want to hold in some heat.

■ Because microwave ovens perform differently from each other, even those with the same wattage, you cannot depend on the time given in the recipe as your only cooking guide. Be sure to follow the recipes' instructions for stopping to check the progress of cooking, stirring the food if required.

POWER SETTINGS

The recipes in this book were tested in microwave ovens with a power level of 650 to 700 watts. If your oven's maximum is 600 watts or less, adjust the cooking time accordingly – add a minute or so, and test constantly.

High	100%
Medium-high	70%
Medium	50%
Medium-low	30%
Low (defrost)	10%

Top 10 time savers

Put your microwave oven to work in cutting preparation time, even when you're making a recipe using conventional methods. Here are the most useful ways in which it can help you.

1 To get the most juice from an orange, lemon or lime, heat it in the microwave oven on high power (100%) for about 30 seconds until just warm. Slice it in half and squeeze to release the juice.

2 To cook bacon, place a double sheet of paper towels on a microwave-safe plate. Arrange the bacon in a single layer on the paper towels and cover it with another paper towel. Cook on high power (100%) for some $1\frac{1}{2}$ to 2 minutes, then leave to stand for 5 minutes. Thinly sliced bacon cooks more rapidly than thick slices do, and a few pieces will cook faster than many done at the same time.

3 Frozen vegetables packaged in plastic bags can be cooked in their bags in the microwave oven. Pierce the package several times for venting and cook for 5 to 8 minutes on high power (100%).

4 Fresh vegetables wrapped in damp paper towels steam very well in the microwave oven. Use vegetables of similar size or density, such as broccoli and cauliflower florets, or cut them into pieces of uniform size. Cook on high power (100%) for 4 to 5 minutes per 250g of vegetables until crisp-tender.

5 When heating muffins or bread, place in a microwave-safe container with a tightly fitting lid and heat for 20 to 30 seconds on medium low power (30%). This will keep them from becoming hard.

6 Butter can be softened on a microwave-safe plate. Remove the wrapper if it's made of foil. Heat the butter on medium-low power (30%) for 30 to 40 seconds per 120g until spreadable. (Cream cheese may be softened in the same way.) To melt 120g butter, heat it on medium power (50%) for 30 seconds at a time until completely melted.

7 Toast nuts in a shallow microwave-safe dish. Heat 75g shelled nuts on high power (100%) for $2\frac{1}{2}$ to 4 minutes, stirring occasionally, until lightly browned.

8 To heat the syrup for pancakes, transfer the syrup to a microwave-safe jug. Microwave on high power (100%) for $1\frac{1}{2}$ to 2 minutes for each 1 to 2 cups of syrup.

9 When ice cream is too hard to scoop, soften it slightly by placing an unopened 1-litre container of ice cream in the microwave oven. Heat it on medium-low power (30%) for about 10 to 20 seconds until the ice cream begins to soften.

10 Melting chocolate in the microwave oven is a quick and convenient way to avoid having to use a double-boiler. Place 30g chocolate in a small microwave-safe bowl. Heat it on high power (100%) for approximately 1 to 2 minutes until it is shiny, stopping once to stir it (the chocolate will still hold its shape). Stir the chocolate gently until it is melted and completely smooth.

Make-ahead recipes

Often the shortest way to a quick meal is by advance preparation. For those who prefer to start from scratch, here are 10 recipes and variations that you can freeze or keep in your refrigerator for weeks. Most of these make-ahead recipes refer to one of the special features you'll find throughout the book. For some great ideas on how to turn the basic into something special, turn to the page mentioned at the beginning of the recipe.

Vegetable stock *Makes 3 to 4 cups*

See page 80, Start with a Stock

2 large carrots, coarsely chopped
1 large onion, coarsely chopped
2 stalks celery, coarsely chopped
1 large tomato, cut into 2,5cm chunks
1 medium turnip, coarsely chopped
1 small parsnip, coarsely chopped
1 cup finely chopped lettuce
6 sprigs parsley
1 clove garlic
1 bay leaf
¾ teaspoon dried thyme
6 cups (1,5 litres) water

1. Place the carrots, onion, celery, tomato, turnip, parsnip, lettuce, parsley, garlic, bay leaf and thyme in a large pot. Add the water and bring the mixture to the boil over moderate heat. Skim the foam off the surface if necessary.

2. Reduce the heat to low and simmer the stock, partially covered, for 2 hours. Line a strainer with two layers of dampened muslin. Strain the stock and allow it to cool. Discard the vegetables and herbs.

3. Pour the stock into 500ml freezer containers, leaving 1cm of space at the top. Seal the containers, label with date and contents, and freeze for up to 6 months.

BEEF STOCK *Makes 8 cups*

See page 80, Start with a Stock

2kg to 2,5kg meaty beef bones, cut into pieces by the butcher
2 large onions, cut into chunks
2 stalks celery with leaves, coarsely chopped
2 large carrots, cut into chunks
1 large tomato, cut into chunks
1 teaspoon black peppercorns
1 bay leaf
6 sprigs parsley
12 to 16 cups (3 to 4 litres) water

1 In a large pot, combine all the ingredients, adding enough water to cover completely. Bring to the boil over a moderate heat, skimming off the foam as it accumulates.

2 Reduce the heat to low and simmer the stock, uncovered, for 4 to 5 hours, skimming off the foam occasionally. Do not stir or allow the stock to boil vigorously.

3 With a slotted spoon, remove the bones. Use two layers of dampened muslin to line a strainer. Strain the stock and leave it to cool. Discard the vegetables and herbs. Chill the stock for 2 to 8 hours until the fat solidifies and can be removed. (Save the meat for another use, if desired.)

4 Pour the stock into 500ml freezer containers, leaving 1cm of space at the top. Seal the containers, label and freeze for up to 6 months.

Chicken Stock *Makes 10 cups*

See page 80, Start with a Stock

2kg chicken necks, wings, or bones and giblets without the liver (or a whole chicken, cut into pieces)
2 large onions, cut into chunks
2 stalks celery with leaves, coarsely chopped
2 large carrots, cut into chunks
1 large tomato, cut into chunks
1 teaspoon black peppercorns
1 bay leaf
6 sprigs parsley
12 to 16 cups (3 to 4 litres) water

1. Combine the chicken, vegetables, peppercorns and the herbs in a large pot. Add enough water to cover. Slowly bring the mixture to the boil over moderate heat, skimming off the foam as it accumulates.

2. Reduce the heat slightly and simmer the stock, uncovered, for 2 to 3 hours, skimming occasionally. Do not stir or boil vigorously as this will cloud the stock.

3. Using a slotted spoon, lift the chicken meat and bones from the stock and set it aside. Line a strainer with two layers of dampened muslin. Strain the stock and allow it to cool. Discard the vegetables and herbs. Chill the stock until the fat solidifies and can easily be removed with a spoon, 2 to 8 hours. (Save the meat for another use, if desired.)

4. Pour the stock into 500ml freezer containers, leaving 1cm of space at the top. Seal the container, label it with date and contents, and freeze for up to 6 months.

Basic Roast Chicken *Yields about 1kg meat*

See page 142, Start with a Roast Chicken

1 roasting chicken (1,5kg to 2kg)
Salt and ground black pepper
1 small onion, quartered
1 stalk celery, halved

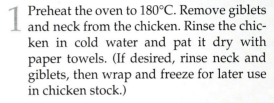

1. Preheat the oven to 180°C. Remove giblets and neck from the chicken. Rinse the chicken in cold water and pat it dry with paper towels. (If desired, rinse neck and giblets, then wrap and freeze for later use in chicken stock.)

2. Sprinkle salt and pepper in the chicken's body cavity and stuff it with the onion and celery. Truss the chicken, if desired. (It is not necessary to truss, or tie the legs together, if the bird is being carved to use for cooked meat. An untrussed chicken roasts faster.) Place the chicken on the rack of a large roasting pan. Tuck the neck skin and wings under the bird to secure.

3. Roast the chicken for 1½ to 2 hours, basting it with its pan juices every 20 minutes. Check if cooked by piercing the leg with a knife; the chicken is done when the juices run clear.

4. Let the chicken cool until it is easy to handle. Slice the meat or cut it into cubes. Wrap the chicken in freezer storage bags or place it in plastic storage containers. Seal the containers, label them with the date and contents, and freeze for up to 3 months.

Prebaked Pizza Bases *Makes 3 large or 6 small bases*

See page 62, Start with a Pizza Base

- 2 envelopes active dry yeast
- 1 tablespoon sugar
- 1¾ cups lukewarm water
- ¼ cup olive oil
- 5½ to 6 cups unsifted flour
- 2 teaspoons salt
- Extra olive oil for coating
- A sprinkling of maize (mealie) meal (optional)

1. In a large bowl, dissolve the yeast and sugar in the water. Let the yeast mixture stand for about 10 minutes until foamy.

2. Add the olive oil, 2 cups flour and the salt to the yeast mixture. Stir until well mixed. Add 2 to 3 cups of the remaining flour, kneading until the dough comes away from the bowl and holds together.

3. On a floured surface, knead dough, adding flour, if necessary, for about 5 minutes until smooth and elastic. Coat the inside of a large bowl with olive oil. Place the dough in the bowl, turning it so the top of the dough is lightly oiled. Cover the bowl with a tea towel and leave the dough to rise in a warm place until it is doubled in size (about 1 hour).

4. Punch the dough down and divide it into three equal pieces for large pizzas or six pieces for smaller pizzas. Shape each into a ball and set aside for 15 minutes.

5. Preheat the oven to 250°C. Grease three 30cm pizza tins or large baking sheets. If desired, dust each tin with maize meal. For large bases, roll out each ball into a 30cm round. For small bases, roll each into a 20cm round. Place them on the baking sheets and brush with the extra olive oil.

6. Bake, preferably on the lowest shelf of the oven, for 10 to 12 minutes until lightly browned. If baking two bases at once, switch the tins' position halfway through the baking time. If the dough puffs up while baking, puncture it with a fork. Cool on wire racks. Wrap the bases in plastic wrap and freeze for up to 3 months.

To make pizzas: Preheat the oven to 250°C. Place the frozen, uncooked pizza bases onto lightly greased pizza tins or baking sheets. Add the topping of your choice. Bake for about 15 minutes or until lightly browned and the topping is bubbly.

Variation

Whole-wheat pizza base: Replace 2 cups white flour with 2 cups whole-wheat flour.

Basic scone mixture *Makes 10 cups*

9 cups unsifted flour
1/3 cup baking powder
1 tablespoon salt
1 1/3 cups (320g) butter or margarine

1. In a large bowl, combine the flour, baking powder and salt. Using a pastry blender or two knives held like a pair of scissors, cut in the butter until the mixture resembles fine bread crumbs.

2. Measure 2-cup portions, place each portion in a plastic food-storage bag and seal tightly. Freeze for up to 6 months.

To make scones: Preheat the oven to 250°C. Place a 2-cup portion of the Basic Scone Mixture into a bowl and stir in enough milk (about 3/4 cup) to form a soft dough. Turn the dough out onto a lightly floured surface. Knead lightly and roll out to a 1cm thickness. Using a 6cm biscuit cutter, cut out the scones. Place them on an ungreased baking sheet and bake for 12 to 15 minutes. (Makes 6 to 8 scones.)

Basic crêpes *Makes 12*

See page 328, Start with a Crêpe

1 1/2 cups milk
3 large eggs
2/3 cup unsifted flour
2 tablespoons (30g) butter or margarine, melted
1/8 teaspoon salt
Extra melted butter or nonstick cooking spray for coating

1. In a medium-sized bowl, whisk together the milk, eggs, flour, melted butter and salt until smooth. (You may blend the ingredients in a blender.) Cover and refrigerate for 30 minutes.

2. Coat a nonstick 20cm frying pan with the butter or nonstick cooking spray. Heat over moderate heat until a drop of water spatters in the pan. Pour in 1/4 cup batter.

3. Swirl the pan to spread the batter to make a 15cm crêpe. Cook for about 1 minute until the underside is golden. Turn the crêpe over and cook a few seconds until set. Slide it onto a plate and cover with wax paper. Repeat until all batter is used, placing wax paper between each crêpe.

4. Leave to cool. Place in a freezer storage bag and freeze for up to one month.

BASIC BUTTER CAKE *Makes 2 loaves*

See page 338, Start with a Butter Cake

2 cups (480g) butter, softened
2 cups sugar
9 large eggs
4 cups sifted cake flour
1 tablespoon baking powder
½ teaspoon salt
1 cup milk
2 teaspoons vanilla essence

1. Preheat the oven to 180°C. Lightly butter two 23cm x 13cm loaf tins and set aside.

2. In a large bowl, using an electric mixer, cream the butter with the sugar until light and fluffy. Add the eggs, one at a time, beating well after each addition.

3. In a small bowl, combine the cake flour, baking powder and salt. Add the flour mixture alternately with the milk to the butter mixture, beginning and ending with the flour mixture. Beat the batter until smooth. Add the vanilla essence and mix well. Pour an equal amount of batter into the prepared tins. Bake for 55 to 60 minutes or until a toothpick inserted in the centre of the cake comes out clean.

4. Cool the cakes in the tins on wire racks for 10 minutes. Remove the cakes from the tins. Leave to cool completely. Place in freezer storage bags. (Alternatively, slice each cake, then reassemble it with wax paper between each slice. Remove single slices and defrost for quick desserts.) Freeze the cakes for up to 4 months.

CRUMB CRUST *Makes 1 crust*

See page 384, Start with a Crumb Crust

200g Tennis or digestive biscuits
¼ cup sugar
⅓ cup (80g) melted butter or margarine

1. Preheat the oven to 190°C. Using a blender or food processor, process the biscuits to make 1½ cups crumbs. In a medium-sized bowl, mix the crumbs, sugar and butter.

2. With the back of a spoon, press the mixture into the bottom and against the side of a 23cm pie plate, forming a rim. Press a second pie plate into the crust to spread it evenly, then remove the second pie plate. Bake the crust for 8 minutes. Place on a wire rack to cool.

3. Wrap the cooled crust with plastic wrap and store in the refrigerator for no more than 2 weeks.

To prepare tart: Fill the crumb crust according to recipe directions. Refrigerate if necessary until ready to serve.

VARIATIONS

Vanilla or chocolate biscuit crumb crust: Substitute plain vanilla or chocolate biscuits (1½ cups crumbs) for the Tennis or digestive biscuits. Omit the sugar. Mix with ⅓ cup (80g) melted butter. Bake, cool and refrigerate as in Steps 2 and 3 above.

Basic pancake and waffle mixture *Makes 6 cups*

9 1/3 cups unsifted flour
1 2/3 cups skimmed milk powder
2/3 cup sugar
1/3 cup baking powder
2 teaspoons salt
1 cup (240g) butter or margarine

1. In a large bowl, combine the flour, milk powder, sugar, baking powder and salt. Using a pastry blender or two knives held like a pair of scissors, cut in the butter thoroughly until the mixture resembles fine bread crumbs.

2. Measure 6 x 1-cup portions and place each portion in a plastic food-storage bag. Seal tightly. Freeze for up to 6 months.

To make pancakes: In a large bowl, combine 1 large egg with 1 cup water. Stir in 1 cup of the Basic Pancake and Waffle Mixture until just moistened. If the batter is overly thick, add more water, 1 tablespoon at a time. For each pancake, pour approximately 1/4 cup batter into a greased hot frying pan, forming a 12,5cm pancake. (Makes about 12 pancakes.)

To make waffles: Combine 2 large eggs, 3/4 cup water and 2 tablespoons sunflower oil. Stir in 1 cup Basic Pancake and Waffle Mixture until just mixed. Pour enough of the batter into the centre of a hot waffle maker to reach within 2,5cm of the edge. (Makes about 3 x 22,5cm square waffles.)

Mixture variations

Whole-wheat mixture: Substitute 3 cups whole-wheat flour for 3 cups flour. Follow Steps 1 and 2 above.

Batter variations

Banana: Fold 1 cup mashed or chopped ripe bananas into the prepared batter.
Blueberry: Stir 1 cup fresh blueberries into the prepared batter.
Cinnamon nut: Before adding the liquid ingredients to the basic batter, stir 1 teaspoon ground cinnamon and 1/2 cup finely chopped almonds, pecan nuts or walnuts into the basic mixture.

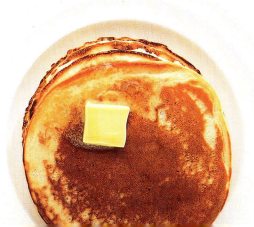

Easy entertaining

The best parties are those in which the host feels relaxed and confident, and doesn't have to disappear into the kitchen for hours at a time. Plan a party where you will feel most comfortable and your guests will follow suit. The Quick Cook keeps some of these ideas in mind for making a successful party without the hassles.

Skilful menu planning, time-saving techniques and easy presentation ideas all add up to a good time for everyone – and that includes the host.

Menu planning

1 The golden rule: Don't make everything from scratch yourself. Plan to make some of the food, the main dish and dessert, for example, then purchase cheese and savoury biscuits, bread and a couple of side dishes from a good delicatessen.

2 Choose recipes in which you can do some of the work ahead of time, rather than all at the last minute. For example, you can't toss a salad ahead of time, but you can certainly rinse and tear the lettuce and chop all the extras that accompany it, then store the ingredients in plastic bags or containers in the refrigerator.

3 There is no substitute for lists. Write down the menu, the shopping list and a reminder of anything that can be made ahead of time. This will help to avoid any last-minute panic.

4 Work out a time schedule. Organize your time so you will know the order in which to prepare the food. This way you will avoid, for example, chopping nuts or whipping cream when you could be enjoying the company of your friends.

5 Plan the meal according to your own equipment and dinner service rather than borrowing and improvising to accommodate the menu. For example, if you have no soup bowls but own two dozen salad plates, don't go to the trouble of borrowing; opt for serving salad instead. Make things easy for yourself.

What kind of party?

Buffets are always easier on the host than a sit-down meal. The atmosphere tends to be more casual and the food can be laid out all at once. On the other hand, if you prefer the intimacy of a sit-down meal, remember to keep the courses simple so that they can flow from the kitchen without too much last-minute attention. In either case, have the buffet or table set as thoroughly as possible before guests arrive.

Another kind of party can be a life-saver for the Quick Cook: a cooking party, in which the guests cook their food themselves. If the size of your kitchen allows it, have an omelette party or a pizza party. You provide the ingredients and set them out in bowls,

then let your guests create their own concoctions. A simpler variation, in which there is no cooking involved, is to have a dessert party with a selection of ice creams and imaginative toppings laid out buffet-style.

NO-COOK PARTY FOOD

Scout your supermarket for interesting foods that will complement your own cooking, especially when it comes to appetizers and desserts. Here are a few suggestions:

Appetizers
- A tray of olives and crudités, some almonds or a mixture of party nuts.
- Salami rolled around a stick of cheese or prosciutto (raw smoked ham) with melon.

IMAGINATIVE CONTAINERS

Add character to your table by serving food in one of these creative containers:

Fruit salads Cut a large melon in half horizontally and remove a thin slice from the top and bottom so that both halves will stand upright. Scoop out the seeds and discard. Scoop out about half of the flesh for a small bowl shape.

Dips Cut off the top third of a red cabbage. Using a small curved knife, scoop out enough of the cabbage to leave a shell about 4cm thick. Cut a thin slice off the base so that it will stand upright.

Salads Hollow out tomatoes, cucumbers or avocado pear halves.

- Prepared dips or package mixtures served with chopped fresh vegetables, toasted sliced pita bread and bread sticks.
- A wedge of cheese served with a bunch of grapes and a basket of savoury biscuits.

Desserts
- A cake, pie or fruit tart from a good bakery, served with coffee.
- Crisp biscuits with sliced fresh fruit.
- The most chocolaty truffles available.

Menus

Good food does not necessarily mean fussy food. The Quick Cook can give a buffet supper, an afternoon tea or a Sunday brunch – no need to forgo get-togethers because of lack of time. The key is in advance planning and presenting food attractively.
The menus on these pages have been created with a combination of recipes from this book and some store-bought items.

Winter supper for four

Chicken Provençale, page 138
Rice Pilaff, page 236
Assorted savoury biscuits with cheese
Coffee and Pecan Tartlets, page 387

◆

■ Bake the pecan tartlets the day before the party. Store them at room temperature.
■ Prepare the rice pilaff on the morning of the party, then reheat just before serving.
■ Arrange the cheese and savoury biscuits on a large platter garnished with grape clusters.

Sunday brunch

Eggs with Cream Cheese and
Smoked Salmon, page 255
Roasted Potatoes, page 277
Minty Fruit Salad, page 308
Warm croissants and assorted muffins
Orange juice

◆

■ If orange juice is to be made from a frozen concentrate, make it the day before and refrigerate. Pour it into a jug and stir before serving.
■ Prepare the melon salad the day before, cover and refrigerate.
■ Place warm croissants and muffins in baskets lined with cloth napkins or tea towels. Serve them with sweetened butter made by mixing fruit preserves or a little jam into softened butter or margarine.

Patio party

Tortilla chips with
tomato salsa
Pita Burgers, page 183
Mealies
Chocolate Ice Cream Pie, page 360

◆

■ Serve chips and salsa on a festive platter.
■ Clean the mealies and cook them the day before. Wrap and refrigerate.
■ Prepare the hamburger patties the day before, wrap and refrigerate. If you prefer, braai the hamburgers.
■ Prepare the ice cream pie the day before and freeze. Leave the pie to stand for a few minutes to soften before serving.

Casual lunch for four

Chicken Club Sandwich, page 64
ready-made pasta salad
Cheesecake Cups, page 373

■ Prepare the sandwich fillings on the morning of the party, then reheat the chicken and bacon before assembling. Save toasting the bread and assembling the sandwiches until just before serving.
■ To serve the pasta salad, line a shallow salad bowl with large lettuce leaves. Gently toss the salad, then spoon it on top of the lettuce. Garnish with tomato wedges or black olives.
■ Prepare the cheesecake cups the day before, cover and refrigerate.
■ Arrange the cheese and savoury biscuits on a large platter garnished with small bunches of grapes.

Afternoon Tea Party

Open-faced Cucumber Tea Sandwiches, page 58
Pear and Prosciutto Sandwiches, page 65
Assorted ready-made biscuits and pastries
Chocolate-dipped Strawberries, page 350

◆

■ Prepare the cucumber topping and slice the bread for the tea sandwiches on the morning of the party. Assemble them just before you are ready to serve tea.
■ Prepare the pear sandwiches shortly before serving. If you prefer, slice them into quarters for easier handling.
■ Make the biscuits and pastries look appealing by arranging them decoratively on platters lined with paper doilies, or in a shallow basket lined with a linen cloth.
■ Offer two or three choices of teas.
■ Prepare the chocolate-dipped strawberries on the morning of the party and refrigerate.

Candlelight Dinner for Two

Asparagus Dijonnaise, page 272
Crispy rolls
Salmon Véronique, page 105
Packaged rice mixture
Ready-made chocolate cake

◆

■ Halve the Asparagus Dijonnaise recipe to serve two. Cook the asparagus on the morning of the dinner, wrap it in plastic and refrigerate. Prepare the sauce just before serving.
■ Serve the rolls with softened butter mixed with finely chopped fresh parsley.
■ Halve the Salmon Véronique recipe. Prepare the salmon just before serving.
■ The rice mixture may also be prepared in the morning, then sealed and refrigerated. Add a few drops of water to the rice before reheating on the stove or in the microwave oven to keep it moist.
■ To serve the cake, place a slice of cake on each dessert plate, then pour a little cream around each slice. Garnish with a light sprinkling of cocoa powder.

Italian Dinner for Four

Bruschetta, page 53
Spaghetti Tuscan Style, page 230
Green salad
Blue cheese with ripe pears
After-dinner chocolates

◆

■ The pasta and the sauce may be made the day before the dinner (see page 212), then reheated just before serving.
■ Purchase pre-washed and torn salad leaves from the supermarket. Add croutons, sliced radishes and artichoke hearts, then toss with an Italian-style dressing.
■ For an authentic touch, place a wedge of Parmesan cheese on the table with a cheese grater and let guests grate their own cheese.
■ Choose gorgonzola or a local blue cheese. The cheese and fruit should be served at room temperature for the best flavour.
■ Arrange the chocolates on a pretty plate and serve them with coffee.

After-Theatre Supper

Spinach Salad with Oranges, page 294
Cheese Fondue, page 268
Ready-made fruit tart

◆

■ Rinse the spinach and slice the oranges for the salad on the morning of the supper. Wrap separately and refrigerate. (You can save even more time by buying pre-packed, ready-washed spinach.)
■ Prepare the salad dressing in the morning. Shake well just before serving.
■ Grate the cheese for the fondue and mix it with the dry ingredients the day before. Place the mixture in a plastic container, seal tightly and refrigerate until needed.
■ Prepare an assortment of bread cubes and fresh vegetables to be used for the fondue in the morning. Store separately and refrigerate.
■ Garnish the fruit tart with fresh mint and serve it with a jug of sweetened whipped cream or ready-whipped cream bought from the supermarket.

Appetizers and Snacks

Baked stuffed mushrooms (page 41)

APPETIZERS

These hors d'oeuvres and first courses make quick work of preparing party food, so you have more time to spend with guests.

BITE-SIZED CHEESE AND RED PEPPER QUICHES Makes 18

1 tablespoon (15g) butter or margarine

½ cup finely chopped sweet red pepper

¼ cup spring onion, including tops, finely chopped

3 large eggs

2 tablespoons milk

½ cup (60g) coarsely grated Cheddar cheese

¼ teaspoon salt

⅛ teaspoon ground black pepper

 Preparation time 20 minutes

 Cooking time 10 minutes

SERVING SUGGESTION *These bite-sized quiches are easier to handle than slices of a large quiche – making them ideal finger food.*

1 Preheat the oven to 230°C. Grease one 24-cup mini muffin tin. In a small saucepan, melt the butter over moderate heat. Add the red pepper and spring onion and sauté for about 5 minutes until soft. Remove from the heat and let the mixture cool slightly.

2 In a medium-sized bowl, mix the eggs, milk, cheese, salt and black pepper. Stir in the red pepper and spring onion. Spoon about 1 tablespoon of the mixture into each muffin cup. (The mixture will fill 18 to 22 cups.)

3 Bake for 8 to 10 minutes until the centres are set. Allow the quiches to cool for 1 minute. Using a knife, loosen the quiches around the edges and remove from the tin. Arrange them on a platter and serve.

CAVIAR CORN FRITTERS Makes 16

2 or 3 extra-large eggs, separated

Salt and freshly ground black pepper

1 tin (410g) whole kernel corn

Pinch of sugar

1 teaspoon baking powder

1 cup (60g) fresh bread crumbs

Sunflower oil

6 tablespoons sour cream

1 jar (100g) red caviar

Chopped chives (optional)

 Preparation time 10 minutes

 Cooking time 20 minutes

1 In a medium-sized bowl, beat the egg yolks with the salt and pepper. Drain the liquid from the corn kernels and add the kernels, with the sugar, to the egg mixture. Whisk the egg whites until stiff and fold into yolk mixture, together with the baking powder and bread crumbs.

2 Heat the oil in a frying pan over moderate heat until a drop of water sizzles on the surface. Lightly mould the batter into fritter shapes and drop them into the pan to make several 5cm fritters.

3 Fry the fritters for about 2 minutes until golden brown. Turn over and repeat until the second side is set and golden. Drain well on paper towels and transfer the fritters to a large platter. Repeat to cook the remaining batter. Top each fritter with some of the sour cream, caviar and chives, if desired, and serve.

APPETIZERS AND SNACKS

DEVILLED EGGS *Makes 16*

8 large eggs

¼ cup mayonnaise or sour cream

1 teaspoon Dijon mustard

¼ teaspoon curry powder

Salt and ground white pepper to taste

Paprika (optional)

Parsley sprigs (optional)

 Preparation time 20 minutes

 Cooking time 25 minutes

SERVING SUGGESTION *Add variety to these perennial favourites by garnishing them with crumbled fried bacon or sliced olives.*

1 Place the eggs in a small saucepan and cover them with cold water. Bring the water to the boil over high heat. Remove the saucepan from the heat and leave the eggs to stand, covered, for 15 minutes.

2 Drain the eggs and rinse them under cold water. Leaving the eggs in the pan, cover them with cold water and let them stand for a further 5 minutes. Shell the eggs and cut them in half lengthwise. Remove the yolks and place the whites on a baking tray covered with a sheet of paper towels.

3 Using the back of a fork, mash the yolks in a small bowl. Stir in the mayonnaise, mustard and curry powder, and season to taste with salt and white pepper. Fit a pastry bag with a large star-shaped nozzle and fill it with the yolk mixture. Pipe the mixture into the egg cavities.

4 Carefully transfer the eggs to a serving platter. Sprinkle the yolks with paprika and garnish the platter with sprigs of parsley, if desired. Serve immediately or refrigerate until ready to serve.

SHELF MAGIC

These quick appetizers make delicious light snacks for a casual get-together. Serve them warm and watch them disappear.

FRIED TORTELLINI

In a medium-sized frying pan, heat *2 tablespoons olive oil*. Add *250g fresh, uncooked, cheese-filled tortellini*. Fry them for 5 to 7 minutes until they are crisp and golden, turning them frequently so that they cook evenly. Drain the tortellini briefly on paper towels. Place them in a serving bowl and toss gently with *2 tablespoons grated Parmesan cheese*. Spear with toothpicks and serve immediately. Serves 4

TORTILLA CHIPS

Preheat the oven to 180°C. With *2 tablespoons oil*, brush a light coating of oil on one side of each of *twelve 20cm flour* or *corn tortillas*. Stack the tortillas, oiled side up, and slice the stack into eight with a sharp knife. Separate the tortilla pieces and arrange them, oiled side up, on two lightly greased baking trays. Bake the chips for about 10 minutes until they are crisp and lightly browned. Serve with *fresh tomato salsa*. Serves 6

CHEDDAR QUESADILLAS

CHEDDAR QUESADILLAS *Makes 16*

 Preparation time
6 minutes

 Cooking time
20 minutes

4 tablespoons sunflower oil

8 small flour tortillas (18cm to 20cm in diameter)

2 cups (250g) coarsely grated Cheddar cheese

125g bottled green chillies, drained and chopped

1 small ripe avocado pear

⅓ cup ready-made thick-style tomato salsa

FOOD NOTE Queso *is the Spanish word for cheese – which gives these traditional Tex-Mex appetizers their irresistible flavour.*

1. In a large frying pan, heat 1 tablespoon of the oil over moderate heat. Place one flour tortilla in the pan and sprinkle it with ½ cup cheese and one-quarter of the green chillies. Place another tortilla on top and press it gently to seal the tortillas together.

2. Cook the tortilla sandwich or quesadilla for about 5 minutes, turning it once with a broad spatula, until the cheese begins to melt. Transfer the quesadilla to a cutting board and slice it into four wedges. Repeat to cook the remaining quesadillas.

3. Transfer the quesadillas to a serving platter. Peel and remove the pip from the avocado pear and slice it into 16 thin slivers. Garnish each quesadilla wedge with an avocado slice and about 1 teaspoon of tomato salsa. Serve immediately.

PIZZA PITA TRIANGLES

PIZZA PITA TRIANGLES *Makes 16*

125g small mushrooms

60g thinly sliced pepper salami

1 small red onion

2 whole-wheat pita breads

2 tablespoons chopped fresh basil (or 2 teaspoons dried basil)

1 cup (125g) coarsely grated mozzarella cheese

2 tablespoons (40g) grated Parmesan cheese

 Preparation time
20 minutes

 Cooking time
12 minutes

COOK'S TIP If you prefer to prepare these ahead of time, cover and refrigerate them and bake just before serving.

1. Preheat the oven to 220°C. Slice the mushrooms and cut the salami into matchstick-sized strips. Thinly slice the onion and separate the rings.

2. Using a sharp knife, carefully slice each pita bread around the edges to split it into two layers. Place the pita halves, cut sides up, on an ungreased baking sheet. Scatter an equal amount of the mushrooms, salami, onion and basil over the pita halves. Sprinkle them with the grated mozzarella and Parmesan cheeses.

3. Bake for 10 to 12 minutes until the cheese is melted. Slice each pita into 4 wedges, arrange them on a platter and serve.

APPETIZERS AND SNACKS

CHEDDAR CHEESE FRITTERS *Makes 12*

1 cup flour
1 teaspoon baking powder
¼ teaspoon salt
⅛ teaspoon cayenne pepper
1 large egg
½ cup milk
1 cup (125g) coarsely grated mature Cheddar cheese
Sunflower oil for frying

 Preparation time 6 minutes

 Cooking time 5 minutes

COOK'S TIP Be sure the cooking oil is at the correct temperature before you begin frying the fritters, so that they turn out light and crispy.

1. In a medium-sized bowl, use a wire whisk to blend the flour, baking powder, salt and cayenne pepper until well mixed. Form a well in the centre and break the egg into the well.

2. Pour ¼ cup of the milk into the well in the flour; stir until the mixture is smooth. Add just enough of the remaining milk to make the mixture soft enough to drop from a spoon. Stir in the grated Cheddar cheese until the batter is well mixed.

3. In a large, heavy-based saucepan or deep fryer, heat 5cm of oil to 180°C. Drop tablespoonfuls of the mixture, 6 to 8 at a time, into the hot oil and fry for 1 to 2 minutes until golden brown. Drain the fritters on paper towels, transfer them to a warmed platter and serve immediately.

BAKED STUFFED MUSHROOMS *Makes 24* (PICTURE PAGE 35)

24x5cm mushrooms (about 500g)
1 tablespoon olive oil
2 tablespoons (30g) butter or margarine
3 tablespoons finely chopped spring onion
⅓ cup (40g) packaged bread crumbs
2 tablespoons chopped parsley
⅛ teaspoon ground white pepper
½ cup (60g) crumbled feta cheese
Parsley sprigs

 Preparation time 20 minutes

 Cooking time 10 minutes

COOK'S TIP Chop the mushroom stems in a food processor to prepare these party appetizers even more quickly.

1. Preheat the oven to 230°C. Remove the stems from the mushrooms. Finely chop enough of the stems to measure ¾ cup and set aside. Place the mushroom caps and the oil in a large bowl and toss to coat evenly. Arrange the mushroom caps, stemless ends up, on a Swiss roll tin and set them aside.

2. In a medium-sized saucepan, melt the butter over moderate heat. Add the spring onion and sauté for about 2 minutes until soft and translucent. Add the chopped mushroom stems and sauté for approximately 2 minutes more until softened. Stir in the bread crumbs, parsley and pepper until well mixed. Remove the saucepan from the heat.

3. Stir the cheese into the crumb mixture. Spoon about 1 teaspoon of the mixture into each mushroom cap. Bake the stuffed mushrooms for about 10 minutes until they are heated through and lightly browned. Transfer the mushrooms to a serving platter. Garnish each with a tiny sprig of parsley and serve.

DILLED MEATBALLS Makes 42

3 large (about 500g) skinned chicken-breast fillets, minced

1 cup (60g) fresh bread crumbs

1 tablespoon grated onion

1 tablespoon chopped dill (or 1 teaspoon dried dill)

½ teaspoon salt

¼ teaspoon ground white pepper

2 tablespoons (30g) butter or margarine

1 tablespoon sunflower oil

1 teaspoon cornflour

½ cup plus 1 tablespoon chicken stock

½ cup sour cream

Additional chopped fresh dill or dried dill (optional)

 Preparation time 15 minutes

 Cooking time 25 minutes

COOK'S TIP You can prepare these meatballs a day ahead, if you prefer. Serve them chilled or reheated, speared with toothpicks.

1 In a medium-sized bowl, combine the chicken, bread crumbs, onion, dill, salt and pepper. Shape the chicken mixture into 2cm balls, making 42 to 46 meatballs.

2 In a large frying pan, heat the butter and oil over moderate heat until the butter is melted. Cook half the meatballs for about 10 minutes until they are well browned. Using a slotted spoon, transfer them to a bowl. Repeat to cook the remaining meatballs, and add them to the bowl.

3 In a cup, blend the cornflour with 1 tablespoon of the chicken stock until smooth; set the mixture aside. Gradually stir the remaining chicken stock into the drippings in the frying pan. Bring the mixture to the boil.

4 Add the cornflour mixture to the stock in the frying pan, stirring until it is smooth and slightly thickened. Return the meatballs and any accumulated juices to the pan and bring to the boil.

5 Stir the sour cream into the mixture (do not boil). Remove the frying pan from the heat. Transfer the meatballs and sauce to a serving bowl. Sprinkle with dill, if desired, and serve.

GRILLED CHICKEN NUGGETS Makes 48

4 large (about 700g) skinned chicken-breast fillets

⅓ cup (80g) butter or margarine

3 cloves garlic, finely chopped

1 teaspoon paprika

1 teaspoon dried tarragon

½ teaspoon salt

⅛ teaspoon ground black pepper

Watercress (optional)

 Preparation time 6 minutes

 Cooking time 6 minutes

1 Preheat the grill. Slice each chicken breast in half lengthwise, then slice each half into 6 portions. Set them aside. In a medium-sized saucepan, melt the butter over moderate heat. Add the garlic and sauté for 15 seconds. Remove the saucepan from the heat. Add the paprika, tarragon, salt and pepper to the garlic butter. Add the chicken and stir until it is coated with the garlic mixture.

2 Arrange the chicken in a single layer on a rack over a grill pan. Grill the portions 10cm from the heat for about 4 minutes until the chicken is lightly browned. Turn the pieces over and continue grilling for approximately 1 more minute until tender.

3 Arrange the chicken pieces on a serving platter and decorate with watercress, if desired. Serve pierced with toothpicks.

DILLED MEATBALLS (RIGHT) AND ROAST BEEF CANAPÉS

ROAST BEEF CANAPÉS *Makes 24*

250g thinly sliced rare roast beef

2 tablespoons olive oil

1 tablespoon red wine vinegar

1 tablespoon chopped chives or dill

¼ teaspoon salt

1 loaf French bread

½ cup mayonnaise

24 small strips pimento or roasted sweet red pepper

Chive or dill sprigs (optional)

 Preparation time 20 minutes

 Cooking time 0 minutes

SERVING SUGGESTION Instead of French bread, try serving these canapés on small bagels, sliced in half and toasted.

1. Cut the slices of beef crosswise into 5cm-wide strips. In a bowl, combine the oil, vinegar, chives and salt until well mixed. Add the sliced beef and toss to coat thoroughly with the oil mixture. Leave to stand for about 10 minutes to marinate.

2. Meanwhile, slice the French bread into 24x1cm-thick slices. Spread one side of each slice of bread with 1 teaspoon of the mayonnaise.

3. Place the roast-beef strips over the mayonnaise, folding them to fit each slice of bread neatly. Garnish the top of each canapé with a strip of pimento and a sprig of chive or dill, if desired.

4. Arrange the canapés on a platter and serve immediately, or cover and refrigerate until ready to serve.

APPETIZERS AND SNACKS

PARMESAN PITA CHIPS *Makes 48*

6 pita breads
4 tablespoons (60g) butter or margarine
¼ cup olive oil
1 clove garlic, finely chopped
½ teaspoon dried thyme
⅓ cup (30g) grated Parmesan cheese

 Preparation time 15 minutes

 Cooking time 10 minutes

FOOD NOTE These home-made pita chips are tastier than any cheese-flavoured crisps you may buy. They'll soon become a family favourite.

1. Preheat the oven to 230°C. Using a sharp knife, slice each pita bread into quarters. Cut through the middle and split each quarter into two, for a total of 48 pieces. Arrange the pieces, sliced-side up, on an ungreased baking sheet.

2. In a small saucepan, heat the butter and oil over moderate heat. Add the garlic and thyme, and sauté for 15 seconds. Remove the butter mixture from the heat. Brush the mixture over the sliced side of the pita pieces and top with grated Parmesan cheese.

3. Bake the pita breads for about 10 minutes until the pieces are crisp and lightly browned. Transfer the chips to a rack to cool. If you are not planning to serve the chips immediately, store them in an airtight container.

HERBED YOGHURT DIP *Serves 5*

2 tablespoons chopped spring onion tops or chives
2 tablespoons chopped parsley
1 tablespoon chopped fresh tarragon or dill
1 clove garlic
1 cup plain low-fat yoghurt
¼ cup mayonnaise
Salt and ground black pepper to taste

 Preparation time 10 minutes

 Cooking time 0 minutes

COOK'S TIP This low-fat dip is a mouthwatering accompaniment for Parmesan pita chips (above) or assorted raw vegetables.

1. Using an electric blender or food processor fitted with the chopping blade, process the spring onion tops, the parsley, tarragon and garlic to a smooth paste. Add the yoghurt and mayonnaise, stirring with a wooden spoon or a rubber spatula to blend well.

2. Season the herbed yoghurt dip with salt and ground black pepper to taste. Transfer to a small decorative bowl, garnish as desired and serve. (Makes 1¼ cups.)

YOGHURT CREAM-CHEESE DIP

Using a medium-sized bowl and an electric mixer or wooden spoon, beat *one 227g carton cream cheese*, at room temperature, until smooth. Add *½ cup plain low-fat yoghurt* with *⅛ teaspoon caraway seeds, ground cumin seeds* or *ground fennel seeds*. Beat until well blended. Season to taste with *salt* and *ground black pepper*. Transfer to a small bowl and serve. (Makes 1½ cups.)

SMOKED SALMON PÂTÉ

SMOKED SALMON PÂTÉ *Serves 5*

125g sliced smoked salmon

½ cup (125g) cream cheese, softened

1 tablespoon lemon juice

1 tablespoon chopped fresh chives

1 tablespoon chopped dill (or 1 teaspoon dried dill)

Ground black pepper to taste

Fresh dill (optional)

 Preparation time
7 minutes

 Cooking/chilling time
15 minutes

Serving suggestion This hors d'oeuvre is delicious served on bite-sized slices of pumpernickel bread or with water biscuits. Place the serving bowl in the refrigerator while preparing the pâté; it will keep the mixture cool much longer.

1 Slice the smoked salmon into narrow strips. Using an electric blender or a food processor fitted with the chopping blade, process the salmon, cream cheese, lemon juice, chives and dill until fairly smooth.

2 Season the pâté with pepper and spoon it into a small serving bowl. Cover and refrigerate for 15 minutes or until ready to serve. Garnish with dill, if desired. (Makes 1⅓ cups.)

APPETIZERS AND SNACKS

BLUE CHEESE DIP *Serves 6*

½ cup mayonnaise
½ cup sour cream
1 cup (125g) crumbled blue cheese
2 to 4 tablespoons milk
1 teaspoon Worcestershire sauce
¼ teaspoon dry mustard
Dash of Tabasco sauce

 Preparation time
7 minutes

 Cooking/chilling time
20 minutes

SERVING SUGGESTION Serve this dip with assorted sliced vegetables, such as cauliflower florets, sliced baby marrow and strips of red and green sweet pepper.

1 In a small bowl, combine the mayonnaise, sour cream, blue cheese, 2 tablespoons milk, Worcestershire sauce, mustard and Tabasco sauce. Stir in more milk if the dip is too thick.

2 Cover the bowl with plastic wrap and refrigerate for about 20 minutes. Just before serving, spoon the dip into a decorative bowl and serve. (Makes 1½ cups.)

GUACAMOLE *Serves 7*

1 large ripe avocado pear
1 ripe plum tomato
1 fresh or tinned jalapeño pepper
1 tablespoon lemon juice
1 tablespoon chopped fresh coriander
½ teaspoon Tabasco sauce
Salt and ground black pepper to taste

 Preparation time
10 minutes

 Cooking time
0 minutes

SERVING SUGGESTION Serve this robust dip with crisp tortilla chips or use it to enhance a hamburger.

1 Cut the avocado pear in half, remove the pip and peel. Finely chop the tomato. Core, seed and finely chop the jalapeño pepper.

2 In a large bowl, using a potato masher or fork, mash the avocado pear with the lemon juice until it is fairly smooth. Stir in the chopped tomato and jalapeño pepper, coriander and Tabasco sauce.

3 Season the mixture with salt and pepper. Transfer the guacamole to a small bowl and serve. (Makes 1¾ cups.)

TIME SAVERS

APPETIZERS
■ Before making creamy dips, remove the cream cheese from the refrigerator and bring it to room temperature so that it is soft enough to blend with the rest of the ingredients.

■ Crumbled bacon pieces can be made ahead to use as a topping on various appetizers. Fry the bacon, let it cool and crumble it. Refrigerate the crumbles in a tightly sealed plastic bag for up to a week.

■ To clean mushrooms quickly and to keep them fresh for crudités, dip a cloth into lemon juice and use it to wipe away the dirt, leaving the mushrooms clean and impervious to discoloration.

Start with Dips

Here are some irresistible dips to serve as appetizers at your next party. The recipes can easily be halved or doubled to accommodate the number of guests.

◀ **Chunky salsa** In a medium-sized bowl, combine *4 medium tomatoes,* peeled and diced, *½ cup chopped onion, ½ cup chopped celery, ¼ cup chopped sweet green pepper, 1 chopped fresh green chilli* and *1 tablespoon chopped coriander,* if desired. In a small bowl, combine *¼ cup olive oil, 2 tablespoons red wine vinegar, 1 teaspoon mustard seed, 1 teaspoon salt, a pinch of pepper, ¼ teaspoon chilli powder* and *Tabasco sauce* to taste. Pour the oil mixture over the vegetables and toss until coated. Cover salsa and chill for at least 25 minutes or until ready to serve. Serve with *corn chips*. (Makes 4 cups.)

▶ **Hot artichoke dip** Preheat oven to 180°C. Chop *one 400g tin artichoke hearts,* drained. Place them in a bowl and add *½ cup plain yoghurt, ½ cup mayonnaise* and *1 cup grated Parmesan cheese;* mix well. Spoon the mixture into a 1-litre casserole dish, sprinkle with *paprika* and bake for 30 minutes. Serve hot or cold with crisp *savoury biscuits.* (Makes 2 cups.)

▶ **Spicy vegetable dip** Place *¼ cup seedless raisins* in a small bowl, cover with hot water and leave to stand for 10 minutes. Meanwhile, in a blender or food processor, mix *1 cup cottage cheese, 2 tablespoons cider vinegar, ½ small onion,* coarsely chopped, *1 teaspoon chilli powder, ½ teaspoon curry powder, ½ teaspoon salt* and *⅛ teaspoon ground black pepper.* Blend until smooth. Drain raisins and stir them into the cheese mixture. If the mixture is too thick for dipping, add *1 tablespoon raisin water* or *milk.* Chill for at least 20 minutes or until ready to serve. Serve with crisp *savoury biscuits* or *sliced raw vegetables.* (Makes 1½ cups.)

◄ **Hot smoked snoek dip** Bring water to a simmer in the bottom portion of a double boiler. Meanwhile, in the top portion of the double boiler, combine *two 250g cartons of cream cheese*, softened, *½ cup cream* or *milk*, *1½ tablespoons prepared horseradish*, *2 teaspoons Worcestershire sauce*, *¼ cup chopped spring onions* and *salt* and *ground black pepper* to taste. Cook for 10 minutes. Do not allow the water to boil. Stir in *300g flaked smoked snoek* and *2 tablespoons white wine*. Continue cooking for 10 minutes. Spoon mixture into a small serving dish and serve immediately with crisp *savoury biscuits*. (Makes 4 cups.)

► **Hot Mexican dip** Preheat oven to 180°C. In a 30cm frying pan, sauté *250g lean minced beef*, *1 small onion*, chopped and *½ small sweet red pepper*, seeded and chopped, for about 7 minutes until beef is lightly browned. Drain if necessary and stir in *one package taco seasoning mixture*; cook for 1 minute. Add *one 400g tin chilli beans* to meat mixture and mix thoroughly. Spoon mixture into a 1½-litre casserole dish, spreading it evenly. Layer *½ cup sour cream*, *½ cup grated mozzarella cheese* and *½ cup grated Cheddar cheese* over the meat mixture. Bake until hot and bubbly, 25 to 30 minutes. Serve with *corn chips*. (Makes 4 cups.)

◄ **Spinach dip** In a large bowl, combine *two 250g packages frozen creamed spinach*, thawed and drained (or *one 400g tin creamed spinach*, drained) and *one 100g package blue cheese*, crumbled. Stir in *one 230g tin sliced water chestnuts*, drained and coarsely chopped, *½ cup chopped celery*, *¾ cup chopped sweet red pepper*, *½ cup chopped spring onions* and *2 cloves crushed garlic*. In a small bowl, combine *1 cup sour cream* and *1 cup mayonnaise*. Gradually stir sour cream mixture into spinach mixture until ingredients are easy to spread. Serve with crisp *savoury biscuits*. (Makes 6 cups.)

APPETIZERS AND SNACKS

HOT SHRIMP DIP *Serves 5*

1 tablespoon (15g) butter or margarine

1 tablespoon flaked almonds

½ small onion, finely chopped

150g frozen tiny shrimps, cooked

1 cup (250g) cream cheese, softened

2 teaspoons lemon juice

1 teaspoon prepared white horseradish

½ teaspoon Worcestershire sauce

Salt and ground white pepper to taste

 Preparation time 6 minutes

 Cooking time 12 minutes

COOK'S TIP This dip is also delicious chilled – cover the bowl with plastic wrap and refrigerate it until ready to serve. Chinese prawn crackers or raw vegetables would be an ideal accompaniment.

1 In a medium-sized saucepan, melt the butter over moderate heat. Add the almonds and sauté for about 3 minutes until golden brown. Using a slotted spoon, transfer the almonds to a small bowl.

2 Add the onion to the remaining butter in the saucepan and sauté for about 3 minutes until soft. Stir in the shrimps and cook until nearly all of the juices have evaporated. Stir in the cream cheese, lemon juice, horseradish and Worcestershire sauce. Cook until just heated through.

3 Season the hot shrimp dip with salt and pepper. Transfer it to a serving bowl, sprinkle with the sautéed almonds and serve. (Makes 1¼ cups.)

VEGETABLE ANTIPASTO *Serves 4*

¼ cup olive oil

3 tablespoons red wine vinegar

½ teaspoon dried origanum

¼ teaspoon salt

⅛ teaspoon ground black pepper

1 clove garlic, finely chopped

1 brinjal (about 350g)

350g baby marrows

2 large red or yellow sweet peppers

¼ cup (25g) finely grated Parmesan cheese

 Preparation time 15 minutes

 Cooking time 15 minutes

1 Preheat the grill. In a small bowl, combine the oil, vinegar, origanum, salt, pepper and garlic.

2 Cut the brinjal crosswise into thin slices. Place the slices in a single layer on the rack over a grill pan. Brush with some of the oil mixture. Grill the brinjal about 10 cm from the heat for about 8 minutes until lightly browned and tender, turning once and brushing with more of the oil mixture.

3 Meanwhile, halve the baby marrows along their length. Core and seed the red pepper and cut it into 2,5cm-wide strips.

4 Transfer the grilled brinjal slices to a plate. Place the baby marrows and peppers on the grill rack and brush with some of the oil mixture. Grill for about 3 minutes until lightly browned on one side. Turn them over, brush them with more of the oil mixture and grill for 3 more minutes.

5 Arrange the vegetables on four serving plates and drizzle them with any remaining oil mixture. Top each with a little finely grated Parmesan cheese and serve immediately.

MELON WITH PROSCIUTTO

MELON WITH PROSCIUTTO *Serves 8*

½ small winter melon, chilled

½ large spanspek, chilled

250g thinly-sliced prosciutto (raw smoked ham)

Freshly ground black pepper

Mint sprigs (optional)

 Preparation time 20 minutes

 Cooking time 0 minutes

FOOD NOTE Prosciutto is famous for its delicately smoky flavour, which is due to the long time it is allowed to mature. It is the perfect contrast to ripe, sweet melon.

1. Cut the winter melon and the spanspek lengthwise into 1cm-thick, wedge-shaped slices (about 12 slices each). Cut off the rind. Arrange the melon on 8 serving plates, alternating slices of winter melon and spanspek.

2. Halve each slice of prosciutto lengthwise. Loosely roll each slice of prosciutto into a cone shape to resemble a rose. Arrange in the centre of the winter melon and spanspek slices. (Alternatively, place the prosciutto informally between the melon slices.) Sprinkle with pepper, garnish with mint, if desired, and serve.

APPETIZERS AND SNACKS

MARINATED VEGETABLES Serves 4

2 large (about 250g) carrots

½ small head (about 350g) cauliflower

1 tin artichoke hearts, drained and quartered, or 180g cooked, fresh artichoke hearts, quartered

½ cup black olives

2 tablespoons lemon juice

¼ cup extra-virgin olive oil

Salt and ground black pepper to taste

1 tablespoon chopped parsley

 Preparation time
5 minutes

 Cooking time
10 minutes

SERVING SUGGESTION *This refreshing antipasto platter makes an ideal starter for an Italian-style meal.*

1. In a large frying pan, bring 2,5cm of water to the boil over high heat. Meanwhile, peel the carrots and chop them diagonally into 5mm-thick slices. Add the carrots to the boiling water. Reduce the heat to moderate, cover and cook for about 2 minutes until the carrots are almost crisp-tender.

2. Trim the cauliflower and cut it into florets. Add the cauliflower florets to the carrots in the pan. Continue cooking the vegetables for about 3 more minutes.

3. Drain the vegetables and rinse them with cold water. Transfer them to a large bowl. Stir in the artichoke hearts, olives, lemon juice and olive oil. Season the vegetables with salt and pepper and toss gently.

4. Spoon the vegetables into a serving bowl and sprinkle them with the parsley. Serve them warm or refrigerate to serve chilled.

BRUSCHETTA Serves 4

5 tablespoons olive oil

1 tablespoon finely chopped spring onion

½ cup fresh basil, coarsely chopped

½ teaspoon lemon juice

6 ripe (about 350g) plum tomatoes

Salt and ground black pepper to taste

2 cloves garlic, slivered

8x2cm-thick slices French bread

Basil leaves (optional)

 Preparation time
22 minutes

 Cooking time
7 minutes

COOK'S TIP *Garlic can be slivered or crushed and stored for a couple of weeks. Place it in a tightly lidded jar, cover with olive oil and keep in the refrigerator.*

1. In a small bowl, combine 3 tablespoons of the olive oil, the spring onion, basil and lemon juice. Chop the tomatoes into 5mm pieces; add them to the oil and onion mixture. Season with salt and pepper and set aside.

2. In a small frying pan, heat the remaining 2 tablespoons oil over moderate heat. Add the garlic slivers and sauté for about 1 minute until a light golden brown. Remove the garlic from the oil and discard.

3. Toast the sliced French bread and arrange two slices of toast on each of four serving plates. Brush the garlic-flavoured oil over each slice. Using a slotted spoon, place an equal amount of the tomato mixture on each slice. Garnish each serving with basil leaves, if desired, and serve.

◄ MARINATED VEGETABLES

Snacks

Whether you want a casual meal, a packed lunch or simply a quick bite to eat, choose one of these mouthwatering savoury snacks.

Spiced nuts *Serves 12*

- 2 tablespoons (30g) butter or margarine
- 1 cup pecan nuts, halved
- 1 cup whole almonds
- 1 cup dry-roasted unsalted peanuts
- 1 tablespoon Worcestershire sauce
- 1 teaspoon chilli powder
- ½ teaspoon garlic salt
- ¼ teaspoon cayenne pepper

 Preparation time 2 minutes

 Cooking time 30 minutes

Serving suggestion You'll need a long cool drink to complement this hot, spicy hors d'oeuvre. Adjust the seasoning according to your taste.

1. Preheat the oven to 150°C. Place the butter in a 32,5cm x 22,5cm baking tin and place the tin in the oven to melt the butter. Remove from the oven and add the pecan nuts, almonds, peanuts and Worcestershire sauce to the melted butter. Stir until well mixed.

2. Bake the nut mixture for about 30 minutes until it is toasted, stirring occasionally. Remove the nuts from the oven and sprinkle the mixture evenly with the chilli powder, garlic salt and cayenne pepper. Toss until well mixed.

3. Transfer the warm nuts to a bowl and serve immediately, or leave to cool and store them at room temperature in an airtight container. (Makes 3 cups.)

Herbed popcorn-cereal bites *Serves 10*

- 2 tablespoons (30g) butter or margarine
- 1 tablespoon Worcestershire sauce
- 1 tablespoon dried basil or origanum
- Dash of Tabasco sauce
- 4 cups bite-sized wheat cereal squares or chunks of Weetbix
- 1 cup pretzels
- 1 cup unsalted peanuts
- 4 cups popped popcorn

 Preparation time 5 minutes

 Cooking time 25 minutes

Serving suggestion Serve this glamorous savoury popcorn mixture as a snack when braaiing or as a treat for special occasions.

1. Preheat the oven to 150°C. Place the butter in a 37,5cm x 26,5cm baking tin and set the tin in the oven to melt the butter. Remove the tin from the oven and stir the Worcestershire sauce, basil and Tabasco sauce into the melted butter.

2. Add the cereal squares, pretzels and peanuts and toss to coat well. Bake for 15 minutes, stirring occasionally.

3. Stir the popcorn into the cereal mixture and bake for about 10 more minutes until heated through. Pour the mixture into a large bowl and serve immediately, or leave to cool and store at room temperature in an airtight container. (Makes 10 cups.)

APPETIZERS AND SNACKS

CRISPY POTATO SKINS *Makes 16*

4 large potatoes, unpeeled

2 tablespoons (30g) butter or margarine

2 tablespoons sunflower oil

Salt and ground black pepper to taste

Sour cream (optional)

Chopped chives (optional)

 Preparation time
5 minutes

 Cooking time
63 minutes

COOK'S TIP *The potato flesh scooped out of the skins shouldn't be wasted – save it to make mashed potatoes.*

1. Rinse and dry the potatoes. Using a fork, pierce the potatoes several times. Bake in a conventional oven at 200°C for about 1 hour until cooked, or microwave on high power for about 20 to 25 minutes, rotating them several times during cooking.

2. Meanwhile, in a small saucepan, heat the butter and oil over low heat until the butter melts. Remove the pan from the heat.

3. Remove the potatoes from the oven and let them cool slightly. Preheat the grill. Cut the baked potatoes in half along their length and scoop out the flesh, leaving a shell of approximately 6mm around the edge.

4. Slice the skins lengthwise in half again. Place them on the rack over the grill pan, cut surfaces up. Brush each with the oil mixture and grill 10cm from the heat for about 3 minutes until crisp. Transfer the skins to a platter and season with the salt and pepper. Serve with sour cream and chives, if desired.

HAM ROLLS *Makes 32*

1 small cucumber, unpeeled

250g cream cheese, softened

2 tablespoons coarse-grained prepared mustard

1 tablespoon chopped dill (or 1 teaspoon dried dill)

8 rectangular slices (about 250g) cooked ham

 Preparation time
24 minutes

 Cooking/chilling time
20 minutes

1. Cut the cucumber in half along its length. Using a spoon, scoop out and discard the seeds. Cut the seeded cucumber lengthwise into about eight 1cm-thick strips.

2. In a medium-sized bowl, blend the cream cheese and mustard until smooth. Stir in the dill and blend until well mixed. Spread about 2 tablespoons of the cream-cheese mixture evenly over each slice of the cooked ham, spreading it to the edges.

3. Place a cucumber strip on the short edge of one slice of cheese-coated ham. Trim the ends of the cucumber until even with the edges of the ham and roll up securely. Secure with toothpicks, if necessary. Repeat with the remaining cucumber and ham slices. Refrigerate the rolls for 20 minutes.

4. Using a serrated knife, carefully cut the chilled ham rolls crosswise into four 2,5cm-thick slices. Arrange the ham-roll slices on a serving platter and serve.

SAUTÉED BRINJAL SANDWICHES

SAUTÉED BRINJAL SANDWICHES *Makes 4*

1 large brinjal (about 600g), unpeeled

¼ cup flour

¼ teaspoon salt

¼ cup sunflower oil

8 slices (about 250g) mozzarella cheese

4 large slices ripe tomato

8 anchovy fillets

1 teaspoon chopped parsley

 Preparation time 10 minutes

 Cooking time 12 minutes

Serving suggestion Serve this filling snack with a salad of red oak leaf lettuce and onion as a quick and delicious meal.

1. Slice the brinjal crosswise into eight 1cm-thick slices. Mix the flour and salt in a pie plate. Dip the brinjal slices into the flour mixture to coat evenly.

2. Heat 2 tablespoons of the oil in a large frying pan over moderate heat. Working in batches, add the brinjal and sauté for about 2 minutes on each side until tender and browned on both sides, adding more oil if necessary. Remove the brinjal from the pan and drain on paper towels.

3. On each of four brinjal slices, place a slice of cheese, a slice of tomato and two anchovies, and top with the remaining slices of cheese. Cover with the remaining brinjal slices.

4. Return the pan to moderate heat and fry the brinjal sandwiches for about 3 minutes until the cheese melts slightly, turning once (use two egg lifters). Transfer the brinjal sandwiches to serving plates, sprinkle with the parsley and serve immediately.

APPETIZERS AND SNACKS

OPEN-FACED CUCUMBER TEA SANDWICHES *Makes 24*

½ small cucumber

125g cream cheese, softened

1 teaspoon finely chopped chives or spring onion

Salt and ground white pepper to taste

6 slices firm whole-wheat bread

24 thin slices cucumber, unpeeled

 Preparation time
15 minutes

 Cooking time
0 minutes

1. Peel the whole cucumber. Slice it in half lengthwise and discard the seeds. Finely chop the cucumber and let it drain (about ¼ cup flesh). In a small bowl, mix the cucumber with the cream cheese and chives. Season the mixture with the salt and pepper.

2. Using a sharp knife, trim the crusts from the bread slices. Spread one side of each slice with some of the cream-cheese mixture. Cut into quarters.

3. Top each sandwich with a slice of unpeeled cucumber. Arrange on a platter and serve immediately.

SNOEK PATÈ SANDWICHES *Makes 16*

250g smoked snoek, deboned and flaked

¼ cup cream

2 tablespoons (30g) butter, softened

1 tablespoon lemon juice

Salt and black pepper

8 slices whole-wheat bread

2 tablespoons (30g) butter for spreading

Dill sprigs (optional)

 Preparation time
20 minutes

 Cooking/chilling time
20 minutes

1. In a blender or food processor, purée the smoked snoek, cream, butter and lemon juice to form a thick, smooth paste. Add salt and a grinding of black pepper to season (if necessary). Chill the mixture for about 20 minutes.

2. Butter each slice of bread. Spread 4 of the slices with the filling and top with the remaining buttered slices. Using a sharp knife, slice each sandwich diagonally into quarters. Garnish with dill sprigs, if desired, and serve immediately.

MOZZARELLA, TOMATO AND PESTO SANDWICHES *Makes 4*

For the pesto:

1 cup fresh basil leaves

1 clove garlic, crushed

1 tablespoon olive oil

⅛ teaspoon black pepper

For the sandwich filling:

2 small loaves French bread or large whole-wheat rolls

2 tablespoons (30g) butter, softened

120g sun-dried tomatoes

250g mozzarella cheese, thinly sliced

 Preparation time
10 minutes

 Cooking time
0 minutes

1. To make the pesto: In a food processor, combine the basil, garlic, olive oil and black pepper and blend until smooth.

2. Cut each French loaf in half horizontally and butter each half sparingly. Blanch the sun-dried tomatoes by placing them in boiling water for a few seconds. Remove and pat them dry on paper towels.

3. Spread the pesto thinly on the bottom half of each loaf, and top with the blanched sun-dried tomatoes and mozzarella cheese. Cover with the top of the loaf and slice in half to make 4 hearty sandwiches. Serve immediately.

OPEN SMOKED CHICKEN SANDWICHES

OPEN SMOKED CHICKEN SANDWICHES *Makes 8*

8x1cm-thick diagonal slices French bread

1 tablespoon olive or sunflower oil

2 small ripe tomatoes

180g thinly sliced smoked chicken

3 to 4 tablespoons mayonnaise

Ready washed watercress for garnishing

 Preparation time
10 minutes

 Cooking time
5 minutes

SERVING SUGGESTION With a serving of salad or a mug of hot soup, these sandwiches provide a satisfying lunch.

1 Preheat the oven to 200°C. Brush each slice of bread with a little of the oil. Place the bread on a baking sheet and bake for 4 to 5 minutes until golden brown.

2 Meanwhile, using a sharp knife, slice the tomatoes crosswise into thin slices.

3 Top each slice of toasted French bread with an equal amount of the thinly sliced smoked chicken, folding or trimming the chicken to fit, if necessary. Drop a spoonful of the mayonnaise on each slice of chicken and arrange two or three slices of tomato on top. Garnish each open-faced sandwich with a sprig of watercress.

4 If desired, arrange the remaining watercress to cover a serving platter and place the open-faced chicken sandwiches on top. Garnish the platter with any leftover slices of tomato and serve them immediately.

APPETIZERS AND SNACKS

SALMON-FILLED CROISSANTS *Makes 4*

4 large croissants

100g cream cheese, softened

1 tablespoon chopped fresh dill (or 1 teaspoon dried dill)

1 teaspoon lemon juice

250g thinly sliced smoked salmon

Coarsely ground black pepper

Dill sprigs (optional)

 Preparation time 10 minutes

 Cooking time 3 minutes

SERVING SUGGESTION Follow with a fruit salad of melon, strawberries and oranges for a special occasion treat.

1. Preheat the oven or a toaster oven to 200°C. Place the croissants on a small baking sheet and bake for about 3 minutes until warmed.

2. Meanwhile, in a small bowl, combine the cream cheese, dill and lemon juice until the mixture is very soft. Using a serrated knife, slice each croissant in half horizontally. Spread the bottom halves with the cream-cheese mixture.

3. Cover the cream cheese with the smoked salmon. Sprinkle with the ground black pepper and garnish with dill, if desired. Cover the croissant sandwiches with their top halves and serve immediately.

CHICKEN SALAD PITAS *Makes 4*

4 pita breads

300g cooked chicken, cubed

²⁄₃ cup mayonnaise

½ cup chopped celery

½ cup coarsely grated carrots

Salt and ground black pepper to taste

2 small ripe tomatoes

½ small cucumber

2 cups alfalfa sprouts

 Preparation time 7 minutes

 Cooking time 10 minutes

1. Preheat the oven to 180°C. Wrap the pita breads tightly in aluminium foil and warm them in the oven for about 10 minutes while preparing the other ingredients.

2. In a medium-sized bowl, mix the chicken, mayonnaise, celery and carrots. Season the chicken salad mixture with the salt and black pepper. Cut the tomatoes into wedges and slice the cucumber thinly.

3. Cut each pita bread in half and open up the pockets. Fill the pockets with the chicken mixture, tomatoes, cucumber slices and the alfalfa sprouts. Serve immediately.

TIME SAVERS

FREEZING SANDWICHES
Many sandwiches can be frozen ahead, reducing last-minute preparations to a minimum. For the best results, use dense breads, such as whole-wheat, which won't become soggy when thawed. Spread the bread with butter to prevent the filling from soaking into the bread. (Spreads to avoid are salad dressings and mayonnaise.) Freeze for no longer than two weeks.

Start with a Pizza Base

Make one of these creative pizzas for a party or a satisfying weekend snack. If you'd like to make your own base, turn to the recipe on page 26, or buy one ready-made from your supermarket. Each of these toppings makes enough for one large or four small pizzas.

◄ **Sesame spinach pizza** In a medium-sized saucepan, heat *2 tablespoons sunflower oil* and sauté *½ cup chopped onion* for about 5 minutes until soft. Add *one 250g package frozen creamed spinach*. Cover and simmer for about 5 minutes until cooked, stirring occasionally. Stir in *1 cup cottage cheese* and *125g crumbled feta cheese*. Season with *salt* and *black pepper*. Spoon onto the pizza base and sprinkle with *1 tablespoon sesame seeds*. Bake at 200°C until the topping is bubbly and crust is golden (10 to 15 minutes).

► **Ham and cheese pizza** Strain *one 410g tin chopped tomatoes* and spread it over the pizza base. Thinly slice *180g ham* or *salami* and arrange the meat over the tomatoes. Slice *250g mozzarella cheese* and place over the meat. Bake at 200°C until the topping is bubbly and crust is golden (10 to 15 minutes).

◄ **Sausage pizza** Remove the casings from *500g sausage*. Place the meat in a frying pan and brown, stirring to break into small pieces. Drain the fat. Strain *one 410g tin chopped tomatoes* and spoon over the pizza base. Spread the sausage over the tomatoes and sprinkle with *Parmesan cheese*. Bake at 200°C until the topping is bubbly and the crust is golden (10 to 15 minutes).

➤ **Tuna and tomato pizza** Strain *one 410g tin chopped tomatoes* and spread over the pizza base. Drain *two 185g tins tuna packed in water* and flake over the tomato. Sprinkle with *1 teaspoon dried origanum*. Season with *ground black pepper* and top with *½ cup grated Parmesan cheese*. Bake at 200°C until the topping is bubbly and crust is golden (10 to 15 minutes).

◄ **Chilli beef pizza** In a large frying pan, brown *500g lean minced beef*. Add *½ cup Italian-style tomatoes*, *½ cup frozen peas* and *½ cup frozen sweetcorn*. Add *½ teaspoon crushed chillies* (or to taste). Cook for 10 minutes, stirring occasionally. Spoon onto the pizza base and top with *½ cup chopped coriander*, if desired. Sprinkle with *½ cup grated light Cheddar cheese*. Bake at 200°C until the topping is bubbly and crust is golden (10 to 15 minutes).

◄ **Bacon and mushroom pizza** Cook *4 slices bacon* in a medium-sized frying pan. Meanwhile, in a large frying pan, heat *2 tablespoons sunflower oil*. Add *500g sliced mushrooms* and sauté for about 5 minutes until soft, stirring occasionally. Add *2 tablespoons Worcestershire sauce, 2 tablespoons soy sauce* and *1 tablespoon Dijon mustard*. Cook over moderate heat for 5 to 10 minutes until the sauce thickens. Slice *4 spring onions*. Add the green part to the mushroom mixture. Spoon onto the pizza base and sprinkle with the white part of the onions. Slice the bacon. Top the mushrooms with the bacon. Bake at 200°C until the topping is bubbly and crust is golden (10 to 15 minutes).

Chicken club sandwich

Chicken club sandwich *Makes 16*

8 rashers bacon

2 skinless chicken-breast fillets (about 180g each)

8 slices firm white bread

4 slices firm brown bread

6 tablespoons mayonnaise

8 butter lettuce leaves

8 large slices ripe tomato

Ground black pepper to taste

 Preparation time 10 minutes

 Cooking time 12 minutes

1. In a large frying pan, cook the bacon over moderate heat for about 5 minutes until crisp. Drain the bacon on paper towels and slice each rasher in half crosswise. Place the chicken-breast fillets in the pan and sauté them in the bacon drippings for about 3 minutes on each side until the juices run clear when pierced with a fork. Transfer the chicken to a plate and slice crosswise.

2. Meanwhile, lightly toast the slices of white and brown bread in a toaster or toaster oven. Spread each slice of toast with a little of the mayonnaise. Arrange half of the lettuce leaves and all of the halved bacon rashers on four of the white-bread slices. Top with half of the slices of tomato. Cover the tomato with the slices of brown-bread toast.

3. Place some of the chopped chicken on each slice of toasted brown bread. Season to taste with ground black pepper. Top with the remaining slices of tomato, lettuce and, finally, with the remaining white-bread toast. Cut the sandwiches diagonally into quarters and serve immediately.

APPETIZERS AND SNACKS

BACON AND LETTUCE PITA SANDWICH *Makes 4*

12 rashers bacon
4 pita breads
3 tablespoons mayonnaise
2 cups finely chopped crisp lettuce
1 large ripe tomato, diced
1 small avocado pear, sliced

 Preparation time
10 minutes

 Cooking time
5 minutes

1. In a large frying pan, cook the bacon over moderate heat for about 5 minutes until crisp. Drain on paper towels and slice each rasher in half crosswise.

2. Cut each pita bread in half and open up the pockets. Spread the inside surface of each pocket with some of the mayonnaise. Fill the pockets with the lettuce, tomato, avocado pear slices and the bacon. Serve immediately.

SCRAMBLED-EGG SANDWICHES *Makes 4*

1/3 cup mayonnaise
1 tablespoon Dijon mustard
4 poppy-seed rolls, halved and toasted
4 large eggs
1/4 teaspoon salt
1/4 teaspoon ground black pepper
2 tablespoons (30g) butter or margarine
1 stalk celery, sliced
4 slices Cheddar cheese
4 slices ripe tomato

 Preparation time
10 minutes

 Cooking time
7 minutes

1. Mix the mayonnaise and mustard in a small bowl. Spread the mayonnaise mixture over the sliced surfaces of the rolls. Place the bottom halves on a serving platter and set the top halves aside.

2. In a medium-sized bowl, beat the eggs with the salt and pepper. Melt the butter in a large frying pan over moderate heat. Add the celery and sauté for about 2 minutes until soft. Stir in the eggs and cook, stirring occasionally, until almost set. Remove the pan from the heat and spoon the eggs over the bottom halves of the rolls. Top with the slices of cheese and tomato and the top halves of the rolls. Serve immediately.

PEAR AND PROSCIUTTO SANDWICHES *Makes 8*

1 ripe pear, unpeeled
1 tablespoon lemon juice
8 slices pumpernickel bread
3 tablespoons coarse-grained prepared mustard
250g prosciutto (raw smoked ham), thinly sliced and trimmed of all fat
125g creamy blue cheese, cut into small pieces

 Preparation time
15 minutes

 Cooking time
0 minutes

1. Remove the core from the pear and slice the flesh thinly along its length. In a small bowl, toss the pear slices in the lemon juice to prevent discoloration. Drain and set aside.

2. Thinly spread the slices of bread with the mustard. Arrange half of the prosciutto on four of the slices of bread. Sprinkle with the blue cheese, and top with the remaining prosciutto and the drained slices of pear.

3. Cover the sandwiches with the remaining slices of bread, mustard side down. Cut each sandwich in half diagonally and serve immediately.

APPETIZERS AND SNACKS

TUNA MUFFIN MELTS *Makes 8*

2 tins (185g each) tuna, packed in water

²⁄₃ cup mayonnaise

½ cup sliced celery

¼ cup chopped sweet red pepper

Dash of Tabasco sauce

4 English muffins

125g Gruyère cheese, sliced

Sweet red pepper strips (optional)

 Preparation time
10 minutes

 Cooking time
5 minutes

SERVING SUGGESTION Make a quick supper out of these simple tuna melts by serving them with sliced raw vegetables.

1 Preheat the grill. Drain the tuna thoroughly. In a medium-sized bowl, combine the tuna, mayonnaise, celery, red pepper and Tabasco sauce.

2 Split each muffin in half horizontally. Place the muffins, split surfaces up, on the rack over the grill pan. Grill the muffins about 10cm from the heat until lightly browned.

3 Remove the muffins from the grill and spread each with an equal amount of the tuna mixture. Top the tuna with a slice of the cheese. Return the muffins to the grill and continue grilling until the cheese melts.

4 Transfer the muffins to a serving platter and garnish each with a few strips of red pepper, if desired. Serve immediately.

STACKED SANDWICH LOAF *Serves 4*

2 cups baby spinach or rocket leaves

¼ cup pitted black olives

¼ cup pimiento-stuffed green olives

2 tablespoons parsley

2 tablespoons olive oil

1 tablespoon red wine vinegar

½ teaspoon dried origanum

1 loaf round bread (about 18cm in diameter)

2 medium ripe tomatoes, sliced

100g provolone cheese, sliced

100g salami, thinly sliced

 Preparation time
15 minutes

 Cooking time
0 minutes

1 Rinse and dry the spinach leaves thoroughly. Remove the tough stems and set the spinach aside. Using a blender or food processor fitted with the chopping blade, coarsely chop the black and pimiento-stuffed olives with the parsley, olive oil, vinegar and origanum. Set the mixture aside.

2 Using a serrated knife, slice through the bread horizontally, removing the top third of the loaf. Scoop out the centre of the loaf and the top piece, leaving a 2,5cm-thick shell. (Refrigerate or freeze the scooped-out bread to be used later for crumbs, if desired.)

3 Spoon most of the olive mixture into the hollowed-out loaf, spreading it evenly over the inside. Into the cavity, layer half of the spinach, half of the tomatoes, all of the cheese and the salami; continue with the remaining spinach and tomatoes. Spread the remaining olive mixture on the inside of the top 'lid' of the loaf.

4 Cover the loaf with the top crust of the bread and press down firmly. Place on a cutting board and slice it into quarters, using a serrated knife. Serve immediately.

FRENCH-TOASTED SANDWICHES

FRENCH-TOASTED SANDWICHES *Makes 4*

3 large eggs

¾ cup milk

½ teaspoon mustard powder

250g Gruyère or Emmenthal cheese, sliced

8 slices day-old white bread

125g ham, thinly sliced

3 to 4 tablespoons (45g to 60g) butter or margarine

For the topping (optional):

¼ cup mayonnaise

1 tablespoon finely chopped chives or spring onion top

1 tablespoon Dijon mustard

1 teaspoon paprika

Preparation time 20 minutes

 Cooking time 16 minutes

FOOD NOTE *This sizzling ham-and-cheese sandwich is better known in France as* Croque Monsieur.

1 Preheat the oven to 120°C. Place the eggs in a shallow dish or pie plate and beat well. Stir in the milk and mustard powder until well blended.

2 Arrange half of the cheese slices on four slices of the bread, trimming the cheese to fit. Top the cheese with the ham and the remaining cheese and cover with the remaining bread. Carefully dip each sandwich into the egg mixture and, using a spatula, turn the sandwich over to soak both slices of bread.

3 In a large frying pan, melt 1 tablespoon of the butter over moderately low heat. Sauté the sandwiches, two at a time, for 3 to 4 minutes on each side until lightly browned. Add more butter if needed. Keep the toasted sandwiches warm in the oven while cooking the remaining sandwiches.

4 To make the topping: Mix the mayonnaise, chives, mustard and paprika in a small bowl and pass around separately, if desired.

BEAN TOSTADAS

BEAN TOSTADAS *Makes 8*

Sunflower oil for frying

8 tortillas

1 small onion, chopped

1 tin (410g) chilli beans, mashed

1 small green chilli, chopped

1 cup (125g) coarsely grated mild Cheddar or Gouda cheese

2 cups finely chopped lettuce

¼ cup sliced red radish

¼ cup sliced pitted black olives

¾ cup ready-made chunky tomato salsa

 Preparation time
15 minutes

 Cooking time
28 minutes

COOK'S TIP You can skip Step 1 completely if you purchase ready-made taco shells; wrap them in foil and warm them in the oven.

1. In a large frying pan, heat 5mm sunflower oil over moderately high heat. Add the tortillas, one at a time, and fry each for about 2 minutes until crisp on both sides, turning once. Drain the fried tortilla, or tostada shell, on paper towels and repeat to fry the remaining tortillas.

2. Drain all but 2 tablespoons of the oil from the frying pan. Add the onion and sauté over moderate heat for about 5 minutes until soft. Stir in the chilli beans and chilli and simmer for a further 1 to 2 minutes until heated through. Stir half of the grated cheese into the beans until melted. Remove from the heat.

3. Spread the bean mixture on the tostada shells. Top each with some of the lettuce, radishes, olives, the remaining cheese and salsa. Serve immediately.

APPETIZERS AND SNACKS

SMOKED SAUSAGE AND SAUERKRAUT SANDWICHES *Makes 4*

4 large (about 500g) smoked sausages

⅓ cup mayonnaise

4 oval slices dark rye or pumpernickel bread

250g sauerkraut, drained and rinsed

4 slices (about 180g) Gruyère or Emmenthal cheese

Dill pickles (optional)

 Preparation time 6 minutes

 Cooking time 7 minutes

1. Preheat the grill. Without cutting all the way through, slice each sausage almost in half along its length. Place the split sausages, cut sides down, on the greased rack over a grill pan. Grill them 10cm from the heat for about 6 minutes until lightly browned, turning once during grilling.

2. Meanwhile, spread the mayonnaise on one side of each slice of bread. Place one sausage, split side up, on each slice of bread. Top each with one-quarter of the sauerkraut and a slice of cheese.

3. Return the sandwiches to the grill and grill for about 1 minute until the cheese melts. Transfer the sandwiches to serving plates and serve with pickles, if desired.

ROAST BEEF ROLLS *Makes 4*

4 sesame-seed rolls

180g prepared coleslaw

1 tablespoon prepared white horseradish, drained

250g rare roast beef, thinly sliced

¼ cup sliced red radish

Red radishes with their leaves (optional)

 Preparation time 15 minutes

 Cooking time 2 minutes

1. Preheat the grill or toaster oven. Using a serrated knife, slice each roll in half horizontally. Place the rolls, sliced sides up, on a small baking sheet and grill 10cm from the heat for about 2 minutes until lightly browned.

2. Combine the ready-made coleslaw and the horseradish in a small bowl until well blended. Spread a 5mm-thick layer of the coleslaw-horseradish mixture on the bottom half of the rolls. Top with the thinly sliced roast beef, folding or trimming it to fit on the roll neatly.

3. Spoon a little more of the coleslaw over the roast beef and top it with a layer of radish slices. Add the top half of the rolls. Place the beef rolls on serving plates, garnish with whole radishes, if desired, and serve.

TIME SAVERS

LUNCHBOX TIPS

▪ Weekday mornings will be more relaxed if you pack lunchboxes the night before and keep them in the refrigerator. For the freshest sandwiches, pack lettuce and tomatoes separately from the bread and add them just before eating.

Avoid refrigerating biscuits and crackers – they will lose their crispness when chilled. Add them to the lunchbox in the morning.

SAVOURY MINCE ROLLS *Makes 4*

2 tablespoons sunflower oil

1 small onion, chopped

1 small sweet green pepper, cored, seeded and chopped

500g lean beef mince

1½ teaspoons ground cumin

½ teaspoon garlic powder

1 cup tomato sauce

1 cup diced fresh or tinned tomatoes

Salt and ground black pepper to taste

4 rolls

 Preparation time
8 minutes

 Cooking time
22 minutes

1. Heat the oil over moderate heat in a large frying pan. Add the onion and the sweet green pepper and sauté for about 5 minutes until soft. Stir in the beef mince, cumin and garlic powder and cook for about 7 minutes until the meat is lightly browned.

2. Remove the frying pan from the heat and drain any excess drippings from the beef mixture. Return the frying pan to the heat and stir the tomato sauce and tomatoes into the beef mixture. Bring to the boil. Reduce the heat to low. Cook the mixture for 5 more minutes, stirring constantly. Season with salt and pepper. Remove the meat mixture from the heat.

3. Toast the rolls in a toaster or toaster oven. Place them on serving plates, top each with an equal amount of the beef mixture and serve immediately.

CRUSTY HOT DOGS *Makes 20*

1 package ready-rolled pastry

¼ cup prepared mustard

10 frankfurters

1 large egg

1 tablespoon water

Sesame or poppy seeds (optional)

Additional prepared mustard (optional)

 Preparation time
13 minutes

 Cooking time
25 minutes

SERVING SUGGESTION *These hot-dog snacks make a warm and tasty treat for children. Serve them with a bowl of vegetable soup for a filling and wholesome lunch.*

1. Preheat the oven to 200°C. Unwrap the pastry according to the directions on the package and, using a floured rolling pin, roll it out once or twice to make it slightly thinner. With a rubber spatula, spread the pastry with a light coating of the prepared mustard. Cut into a large circle and then slice it into 20 equally-sized wedges.

2. Slice each frankfurter in half crosswise. Place a halved frankfurter on the wide end of each wedge-shaped piece of pastry. Roll the pastry around the frankfurter from the wide side of the wedge towards its point. Place it, with its pointed end underneath, on a greased baking sheet. Repeat with the remaining frankfurters.

3. Mix the egg and the water in a cup or small bowl. Brush the pastry-wrapped frankfurters with the egg-and-water mixture. Sprinkle with sesame or poppy seeds, if desired, and bake for 20 to 25 minutes until lightly browned. Transfer to a warmed platter and serve with additional prepared mustard, if desired.

Soups

Pumpkin and orange soup (page 87)

First-course soups

Served with a sandwich or as a starter to a ready-made meal, these quick soups will add a touch of home-made goodness.

Middle Eastern tomato soup Serves 4

1 tablespoon olive oil

1 baby marrow, sliced into narrow strips

½ cup cracked wheat

4 cups chicken stock

2 teaspoons dried mint

2 large (about 500g) ripe tomatoes, skinned and chopped (or one 410g tin chopped tomatoes, drained)

1 spring onion, slivered

2 pita breads, toasted and cut into 6 triangles each

 Preparation time
12 minutes

 Cooking time
23 minutes

FOOD NOTE *Serve this delicious soup with a green salad and toasted pita bread for a filling meal.*

1. In a medium-sized saucepan, heat the oil over moderate heat. Add the baby marrow and sauté for 2 minutes. Add the cracked wheat and stir to coat with the oil. Add the stock and mint and bring the mixture to the boil over high heat. Reduce the heat to low, cover and simmer for 5 minutes.

2. Stir the chopped tomatoes into the cracked wheat mixture. Cover the saucepan and simmer the mixture for 10 more minutes. Garnish the soup with the spring onion and serve with toasted pita bread triangles.

Easy mushroom soup Serves 4

2 tablespoons (30g) butter or margarine

1 large onion, finely chopped

½ cup chopped sweet green pepper

1 small clove garlic, finely chopped

1½ cups (about 125g) sliced mushrooms

2 tablespoons flour

2 cups chicken stock

½ cup milk

Salt and ground black pepper to taste

1 tablespoon chopped parsley

 Preparation time
17 minutes

 Cooking time
20 minutes

DIET NOTE *This simple soup can be adapted for vegetarians by replacing the chicken stock with vegetable stock, made with vegetable stock cubes (or powder) and boiling water. Either stock mingles deliciously with the earthy flavour of the mushrooms.*

1. In a large saucepan, melt the butter over moderate heat. Add the onion, green pepper and garlic. Sauté for about 5 minutes, stirring occasionally, until the onion is soft. Stir in the mushrooms and sauté, stirring constantly, for about 3 minutes until they are just softened.

2. Stir the flour into the mushroom mixture until well mixed. Add the stock and bring the mixture to the boil over high heat, stirring for about 5 minutes until thickened.

3. Reduce the heat to moderate. Add the milk and season to taste with the salt and pepper. Heat the soup, stirring frequently, until it is hot, taking care not to let it boil. Stir in the chopped parsley and serve immediately.

LEEK AND POTATO SOUP

LEEK AND POTATO SOUP *Serves 4*

2 tablespoons (30g) butter or margarine

2 medium leeks, white part only, sliced and rinsed

1 small onion, chopped

1 large (350g) potato, peeled and diced

2 cups water

½ cup milk

½ teaspoon salt

1 tablespoon chopped fresh chives

Ground black pepper to taste

 Preparation time 10 minutes

 Cooking time 30 minutes

COOK'S TIP Based on the classic creamy potato soup called vichyssoise, this soup is just as delicious served cold. If it thickens too much when chilled, dilute it with a little milk.

1 In a large saucepan, melt the butter over moderate heat. Add the leeks, onion and potato, and sauté for 5 minutes, stirring occasionally. Add the water. Cover the saucepan and bring the mixture to the boil over high heat. Reduce the heat and, still covered, simmer the soup for about 15 minutes until the potato is cooked through.

2 Using a food processor or electric blender, purée the soup, half at a time, until smooth. Pour into a medium-sized saucepan.

3 Stir in the milk and salt. Reheat the soup over moderate heat until it is hot but not boiling. Ladle into individual bowls. Sprinkle each serving with an equal amount of the chives and a pinch of black pepper. Serve immediately.

SOUPS

GREEN PEA SOUP *Serves 5*

4 cups vegetable stock (made with vegetable stock cubes or powder, and water)

2 cups frozen green peas

2 heads butter lettuce, cored and finely chopped (about 6 cups)

3 spring onions, chopped

½ teaspoon dried tarragon

¼ teaspoon ground white pepper

Salt to taste

Croutons (optional)

 Preparation time
10 minutes

 Cooking time
28 minutes

SERVING SUGGESTION This warming, low-kilojoule soup is best served in a mug accompanied by a whole-wheat ham and salad sandwich.

1. In a large saucepan, combine the stock, peas, lettuce, spring onions and tarragon. Bring to the boil over high heat. Reduce the heat, cover and simmer for 5 minutes.

2. Using a food processor or electric blender, purée the soup, one-third at a time. Pour the soup into a medium-sized saucepan. Reheat over moderate heat until the soup is hot but not boiling.

3. Stir in the pepper and season with salt to taste. Ladle the soup into mugs or bowls and top each serving with a few croutons, if desired. Serve immediately.

SWEETCORN DUMPLING SOUP *Serves 4*

3 cups chicken or beef stock

3 cups water

2 cups fresh or frozen corn kernels

For the dumplings:

⅔ cup flour

½ teaspoon salt

2 large eggs

 Preparation time
5 minutes

 Cooking time
25 minutes

1. In a large saucepan, bring the stock, water and corn kernels to the boil over high heat.

2. Meanwhile, to make the dumplings, combine the flour and salt in a small bowl. In a second small bowl, whisk the eggs thoroughly. Stir the eggs into the flour mixture to form a soft dough. Dip a teaspoon into cold water and spoon up some of the dough. Using a knife, push off ½-teaspoon-sized pieces of the dough into the boiling stock.

3. Reduce the heat, cover and simmer the soup for approximately 15 minutes until the dumplings have risen and are cooked through. Serve immediately.

MEATBALL SOUP

Prepare the soup as in Step 1 above. To make meatballs instead of the dumplings, soak *2 slices of whole-wheat bread* in *water* or *beef stock*. Squeeze until nearly dry and crumble. In a food processor or electric blender, mix the bread, *125g lean minced beef, 1 tablespoon grated* or *finely chopped onion, 1 teaspoon chopped parsley, a pinch of cayenne pepper, a dash of soy sauce* and *1 large egg*. Purée for a few seconds until smooth. Roll the meat mixture into 2,5cm balls and drop them into the boiling soup. Simmer for 10 to 15 minutes until cooked through.

CAULIFLOWER YOGHURT SOUP *Serves 4*

2¼ cups water
500g frozen cauliflower
2 tablespoons (30g) butter or margarine
2 tablespoons slivered almonds
1 small onion, chopped
1 tablespoon flour
½ teaspoon salt
½ teaspoon sugar
⅛ teaspoon ground nutmeg
1 cup plain low-fat yoghurt
1 cup milk
Chopped parsley

 Preparation time 10 minutes

 Cooking time 32 minutes

SERVING SUGGESTION *Save a little yoghurt to swirl into each serving. This elegant soup makes a fine appetizer for roast chicken or lamb.*

1. Pour the water into a large saucepan, add the cauliflower and bring the mixture to the boil over high heat. Reduce the heat to low, cover and simmer for 6 to 8 minutes until the cauliflower is soft. Over a medium-sized bowl, drain the cauliflower and reserve 2 cups of the cooking liquid. Remove the cauliflower from the saucepan and set aside.

2. In the same saucepan, melt the butter over moderate heat. Add the almonds and sauté for 1 to 2 minutes until brown. Using a slotted spoon, remove the almonds and set aside. Add the onion to the remaining butter in the saucepan and sauté for about 5 minutes over moderate heat until soft.

3. Stir in the flour, salt, sugar and nutmeg. Stir in the reserved liquid and continue cooking until the soup is thickened and bubbly. Remove from the heat and stir in the cauliflower.

4. Using a food processor or electric blender, purée the cauliflower mixture with the yoghurt, combining one-third of each at a time.

5. Pour the soup into a medium-sized saucepan and stir in the milk. Over moderate heat, reheat the soup (do not boil). Ladle the soup into bowls. Sprinkle each serving with some of the almonds and a pinch of parsley and serve immediately.

QUICK BORSCHT *Serves 4*

2 cups (250g) sliced bottled beetroot, undrained
1 cup chicken stock
¾ cup sour cream
2 tablespoons lemon juice
2 tablespoons chopped onion
2 teaspoons sugar, or to taste
½ teaspoon dried dill
Salt to taste

 Preparation time 7 minutes

 Cooking time 5 minutes

1. Using a food processor or electric blender, purée the sliced beetroot with its liquid for 1 minute.

2. Add the stock, ½ cup of the sour cream, the lemon juice, onion, sugar and dill to the beetroot. Season with salt and purée the mixture until it is smooth, stopping occasionally to scrape the sides of the container with a rubber spatula.

3. Pour the soup into a medium-sized saucepan and heat gently over moderate heat for about 5 minutes until it is hot but not boiling. Ladle into bowls and swirl a spoonful of the remaining ¼ cup sour cream into each serving. Serve immediately.

SOUPS

SPICY CREAM OF CARROT SOUP *Serves 6*

3 to 3½ cups chicken stock
4 medium carrots, sliced
1 medium onion, thickly sliced
1 medium stalk celery, sliced
3 tablespoons long-grain white rice
½ teaspoon sugar
⅛ teaspoon cayenne pepper, or to taste
½ cup milk
½ cup sour cream
Salt to taste
Diced sweet red pepper (optional)

 Preparation time
10 minutes

 Cooking time
32 minutes

DIET NOTE This nutritious soup is rich in vitamin A, which is essential for strong bones, healthy skin and good vision. Enjoy it freshly made and hot, or chilled and served cold. Either way, it makes a tasty first course or light lunch.

1. In a large saucepan, combine 3 cups of the stock, the carrots, onion, celery, rice, sugar and cayenne pepper. Cover and bring to the boil over high heat. Reduce the heat to low and simmer for 15 to 20 minutes until the rice and carrots are tender.

2. Stir the milk and sour cream into the carrot mixture. Using a food processor or electric blender, purée the soup, half at a time, until it is smooth. If a thinner soup is desired, blend in ½ cup of additional chicken stock.

3. Return the soup to a medium-sized saucepan. Stir in the salt and additional cayenne pepper, if desired. Reheat the soup over moderate heat until it is hot but not boiling. Ladle the soup into bowls and top each serving with diced red pepper, if desired. Serve immediately.

SHELF MAGIC

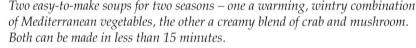

Two easy-to-make soups for two seasons – one a warming, wintry combination of Mediterranean vegetables, the other a creamy blend of crab and mushroom. Both can be made in less than 15 minutes.

MEDITERRANEAN VEGETABLE SOUP

In a medium-sized saucepan, with a potato masher, crush the contents of *one 410g tin Italian-style tomatoes*. Add *one 400g tin Mediterranean-style ratatouille, one 400g tin green beans*, drained, and *2 cups vegetable stock*. Add *1 clove crushed garlic* and bring to the simmer. Add about *30 strands of spaghettini*, broken. Cook, stirring regularly, for about 10 minutes until the pasta is tender. Season with *black pepper* and *salt*. Garnish with *chopped basil* and *grated Parmesan cheese*. Serves 4

CRAB AND MUSHROOM BISQUE

In a large saucepan, heat together *one 425g tin cream of mushroom soup, one 425g tin asparagus soup, 1 cup full cream milk* and *½ cup cream*. Heat over moderate heat, stirring constantly to mix thoroughly. Add *one 227g tin crabmeat*, finely chopped. Stir in *3 tablespoons sherry*. Heat gently. Just before serving, add a grinding of *black pepper* (or use *lemon pepper* for added flavour). Serve hot or chilled, garnished with *chopped dill* or *chives*, if desired. Serves 4

VEGETABLE CONSOMMÉ

VEGETABLE CONSOMMÉ *Serves 4*

- 6 sprigs parsley
- 2 cloves garlic
- 2 bay leaves
- 1 teaspoon black peppercorns
- 1 tablespoon (15g) butter or margarine
- 1 medium leek, white part only, sliced and rinsed
- 4 cups water
- 2 vegetable stock cubes
- 2 medium stalks celery
- 2 medium carrots, peeled
- 125g mange-tout, trimmed

 Preparation time
6 minutes

 Cooking time
20 minutes

SERVING SUGGESTION This light soup makes an elegant introduction to a main dish of beef or poultry. It's best served in shallow bowls so that the colourful vegetables are clearly visible.

1. Using a piece of muslin and string, tie the parsley, garlic, bay leaves and peppercorns together tightly to form a small parcel, called a bouquet garni.

2. In a large saucepan, melt the butter over low heat. Add the leek and sauté for about 5 minutes until soft. Add the water, stock cubes and the bouquet garni. Increase the heat to high, cover and bring to the boil.

3. Meanwhile, slice the celery and carrots into matchstick strips. Add them to the boiling consommé. Reduce the heat to moderate and simmer for 5 to 8 minutes until the vegetables are just tender. Slice the mange-tout into thirds lengthwise, if desired. Remove the bouquet garni, stir in the mange-tout and cook for 1 minute. Ladle into bowls and serve immediately.

START WITH A STOCK

Stock forms the base for most soups (in fact, the French call it fond, *which literally means 'foundation') and having a supply on hand makes it easy to create a quick, tasty and healthy meal. Start with ready-made or home-made stock (see pages 22 to 24), allowing about one cup per person. Add one or more ingredients, using the food in your refrigerator and the staples in your cupboard as your guide. Experiment with a variety of flavours and textures. Always bring the stock to a rolling boil and skim off any foam (in the case of home-made stocks) before adding the other ingredients. Each of the following recipes serves four.*

◄ **Vegetable and pasta soup** In a large saucepan, boil *4 cups vegetable stock*. Slice *2 or 3 mushrooms* and *¼ leek*; peel and dice *1 small tomato*. Add *¼ cup pastina* (tiny pasta shapes) to the boiling stock and simmer for about 4 minutes until the pasta is partially cooked. Add the vegetables and continue to simmer until the vegetables are crisp-tender. Stir in *1 tablespoon chopped parsley*; season with *salt* and *pepper*. Serve with *savoury biscuits*.

► **Oriental-style fish soup** Bring *4 cups fish* or *vegetable stock* to the boil in a medium-sized saucepan. Slice *4 spring onions*, finely chop *1 small clove garlic*, and peel and finely chop a *1cm piece of fresh ginger*. Add the spring onions, garlic, ginger, *1 teaspoon soy sauce* and *1 teaspoon crushed chillies* to the stock. Add *½ cup cooked chopped shrimps* or *one 200g tin baby clams*, drained and chopped. Simmer for 2 minutes. Garnish with *fresh coriander*.

◄ **Chopped-spinach soup** In a medium-sized saucepan, bring *4 cups vegetable stock* to the boil. Roll *1 bunch young spinach leaves* into a cigar shape and cut the leaves crosswise into very thin strips. Add the spinach to the boiling stock and simmer for 1 minute. Season with *salt*, *pepper* and a *pinch of nutmeg*. Sprinkle with *toasted slivered almonds*.

◄ **Ham and cheese soup** Bring 4 *cups of beef stock* to the boil in a large saucepan. Slice *1 stalk celery*, cube *2 slices cooked ham* and dice *60g mozzarella cheese*. Add the celery to the boiling stock and simmer for 1 to 2 minutes. Add the ham and cook for 1 minute. Season to taste with *salt* and *pepper*. Place some of the cheese in each serving bowl and ladle the soup over it. Garnish with *croutons* and *fresh basil*.

► **Lima bean soup** Bring *4 cups of chicken stock* to the boil in a large saucepan. Chop *1 medium onion* and slice *2 bratwurst* or other mild cooked sausage. Add the onion and sausage to the boiling stock. Add *one 400g tin lima beans*, drained, and *1 clove garlic*, crushed. Simmer for about 5 minutes until the onion is soft and the sausage is heated through. Season with *salt* and *pepper*.

◄ **Chicken soup** In a large saucepan, boil *4 cups chicken stock*. Thinly slice *1 small carrot*, *½ small leek* and *1 small stalk celery*. Slice *1 small skinned chicken-breast fillet* into thin strips and add it to the boiling stock. Simmer for 2 minutes. Add the vegetables and simmer for about 2 to 3 minutes until the chicken is cooked through and the vegetables are crisp-tender. Season with *salt* and *pepper*.

INGREDIENTS TO ADD TO STOCKS

Beef stock	Chicken and Vegetable Stocks	Fish stock
Sliced sausage	Croutons	Cooked fish or seafood
Cubed cheese	Toasted nuts	Fresh herbs
Diced potato	Oriental noodles	Soy sauce
Tinned beans	Diced chicken	Oriental vegetables, eg bean sprouts
Tinned tomatoes	Finely chopped vegetables	Toasted sesame seeds
Noodles or pasta shapes		

Main-course soups

Hearty and aromatic, these easy soups need only a tossed salad and a basket of warm bread to satisfy a hungry family.

Creamy peanut soup *Serves 4*

1 tablespoon peanut or sunflower oil

1 medium onion, finely chopped

1 clove garlic, finely chopped

2 medium potatoes, peeled and chopped

2 medium carrots, sliced

1 medium stalk celery, sliced

3½ cups chicken stock

½ cup smooth peanut butter

¼ teaspoon cayenne pepper

¼ cup sour cream

 Preparation time 12 minutes

 Cooking time 30 minutes

FOOD NOTE *Protein-rich peanut butter is the unusual ingredient that makes this soup so tasty and filling. If you prefer to make a vegetarian soup, vegetable stock (made with stock cubes and water) may be substituted for the chicken stock.*

1 In a large saucepan, heat the oil over moderate heat. Add the onion and garlic and sauté for approximately 1 minute. Stir in the vegetables. Add the stock and bring to the boil. Reduce the heat, cover the saucepan and simmer for about 15 minutes until the vegetables are tender.

2 Remove the soup from the heat. Stir in the peanut butter and cayenne pepper until well blended. Using a food processor or electric blender, purée the soup, half at a time, until smooth.

3 Return the soup to a medium-sized saucepan. Reheat over moderate heat (do not boil). Ladle the soup into bowls and top with a swirl of the sour cream. Serve immediately.

Time Savers

Soup

■ If your soup has too much liquid in proportion to the amount of solid ingredients, press a large strainer into the saucepan and hold it over the solids. Use a ladle to remove the excess liquid that filters into the strainer.

■ Don't discard leftover stock – freeze it in an ice cube tray to use later to add flavour to casseroles, rice and pasta dishes, or when cooking vegetables.

■ A hand-held blender is a convenient appliance for puréeing soups. It allows you to blend the soup directly in the saucepan instead of transferring it to a blender container.

■ To thicken the liquid in chunky soups quickly, place a slice of toasted French bread on the bottom of each serving bowl, then add the soup. The bread absorbs the liquid and disintegrates into the soup, making it thick.

■ Quickly preheat bowls or mugs in order to keep soups hot. An easy way to warm the dishes is to fill them with boiling water and leave them to stand for a few minutes while you finish preparing the soup.

■ Soups can easily be prepared ahead of time – most taste even better a couple of days after they're made. Chill them in airtight containers and simply reheat.

SOUPS

Cheddar cheese soup *Serves 4*

- 2 stalks celery, sliced
- 1 small sweet green pepper, cored, seeded and chopped
- 2 medium carrots, diced
- 1 cup chopped cauliflower
- 2 cups chicken stock
- 4 tablespoons (60g) butter or margarine
- ½ cup flour
- 3 cups milk
- 1½ cups (180g) coarsely grated mature Cheddar cheese
- 1 teaspoon Worcestershire sauce
- Paprika for garnishing

 Preparation time
12 minutes

 Cooking time
21 minutes

Serving suggestion Turn this cheesy soup into a complete meal by complementing it with a mixed green salad topped with raisins and chopped nuts.

1. In a large saucepan, combine the celery, green pepper, carrots, cauliflower and stock. Bring to the boil over high heat. Reduce the heat, cover and simmer for about 10 minutes until the vegetables are tender.

2. Meanwhile, in a medium-sized saucepan, melt the butter over moderate heat. Stir in the flour and cook for about 1 minute until just bubbling. Remove the saucepan from the heat. Using a wire whisk, gradually blend in the milk.

3. Cook the milk mixture over moderate heat, stirring constantly, for about 5 minutes until slightly thickened (do not boil). Stir in the cheese until it is just melted and smooth.

4. Stir the cheese mixture and Worcestershire sauce into the vegetable mixture until it is thoroughly mixed. Ladle the soup into bowls and sprinkle each serving with a pinch of paprika. Serve immediately.

French onion soup *Serves 4*

- 3 tablespoons (45g) butter or margarine
- 4 large onions, sliced
- 1 tablespoon flour
- 2 cups beef stock
- 2 cups water
- 1 teaspoon Worcestershire sauce
- 4x1cm-thick slices French bread
- 4 slices (about 30g each) Gruyère cheese

 Preparation time
8 minutes

 Cooking time
27 minutes

Cook's tip Try adding a glass of dry red wine to the stock to create an even richer flavour in this ever-popular classic.

1. In a large saucepan, melt the butter over moderate heat. Add the onions and sauté, covered, for about 10 minutes, stirring frequently to prevent them from sticking. Stir in the flour.

2. Add the stock, water and Worcestershire sauce. Bring to the boil. Reduce the heat, cover and simmer for about 10 minutes.

3. Meanwhile, preheat the grill. Place the bread on a baking tray and toast it on both sides. Cover each slice with a slice of the cheese. Return to the oven and grill for a few seconds until the cheese is just melted and browned.

4. Place a cheese-topped slice of bread in each serving bowl. Ladle the soup over the bread and serve immediately.

BACON AND CORN CHOWDER

BACON AND CORN CHOWDER *Serves 4*

3 slices bacon, sliced into 1cm strips

1 large onion, chopped

2 medium potatoes, peeled and diced

1½ cups chicken stock

1½ cups fresh or frozen corn kernels

3 cups milk

Salt and ground white pepper to taste

Chopped parsley for garnishing

 Preparation time
15 minutes

 Cooking time
30 minutes

SERVING SUGGESTION Serve this chowder with easily prepared quesadillas – slices of mild Cheddar cheese melted between two flour tortillas. For even simpler fare, serve it with crispy tortilla chips.

1. In a large saucepan, fry the bacon for about 4 minutes until crisp. With a slotted spoon, remove the bacon and drain it on a paper towel. Pour off all but 1 tablespoon of the drippings in the pan.

2. Add the onion and sauté for about 5 minutes until soft. Add the potatoes and stock and bring to the boil over high heat. Reduce the heat, cover, and simmer for about 10 minutes until the potatoes are very soft.

3. Stir in the corn kernels and milk. Heat the soup over moderate heat (do not boil). Season with salt and pepper. Ladle the soup into bowls and crumble some of the bacon over each serving. Garnish with the chopped parsley and serve immediately.

SALMON CHOWDER

SALMON CHOWDER *Serves 4*

2 tablespoons (30g) butter or margarine

1 medium onion, chopped

1½ cups water

2 to 3 large (about 380g) potatoes, unpeeled, scrubbed and diced

½ teaspoon salt

¼ teaspoon ground white pepper

500g salmon or salmon trout fillets, sliced into 2,5cm chunks

2 cups milk

Chopped fresh dill or parsley for garnishing

 Preparation time
7 minutes

 Cooking time
31 minutes

FOOD NOTE This subtle chowder tastes best when made with fresh salmon. Substitute two 212g tins of salmon if fresh is unavailable.

1 In a large saucepan, melt the butter over moderate heat. Add the onion and sauté for about 5 minutes, stirring occasionally, until softened.

2 Add the water, potatoes, salt and pepper. Increase the heat to high and bring the mixture to the boil. Reduce the heat to low. Cover and simmer the soup for about 10 minutes, or until the potato pieces are soft when pierced with a fork.

3 Increase the heat to high and bring the soup to the boil. Stir in the salmon. Reduce the heat and cook for 3 to 5 minutes until the fish flakes easily when pulled apart with a fork. Stir in the milk and continue cooking the soup until it is heated through but not boiling. Sprinkle with the dill or parsley and serve immediately.

SOUPS

HEARTY CHILLI CORN SOUP *Serves 4*

2 tablespoons (30g) butter or margarine

1 small onion, chopped

1 tablespoon flour

2 cups chicken stock

2 cups diced baby marrows

2 cups fresh or frozen corn kernels

2 green chillies, chopped

¼ teaspoon ground black pepper

1 cup milk

½ cup (60g) coarsely grated mild Cheddar cheese

 Preparation time
15 minutes

 Cooking time
25 minutes

COOK'S TIP Try making this filling soup using succulent corn kernels freshly sliced off the cob. Using a sharp knife, slice along the rows of kernels, letting them fall onto a plate. With the dull side of the knife, press along the rows, squeezing out the juice and heart of the kernels.

1. In a large saucepan, melt the butter over moderate heat. Add the onion and sauté for about 5 minutes until soft. Stir in the flour until well mixed.

2. Stir in the stock, baby marrows, corn kernels, chillies and pepper. Bring the mixture to the boil over high heat, stirring occasionally. Reduce the heat, cover and simmer for 5 minutes.

3. Add the milk and heat the soup over moderate heat, stirring frequently, until it is hot but not boiling. Ladle the soup into bowls and garnish each serving with some of the grated cheese. Serve immediately.

PUMPKIN AND ORANGE SOUP *Serves 4 (PICTURE PAGE 71)*

1 tablespoon olive oil

1 onion, chopped

1 clove garlic, crushed

500g pumpkin, diced

1 tablespoon chopped fresh sage

Salt and ground black pepper

3 cups vegetable or chicken stock

Grated rind and juice of 1 orange

Chopped parsley for garnishing

 Preparation time
15 minutes

 Cooking time
35 minutes

COOK'S TIP If you prefer a thicker soup, cook a peeled and cubed medium potato with the pumpkin.

1. Heat the oil in a large, heavy-based saucepan. Add the onion and sauté gently for about 5 minutes until softened. Stir in the garlic, pumpkin and sage. Season with some of the salt and pepper, cover and cook gently for about 5 minutes.

2. Pour the stock into the saucepan and simmer for approximately 20 minutes or until the pumpkin is very tender. Remove from the heat and purée the soup with a hand-held blender.

3. Add the orange rind and juice and reheat. Check the seasoning and adjust according to taste. Garnish with the chopped parsley and serve immediately.

VARIATION

As a spicy alternative, omit the sage and orange flavourings and stir *1 teaspoon curry powder* and *1 teaspoon ground cumin* into the garlic mixture. Garnish with *fresh coriander* and serve immediately.

SOUPS

SPICY SHRIMP SOUP *Serves 4*

350g frozen, uncooked, shelled and deveined shrimps

1 tin (410g) whole peeled tomatoes

2 tablespoons (30g) butter or margarine

1 medium onion, finely chopped

1 medium sweet green pepper, seeded and coarsely chopped

1 teaspoon finely chopped parsley

½ teaspoon dried thyme

1 small bay leaf

¼ teaspoon Tabasco sauce (or to taste)

2½ teaspoons flour

1½ cups water

 Preparation time 17 minutes

 Cooking time 19 minutes

FOOD NOTE Add as much Tabasco sauce as your taste buds will tolerate, if desired. Although the soup tastes wonderful when made with frozen shrimps, the flavour of fresh shrimps raises it above the ordinary. Serve with a loaf of crusty bread.

1 Thaw the shrimps by placing them in a colander and holding it under lukewarm running water. Meanwhile, chop the tomatoes roughly, reserving the liquid.

2 In a large saucepan, melt the butter over moderate heat. Add the onion and sauté for about 5 minutes until soft. Stir in the green pepper, parsley, thyme, bay leaf and Tabasco sauce and sauté for 1 minute. Stir in the flour until well mixed.

3 Add the tomatoes with their liquid and the water. Bring the mixture to the boil over high heat. Reduce the heat, cover and simmer for 5 minutes. Add the shrimps and continue simmering, covered, for about 5 more minutes until the shrimps are cooked. Discard the bay leaf and season the soup with salt to taste. Ladle the soup into bowls and serve immediately.

HEARTY VEGETABLE SOUP *Serves 4*

2 tablespoons olive oil

1 medium onion, chopped

1 stalk celery, chopped

1 large carrot, chopped

1 cup dried split red lentils, rinsed and sorted

2 cups vegetable stock (made with vegetable stock cubes or powder, and water)

2 cups water

1 bay leaf

½ teaspoon dried thyme

1 medium ripe tomato, seeded and chopped

1 spring onion, thinly sliced

 Preparation time 8 minutes

 Cooking time 30 minutes

FOOD NOTE Split red lentils cook quickly and give the soup the body it needs to become a filling main dish. It's best not to skimp on the bay leaf and dried thyme in this recipe – the lentils absorb the delicate flavours of the herbs beautifully.

1 In a large saucepan, heat the oil over moderate heat. Add the chopped onion, celery and carrot and sauté for 1 minute until the vegetables become slightly softened. Stir in the lentils, vegetable stock, water, bay leaf and thyme.

2 Bring the mixture to the boil over high heat. Reduce the heat, cover the saucepan and simmer for about 15 minutes until the vegetables are tender.

3 Stir in the tomato. Continue cooking, covered, for approximately 10 minutes until the lentils are tender. Discard the bay leaf. Ladle the soup into bowls and sprinkle each serving with an equal amount of the spring onion. Serve immediately.

SOUPS

Chicken vegetable soup *Serves 3*

3 tablespoons (45g) butter or margarine

3 large (about 500g) potatoes, peeled and cut into 2,5cm chunks

250g carrots, sliced

3 spring onions, sliced diagonally into 1cm lengths, white and green parts separated

2 tablespoons flour

¹/₂ teaspoon sugar

¹/₄ teaspoon dried tarragon

¹/₈ teaspoon ground black pepper

4 cups chicken stock

250g skinless chicken-breast fillets, cut into 1cm slices

 Preparation time 12 minutes

 Cooking time 30 minutes

1 In a large saucepan, melt the butter over moderate heat. Add the potatoes and carrots. Stir to coat the vegetables with the butter. Add the white part of the spring onions and sauté for 1 minute.

2 Add the flour, sugar, tarragon and pepper to the vegetables and stir to mix. Add the stock and bring to the boil over high heat.

3 Reduce the heat and add the chicken to the saucepan. Cover and simmer for about 20 minutes until the vegetables are tender and the chicken is cooked through. Stir in the green part of the spring onions and serve immediately.

Microwave oven version

In a microwave-safe, 3-litre casserole dish, microwave the butter, covered, for about 1 minute on high power, until melted. Stir in the potatoes, carrots and the white part of the spring onions. Cook on high, covered, for about 8 minutes until the vegetables are tender. Stir in the flour, sugar, tarragon and pepper. Cook on high, covered, for 1 minute. Stir in the stock and the chicken. Cook on high, covered, for about 8 to 10 minutes until the chicken is cooked through, stirring twice during cooking.

SHELF MAGIC

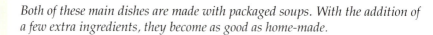

Both of these main dishes are made with packaged soups. With the addition of a few extra ingredients, they become as good as home-made.

Seafood noodle soup

In a large saucepan, bring *4¹/₂ cups water* and the seasoning packet from one of *two 85g packages of chicken-flavoured ramen noodle soup* to the boil. Add the noodles from both packages and *180g mangetout*, rinsed and trimmed. Simmer for about 2 minutes, stirring frequently, until the noodles are soft and the peas are cooked. Add *250g frozen mixed seafood*, thawed. Remove from the heat when the water returns to the boil. Serve immediately. Serves 4

Chicken vegetable soup

In a medium-sized saucepan, bring *1 cup water* and *250g frozen mixed vegetables* to the boil over high heat. Stir in *two 295g tins condensed cream of chicken soup*, *1¹/₂ cups milk* and *150g finely chopped cooked chicken*. Bring the mixture to the boil over moderately high heat, stirring occasionally. Pour into bowls, top with *chopped parsley*, if desired, and serve immediately with *breadsticks* or *savoury biscuits*. Serves 4

QUICK VEGETABLE BEEF SOUP

QUICK VEGETABLE BEEF SOUP *Serves 6*

500g lean minced beef

1 medium onion, sliced

4 cups beef stock

1 tin (410g) chopped tomato and onion mixture

1 package (500g) frozen mixed vegetables (such as broccoli, carrots and cauliflower)

1 cup fresh or frozen corn kernels

½ teaspoon dried origanum

Salt and ground black pepper to taste

 Preparation time
3 minutes

 Cooking time
35 minutes

COOK'S TIP Taste the soup before adding any salt – beef stock is particularly salty and you will probably not need to add more. Because it freezes well and can be reheated quickly, this is an excellent meal to make ahead of time.

1 In a large saucepan, cook the minced beef and the onion over moderate heat for about 10 minutes, stirring occasionally, until the beef is well browned and the onion is soft.

2 Stir in the stock, tomato and onion mixture, mixed vegetables, corn kernels and origanum, and season to taste with salt and pepper. Cover and bring to the boil over high heat.

3 Reduce the heat to low; simmer until the vegetables are tender, stirring occasionally, for 10 to 15 minutes. Serve immediately.

TORTELLINI MINESTRONE Serves 6

2 tablespoons (30g) butter or margarine

1 medium onion, sliced

250g large pattypan squash or baby marrows, sliced

1 clove garlic, chopped

5 cups beef stock

2 cups (about 60g) cubed day-old focaccia (Italian bread)

250g refrigerated or frozen meat-filled tortellini

250g frozen chopped broccoli, partially thawed under warm running water

Salt and ground black pepper to taste

12 cherry tomatoes, halved

 Preparation time
6 minutes

 Cooking time
28 minutes

FOOD NOTE Tortellini are the round pockets of pasta, filled with minced meat or a mixture of cheese and spinach, that may be found in the pasta or refrigerator sections of many supermarkets. Either may be used to create this satisfying meal-in-a-bowl. The soup thickens as it stands – add a little more stock if a thinner soup is desired.

1 In a large saucepan, melt the butter over moderate heat. Add the onion and sauté for about 5 minutes until soft. Stir in the squash and the garlic. Sauté for 2 minutes.

2 Add the stock and bread. Increase the heat to high, cover and bring to the boil over high heat, stirring occasionally. Reduce the heat to low and simmer the soup for 2 to 3 minutes.

3 Add the tortellini and simmer for 7 minutes. Increase the heat to high and bring the soup to the boil. Add the broccoli and cook for 3 to 4 minutes until it is tender. Season the soup with salt and pepper, stir in the cherry tomatoes and serve immediately.

HUNGARIAN CABBAGE SOUP Serves 4

½ teaspoon caraway seeds

1½ teaspoons paprika

½ cup sour cream

2 tablespoons (30g) butter or margarine

1 large onion, finely chopped

4 cups beef stock

250g cooked ham, diced

Salt and ground black pepper to taste

½ small head cabbage, cored and shredded (about 6 cups)

1 tablespoon chopped parsley

 Preparation time
12 minutes

 Cooking time
17 minutes

DIET NOTE Cabbage offers a wealth of benefits for the health-conscious – it provides a rich source of vitamin A for healthy skin and good eyesight, vitamin C for cell growth and fibre to aid proper digestion. Here it is combined with cooked ham to create a satisfying main-dish soup.

1 Using a mortar or rolling pin, crush the caraway seeds. In a small bowl, combine the caraway seeds, paprika and sour cream. Refrigerate until the soup is ready to serve.

2 In a large saucepan, melt the butter over moderate heat. Add the onion and sauté for about 5 minutes until softened, stirring occasionally.

3 Add the stock and ham. Season to taste with salt and ground black pepper. Bring to the boil over high heat. Reduce the heat, stir in the shredded cabbage and continue cooking for about 5 more minutes until the cabbage is tender but still firm to the bite. Stir in the chopped parsley. Ladle the soup into bowls and garnish each serving with a spoonful of the sour-cream mixture. Serve immediately.

SOUPS

GOULASH SOUP *Serves 5*

2 tablespoons sunflower oil

1 small onion, chopped

1 medium potato, peeled and diced

1 small carrot, sliced

1 clove garlic, finely chopped

2 knackwurst (or other smoked sausage), sliced

1½ teaspoons paprika

½ teaspoon dried dill

Salt and ground black pepper to taste

4 cups water

1 tin (410g) whole, peeled tomatoes, drained and coarsely chopped

½ cup medium-width egg noodles

 Preparation time
10 minutes

 Cooking time
35 minutes

1 In a large saucepan, heat the oil over moderate heat. Add the onion, potato, carrot and garlic. Sauté gently for about 10 minutes until the onions are soft, stirring occasionally.

2 Add the knackwurst, paprika and dill to the vegetables. Season to taste with salt and pepper. Stir until well mixed.

3 Add the water and tomatoes to the mixture and bring to the boil. Reduce the heat, cover and simmer for 10 minutes.

4 Increase the heat to high and return the soup to the boil. Stir in the noodles and continue cooking for about 5 minutes until the noodles are just tender. Serve immediately.

MICROWAVE OVEN VERSION

In a microwave-safe, 4-litre casserole dish, microwave the oil, onion, potato, carrot and garlic on high power, covered, for about 5 minutes until tender, stirring once. Add the knackwurst, paprika and dill. Cook on high, uncovered, for 1 minute. Season to taste with salt and pepper. Add the water and tomatoes. Cook on high, covered, for 8 to 13 minutes until the mixture is boiling. Stir in the noodles. Cook on high, uncovered, for 5 to 7 minutes until the noodles are tender.

BEAN AND HAM SOUP *Serves 6*

2 slices bacon

1 large onion, chopped

2 medium carrots, peeled and sliced

4 cups water

2 tins (410g each) white kidney beans (or two 410g tins baked beans), drained and rinsed

1 cup tinned Italian-style tomatoes, crushed

250g cooked ham, cubed

1 bay leaf

Salt and ground black pepper to taste

 Preparation time
7 minutes

 Cooking time
36 minutes

1 In a large saucepan (preferably with nonstick coating), cook the bacon over moderately high heat until lightly browned on both sides. Using a slotted spoon, remove the bacon and drain it on a paper towel. Reduce the heat to moderate. Add the onion and carrots to the drippings in the pan and sauté for 5 minutes.

2 Stir in the water, half of the beans, the tomatoes, ham and bay leaf. Increase the heat to high, cover and bring the soup to the boil. Reduce the heat to low. Still covered, simmer the soup for 20 to 25 minutes, stirring occasionally, until the carrots are tender.

3 Discard the bay leaf. Stir in the remaining beans and season with salt and pepper. Increase the heat to high and bring the soup to the boil. Ladle the soup into bowls and crumble some of the bacon over each serving. Serve immediately.

IBERIAN POTATO SOUP

IBERIAN POTATO SOUP *Serves 4*

2 tablespoons olive oil

1 large onion, chopped

2 cloves garlic, finely chopped

4 medium (about 350g) potatoes, peeled and diced

3 cups chicken stock

1 bay leaf

2 chorizo sausages (or 250g kielbasa sausage)

2 cups thinly sliced kale, cabbage or Swiss chard, hard stems removed

 Preparation time
12 minutes

 Cooking time
32 minutes

FOOD NOTE Chorizo sausage gives this soup its spicy flavour. Kielbasa – a Polish sausage seasoned with paprika – makes a fine substitute, but, as it's milder, you may wish to add a pinch of cayenne pepper.

1. In a large saucepan, heat the oil over moderate heat. Add the onion and garlic and sauté for 2 minutes. Stir in the potatoes. Add the stock and bay leaf, cover and bring to the boil over high heat. Reduce the heat to low and simmer for 18 to 20 minutes until the potatoes are very tender.

2. Meanwhile, cut the sausages into 1cm slices. When the soup is cooked, discard the bay leaf. Using the back of a fork, mash some of the potatoes in the soup to thicken it slightly, if desired.

3. Stir in the sausage and kale. Continue cooking for about 5 minutes until the sausage is hot. Serve immediately.

SOUPS

CHINESE CHICKEN SOUP Serves 4

250g skinless chicken-breast fillets

2 tablespoons dry sherry

4 cups chicken stock

1½ cups (about 125g) sliced mushrooms

1 teaspoon crushed fresh ginger (or ⅛ teaspoon ground ginger)

1 tablespoon light soy sauce

3 spring onions, sliced diagonally into 1cm portions

125g Chinese cabbage, sliced into 1cm strips

½ cup thinly sliced, tinned water chestnuts

 Preparation time 18 minutes

 Cooking time 13 minutes

FOOD NOTE *Mushrooms, ginger, soy sauce and chicken merge to create a delicate soup redolent of some of Asia's favourite flavours.*

1. Cut the chicken across the grain into 5mm-thick slices. In a medium-sized bowl, mix the chicken and the dry sherry, and leave to stand for about 10 minutes to marinate.

2. Meanwhile, in a large saucepan, combine the chicken stock, mushrooms, ginger and soy sauce. Bring the mixture to the boil over high heat.

3. Add the chicken and cook for 1 minute. Stir in the spring onions, cabbage and water chestnuts. Cook for about 5 minutes until the cabbage is just crisp-tender. Serve immediately.

PORK EGG DROP SOUP Serves 4

2x1cm-thick (about 600g) pork loin chops

1 tablespoon peanut or sunflower oil

2 cups beef stock

2 cups water

3 spring onions, sliced

½ cup tinned bamboo shoots, drained

1 tablespoon crushed fresh ginger

250g frozen peas

Salt to taste

2 large eggs

 Preparation time 11 minutes

 Cooking time 32 minutes

FOOD NOTE *The pungent taste of fresh ginger is infinitely preferable for a really authentic flavour. However, if fresh is unavailable, dried ginger will still help create this Chinese classic.*

1. Debone the pork chops and trim and discard any visible fat. Slice the meat into strips. In a 5-litre flameproof casserole dish or large saucepan, heat the oil over high heat. Add the pork meat and the bones and sauté for 8 to 10 minutes until well browned.

2. Add the stock, water, spring onions, bamboo shoots and ginger to the pork. Cover the casserole dish and bring the mixture to the boil over high heat. Reduce the heat to low and simmer the soup for 10 minutes.

3. Meanwhile, to thaw the peas, place them in a colander under warm running water for about 2 minutes.

4. Discard the pork bones. Add the peas to the soup and season with salt to taste. Increase the heat to high and cook for about 4 more minutes until the peas are tender.

5. Beat the eggs in a small bowl. Slowly stir the eggs into the soup and cook until they are just set. Remove the dish from the heat. Ladle the soup into Chinese bowls and serve immediately.

Seafood

Mussels with tomatoes and rice (page 128)

Seafood

From angelfish and yellowtail to calamari and prawns, seafood forms an essential part of the quick cook's repertoire. Readily available, it is a tasty source of protein and essential vitamins.

Herbed baked whole fish *Serves 4*

⅓ cup fresh basil (do not use dried)

⅓ cup parsley, lightly packed (do not use dried)

1 clove garlic

⅓ cup olive oil

Salt and ground black pepper to taste

½ cup sour cream

1 teaspoon dried rosemary

2 whole (about 750g each) red roman, cleaned

Lemon slices (optional)

Additional fresh herbs (optional)

 Preparation time 10 minutes

 Cooking time 20 minutes

Serving suggestion Serve this fish with boiled new potatoes – a perfect foil for this tasty dish with its sour-cream sauce.

1. Preheat the oven to 180°C. Line a baking tray large enough to hold the fish with heavy-duty aluminium foil.

2. Using a food processor or electric blender, purée the basil, parsley and garlic with the oil. Season the mixture with salt and pepper. Stir 2 tablespoons of the herb mixture into the sour cream. Cover and refrigerate the sauce until the fish is ready to serve. Add the rosemary to the remaining herb mixture and continue to purée for 1 minute.

3. Using a sharp knife, make three shallow diagonal slashes on each side of both fish. Rub the herb mixture into the slashes and cavity of each fish. Carefully place the fish on the prepared baking tray.

4. Bake the fish, uncovered, for about 20 minutes or until it flakes easily when pierced with a fork. Using the foil to lift it, transfer the fish to a serving platter. Cut away the foil and discard. Garnish the fish with slices of lemon and fresh herbs, if desired, and serve immediately with the chilled sour-cream sauce.

Time Savers

Fish
■ The quickest way to estimate the cooking time for any fish is to calculate 10 minutes for every 2,5cm of its thickness. Place the fish on the counter and measure it across its thickest part. This estimate applies to any cooking method.

■ If fresh fish is not available or if you are short of time, you may substitute some of the excellent pre-packed frozen fish fillets available in the supermarkets. Simply check the cooking instructions on the package and adjust the cooking times accordingly.

■ When fish is being fried, it will cook faster and taste better if you cook only one or two pieces at a time. If the pan is overloaded, the cold fish will reduce the temperature of the oil. The fish will not only become greasy and soggy, it will also take longer to cook.

SEAFOOD

Trout with mushroom sauce Serves 4

- ⅓ cup flour
- ½ teaspoon salt
- ¼ teaspoon ground black pepper
- 4 trout (about 250g each), cleaned, with heads and tails left on
- 1 tablespoon sunflower oil
- 4 tablespoons (60g) butter or margarine
- 1 medium onion, chopped
- 2 cups (250g) small mushrooms, halved
- 1 cup milk
- 1 tablespoon chopped parsley

 Preparation time 11 minutes

 Cooking time 34 minutes

1. Mix the flour, salt and pepper in a pie plate, placing 2 teaspoons of the flour mixture to one side. Rinse the trout and pat them dry. Roll the fish in the seasoned flour mixture until they are coated thoroughly.

2. In a large frying pan, heat the oil and half the butter over moderate heat. Fry the trout, two at a time, for 5 to 6 minutes on each side until they are well browned. Transfer the trout to a serving platter and keep them warm. Repeat, adding more butter if necessary, to cook the remaining trout.

3. In the same frying pan, melt the remaining butter over moderate heat. Add the onion and sauté for 3 minutes. Add the mushrooms and sauté until softened. Stir in the reserved flour mixture until well mixed. Gradually stir the milk into the mushroom-flour mixture and cook, stirring, until the mixture boils and thickens slightly.

4. Spoon some of the mushroom sauce over the trout. Pour the remaining sauce into a serving bowl. Sprinkle the trout with the parsley and serve, passing the sauce separately.

Pan-fried trout with lemon butter Serves 4

- ¼ cup flour
- ½ teaspoon salt
- ¼ teaspoon ground black pepper
- 4 trout (about 250g each), cleaned, with heads removed
- Sunflower oil for frying
- 4 tablespoons (60g) butter or margarine
- 1 tablespoon lemon juice
- Chopped parsley (optional)
- 8 lemon slices

 Preparation time 10 minutes

 Cooking time 28 minutes

COOK'S TIP *This is the classic way to serve fresh, succulent trout – the lemon butter enhances the mild flavour of the fish.*

1. Mix the flour, salt and pepper in a pie plate. Rinse the trout and pat them dry. Roll the fish in the flour mixture until they are coated thoroughly.

2. Pour enough oil into a large frying pan to cover the base to a depth of about 5mm. Heat the oil over moderate heat until it is hot. Add the trout, two at a time and fry for 5 to 6 minutes on each side until well browned. Transfer the trout to serving plates and keep them warm. Repeat to cook the remaining two trout.

3. Meanwhile, in a small saucepan, melt the butter and cook for about 1 minute until lightly browned. Stir in the lemon juice. Pour an equal amount of the lemon butter over each trout and garnish with parsley, if desired, and the slices of lemon. Serve immediately.

TUNA CAKES WITH CUCUMBER-YOGHURT SAUCE

TUNA CAKES WITH CUCUMBER-YOGHURT SAUCE *Serves 4*

1 medium cucumber

1¼ teaspoons salt

2 tins (185g each) tuna packed in water, drained and flaked

½ cup (60g) packaged bread crumbs

½ cup thinly sliced spring onion

1 large egg

2 tablespoons mayonnaise

¼ teaspoon ground black pepper

½ cup plain yoghurt

1 tablespoon chopped fresh dill (or 1 teaspoon dried dill)

Additional salt and ground black pepper to taste

1 tablespoon sunflower oil

Fresh dill sprigs (optional)

 Preparation time 30 minutes

 Cooking time 4 minutes

COOK'S TIP This recipe makes enough for four first-course servings, but it can easily be doubled to create a filling main dish.

1. Peel the cucumber, cut it in half lengthwise and seed and coarsely grate it. Place it in a strainer, sprinkle it with 1 teaspoon salt and toss well. Place the strainer over a bowl and set it aside to drain.

2. Meanwhile, in a large bowl, mix the tuna, bread crumbs, spring onions, egg, mayonnaise, pepper and the remaining ¼ teaspoon of salt until thoroughly blended. Shape the tuna mixture into four 2,5cm-thick cakes.

3. Rinse the grated cucumber under cold water. Drain and squeeze it to remove the excess moisture. In a small bowl, mix the cucumber with the yoghurt and dill, and season with salt and pepper. Cover and refrigerate the mixture until ready to cook.

4. In a large frying pan, heat the oil over moderate heat. Add the tuna cakes and cook for about 2 minutes on each side until they are browned. Transfer to serving plates and garnish with fresh dill, if desired. Serve immediately with the cucumber sauce.

SEAFOOD

BAKED TUNA WITH BROCCOLI Serves 4

- 250g frozen broccoli florets
- 3 tablespoons (45g) butter or margarine
- ¼ cup slivered blanched almonds
- ¼ cup flour
- ¼ teaspoon salt
- ⅛ teaspoon ground black pepper
- 2 cups milk
- 2 tins (185g each) tuna packed in water, drained and flaked
- Paprika

 Preparation time
10 minutes

 Cooking time
30 minutes

SERVING SUGGESTION A chopped salad of lettuce, avocado pear and tomato would make a refreshing accompaniment to this easy and economical main dish.

1 Preheat the oven to 180°C. Grease a 30cm x 20cm baking dish. Partially thaw the broccoli florets under warm running water or in the microwave oven until the florets can easily be separated.

2 Meanwhile, in a large saucepan, melt the butter over moderate heat. Add the almonds and sauté for about 1½ minutes until lightly browned. Blend in the flour, salt and pepper. Gradually add the milk and cook, stirring constantly, for 4 to 5 minutes until the mixture thickens. Remove the almond sauce from the heat.

3 Pat the broccoli dry. Arrange the floret end of each spear down the long sides of the prepared baking dish, with the stems turned toward the centre of the dish. Place the tuna over the broccoli in the centre of the dish. Pour the almond sauce over the tuna.

4 Cover the dish with aluminium foil and bake for 20 to 25 minutes until the broccoli is cooked. Remove the foil, sprinkle with paprika and serve.

BLACKENED FISH Serves 4

- 2 tablespoons paprika
- 2 teaspoons salt
- 2 teaspoons finely ground onion flakes
- 2 teaspoons garlic powder
- 1½ teaspoons ground black pepper
- 1 teaspoon cayenne pepper
- 1 teaspoon dried thyme
- 1 teaspoon dried origanum
- 4 tablespoons (60g) unsalted butter or margarine
- 4 fish fillets (about 180g each)
- 4 lemon wedges

 Preparation time
5 minutes

 Cooking time
12 minutes

COOK'S TIP The secret of the popular Cajun dish of blackened fish is to use a cast-iron frying pan and to fry the fish only when the pan is very hot, sealing the succulent juices inside.

1 Mix the paprika, salt, onion flakes, garlic powder, black and cayenne peppers, thyme and origanum in a pie plate or shallow dish. Melt the butter and pour it into a second shallow dish.

2 Heat a large cast-iron frying pan until very hot. Dip the fish fillets into the melted butter, then into the paprika mixture, until they are coated on both sides. Place the fillets, two at a time, into the frying pan and cook each side for 2 to 3 minutes until blackened.

3 Transfer the fillets to a serving platter and keep them warm. Repeat to cook the remaining two fillets. Garnish with the lemon.

PECAN FRIED ANGELFISH FILLETS

PECAN FRIED ANGELFISH FILLETS *Serves 4*

⅓ cup ground pecan nuts

⅓ cup yellow maize (mealie) meal

3 tablespoons flour

½ teaspoon salt

¼ teaspoon cayenne pepper

1 large egg

1 tablespoon water

4 angelfish fillets (about 180g each)

3 tablespoons sunflower oil

2 tablespoons (30g) butter or margarine

Lemon wedges

 Preparation time 15 minutes

 Cooking time 16 minutes

SERVING SUGGESTION Serve this crispy fish dish with buttered green beans sprinkled with additional chopped pecan nuts.

1 Mix the pecan nuts and maize meal together in a pie plate. Sift together the flour, salt and cayenne pepper on a large plate. Mix the egg and water in a separate pie plate or shallow dish.

2 Dredge each angelfish fillet in the flour mixture, shaking off the excess. Dip the floured fillets into the egg mixture, then coat each one with the pecan-maize meal mixture.

3 In a large frying pan, heat half of the oil and half of the butter over moderate heat. Add two fillets and fry for about 3 to 4 minutes on each side until golden brown.

4 Transfer the fillets to a serving platter and keep them warm. Repeat to cook the remaining fillets using the remaining oil and butter. Serve immediately, with lemon wedges.

SEAFOOD

Foil-wrapped Angelfish Serves 4

2 tablespoons dry sherry
2 tablespoons sunflower oil
1 tablespoon finely sliced spring onion tops
1 tablespoon soy sauce
¼ teaspoon ground ginger
4 angelfish fillets (about 180g each)
1 small tomato, thinly sliced
1 baby marrow, thinly sliced

 Preparation time
13 minutes

 Cooking time
20 minutes

1. Preheat the oven to 230°C. In a small bowl, combine the sherry, oil, spring onion, soy sauce and ginger. Cut four 30cm squares of heavy-duty aluminium foil.

2. Place an angelfish fillet in the centre of each square, and cover each with an equal amount of the tomato and baby marrow. Spoon the sherry mixture over each fillet and fold the foil in half diagonally to form a triangle. Crimp the edges to seal tightly.

3. Place the fish parcels on a baking sheet. Bake for 15 to 20 minutes until the fish flakes easily when the parcels are opened and the fish is tested with a fork. Transfer the fish and vegetables to individual serving plates and serve immediately.

Angelfish with Almonds Serves 4

¼ cup flour
¼ teaspoon salt
¼ teaspoon ground black pepper
4 angelfish fillets (about 125g each)
2½ tablespoons sunflower oil
3 tablespoons slivered almonds
2 tablespoons (30g) butter
½ cup dry white wine
2 tablespoons chopped parsley

 Preparation time
4 minutes

 Cooking time
21 minutes

SERVING SUGGESTION *The addition of almonds, gently sautéed to release their subtle flavour, complements this dish perfectly. Serve with a tossed salad and steamed baby potatoes for an elegant luncheon or light evening meal.*

1. Mix the flour, salt and pepper on a plate. Dredge each angelfish fillet in the flour mixture, shaking off the excess. Transfer the fillets to a plate and set aside.

2. In a large frying pan, heat ½ tablespoon of the oil over moderate heat. Add the almonds and sauté for 2 to 3 minutes until lightly browned. With a slotted spoon, transfer the almonds to a bowl and set aside.

3. Add the remaining oil and butter to the frying pan and heat over moderately high heat. Place two of the angelfish fillets in the pan and fry for about 3 minutes on each side until they are golden brown and cooked through. Transfer the fish to individual serving plates and keep them warm. Repeat to cook the remaining two fillets.

4. Stir the wine into the drippings in the pan and bring the mixture to the boil. Continue boiling for about 4 minutes more until the sauce is slightly thickened. Spoon an equal amount of the sauce over each angelfish fillet, sprinkle with the almonds and parsley and serve immediately.

SALMON VÉRONIQUE

Salmon Véronique *Serves 4*

1 cup water

⅓ cup dry white wine

1 small onion, sliced

1 clove garlic, halved

1 bay leaf

½ cup seedless green or black grapes

4 salmon fillets (about 180g each)

1 tablespoon (15g) butter or margarine

1 tablespoon flour

¼ cup cream

Salt and ground white pepper to taste

1 tablespoon chopped walnuts (optional)

Small bunches of grapes (optional)

 Preparation time 5 minutes

 Cooking time 21 minutes

FOOD NOTE Created at the Ritz hotel in Paris, the Véronique method combines fish with grapes; here the grapes blend subtly with salmon to make an elegant dish. Serve with brown rice and lemon wedges.

1. In a large frying pan, bring the water, wine, onion, garlic and bay leaf to the boil. Reduce the heat to low, cover the pan and simmer the liquid for 5 minutes. Meanwhile, cut each grape in half.

2. Add the salmon fillets to the liquid. Return to the boil and poach, covered, for 8 to 10 minutes until the fish is cooked and flakes easily when tested with a fork. Transfer the fish to a serving platter and keep it warm. Strain the poaching liquid into a cup or small bowl.

3. In the same pan, melt the butter over moderate heat. Stir in the flour and cook until bubbly. Whisk in ¾ cup of the strained liquid and bring to the boil, stirring constantly. Add the grapes and cream and heat through (do not boil). Season to taste.

4. Spoon the sauce over the salmon. Sprinkle with the walnuts and garnish with clusters of grapes, if desired. Serve immediately.

SEAFOOD

SALMON-STUFFED SOLE *Serves 4*

3 tablespoons mayonnaise

1 heaped tablespoon grated onion

2 teaspoons Dijon mustard

1 teaspoon dried tarragon

¼ teaspoon ground black pepper

½ cup watercress leaves

4 thin (about 250g) red salmon trout fillets

4 sole fillets (about 125g each)

2 teaspoons (10g) butter or margarine, cut into small pieces

Pinch of paprika

 Preparation time
18 minutes

 Cooking time
25 minutes

SERVING SUGGESTION *This light springtime dish pairs well with fresh steamed asparagus topped with a dollop of extra mayonnaise, or brown rice mixed with sautéed slivered almonds.*

1. Preheat the oven to 180°C. Grease a 25cm x 15cm baking dish. In a small bowl, blend the mayonnaise, onion, mustard, tarragon and pepper. Rinse the watercress leaves and pat them dry on paper towels. Slice the salmon trout into four thick strips.

2. Spread some of the mayonnaise mixture over the darker side of each sole fillet, and cover each fillet with a thin layer of watercress leaves. Place a strip of salmon across one short end of each sole fillet and roll up each one.

3. Place the rolled fillets, seam sides down, in the prepared baking dish. Dot the fillets with the butter and sprinkle with paprika. Cover the dish with aluminium foil, place it in the oven and bake for 20 to 25 minutes until the fish flakes easily when tested with a fork. Transfer the cooked fillets to a warmed serving platter and serve immediately.

TERIYAKI CAPE SALMON *Serves 4*

3 tablespoons soy sauce

1 tablespoon lemon juice

2 teaspoons sugar

1 teaspoon Oriental sesame oil

½ teaspoon ground ginger

4x2,5cm-thick (about 300g each) Cape salmon steaks

Lemon slices (optional)

 Preparation time
12 minutes

 Cooking time
12 minutes

SERVING SUGGESTION *Cape salmon gets the Oriental treatment with the addition of soy sauce, sesame oil and ginger. Serve it with fried rice and crispy stir-fried vegetables, and end the meal with a mouthwatering fruit salad of litchis and mandarin oranges.*

1. Preheat the grill. Mix the soy sauce, lemon juice, sugar, sesame oil and ground ginger together in a large shallow dish. Add the Cape salmon steaks, turning them in the mixture until they are thoroughly coated. Set them aside for 10 minutes to marinate, turning once more.

2. Place the salmon steaks on the rack over a grill pan. Grill them 10cm from the heat for 5 minutes. Turn the salmon over and baste it with any leftover marinade. Continue grilling the steaks for a further 5 to 7 minutes until the fish is cooked through and flakes easily when tested with a fork. Place the steaks on warmed serving plates and garnish with slices of lemon, if desired. Serve immediately.

VARIATIONS ON THE BASIC BAKED FISH

Baked fish is a simpler dish to create than you may think, and the rewards are wonderful. It can become a mouthwatering main dish and, since it is low in fat, fish offers one of the healthiest sources of protein available. You may enjoy the fish on its own with a squeeze of lemon juice, or you may enhance its delicate flavour with one of the tasty sauces given here.

Once the fish is in the oven, begin preparing one of these easy sauces to serve as an accompaniment. The sauces are endlessly adaptable – they will lift whole fish or fish steaks out of the ordinary, and are especially delicious when served with succulent fish fresh off the braai grid.

Basic baked fish fillets Select *1,5 to 2kg line fish fillets*. Preheat the oven to 200°C. On the kitchen counter, spread a piece of aluminium foil large enough to wrap the fish completely. Brush the foil with *olive* or *sunflower oil*. Place the fillets in the centre of the foil and brush them with more oil. Season with *salt* and *pepper*, and place a few *thin slices of lemon* between the fillets. Wrap the foil loosely around the fish, sealing the parcel securely so that the juices do not evaporate. Bake the fish for 10 minutes for each 2,5cm of the total thickness of the combined fillets. The fish should flake easily when tested with a fork.

Using a spatula, transfer the fish to a serving platter. Garnish with additional *lemon slices* and *watercress* or *dill*, if desired. Serve with one of the following sauces.

◄ **Green sauce** Using a food processor or electric blender, mix *½ cup mayonnaise, ½ cup plain yoghurt, 2 tablespoons chopped fresh dill* or *1 teaspoon dried dill, 2 tablespoons chopped spring onion tops, 2 tablespoons chopped parsley, 2 teaspoons red wine vinegar* and *¼ teaspoon dried tarragon.* Process or blend all the ingredients until smooth, stopping occasionally to scrape the sides of the container.

◄ **Mushroom-tomato sauce** In a medium-sized saucepan, melt *1 tablespoon (15g) butter* over moderate heat. Add *125g sliced mushrooms, 2 tablespoons chopped onion* and *1 clove garlic,* crushed. Sauté for about 5 minutes until soft. Stir in *one 410g tin whole tomatoes* with their juice and *½ teaspoon dried rosemary.* Bring to the boil, cover, and cook for 10 minutes, stirring occasionally.

► **Cucumber-dill sauce** In a medium-sized bowl, blend *¾ cup seeded and finely chopped unpeeled cucumber, ½ cup sour cream, 2 tablespoons mayonnaise, 2 teaspoons finely chopped onion, ½ teaspoon grated lemon peel* and *½ teaspoon dried dill* until well mixed. Season with *salt* and *ground white pepper.*

▼ **Spicy tomato sauce** In a medium-sized bowl, mix *1 cup tomato sauce* or *ketchup*, *1 to 2 tablespoons prepared horseradish, 1 tablespoon lemon juice, ¼ teaspoon Worcestershire sauce* and *a few drops of Tabasco sauce* until well blended.

▼ **Mustard onion sauce** In a medium-sized saucepan, melt *2 tablespoons butter* or *margarine* over moderate heat. Add *1 medium onion, sliced*, and sauté for about 5 minutes until soft. Stir in *1 tablespoon flour* until well mixed. Add *¾ to 1 cup fish* or *chicken stock* and *1 tablespoon prepared mustard.* Season with *salt* and *pepper.* Cook, stirring constantly, for about 2 to 3 minutes until slightly thickened.

SEAFOOD

SOLE WITH CAPER SAUCE *Serves 4*

¼ cup flour

¼ teaspoon salt

⅛ teaspoon ground black pepper

4 sole fillets (about 180g each)

2 tablespoons olive oil

1 tablespoon (15g) butter or margarine

½ cup water

¼ cup lemon juice

1 teaspoon Worcestershire sauce

1 tablespoon capers, rinsed

Lemon slices (optional)

 Preparation time 10 minutes

 Cooking time 11 minutes

SERVING SUGGESTION Complement this slightly tangy fish dish with grilled tomato halves sprinkled with Parmesan cheese, and a glass of crisp dry white wine.

1. Mix the flour, salt and pepper in a pie plate. Dredge each fish fillet in the flour mixture, shaking off the excess.

2. In a large frying pan, heat half of the oil and half of the butter over moderate heat. Add two of the fish fillets and fry for about 2 minutes on each side until they are golden brown. Transfer to serving plates and keep warm. Repeat to cook the remaining fillets, using the remaining oil and butter.

3. Pour the water, lemon juice and Worcestershire sauce into the frying pan. Bring the mixture to the boil over high heat. Reduce the heat to moderate and simmer the sauce for about 2 minutes until it is slightly thickened. Stir in the capers.

4. Pour an equal amount of the sauce over each sole fillet, garnish with lemon slices, if desired, and serve immediately.

GRILLED SOLE WITH MUSTARD *Serves 4*

4 sole fillets (about 180g each)

1 tablespoon sunflower oil

Pinch of ground black pepper

2 tablespoons mayonnaise

1 tablespoon Dijon mustard

2 teaspoons finely chopped parsley

4 lemon wedges

 Preparation time 5 minutes

 Cooking time 4 minutes

COOK'S TIP Mild and delicate, these thin sole fillets cook so quickly that they do not need to be turned during grilling. Watch them carefully to avoid overcooking. Angelfish fillets may also be used. Serve them with small boiled potatoes and steamed green beans.

1. Preheat the grill. Cover the rack of a grill pan with aluminium foil. Brush both sides of the sole fillets with a little of the sunflower oil, and place them on the foil. Sprinkle the fillets with ground black pepper.

2. In a small bowl, combine the mayonnaise, mustard and parsley. Brush or spread the mixture evenly over the fillets.

3. Grill the sole fillets 10cm from the heat for about 3 to 4 minutes until they are golden brown on top and the fish flakes easily when tested with a fork.

4. Transfer them to warmed individual serving plates, garnish with the lemon wedges and serve immediately.

SPINACH-WRAPPED FILLET OF SOLE

SPINACH-WRAPPED FILLET OF SOLE *Serves 4*

4 sole fillets (about 180g each)

4 teaspoons lemon juice

2 tablespoons (30g) butter or margarine, softened

1 teaspoon dried tarragon

¼ teaspoon ground white pepper

12 large spinach leaves

4 lemon wedges

 Preparation time
15 minutes

 Cooking time
10 minutes

SERVING SUGGESTION Make this low-kilojoule main dish even more nutritious by offering it with a colourful medley of sautéed vegetables.

1 Drizzle each fillet with 1 teaspoon of the lemon juice. Dot with the butter and sprinkle with the tarragon and pepper. Fold the fillets in half and arrange them on a heatproof plate.

2 Pour 2,5cm of water into a large pot, and set a steaming rack into the pot. Bring the water to the boil over high heat. Reduce the heat to moderately low to bring the water to the simmer.

3 Place the fish, on its plate, onto the steaming rack. Cover the pot and steam the fish for 5 to 7 minutes. Meanwhile, remove the large, tough stems from the spinach leaves.

4 Remove the fish and wrap each in three layers of spinach leaves, securing them with toothpicks. Return them to the steamer and cook for about 2 minutes until the leaves are slightly softened but still bright green. Serve immediately with the lemon wedges.

SEAFOOD

BAKED HAKE OVER RICE *Serves 4*

1 cup long-grain white rice

250g frozen green peas

4 hake fillets (about 180g each)

¼ cup dry white wine

1 tablespoon lemon juice

2 tablespoons (30g) butter or margarine, cut into small pieces

2 large ripe plum tomatoes, chopped

½ teaspoon dried thyme

¼ teaspoon salt

¼ teaspoon ground black pepper

 Preparation time
10 minutes

 Cooking time
22 minutes

Food note Fresh tomatoes, white wine and thyme make a colourful and appetizing sauce for hake. If hake isn't available, any white fish fillets may be substituted.

1. Preheat the oven to 230°C. Grease a 30cm x 20cm baking dish. In two separate saucepans, prepare the rice and the peas according to their package directions.

2. Meanwhile, place the hake fillets in a single layer in the prepared dish. Drizzle the fillets with the wine and lemon juice. Dot with the butter and sprinkle with the chopped tomatoes, thyme, salt and pepper. Bake for 8 to 10 minutes until the hake flakes easily when tested with a fork.

3. Drain the cooked peas. Stir the peas into the rice, and ladle onto a serving platter or individual plates. Spoon the fillets and their juices over the rice mixture and serve immediately.

MEXICAN-STYLE HAKE *Serves 4*

4 medium (about 500g) frozen hake fillets

1 small sweet green pepper

2 tablespoons (30g) butter or margarine

1 small celery stalk, chopped

1 small onion, chopped

1 clove garlic, finely chopped

2 tablespoons flour

1 tin (410g) Mexican-style tomatoes

2 tablespoons water

½ teaspoon sugar

1 bay leaf

Celery leaves for garnishing (optional)

 Preparation time
8 minutes

 Cooking time
30 minutes

1. Place the frozen hake in a heavy-duty plastic food-storage bag and seal the bag tightly. Place in a large pan containing very hot water and thaw the fish until it can be sliced. (Alternatively, thaw the fish in a microwave oven.)

2. Meanwhile, core and seed the sweet green pepper and slice it into strips.

3. In a large frying pan, melt the butter over moderately high heat and cook until lightly browned. Add the celery, onion and garlic and sauté for about 5 minutes until lightly browned.

4. Stir the flour into the celery mixture until well mixed. Stir in the tomatoes, water, sugar and bay leaf and bring to the boil, stirring occasionally. Reduce the heat to low and simmer for 5 to 10 minutes, stirring occasionally.

5. Using a sharp knife, cut the fish into four pieces. Place it in the simmering tomato mixture. Add the green pepper, cover the pan and cook the fish for 12 to 15 minutes until it flakes easily when tested with a fork. Discard the bay leaf and garnish with celery leaves, if desired. Serve immediately.

◄ Baked hake over rice

SEAFOOD

STIR-FRIED FISH WITH VEGETABLES *Serves 4*

4 medium (about 500g) fish fillets

2 tablespoons cornflour

¼ cup chicken stock

2 tablespoons dry sherry

2 tablespoons soy sauce

1 teaspoon sugar

4 tablespoons sunflower oil

4 spring onions, cut into 2,5cm lengths

2 to 3 cups (about 250g) sliced mushrooms

1 cup celery, sliced diagonally

1 tin (230g) sliced water chestnuts, drained

2 cloves garlic, finely chopped

 Preparation time
15 minutes

 Cooking time
11 minutes

COOK'S TIP As with most stir-fried dishes, the bulk of the cook's time is spent in preparation rather than in the actual cooking. If the vegetables are prepared ahead and refrigerated, the dish will be ready in less than 15 minutes.

1. Cut the fish fillets into 1cm-wide strips. In a medium-sized bowl, toss the fish strips with 1 tablespoon of the cornflour until coated. In a small bowl, mix the remaining 1 tablespoon of cornflour, the stock, sherry, soy sauce and sugar. Set aside.

2. In a large frying pan or wok, heat 2 tablespoons of the oil over high heat. Add the fish in a single layer and fry for about 3 minutes until lightly browned, using a spatula to turn the strips carefully. Transfer the fish to a plate and keep warm.

3. Heat the remaining 2 tablespoons of oil in the frying pan. Add the spring onions, mushrooms, celery, water chestnuts and garlic and stir-fry for 2 to 3 minutes until the vegetables are just softened. Stir in the cornflour mixture and bring to the boil. Continue boiling for 1 minute.

4. Return the fish to the frying pan. Remove the pan from the heat, toss the fish and vegetables gently and serve immediately.

FISH AND POTATO PIE *Serves 4*

500g potatoes, unpeeled, cut into 5mm-thick slices

4 tablespoons (60g) butter or margarine

2 cloves garlic, finely chopped

2 tablespoons chopped parsley

⅛ teaspoon cayenne pepper

4 medium (about 500g) hake or angelfish fillets

¼ teaspoon salt

3 tablespoons packaged bread crumbs

 Preparation time
10 minutes

 Cooking time
25 minutes

1. Preheat the oven to 200°C. In a large saucepan, boil the potatoes for about 10 minutes until they are almost tender. Meanwhile, in a small saucepan, melt the butter. Add the garlic and cook gently for 10 seconds. Remove the saucepan from the heat and stir in the parsley and cayenne pepper. Cut the fish into 2,5cm slices.

2. Grease a 23cm pie plate. Drain the potatoes and layer them in the pie plate. Brush the potatoes with some of the parsley butter and sprinkle with the salt.

3. Arrange the fish over the potatoes and brush with more parsley butter. Cover with aluminium foil and bake for 15 minutes. Stir the bread crumbs into the remaining parsley butter. Remove the foil and sprinkle with the crumb mixture. Continue baking, uncovered, for about 10 more minutes until the top is golden brown. Serve immediately.

CAPE SEAFOOD STEW

CAPE SEAFOOD STEW *Serves 6*

1 small sweet green pepper

500g monkfish or kingklip

3 tablespoons olive oil

1 medium onion, sliced

2 cloves garlic, chopped

1 cup (about 125g) sliced mushrooms

1 tin (410g) whole, peeled tomatoes, undrained

½ tin (200g) Italian-style tomatoes, puréed

1 cup water

½ cup dry white wine

1 bay leaf

12 fresh mussels

250g frozen prawns

 Preparation time
15 minutes

 Cooking time
27 minutes

SERVING SUGGESTION Serve a loaf of warm crusty bread with this robust stew of monkfish, mussels and prawns.

1. Core, seed and coarsely chop the sweet green pepper. Slice the monkfish or kingklip into medium-sized chunks.

2. In a large saucepan or fish kettle, heat the oil over moderate heat. Add the onion, garlic, green pepper and mushrooms and sauté for 5 minutes. Stir in the whole tomatoes and their liquid, the puréed Italian-style tomatoes, the water, wine and bay leaf.

3. Increase the heat to high and bring the mixture to the boil, stirring to break up the tomatoes. Reduce the heat to low, cover, and simmer for 10 minutes.

4. Meanwhile, scrub and clean the mussels under cold running water to remove any sand. Discard those which are not tightly closed. Add the mussels to the tomato mixture. Cover the saucepan, increase the heat to high and bring to the boil.

5. Add the fish chunks and the prawns. Reduce the heat to moderate and simmer for about 5 more minutes until the mussels open, the fish flakes easily and the prawns are opaque. Discard the bay leaf and serve.

SEAFOOD

BAKED CRUMB-TOPPED KABELJOU Serves 4

4 tablespoons (60g) butter or margarine

2x2,5cm-thick (about 300g each) kabeljou steaks

2 tablespoons sesame seeds

1 cup (60g) fresh bread crumbs

1 tablespoon chopped fresh thyme (or 1 teaspoon dried thyme)

¼ teaspoon ground black pepper

Thyme sprigs (optional)

 Preparation time
5 minutes

 Cooking time
25 minutes

COOK'S TIP *Fresh bread crumbs can be made by processing slices of bread in a blender. Use packaged bread crumbs if you have no fresh bread, or if you are short of time.*

1. Preheat the oven to 180°C. Grease a 23cm square baking dish. In a small saucepan, melt the butter over moderate heat. Remove the saucepan from the heat. Place the fish steaks in the prepared baking dish and brush them with some of the melted butter.

2. Bake the fish steaks for 10 minutes. Meanwhile, in the saucepan with the remaining butter, sauté the sesame seeds over moderate heat for 3 minutes, taking care not to burn the butter. Add the bread crumbs, thyme and black pepper and mix well.

3. Sprinkle the fish steaks with the crumb mixture. Continue to bake the fish for about 15 minutes more until it flakes easily when tested with a fork. Slice each steak in half, place on warmed serving plates and garnish with sprigs of thyme, if desired. Serve immediately.

GRILLED MARINATED FISH STEAKS Serves 4

¼ cup sunflower oil

¼ cup dry white wine

1 teaspoon grated lemon peel

2 tablespoons lemon juice

1 tablespoon finely chopped parsley

1 teaspoon dried thyme

¼ teaspoon salt

4x2cm-thick (about 180g each) yellowtail, kabeljou or tuna steaks

Lemon wedges

 Preparation time
25 minutes

 Cooking time
8 minutes

COOK'S TIP *Fish is marinated before cooking chiefly to enrich its flavour and prevent it from drying during cooking. This pungent combination of lemon and wine also helps to tenderize the firm, dense flesh of yellowtail, kabeljou or tuna. Since the marinade is acidic, be sure to use a glass or porcelain dish (not metal) for marinating.*

1. Combine the oil, wine, lemon peel, lemon juice, parsley, thyme and salt in a large, shallow glass dish. Place the fish steaks in the wine mixture. Turn to coat the fish thoroughly, cover the dish and leave to marinate for 20 minutes at room temperature. (The longer it is left in the marinade, the more flavour it will absorb.)

2. Preheat the grill. Remove the fish steaks from the marinade and place them on the rack over a grill pan. Grill them 10cm from the heat for 3 minutes. Turn the steaks over, drizzle them with a little of the marinade and continue grilling them for about 5 more minutes until the fish is lightly browned and flakes easily when tested with a fork. Garnish with wedges of lemon and serve immediately.

YELLOWTAIL KEBABS

YELLOWTAIL KEBABS *Serves 4*

- 4x2cm-thick (about 180g each) yellowtail steaks
- 3 tablespoons olive oil
- 1 tablespoon red wine vinegar
- 2 cloves garlic, finely chopped
- 1 teaspoon paprika
- ½ teaspoon salt
- ½ teaspoon dried thyme
- ¼ teaspoon ground black pepper
- 1 large sweet green pepper, cored and seeded
- 2 large (about 250g) onions

 Preparation time
25 minutes

 Cooking time
6 minutes

SERVING SUGGESTION Serve these skewers of yellowtail and vegetables on a bed of steamed white rice. In the summer, try grilling them over the braai coals and serving them with baby potatoes.

1. Skin and debone the yellowtail if necessary. Cut the fish into 2,5cm to 3cm cubes. In a bowl, combine the oil, vinegar, garlic, paprika, salt, thyme and pepper. Add the fish and toss until well coated. Leave to stand for 10 minutes to marinate.

2. Meanwhile, slice the green pepper into 3cm squares. Chop the onions in half, cut each half into sixths and separate the layers. Toss the pepper and onion in the marinade with the fish.

3. Preheat the grill. On four long metal skewers, thread alternate chunks of the fish, green pepper and onion until all of the pieces are used. Arrange the kebabs on the rack over a grill pan and brush them with the remaining marinade.

4. Grill the kebabs 10cm from the heat for 3 minutes. Turn them over and continue grilling for about 3 more minutes until the fish is just tender but still firm. Serve immediately.

SEAFOOD

BAKED SNOEK WITH TOMATO AND ONION Serves 6 to 8

1 large snoek, cleaned and butterflied

A little sunflower oil for moistening

Salt and ground black pepper to taste

1 tin (410g) tomato and onion mixture

Fresh coriander leaves or chopped parsley for garnishing

Lemon wedges

 Preparation time
5 minutes

 Cooking time
30 minutes

COOK'S TIP When snoek is in season and freely available, try baking it in the oven as a succulent and healthy alternative to the more often pan-fried method of cooking. Serve with steamed rice and a crisp green salad.

1 Preheat the oven to 190°C. Wash and dry the fish. Moisten all over with the oil and season lightly with the salt and ground black pepper. Place the fish, skin side down, on a well-greased baking sheet.

2 Cover the fish with the tomato-onion mixture. Place in the oven and bake for 25 to 30 minutes or until the fish is springy to the touch, just cooked and still moist.

3 Transfer the fish to a warmed serving platter. Garnish with coriander leaves or chopped parsley and lemon wedges. Serve immediately with steamed rice and a green salad.

SMOORED SNOEK HASH Serves 4

2½ cups diced potatoes

1 large ripe tomato

500g smoked snoek, deboned

½ cup finely chopped onion

3 tablespoons finely chopped parsley

1 teaspoon grated lemon rind

½ teaspoon salt

¼ teaspoon ground black pepper

2 tablespoons sunflower oil

1 large egg

1 egg white

¼ cup milk

Parsley sprigs (optional)

 Preparation time
15 minutes

 Cooking time
21 minutes

1 Bring 1 litre of water to the boil in a large saucepan. Boil the diced potatoes for about 8 minutes until tender but still firm. Drain. Skin and finely chop the tomato.

2 In a large bowl, combine the cooked potatoes, tomato, smoked snoek, onion, parsley, lemon rind, ¼ teaspoon of the salt and ⅛ teaspoon of the ground black pepper.

3 In a frying pan, heat the oil over moderate heat. Add the snoek mixture, flattening it into the base of the pan with a spatula. Cover the pan and cook for 8 to 10 minutes until the underside of the mixture is golden, shaking the pan frequently to prevent the bottom of the hash from sticking.

4 In a large bowl, beat together the egg, egg white, milk and remaining salt and black pepper. With the back of a spoon, make a shallow indentation in the hash, pour in the egg mixture and cook over moderately low heat for 2 to 3 minutes until the eggs are set.

5 Loosen the edges with a spatula, invert a warmed plate over the pan and slide the hash onto the plate. Garnish with sprigs of parsley, if desired, and serve immediately.

FISH AU GRATIN

FISH AU GRATIN *Serves 4*

3 tablespoons (45g) butter

½ cup (30g) fresh bread crumbs

1 medium onion, sliced

500g kingklip or monkfish fillets, cubed

2 to 3 cups (about 250g) sliced mushrooms

3 tablespoons flour

½ cup dry white wine

½ cup water

¾ cup cream

½ cup (60g) grated Gruyère or Emmenthal cheese

 Preparation time 10 minutes

 Cooking time 17 minutes

FOOD NOTE Serve this delicious cheese-topped baked fish dish with steamed broccoli.

1. Preheat the grill. Grease four single-portion ovenproof baking dishes. In a large frying pan, melt 1 tablespoon of the butter over moderate heat. Pour the butter into a small bowl and stir in the bread crumbs. Set the buttered crumbs aside.

2. In the frying pan, heat the remaining 2 tablespoons of butter over low heat. Add the onion and sauté for 5 minutes until softened. Increase the heat to moderate, add the fish and mushrooms and sauté for 5 minutes.

3. Add the flour to the fish and mix well. Gradually stir in the wine and water, bring to the boil and simmer for 2 to 3 minutes, stirring constantly, until the sauce thickens. Add the cream and heat through (do not boil). Remove from the heat.

4. Divide the fish mixture among the baking dishes. Sprinkle each serving with an equal amount of the cheese and top with the bread crumbs. Grill 10cm from the heat for 1 to 2 minutes until lightly browned on top. Serve immediately.

FISH CAKES

FISH CAKES *Serves 4*

½ cup (60g) packaged bread crumbs

½ cup mayonnaise

1 large egg

1 tablespoon lemon juice

½ teaspoon mustard powder

Dash of Tabasco sauce

500g cooked fish, flaked

¼ cup chopped celery

3 tablespoons chopped parsley

1 tablespoon finely chopped onion

2 tablespoons sunflower oil

2 tablespoons (30g) butter or margarine

Lemon wedges

 Preparation time
13 minutes

 Cooking time
16 minutes

SERVING SUGGESTION With a fresh green salad and a glass of white wine, these fish cakes make a delicious lunch or light supper.

1. In a large bowl, combine the bread crumbs, mayonnaise, egg, lemon juice, mustard powder and Tabasco sauce until well mixed. Stir in the fish, celery, parsley and onion.

2. Divide the mixture into eight ⅓-cup portions and shape each portion into a 1cm-thick pattie. In a large frying pan, heat 1 tablespoon of the oil with 1 tablespoon of the butter over moderate heat.

3. Fry four of the fish patties for 3 to 4 minutes on each side until they are golden brown. Transfer them to a serving platter and cover to keep them warm.

4. Wipe the frying pan with a paper towel, add the remaining oil and butter and repeat to cook the remaining fish cakes. Arrange the fish cakes on a warmed serving platter. Serve immediately with lemon wedges.

SEAFOOD

SPICED FISH *Serves 4*

4 large (about 750g) hake fillets
1 teaspoon salt
2 tablespoons sunflower oil
1 onion, thinly sliced
1 teaspoon curry powder
1 clove garlic, crushed
1 tin (410g) Indian-style tomatoes
1 bay leaf
Fresh coriander leaves for garnishing
Garam masala for serving

 Preparation time 10 minutes

 Cooking time 20 minutes

1. Wash and dry the fish and slice it into 2,5cm cubes. Season with the salt.

2. In a large flameproof casserole dish, heat the oil over moderate heat. Sauté the onion gently for about 5 minutes until softened but not browned. Stir in the curry powder and the garlic.

3. Add the cubes of fish to the onion mixture and stir until coated. Add the tomatoes and the bay leaf. Simmer, half-covered, for about 10 minutes or until the fish is opaque, just cooked and still moist. Adjust seasoning, if necessary.

4. Garnish with fresh coriander leaves. Serve with white or basmati rice, chutney and a sprinkling of garam masala.

ROASTED FISH *Serves 4*

½ cup dry white wine
¼ cup olive oil
A few sprigs of rosemary
½ teaspoon dried origanum
1 clove garlic, crushed
¼ teaspoon salt
½ teaspoon ground black pepper
2 large fillets (about 500g each) Cape salmon, yellowtail or kingklip
Finely chopped lettuce for garnishing

 Preparation time 70 minutes

 Cooking time 10 minutes

1. For the marinade, mix together the wine, oil, rosemary sprigs, origanum and garlic in a medium-sized bowl.

2. Wash, dry and lightly salt and pepper the fish fillets. Place the fish in a baking dish just large enough to hold it. Pour half the marinade over the fish and leave for about an hour at room temperature to marinate. Preheat the oven to 230°C.

3. Place in the oven and roast, uncovered, for about 10 minutes until just cooked and still moist. Turn onto a warmed serving platter. Pour the remaining marinade over the fish. Garnish with finely chopped lettuce and serve with salsa, Festive Mexican Rice (page 237) and steamed spinach.

TIME SAVERS

Garam masala is a mixture of hot spices and herbs ground together to sprinkle over Indian foods after cooking. To make your own, blend equal quantities of cinnamon, cloves and black pepper. Add cardamom, cumin, coriander seeds, nutmeg and bay leaves to taste.
Store in a tightly sealed bottle in the refrigerator. Keeps for three months.

Salsa is the Mexican word for sauce, but also refers to a tomato-based relish flavoured with a mixture of onions, chillies and coriander that is used to top Mexican-style dishes.

SEAFOOD

FISH KEBABS WITH ORANGE SAUCE Serves 4

4 medium (about 500g) hake fillets

3 baby marrows

12 medium mushrooms

For the orange sauce:

4 tablespoons (60g) butter or margarine

1 cup orange juice

2 tablespoons lemon juice

1 tablespoon grated orange rind

1½ teaspoons cornflour

1 teaspoon dried thyme

¼ teaspoon salt

 Preparation time
15 minutes

 Cooking time
8 minutes

COOK'S TIP Try cooking these delicious kebabs on the braai. Kingklip or monkfish may be used instead of the hake.

1. Preheat the grill. In a large saucepan, bring 5cm of water to the boil over high heat. Meanwhile, slice the fish fillets into 2,5cm cubes and cut the baby marrows into 2,5cm-thick slices. Add the baby marrows to the boiling water and cook for 2 minutes. Drain and set the saucepan aside.

2. To make the sauce: In a medium-sized saucepan, melt the butter over moderate heat. Stir in the orange juice, lemon juice, orange peel, cornflour, thyme and salt. Bring the mixture to the boil and cook for 5 to 6 minutes until it is slightly thickened. Remove the saucepan from the heat and keep the sauce warm.

3. Divide the fish cubes, baby marrow slices and mushrooms into 4 equal portions. Thread them alternately onto four 30cm metal skewers. Brush with ½ cup of the sauce. Grill them 10cm from the heat for about 6 to 7 minutes until they are lightly browned, turning once during cooking. Serve immediately with the remaining sauce.

CHILLI TARRAGON PRAWNS Serves 4

1 medium sweet red pepper

2 cloves garlic

2 tablespoons olive oil

400g uncooked peeled and deveined prawns, thawed

3 tablespoons lemon juice

2 tablespoons (30g) butter or margarine

1 teaspoon dried tarragon

⅛ teaspoon crushed chillies, or to taste

Salt to taste

2 tablespoons chopped parsley

Cooked long-grain white rice (optional)

 Preparation time
7 minutes

 Cooking time
5 minutes

COOK'S TIP Prawns are at their best when only just cooked through, so take care not to keep them on the stove any longer than necessary. Be sure to heat the oil before adding the prawns so that they will cook as quickly as possible.

1. Core and seed the red pepper and cut it into 5mm-wide strips. Peel and finely chop the garlic.

2. Heat the oil over moderately high heat in a large frying pan or wok. Add the prawns, the red pepper and the garlic, and sauté for 2 to 3 minutes until the prawns turn pink.

3. Add the lemon juice, butter, tarragon and chillies to the prawn and pepper mixture. Cook until the butter melts, stirring constantly, about 1 minute. Season with salt and sprinkle with the parsley. Place the prawns on a warmed serving platter. Serve with hot white rice, if desired.

PRAWNS IN TOMATO-WINE SAUCE

PRAWNS IN TOMATO-WINE SAUCE *Serves 4*

1 cup long-grain white rice

2 medium tomatoes

1 tablespoon cornflour

¾ cup chicken stock

¼ cup dry white wine

3 tablespoons (45g) butter or margarine

400g uncooked peeled and deveined prawns, thawed

1 tablespoon capers, rinsed and drained

 Preparation time
2 minutes

 Cooking time
20 minutes

1. Prepare the rice according to the directions given on the packet. While it is cooking, slice the tomatoes into 1cm chunks. In a small bowl, blend the cornflour with the stock and wine.

2. In a large frying pan, melt the butter over moderately high heat. Add the prawns and sauté for about 2 minutes until they begin to turn pink.

3. Add the cornflour-stock mixture to the prawns in the frying pan, stirring thoroughly. Bring the mixture to the boil, stirring constantly, and continue boiling until the sauce thickens. Add the tomatoes and capers to the prawns. Continue cooking until the tomatoes are just heated through.

4. Transfer the cooked rice to a serving bowl, pour the prawns and tomato sauce over it and serve immediately.

SEAFOOD

Saffron seafood casserole *Serves 6*

3 tablespoons (45g) butter or margarine

1 clove garlic, crushed

1 large onion, chopped

1 leek, thinly sliced

450g hake or monkfish, skinned and cubed

450g baby potatoes

300ml dry white wine

150ml fish or vegetable stock

150ml cream

½ teaspoon saffron threads

400g frozen seafood mixture, thawed

2 tablespoons chopped tarragon

Salt and freshly ground black pepper to taste

 Preparation time 10 minutes

 Cooking time 40 minutes

COOK'S TIP This recipe can be adapted using any fish you choose. Serve it on a bed of steamed white rice and accompanied by a crisp garden salad and a glass of icy dry white wine.

1. Melt the butter in a large, heavy-based saucepan. Add the garlic, onion and leek and cook gently for about 10 minutes until the vegetables are softened. Add the hake and potatoes to the saucepan and stir to mix well.

2. Add the white wine, stock, cream and saffron threads. Bring to the boil, reduce the heat to low and simmer gently, covered, for about 20 minutes until the potatoes are just tender when pricked with a fork.

3. Stir the seafood mixture and the tarragon into the saucepan and return to a gentle simmer. Cook for a further 10 minutes. Season to taste with salt and a grinding of black pepper. Transfer to warmed serving plates and serve immediately with steamed white rice.

Seafood paprika *Serves 4*

2 tablespoons (30g) butter or margarine

400g frozen seafood mixture, thawed

1 tablespoon sunflower oil

1 small onion, chopped

2 to 3 cups (about 250g) sliced mushrooms

2 tablespoons flour

2 teaspoons paprika

¾ cup dry white wine

¾ cup fresh cream

½ cup sour cream

4 to 6 drops Tabasco sauce

Salt and freshly ground black pepper to taste

Parsley sprigs (optional)

Cooked long-grain white rice (optional)

 Preparation time 5 minutes

 Cooking time 15 minutes

1. In a large frying pan melt the butter over moderately high heat. Add the seafood mixture and sauté for about 2 minutes. Transfer to a deep bowl and set aside.

2. Add the sunflower oil to the frying pan and heat over moderate heat. Add the chopped onion and sauté for about 5 minutes until soft. Add the sliced mushrooms and stir to mix well. Cover the pan and cook the mixture for about 4 minutes until softened, stirring occasionally.

3. Stir the flour and paprika into the mushroom mixture until well mixed. Gradually stir in the wine. Bring the mixture to the boil, stirring constantly, until the sauce thickens. Stir in the fresh cream and heat through (do not boil).

4. Reduce the heat to low and stir in the sour cream, Tabasco sauce and the sautéed seafood mixture. Cook, stirring gently, for about 1 minute. Season to taste with salt and pepper. Transfer the seafood to a serving bowl, garnish with sprigs of parsley and serve with rice, if desired.

CURRIED PRAWNS

CURRIED PRAWNS *Serves 4*

2 tablespoons (30g) butter or margarine

1 tablespoon sunflower oil

1 small onion, sliced

1 clove garlic, finely chopped

400g large uncooked peeled and deveined prawns, thawed

1 tablespoon flour

2 teaspoons curry powder

1 cup plain low-fat yoghurt

Salt and ground black pepper to taste

Cooked long-grain white rice (optional)

Chopped parsley

 Preparation time
5 minutes

 Cooking time
11 minutes

COOK'S TIP Long-grain white rice can be left to cook while you prepare the prawns. Serve with poppadums or warmed pita bread.

1. In a large frying pan, heat the butter and oil over moderate heat. Add the onion and sauté for about 5 minutes until soft. Add the garlic and sauté for 2 more minutes.

2. Using paper towels, pat the prawns dry. Place them in a medium-sized bowl and sprinkle the flour and curry powder over them. Toss to coat. Place the prawns in the frying pan and cook for about 2 minutes until they begin to turn pink, stirring constantly.

3. Reduce the heat to low and stir in the yoghurt. Heat for about 1 minute until the mixture becomes bubbly. Season with salt and pepper. Serve over rice, if desired, and garnish with parsley.

SEAFOOD

GRILLED CALAMARI Serves 4

4 calamari (about 200g each)

A little olive oil for moistening

For the dressing:

4 tablespoons olive oil

2 tablespoons lemon juice

1 clove garlic, crushed

1 red chilli, seeded and chopped

½ teaspoon salt

⅛ teaspoon ground black pepper

 Preparation time
10 minutes

 Cooking time
3 minutes

COOK'S TIP Take care not to overcook calamari as it will become tough and unpalatable.

1. Ask your fishmonger to clean the calamari. Cut off the tentacles, rinse, dry well and set aside. Butterfly the calamari by cutting down one side of each and opening out flat. Score the inside in a crisscross pattern, rinse and dry well. Moisten with the olive oil, including the reserved tentacles. Preheat the grill.

2. To make the dressing: Combine the oil, lemon juice, garlic, chilli, salt and pepper in a small bowl. Mix well.

3. Place the calamari on a greased grill rack and grill for 1 to 2 minutes until opaque, just cooked and starting to curl. Turn with tongs and grill for barely 1 more minute on the other side. Turn into a hot serving dish and pour the dressing over it.

4. Serve immediately with Baked Potato Cakes (page 279) and a medley of baby vegetables.

CALAMARI AND VEGETABLE STIR-FRY Serves 4 (PICTURE PAGE 127)

300g calamari rings

2 tablespoons dry sherry

¾ cup fish or chicken stock

1 tablespoon soy sauce

2 teaspoons cornflour

½ teaspoon sugar

1 medium onion

250g mange-tout

2 tablespoons sunflower oil

1 clove garlic, finely chopped

1 teaspoon finely chopped ginger (or ¼ teaspoon ground ginger)

Salt and pepper to taste

 Preparation time
20 minutes

 Cooking time
11 minutes

1. In a medium-sized bowl, combine the calamari rings and sherry and toss to coat evenly. Set the calamari aside for 15 to 20 minutes to marinate, turning occasionally.

2. Meanwhile, in a small bowl, mix ¼ cup of the stock, the soy sauce, cornflour and sugar and set aside. Slice the onion into 2,5cm wedges and the mange-tout into 5cm lengths. Set aside.

3. In a wok or large frying pan, heat the oil over high heat. Add the garlic and ginger and stir-fry for a few seconds. Add the calamari and stir-fry for 2 to 3 minutes until they turn opaque. With a slotted spoon, transfer the calamari to a bowl and set aside.

4. Reheat the wok or frying pan over moderate heat. Add the onion, mange-tout and remaining stock. Cover and cook the vegetables for about 6 minutes until they are tender but still firm to the bite.

5. Add the cornflour mixture to the vegetables, season to taste with the salt and pepper and cook for about 30 seconds until thickened. Stir in the calamari and cook until just heated through. Transfer to a serving dish and serve immediately.

CALAMARI AND VEGETABLE STIR-FRY *(see facing page)*

THAI-STYLE CURRIED CALAMARI *Serves 3 to 4*

2 cups coconut milk

2 tablespoons green curry paste

300g calamari, cleaned and sliced, at room temperature

1 tablespoon Thai fish sauce

Grated rind of 1 large lemon

1 red chilli, seeded and sliced

2 tablespoons basil or coriander leaves

Steamed Thai rice

 Preparation time
5 minutes

 Cooking time
10 minutes

COOK'S TIP Many Thai ingredients are now available at supermarkets. If not, you'll find them at speciality Asian food shops.

1. Pour the coconut milk into a wok or large frying pan. Bring to the boil over moderate heat and simmer for 5 minutes.

2. Stir in the green curry paste and simmer the mixture for a further 3 to 4 minutes.

3. Add the calamari and simmer for barely 1 minute until the calamari is opaque and just cooked. Add the fish sauce and lemon rind. Check the seasoning. If the dish needs more salt, add a little of the fish sauce, which has a high salt content.

4. Garnish with the chilli and basil, and serve immediately on a bed of steamed Thai rice.

SEAFOOD

MUSSELS WITH TOMATOES AND RICE Serves 4 (Picture page 97)

50 fresh mussels
1 cup dry white wine
¼ cup currants
¼ cup olive oil
2 onions, finely chopped
1 tin (410g) chopped tomatoes
½ cup rice
¼ cup pine nuts
¼ teaspoon ground allspice
1 tablespoon chopped fresh dill
Salt and pepper to taste

 Preparation time
2 hours

 Cooking time
30 minutes

Food note Mussels must be absolutely fresh and, if you didn't gather them yourself, check that the bought ones are still alive when purchased. The shells must be tightly closed. Discard those with open shells. Farmed mussels are generally fairly clean and won't take long to scrub.

1. Soak the mussels in cold water for about 2 hours and discard those which are not tightly closed. Scrub them and peel away the beardlike threads.

2. Place the mussels in a large saucepan with the wine. Cover, bring to the boil and cook briskly for about 5 minutes until they open. Discard any that do not open. Strain the cooking liquid and set it aside. Blanch the currants by bringing them to the boil in a little cold, unsalted water. Simmer for a few minutes and drain.

3. Wipe the saucepan, return it to the stove, add the oil and heat it gently. Add the onions and cook gently for about 5 minutes until softened. Add the tomatoes, rice, pine nuts, currants, allspice, dill and the reserved liquid. Simmer for 15 to 20 minutes or until the rice is cooked.

4. Add the mussels and heat gently. Check the seasoning. Serve in deep bowls with crusty bread.

WEST COAST MUSSELS WITH GARLIC BUTTER Serves 4

45 fresh West Coast mussels
½ cup dry white wine
A few sprigs parsley
A few sprigs thyme
½ cup (125g) unsalted butter
4-6 cloves garlic, crushed
2 tablespoons finely chopped fresh parsley
Salt and freshly ground pepper to taste
Steamed rice

 Preparation time
2 hours

 Cooking time
10 minutes

1. Soak the mussels in cold water for about 2 hours and discard those which are not tightly closed. Scrub them and peel away the beardlike threads.

2. Place the cleaned mussels in a wide, shallow saucepan with the wine, parsley and thyme. Cover and bring to the boil over high heat. Cook, shaking vigorously, for about 5 minutes until the shells open. Do not overcook. Discard those that do not open.

3. As soon as they are cool enough to handle, remove the top shells. Arrange the halved mussels on a warmed serving platter.

4. Meanwhile, in a small saucepan, heat the butter with the garlic, parsley and a little salt and pepper until frothy.

5. Pour half of the garlic butter over the mussels and pass around the rest separately. Serve immediately with steamed rice.

Poultry

Orange-glazed chicken (page 134)

Poultry

This all-time favourite bird appears in a mouth-watering selection of quick and economical meals. One of the most versatile of foods, the chicken dishes here are sure to please friends and family.

Buffalo chicken wings *Serves 4*

1kg (approximately 12) chicken wings
Sunflower oil for frying
4 tablespoons (60g) butter or margarine
1 tablespoon Tabasco sauce
1 small bunch celery

For the blue cheese dip:
½ cup sour cream
½ cup mayonnaise
¼ cup (30g) crumbled blue cheese
2 tablespoons chopped parsley
½ teaspoon Worcestershire sauce

 Preparation time
9 minutes

 Cooking time
30 minutes

FOOD NOTE *This tantalizing appetizer originated in Buffalo, New York. Dip the hot chicken in the chilled blue cheese dip and wash it all down with a refreshing beer or a long, cool drink.*

1 Cut the tips off the chicken wings and discard (or freeze to use in soup stock). Split the remaining part of each wing into 2 pieces at the joint. In a large saucepan, heat 5cm of oil over moderate heat to 190°C. Add half of the wing portions and fry them for 12 to 15 minutes until they are golden brown.

2 Meanwhile, make the blue cheese dip. In a small bowl, blend the sour cream, mayonnaise, blue cheese, parsley and Worcestershire sauce until well mixed. Cover the dip and refrigerate it until the chicken is ready to serve.

3 Drain the first batch of fried wings on a baking sheet lined with paper towels. Keep them warm. Repeat to fry the second half of the wings. In a small saucepan, melt the butter over low heat and stir in the Tabasco sauce. Slice the celery in half lengthwise and then into 10cm-long sticks. Drizzle or toss the drained chicken wings with the Tabasco-sauce mixture. Arrange the wings and celery sticks on a platter. Serve with the blue cheese dip.

Time Savers

Poultry
■ For a quick glaze for chicken or turkey, brush the portions with a mixture of ready-made barbecue sauce and one or two tablespoons of orange juice. This citrus glaze is particularly good when brushed over grilled or braaied chicken.

■ Prepared teriyaki sauce, readily available from many supermarkets, is the perfect marinade for poultry. For the best results, slice the deboned meat finely to absorb more of the flavour of the marinade, then stir-fry. Add the marinade shortly before serving.

■ It is worth investing in some poultry shears or strong kitchen scissors for cutting up whole chickens; they slice through joints, bones and meat easily. This will save the extra expense of buying pre-cut poultry. The shears are available in most kitchen-supply shops.

POULTRY

Parsley mustard chicken *Serves 4*

1 chicken (about 1,5kg), cut into serving portions

1 tablespoon (15g) butter or margarine

2 tablespoons finely chopped onion

1 clove garlic, finely chopped

½ cup (30g) fresh bread crumbs

2 tablespoons finely chopped parsley

¼ cup mayonnaise

2 teaspoons Dijon mustard

 Preparation time 10 minutes

 Cooking time 28 minutes

Food note In France, a preparation of finely chopped parsley and bread crumbs is called persillade. *It complements chicken perfectly, as would a side dish of steamed broccoli or cauliflower florets.*

1 Preheat the grill. Arrange the chicken portions, skin side down, on the rack over a grill pan. Grill 12,5cm from the heat for about 20 minutes until lightly browned and almost tender.

2 Meanwhile, in a small saucepan, melt the butter over moderate heat. Add the onion and garlic and sauté for about 5 minutes until soft. Stir in the bread crumbs and parsley. Remove the saucepan from the heat and set it aside. Mix the mayonnaise and the mustard together in a cup or small bowl.

3 Turn the chicken pieces over and continue grilling for about 5 more minutes until they are tender.

4 Spread the mayonnaise mixture over the chicken portions and sprinkle or pat them with the parsley mixture. Continue grilling for about 3 more minutes, or until the crumb coating is golden brown. Serve immediately.

Tangy grilled chicken *Serves 4*

1 chicken (about 1,5kg), cut into quarters

¼ teaspoon each salt and ground black pepper

⅔ cup tomato sauce or ketchup

2 tablespoons soy sauce

1 clove garlic, finely chopped

½ teaspoon ground ginger

¼ teaspoon mustard powder

Parsley sprigs (optional)

 Preparation time 5 minutes

 Cooking time 27 minutes

1 Preheat the grill. Arrange the chicken quarters, skin side down, on the rack over a grill pan. Season the chicken with the salt and pepper. Grill the portions 12,5cm from the heat for about 20 minutes until lightly browned and almost tender.

2 Meanwhile, in a small saucepan, combine the tomato sauce, soy sauce, garlic, ginger and mustard. Bring the mixture to the boil over moderate heat, stirring occasionally.

3 Turn the chicken over and continue grilling for 5 minutes. Brush the chicken generously with some of the tomato sauce mixture and continue grilling for approximately 2 more minutes until the sauce on the chicken is bubbly and lightly browned, taking care not to burn it.

4 Place the chicken on a warmed serving platter and pour any remaining sauce over it. Garnish the chicken with sprigs of parsley, if desired, and serve immediately.

CHICKEN TACOS

CHICKEN TACOS *Serves 4*

1 tablespoon sunflower oil

1 medium onion, chopped

500g minced chicken

1 tablespoon flour

125g bottled green chillies, chopped

1 teaspoon chilli powder

½ teaspoon dried origanum

½ teaspoon salt

8 taco shells

½ cup (60g) coarsely grated mild Cheddar cheese

1 to 1½ cups finely chopped crisp lettuce, eg Iceberg

⅔ cup ready-made tomato salsa

 Preparation time 8 minutes

 Cooking time 13 minutes

SERVING SUGGESTION Mashed chilli beans continue the theme of this Mexican-style meal. For the less adventurous, serve it with a crisp salad of lettuce tossed with chopped tomatoes and slices of avocado pear.

1. In a large frying pan, heat the oil over moderate heat. Add the chopped onion and sauté for about 5 minutes until soft. Increase the heat to moderately high and add the minced chicken. Cook the chicken for about 3 minutes until it is lightly browned, stirring frequently.

2. Sprinkle the flour over the chicken mixture and stir until blended. Stir in the green chillies, chilli powder, origanum and salt and continue cooking, stirring occasionally, for 5 minutes. Remove the chicken mixture from the heat.

3. Spoon the chicken mixture into the taco shells. Sprinkle each with some of the Cheddar cheese, and top with some of the lettuce. Spoon the salsa over the lettuce and serve immediately.

POULTRY

Orange-glazed chicken *Serves 4 (Picture page 129)*

½ cup orange marmalade
⅓ cup firmly packed dark brown sugar
⅓ cup orange juice
¼ cup red wine vinegar
1 tablespoon Dijon mustard
½ teaspoon ground ginger
2 cloves garlic, finely chopped
1 tablespoon plus 2 teaspoons sunflower oil
1 chicken (about 1,5kg), cut into serving portions

 Preparation time 5 minutes

 Cooking time 38 minutes

1. Preheat the oven to 230°C. In a small bowl, blend the marmalade, brown sugar, orange juice, vinegar, mustard, ginger, garlic and 2 teaspoons of the oil until thoroughly mixed. Set aside.

2. In a large flameproof casserole dish, heat the remaining 1 tablespoon of oil over moderately high heat. Fry the chicken portions for about 8 minutes until lightly browned on all sides. Drain the fat. Add the marmalade mixture to the dish and bring it to the boil.

3. Transfer the dish to the oven. Bake until the chicken juices run clear, about 15 minutes for white meat, 30 minutes for dark. Skim the fat from the sauce. Transfer the chicken to a warmed platter, spoon the sauce over it and serve.

Microwave oven version

Omit the sunflower oil and add 2 tablespoons of flour to the ingredients. Remove the skin from the chicken portions. In a microwave-safe 32,5cm x 22,5cm baking dish, mix the sugar and flour until well blended. Add the marmalade, orange juice, vinegar, mustard, ginger and garlic, and mix well. Add the chicken portions and coat with the marmalade mixture. Arrange the chicken in a single layer in the baking dish, with the thickest part of each portion facing towards the outside of the dish.

Cover the baking dish with plastic wrap pierced at one corner to allow the steam to escape. Microwave the chicken on high power for 9 minutes. Spoon some of the sauce over each portion. Replace the cover and microwave on high power for 9 to 12 more minutes until the chicken juices run clear.

Time Savers

Quick-cooked chicken
■ When a recipe calls for cooked chicken, or when making a chicken salad, simmer it gently in stock or water. For two cups of cooked chicken, you will need two 180g skinned and deboned breasts.

■ To cook the chicken conventionally, place the breasts in a large frying pan with 1⅓ cups water or stock. Bring to the boil, then reduce the heat and simmer, covered, for approximately 12 to 14 minutes or until the chicken is tender.

■ To microwave the chicken, wrap each breast in a double layer of paper towels. Moisten with water and place on a microwave-safe plate. Cook on high power for 4 to 5 minutes. Allow to stand for 3 minutes before slicing.

CRUSTY OVEN-BAKED CHICKEN

CRUSTY OVEN-BAKED CHICKEN *Serves 4*

4 tablespoons (60g) butter or margarine

1 clove garlic, chopped

1 cup (60g) fresh bread crumbs

3 tablespoons grated Parmesan cheese

1 tablespoon finely chopped parsley

½ teaspoon dried marjoram

¼ teaspoon dried thyme

⅛ teaspoon ground black pepper

4 large (about 700g) skinless chicken-breast fillets

 Preparation time
10 minutes

 Cooking time
30 minutes

SERVING SUGGESTION A delicate green salad with cucumber and mange-tout is the perfect foil for this crunchy chicken dish.

1 Preheat the oven to 200°C. Lightly grease a baking tray. In a small saucepan, melt the butter over moderate heat. Add the garlic and sauté for 10 seconds. Remove the saucepan from the heat.

2 In a pie plate, mix the bread crumbs, Parmesan cheese, parsley, marjoram, thyme and ground black pepper. Dip the chicken breasts, one at a time, into the garlic butter, letting the excess fall back into the saucepan. Roll them in the crumb mixture, coating them evenly. (If necessary, pat the crumb mixture onto the chicken to make it stick.)

3 Arrange the chicken in a single layer on the baking tray. Pat any remaining crumbs onto the top surface of the chicken portions and drizzle them with any remaining garlic butter. Bake for about 25 to 30 minutes until the chicken is lightly browned and tender. Serve immediately.

POULTRY

HONEY-GLAZED CHICKEN WITH ORANGES Serves 4

1,5kg (about 8) chicken breasts, on the bone
⅓ cup honey
⅓ cup whole fruit apricot jam
2 tablespoons orange juice
1 tablespoon lemon juice
1 teaspoon ground ginger
2 navel oranges
Pinch of salt
Watercress sprigs (optional)

 Preparation time 5 minutes

 Cooking time 29 minutes

SERVING SUGGESTION *Present this elegant creation with steamed green beans tossed with lemon juice, melted butter and finely chopped parsley.*

1. Preheat the grill. Arrange the chicken breasts, skin side down, on the rack over a grill pan. Grill the chicken 12,5cm from the heat for about 15 minutes until lightly browned.

2. Meanwhile, in a cup or small bowl, blend the honey, apricot jam, orange juice, lemon juice and ground ginger. Brush the chicken with some of the honey mixture and grill for approximately 1 more minute.

3. Turn the chicken over and continue grilling for a further 10 minutes until the chicken is tender. Meanwhile, using a sharp knife, peel the oranges and slice them crosswise into 1cm-thick slices. Add the oranges to the grill pan with the chicken and season with the salt.

4. Brush the orange slices and the chicken with the remaining honey mixture and continue grilling them for approximately 2 more minutes until the chicken is lightly browned and the orange slices are glazed.

5. Arrange the chicken and oranges on a warmed serving platter, garnish with watercress, if desired, and serve.

SAVOURY PAN-FRIED CHICKEN BREASTS Serves 4

½ cup ground pecan nuts
⅓ cup (40g) packaged bread crumbs
1 teaspoon dried sage
¼ teaspoon salt
¼ teaspoon cayenne pepper
¼ cup flour
1 large egg
2 tablespoons water
4 large (about 700g) skinless chicken-breast fillets
3 tablespoons sunflower oil
Halved pecan nuts (optional)

 Preparation time 10 minutes

 Cooking time 8 minutes

FOOD NOTE *Tempt your palate with this easy chicken dish, coated with the distinctive flavour and delightful crunch of pecan nuts.*

1. In a pie plate, combine the pecan nuts, bread crumbs, sage, salt and cayenne pepper until well mixed. Place the flour in a second pie plate. In a third pie plate, beat the egg with the water. Coat each chicken breast first with the flour, then the egg mixture, then the pecan nut mixture.

2. In a large frying pan, heat the oil over moderately high heat. Add the chicken breasts and sauté for 3 to 4 minutes on each side until the pieces are golden brown on both sides. Transfer the chicken to a warmed platter. Garnish with pecan halves, if desired, and serve immediately.

CHICKEN PROVENÇALE

CHICKEN PROVENÇALE *Serves 4*

2 tablespoons olive oil

1kg chicken legs and thighs

1 medium onion

2 cloves garlic, finely chopped

½ teaspoon saffron threads (optional)

1 cup chicken stock

½ cup dry white wine

1 tin (410g) whole, peeled tomatoes, drained and halved

1 teaspoon dried rosemary

1 bay leaf

2 baby marrows, sliced

½ cup pitted black olives

Salt and ground black pepper to taste

 Preparation time 5 minutes

 Cooking time 40 minutes

FOOD NOTE Olive oil, tomatoes and garlic are all typical of the cuisine of Provence, combining to give this dish a truly Mediterranean flavour.

1. In a 5-litre flameproof casserole dish or a large, deep, heavy-based saucepan, heat the oil over moderate heat. Add the chicken portions and sauté for about 15 minutes until well browned on all sides. Meanwhile, chop the onion into 8 wedges.

2. Transfer the chicken to a plate, and drain all but 2 tablespoons of the drippings. Combine the onion, garlic and saffron, if desired, in the casserole dish and sauté for 3 minutes. Add the stock and wine to the onion mixture. Increase the heat to high and bring to the boil. Stir in the tomatoes, rosemary and bay leaf. Add the chicken and cover the dish. Reduce the heat to moderate and cook for 10 minutes.

3. Stir the baby marrows and olives into the chicken mixture and cook for 5 minutes. Remove the lid and continue cooking for a further 5 minutes or until the chicken juices run clear. Season with salt and pepper, discard the bay leaf, and serve.

POULTRY

SPICED CHICKEN *Serves 4*

½ teaspoon salt
½ teaspoon ground black pepper
½ teaspoon ground cinnamon
½ teaspoon ground cloves
1kg chicken legs and thighs
1½ tablespoons sunflower oil
1 medium onion, sliced
1 stalk celery, sliced
2 tablespoons raisins
¾ cup orange juice
2 teaspoons cornflour
¼ cup slivered almonds
Salt to taste

 Preparation time 5 minutes

 Cooking time 32 minutes

1. In a small bowl or cup, combine the salt, pepper, cinnamon and cloves. Sprinkle the chicken portions with the spice mixture, top and bottom. In a large frying pan, heat the oil over moderately high heat. Add the chicken portions and sauté for about 10 minutes until lightly browned on one side.

2. Turn the chicken portions over and add the onion and celery to the frying pan. Cook the chicken for approximately 5 more minutes until the second side is browned.

3. Add the raisins and ½ cup of the orange juice to the chicken mixture. Reduce the heat to moderately low, cover the frying pan and cook for 15 minutes until the chicken is tender.

4. Meanwhile, in a cup, combine the cornflour and the remaining ¼ cup orange juice. Stir the cornflour mixture and almonds into the chicken mixture. Bring the sauce to the boil and cook for 1 to 2 minutes until thickened and season with salt. Transfer the chicken to a serving platter, pour the sauce over it and serve.

PAPRIKA CHICKEN *Serves 4* (PICTURE PAGE 2)

2 tablespoons sunflower oil
4 large (about 650g) skinless chicken-breast fillets
1 medium sweet green pepper
1 tin (410g) whole, peeled tomatoes
2 medium onions, coarsely chopped
2 tablespoons paprika
½ cup chicken stock
½ cup sour cream
Salt and ground black pepper to taste
Chopped parsley (optional)

 Preparation time 5 minutes

 Cooking time 35 minutes

1. In a large, heavy-based saucepan, heat the oil over moderate heat. Add the chicken-breast fillets and sauté for about 15 minutes until well browned on all sides. Meanwhile, core and seed the green pepper and slice it into strips. Drain and chop the tomatoes.

2. Transfer the chicken to a plate. Drain all but 2 tablespoons of the drippings in the saucepan. Stir in the onions and pepper strips and sauté for 3 minutes until they begin to soften.

3. Add the tomatoes, paprika and stock to the saucepan. Increase the heat to high and bring the mixture to the boil.

4. Return the chicken to the saucepan. Reduce the heat to low, cover the saucepan and simmer the chicken and vegetables for about 10 minutes until they are tender and cooked through.

5. Stir the sour cream into the chicken mixture and cook for a few seconds until just heated through (do not boil). Season the chicken with the salt and pepper, sprinkle with parsley, if desired, and serve.

POULTRY

GRILLED LEMON CHICKEN *Serves 4*

1 chicken (about 1kg), cut into serving portions

1 tablespoon (15g) butter or margarine

2 cloves garlic, finely chopped

1 teaspoon finely grated lemon rind

¼ cup lemon juice

1 teaspoon coarsely ground black pepper

1 teaspoon dried origanum

¼ teaspoon salt

 Preparation time
5 minutes

 Cooking time
30 minutes

1. Preheat the grill. Arrange the chicken portions, skin side down, on the rack over a grill pan. Grill the chicken 12,5cm from the heat for about 20 minutes until the portions are lightly browned on the exposed side.

2. Meanwhile, in a small saucepan, melt the butter over low heat. Add the garlic and sauté for 10 seconds. Remove the saucepan from the heat and stir in the lemon rind and juice, the pepper, origanum and salt. Brush the chicken portions with some of the lemon mixture.

3. Turn the chicken portions over and brush them with more of the lemon mixture. Continue grilling for a further 5 to 10 minutes until the chicken is tender, brushing frequently with the lemon mixture. Transfer the chicken to a platter and serve immediately.

DEVILLED DRUMSTICKS *Serves 4*

2 tablespoons sunflower oil

1,5kg (approximately 10) chicken drumsticks

2 medium onions, sliced

⅓ cup ready-made barbecue sauce

⅓ cup plus 1 tablespoon water

3 tablespoons light brown sugar

2 tablespoons prepared mustard

½ teaspoon salt

2 teaspoons cornflour

1 small spring onion

 Preparation time
5 minutes

 Cooking time
35 minutes

1. In a 30cm frying pan (preferably with a nonstick coating), heat the sunflower oil over moderately high heat. Add the chicken drumsticks and fry for about 15 minutes until they are well browned on all sides.

2. Move the drumsticks to one side of the frying pan. Add the onions and sauté for 3 minutes.

3. In a small bowl, mix the barbecue sauce, ⅓ cup of the water, the brown sugar, mustard and salt until well blended. Pour the sauce over the drumsticks and onions in the frying pan. Reduce the heat to low, cover and simmer for 10 to 15 minutes until the chicken is tender.

4. Meanwhile, in a cup, blend the remaining 1 tablespoon water with the cornflour and set aside. Slice the spring onion diagonally into 1cm chunks.

5. Using a slotted spoon, transfer the drumsticks to a warmed serving platter. Increase the heat to moderate and stir the cornflour mixture into the sauce in the frying pan. Bring the mixture to the boil and cook until thickened.

6. Pour the sauce over the chicken, garnish with the spring onion and serve immediately.

CHICKEN WITH APPLE RINGS

CHICKEN WITH APPLE RINGS *Serves 4*

¼ cup flour

¼ teaspoon each salt and ground black pepper

4 large (about 600g) skinless chicken-breast fillets

2 tablespoons (30g) butter or margarine

2 Granny Smith apples, unpeeled, cored and sliced into 5mm-thick rings

1 tablespoon sunflower oil

½ cup chicken stock

½ teaspoon dried thyme

½ cup apple juice

1 teaspoon cornflour

¼ cup cream

 Preparation time 5 minutes

 Cooking time 15 minutes

SERVING SUGGESTION Apples lend an appealing flavour to this satisfying dish. Serve it with new potatoes tossed with butter and chopped parsley.

1. Mix the flour, salt and pepper in a pie plate. Dip the chicken breasts into the flour until well coated, shaking off the excess.

2. In a large, heavy-based frying pan, heat 1 tablespoon of the butter over moderate heat. Add the apple rings and cook for 3 minutes, turning once, until slightly softened. Using a slotted spoon, transfer the apples to a bowl and keep them warm.

3. In the same frying pan, heat the remaining 1 tablespoon of butter and the oil over moderate heat. Add the chicken breasts and sauté for 2 to 3 minutes on each side until golden brown. Using a slotted spoon, transfer the chicken to a warmed serving platter.

4. Add the stock and thyme to the pan and bring the mixture to the boil. In a cup, mix the apple juice and cornflour. Stir the cornflour mixture into the stock mixture. Return the sauce to the boil, stirring constantly. Simmer gently for about 1 minute until thickened. Stir in the cream and heat through (do not boil). Pour the sauce over the chicken, top with the apples and serve.

Start with a Roast Chicken

A roast chicken is a healthy starting point for a quick and nourishing meal. It is as good when used in salads and sandwiches as it is when adapted for hot dishes. In fact, you will probably think of many more variations to add to the ideas you find here. Start with a whole, cooked 1,5kg roast chicken. Of course you can cook your own (see page 25), but delicious ready-cooked birds are available from many supermarkets and delicatessens, making the preparation of a last-minute meal much easier. Remove the skin and bones from the chicken before beginning the recipe. Each recipe serves four.

▼**Spinach chicken salad** Finely chop the meat of *1 roast chicken*. Chop *2 large tomatoes* and slice *250g Gruyère* or *mozzarella cheese* into thin strips. Line a platter with *150g spinach leaves*. In a small bowl, mix *½ cup sunflower oil*, *3 tablespoons Dijon mustard* and *2 tablespoons red wine vinegar*. Arrange the chicken, tomatoes and cheese strips over the spinach. Pour some of the dressing over the salad, and serve the remaining dressing separately.

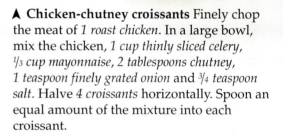

▲ **Chicken-chutney croissants** Finely chop the meat of *1 roast chicken*. In a large bowl, mix the chicken, *1 cup thinly sliced celery*, *⅓ cup mayonnaise*, *2 tablespoons chutney*, *1 teaspoon finely grated onion* and *¾ teaspoon salt*. Halve *4 croissants* horizontally. Spoon an equal amount of the mixture into each croissant.

▼**Barbecued chicken rolls** Finely chop the meat of *1 roast chicken*. Preheat the grill. In a large saucepan, melt *2 tablespoons (30g) butter* or *margarine* over moderate heat. Add *1 medium onion*, chopped, and *1 large sweet green pepper*, diced. Sauté about 5 minutes until soft. Stir in the chicken and *1 cup ready-made barbecue sauce*. Bring the mixture to the boil, stirring frequently. Halve and toast *4 rolls*. Spoon the chicken mixture over the rolls and sprinkle with *½ cup grated Cheddar cheese*. Place under the grill until cheese melts.

◄ **Chicken-feta salad** Finely chop the meat of *1 roast chicken*. Preheat the oven to 200°C. In a small baking tin, spread *¼ cup chopped walnuts* and bake for about 5 minutes until toasted. Meanwhile, in a large salad bowl, combine *2 medium heads crisp lettuce*, torn into small pieces, the chicken and *100g feta cheese*, crumbled. Garnish the salad with the toasted walnuts and *1 tomato*, chopped. Toss gently with prepared *vinaigrette salad dressing*.

► **Chicken tostadas** Finely chop the meat of *1 roast chicken*. In a small saucepan, heat *one 410g tin chilli beans* until hot. In a medium-sized saucepan, heat the chicken and *1 cup ready-made tomato salsa* until hot. Spread one-eighth of the beans on each of *8 tostada shells*. Top each with one-eighth of the chopped chicken mixture. Garnish with *shredded lettuce*, *avocado pear slices* and *sour cream*.

◄ **Curried chicken** Chop the meat of *1 roast chicken*. In a medium-sized saucepan, melt *2 tablespoons (30g) butter* or *margarine*. Add *1 small onion*, chopped, and *2 teaspoons curry powder*; cook for about 5 minutes until the onion is soft. Stir in *2 tablespoons flour* and *½ teaspoon salt*; cook for 1 minute. Gradually stir in *¾ cup milk*. Cook, stirring constantly, for about 5 minutes until the sauce is thickened and bubbly. Stir in the chicken and heat through. Serve over *cooked white rice*.

POULTRY

CHICKEN BREASTS WITH PEPPER SAUCE *Serves 4*

¼ cup flour

¼ teaspoon ground black pepper

4 large (about 600g) skinless chicken-breast fillets

2 tablespoons sunflower oil

1 cup chicken stock

½ teaspoon dried origanum

½ cup sweet red pepper, diced

½ cup sweet green pepper, diced

2 tablespoons dry white wine or water

1 teaspoon cornflour

 Preparation time
14 minutes

 Cooking time
15 minutes

Diet note Sweet peppers are a good source of vitamin A, which is essential for a healthy, glowing skin. This low-kilojoule dish is as appealing to the eye as it is to the taste; complement it with a glass of crisp white wine.

1 Mix the flour and the black pepper on a plate. Dip the chicken-breast fillets into the flour mixture, turn to coat evenly and shake off the excess.

2 In a large frying pan, heat the oil over moderately high heat. Add the chicken and sauté for 2 to 3 minutes on each side until golden brown. Transfer the chicken to a warmed serving platter, cover and keep warm.

3 Wipe the frying pan with paper towels. Add the stock and origanum to the frying pan and bring the mixture to the boil. Add the red and green peppers and cook for 3 minutes.

4 Meanwhile, in a cup, combine the wine and cornflour and stir into the stock mixture in the frying pan. Bring to the boil, stirring constantly. Continue cooking for about 2 minutes until it is thickened. Spoon the sauce over the chicken and serve.

SHELF MAGIC

Ready-smoked chicken forms the basis for these two refreshing salads. Served with a loaf of crusty French bread, each makes a superb entrée for a cool lunch or a light supper.

CHICKEN COLESLAW

In a medium-sized mixing bowl, combine *3 cups cabbage*, finely chopped, *1 medium red* or *green apple*, peeled (if desired) and chopped, and *½ cup salad dressing*. Stir in *300g smoked chicken-breast fillets*, skinned and finely chopped. Toss the coleslaw lightly until it is just mixed. Cover the bowl with plastic wrap and place it in the freezer for 5 minutes to chill slightly. Spoon the coleslaw onto chilled salad plates and serve immediately. Serves 3

CHINESE CHICKEN SALAD

In a large bowl, mix *300g smoked chicken-breast fillets*, skinned and finely chopped, *one 230g tin sliced water chestnuts*, drained, *4 spring onions (green and white parts)*, finely chopped, *1 sweet red pepper*, cored, seeded and thinly sliced, *250g bean sprouts*, *2 tablespoons sesame seeds* and *1 cup cooked instant ramen noodles*. Toss the salad with *½ cup prepared salad dressing* and a generous handful of *cashew nuts*, chopped, until well mixed. Serve immediately. Serves 3

Mushroom chicken *Serves 4*

¼ cup flour

¼ teaspoon each salt and ground black pepper

4 large (about 600g) skinless chicken-breast fillets

2 tablespoons (30g) butter or margarine

1 tablespoon sunflower oil

4 spring onions

2 cups (about 250g) quartered mushrooms

⅓ cup chicken stock

¼ cup dry white wine

½ cup cream

 Preparation time 15 minutes

 Cooking time 16 minutes

1 Combine the flour, salt and pepper on a plate. Dip the chicken into the flour mixture until well coated, shaking off the excess. Reserve the remaining flour mixture.

2 In a large frying pan, heat 1 tablespoon of the butter and the oil over moderate heat. Add the chicken and sauté for about 3 minutes on each side until golden brown. Meanwhile, cut the spring onion tops into 2,5cm lengths, and chop the white parts finely. (Keep the white and green parts separate.)

3 Using a slotted spoon, transfer the chicken to a plate. Add the remaining 1 tablespoon of butter to the frying pan. Add the mushrooms and sauté for about 3 minutes until transparent. Stir in the stock, wine and the white part of the spring onions. Bring the mixture to the boil.

4 Return the chicken to the frying pan. Reduce the heat to low, cover the pan and cook for about 5 minutes until the chicken is tender. Meanwhile, in a cup or small bowl, whisk the cream with 1 teaspoon of the flour mixture.

5 Transfer the chicken to a warmed serving platter and keep warm. Stir the cream mixture and the green spring onion tops into the mushroom sauce in the frying pan. Cook, stirring constantly, for about 1 minute until the sauce is thickened and bubbly. Spoon the mushroom sauce over the chicken and serve.

Mustard chicken *Serves 4*

¼ cup lemon juice

2 teaspoons Worcestershire sauce

¼ teaspoon salt

¼ teaspoon cayenne pepper

4 large (about 600g) skinless chicken-breast fillets

¼ cup coarse-grained prepared mustard

 Preparation time 15 minutes

 Cooking time 16 minutes

1 In a medium-sized bowl, mix the lemon juice, Worcestershire sauce, salt and cayenne pepper. Add the chicken breasts, turn to coat evenly and leave them to marinate for 10 minutes.

2 Preheat the grill. Drain the chicken and arrange the fillets on the rack over a grill pan. Brush or spread half of the mustard on top of each fillet. Grill the chicken fillets 12,5cm from the heat for approximately 8 minutes until they are golden brown on the exposed surface.

3 Turn the chicken breasts over and spread them with the remaining mustard. Continue grilling for a further 5 to 8 minutes until tender and cooked through. Serve immediately.

CRUMBED MEXICAN-STYLE CHICKEN ROLLS

CRUMBED MEXICAN-STYLE CHICKEN ROLLS *Serves 4*

4 large (about 600g) skinless chicken-breast fillets

¼ teaspoon salt

125g Gouda or mild Cheddar cheese

⅓ cup (40g) packaged bread crumbs

2 to 3 tablespoons flour

1 large egg

1 tablespoon milk

¼ cup sunflower oil

Ready-made tomato salsa (optional)

 Preparation time
11 minutes

 Cooking time
25 minutes

SERVING SUGGESTION Sliced avocado pear, topped with finely chopped tomatoes and drizzled with a vinaigrette dressing, is the perfect foil for these chicken rolls.

1 Preheat the oven to 200°C. Place the chicken fillets between two sheets of plastic wrap. Using a mallet, pound each fillet until it is about 5mm thick. Sprinkle with the salt.

2 Slice the cheese into 4 strips. Place one strip of cheese in the centre of each chicken fillet. Fold the sides of the chicken over the cheese to enclose it completely. Secure with wooden toothpicks. Place the bread crumbs and 2 tablespoons of the flour on two separate plates. In a pie plate, beat the egg with the milk. Dip the rolled chicken fillets into the flour, then into the egg mixture and finally into the bread crumbs.

3 Heat the oil in a flameproof casserole dish over moderate heat. Sauté the chicken rolls for 5 minutes until lightly browned. Bake in the oven for 15 to 20 minutes until the chicken feels firm to the touch. Remove the toothpicks. Serve with salsa, if desired.

BRAISED CHICKEN WITH VEGETABLES

BRAISED CHICKEN WITH VEGETABLES *Serves 4*

2 tablespoons sunflower oil

1kg chicken legs and thighs

500g small potatoes, unpeeled

2 small onions, peeled

4 large carrots, peeled and chopped into 2,5cm chunks

1½ cups chicken stock

½ teaspoon dried thyme

¼ teaspoon ground black pepper

2 tablespoons water

2 teaspoons cornflour

1 cup frozen green peas, partially thawed

 Preparation time
5 minutes

 Cooking time
38 minutes

SERVING SUGGESTION Add a continental twist to this traditional dish by serving it with a loaf of garlic bread, warmed to perfection in the oven.

1 In a 5-litre, heavy-based saucepan, heat the oil over moderate heat. Add the chicken portions and sauté for about 15 minutes until well browned on all sides.

2 Meanwhile, slice the potatoes into quarters. Halve the onions. Transfer the chicken to a plate and drain all but 1 tablespoon of the oil from the saucepan. Add the potatoes, onions and carrots to the saucepan and sauté for 3 minutes.

3 Add the stock, thyme and pepper to the vegetables. Increase the heat and bring the mixture to the boil. Return the chicken to the saucepan. Reduce the heat to low, cover and simmer for about 15 minutes until the chicken is tender. Transfer the chicken and vegetables to a warmed platter.

4 In a cup, mix the water and cornflour and add to the saucepan. Bring to the boil, add the peas and cook for about 3 minutes until thickened. Pour the sauce over the chicken and serve.

POULTRY

TERIYAKI CHICKEN WITH BROCCOLI *Serves 4*

4 large (about 600g) skinless chicken-breast fillets

¼ cup prepared teriyaki sauce

¼ cup orange juice

1 teaspoon cornflour

½ teaspoon ground ginger

2 tablespoons sunflower oil

2 cups (300g) small broccoli florets

1 tin (230g) sliced water chestnuts, drained

Hot cooked rice or Chinese noodles (optional)

 Preparation time
8 minutes

 Cooking time
8 minutes

COOK'S TIP You may prefer to substitute fresh mange-tout for the broccoli florets. Whichever you choose, this exotic stir-fry tastes equally delicious with white rice or with noodles.

1. Slice the chicken-breast fillets into 3cm strips and set aside. In a small bowl, combine the teriyaki sauce, orange juice, cornflour and ginger, and set the mixture aside.

2. In a wok or large frying pan, heat the oil over high heat. Add the chicken breasts and stir-fry for about 3 minutes until they are lightly browned. Using a slotted spoon, transfer the chicken to a bowl, leaving the drippings in the wok. Reduce the heat to moderate. Add the broccoli to the wok and stir-fry for 1 minute.

3. Stir the teriyaki mixture and pour it into the wok with the broccoli. Cook the mixture, stirring constantly, for about 1 minute until it is thickened and bubbly. Add the water chestnuts and the cooked chicken with any accumulated juices. Continue cooking until heated through. Serve over hot cooked rice or Chinese noodles, if desired.

ORIENTAL CHICKEN *Serves 4*

1 tablespoon sunflower oil

1kg (about 8) skinless chicken thighs

½ cup chicken stock

¼ cup dry sherry

1 clove garlic, sliced

½ teaspoon ground ginger

180g mange-tout

2 tablespoons soy sauce

2 teaspoons cornflour

½ teaspoon sugar

Pinch of crushed red chillies

 Preparation time
5 minutes

 Cooking time
28 minutes

1. In a large, heavy-based frying pan, heat the oil over moderately high heat. Add the chicken thighs and cook, turning occasionally, for about 15 minutes until they are well browned on all sides.

2. Add ¼ cup of the stock, the sherry, garlic and ginger to the frying pan. Bring the mixture to the boil. Place the mange-tout on top of the chicken. Reduce the heat to low and cover the frying pan. Simmer the chicken and mange-tout for 10 minutes, stirring occasionally.

3. Meanwhile, in a cup or small bowl, mix the soy sauce, cornflour, sugar, red chillies and the remaining ¼ cup of chicken stock. Stir the mixture thoroughly to dissolve the cornflour.

4. Increase the heat to moderately high. Stir the cornflour mixture into the chicken and mange-tout. Mix well. Simmer, stirring occasionally, for approximately 2 minutes until the thighs are tender and the sauce thickens. Transfer to a warmed platter and serve immediately.

POULTRY

Tarragon Chicken *Serves 4*

1 tablespoon sunflower oil

1 tablespoon (15g) butter or margarine

1 chicken (about 1,5kg), cut into serving portions

500g carrots

1 cup chicken stock

1 teaspoon dried tarragon

¼ teaspoon salt

¼ teaspoon ground black pepper

1 teaspoon cornflour

1 cup (1 bunch) watercress sprigs

 Preparation time
5 minutes

 Cooking time
32 minutes

1. In a 5-litre, heavy-based saucepan, heat the oil and butter over moderate heat. Add the chicken portions and fry gently for about 15 minutes until well browned on all sides. Meanwhile, peel the carrots, if desired, and slice them into 3cm sticks.

2. Add ⅔ cup of the stock, the carrot sticks, tarragon, salt and pepper to the chicken. Bring the mixture to the boil. Reduce the heat to low, cover and simmer the chicken for about 15 minutes until tender. Meanwhile, in a cup, blend the remaining ⅓ cup of stock and the cornflour until smooth.

3. Using a slotted spoon, transfer the chicken and carrots to a serving platter and keep them warm. Stir the cornflour mixture and watercress into the saucepan. Increase the heat to moderate and cook the sauce for about 2 minutes until it is thickened and bubbly. Pour the sauce over the chicken and serve.

Hawaiian Chicken *Serves 4*

1 chicken (about 1,5kg), cut into quarters

1 tablespoon (15g) butter or margarine

2 teaspoons cornflour

1 tin (225g) pineapple slices in juice, drained and juice reserved

1 tablespoon light brown sugar

1 teaspoon chopped parsley

½ teaspoon ground ginger

¼ teaspoon dry mustard

Salt and ground black pepper to taste

 Preparation time
5 minutes

 Cooking time
32 minutes

1. Preheat the grill. Arrange the chicken quarters, skin side down, on the rack over a grill pan. Grill the chicken 12,5cm from the heat for 15 to 20 minutes until lightly browned and almost tender when pierced with a fork.

2. Meanwhile, in a small saucepan, melt the butter over moderate heat. Stir in the cornflour until blended. Add the juice drained from the pineapple slices to the cornflour mixture and cook for about 45 seconds until thickened and bubbly.

3. Stir the brown sugar, parsley, ginger and mustard into the pineapple sauce. Remove the saucepan from the heat and season the sauce with salt and ground black pepper.

4. Brush the chicken with some of the pineapple sauce and grill for 2 more minutes. Turn the chicken over and continue grilling for 5 minutes.

5. Brush the chicken generously with more of the pineapple sauce and top the quarters with the pineapple slices. Continue grilling for a further 4 minutes until the sauce on the chicken is bubbly and the pineapple slices are glazed. Place the chicken and pineapple on a warmed platter and serve immediately.

CREAMY CHICKEN AND GRAPES

CREAMY CHICKEN AND GRAPES *Serves 4*

2 tablespoons sunflower oil

4 large (about 600g) skinless chicken-breast fillets

1 tablespoon (15g) butter or margarine

1 small red onion, finely chopped

1 teaspoon cornflour

½ cup dry white wine

½ cup cream

½ cup seedless green or red grapes, halved

Salt and ground black pepper to taste

 Preparation time 10 minutes

 Cooking time 12 minutes

Serving suggestion Serve with a simple but elegant combination of brown rice (cooked in chicken stock), sautéed mushrooms and chopped red onion.

1 In a large frying pan, heat the oil over moderately high heat. Add the chicken and sauté for 2 to 3 minutes on each side until golden brown. Transfer the chicken to a plate and set it aside.

2 Reduce the heat to moderate and place the butter in the frying pan. Add the onion and sauté for 3 minutes. In a cup, blend the cornflour and wine. Add the wine mixture to the frying pan and cook for about 1 minute, stirring continuously, until the mixture is thickened and bubbly. Stir in the cream and grapes and cook for 1 minute.

3 Return the chicken and any accumulated juices to the pan. Cook until heated through. Season with salt and pepper and serve.

CHICKEN SATAY WITH PEANUT SAUCE *Serves 4*

½ teaspoon ground cumin
¼ teaspoon salt
3 tablespoons sunflower oil
3 tablespoons lemon juice
4 large (about 600g) skinless chicken-breast fillets
1 medium onion, sliced
½ cup water
2 tablespoons soy sauce
1 clove garlic, crushed
⅓ cup creamy peanut butter
Coriander sprigs (optional)

 Preparation time
11 minutes

 Cooking time
10 minutes

Food note Traditional Thai satay has the meat skewered and grilled over a charcoal fire, then dipped into the peanut sauce just before eating. Try cooking the chicken breasts over the braai fire in this easy variation.

1. Preheat the grill. In a large bowl, mix the ground cumin, salt, 2 tablespoons of the oil and 2 tablespoons of the lemon juice. Add the chicken-breast fillets and turn to coat evenly. Leave the chicken to marinate for 10 minutes.

2. Meanwhile, in a medium-sized saucepan, heat the remaining 1 tablespoon of oil over moderate heat. Add the onion and sauté for about 7 minutes until golden. Stir in the water, soy sauce, garlic and remaining 1 tablespoon of lemon juice. Bring the mixture to the boil.

3. Remove the saucepan from the heat and, using a wire whisk, beat in the peanut butter until it is melted. Cover the saucepan and set the peanut sauce aside.

4. Arrange the chicken breasts on the rack over a grill pan. Grill 10cm from the heat for approximately 4 minutes. Turn the chicken over and continue grilling for a further 2 to 5 minutes until it is tender. Transfer the chicken to a warmed platter and garnish with coriander sprigs, if desired. Serve with the warm peanut sauce.

BRAISED ITALIAN-STYLE CHICKEN *Serves 4*

2 tablespoons olive oil
4 large (about 1kg) chicken breasts on the bone
2 cups (about 250g) quartered mushrooms
2 cloves garlic, finely chopped
250g frozen sliced green beans
1 cup ready-made tomato pasta sauce
1 cup chicken stock
¼ teaspoon crushed red chillies

 Preparation time
2 minutes

 Cooking time
35 minutes

1. In a 5-litre flameproof casserole dish or large, heavy-based saucepan, heat the oil over moderate heat. Add the chicken breasts and sauté for about 15 minutes until they are well browned on all sides.

2. Transfer the chicken to a plate and set it aside. Pour off all but 1 tablespoon of the oil from the casserole dish. Stir in the mushrooms, garlic and frozen beans and sauté for 3 minutes.

3. Add the tomato pasta sauce, the stock and the red chillies. Increase the heat to high and bring the mixture to the boil. Return the chicken to the casserole dish. Reduce the heat to low, cover and simmer for about 15 minutes until the chicken and beans are tender and cooked through. Serve.

CHICKEN AND BABY MARROW KEBABS

CHICKEN AND BABY MARROW KEBABS *Serves 4*

4 green baby marrows

4 yellow baby marrows

6 large (about 750g) skinless chicken-thigh fillets

3 tablespoons (45g) butter or margarine

3 cloves garlic, finely chopped

6 tablespoons lemon juice

2 tablespoons light brown sugar

½ teaspoon salt

 Preparation time
8 minutes

 Cooking time
15 minutes

SERVING SUGGESTION White rice tossed with a handful of blanched almonds and raisins sets off this low-kilojoule dish.

1 Preheat the grill. In a large saucepan, bring 5cm of water to the boil over high heat. Meanwhile, slice the baby marrows into 2,5cm-thick slices, add them to the boiling water and cook for about 2 minutes until just softened.

2 Meanwhile, cut each chicken-thigh fillet into four chunks. In a medium-sized saucepan, melt the butter over moderate heat. Add the garlic and sauté for 10 seconds. Remove the saucepan from the heat and stir in the lemon juice, brown sugar and salt until well mixed.

3 Add the baby marrows and chicken to the butter mixture. Toss to mix well. On four 30cm metal skewers, alternately thread the chicken and vegetables, reserving the remaining butter mixture.

4 Grill the kebabs 10cm from the heat for 6 to 8 minutes until lightly browned, turning the kebabs occasionally and brushing them with more of the butter mixture. Serve immediately.

POULTRY

BAKED HERBED LEMON CHICKEN *Serves 4*

1 chicken (about 1kg), butterflied (ask your butcher's help, if necessary)

2 teaspoons dried origanum

1 teaspoon dried thyme

1 teaspoon dried rosemary

¼ teaspoon each salt and ground black pepper

2 tablespoons olive oil

2 tablespoons lemon juice

1 tablespoon Worcestershire sauce

Preparation time 10 minutes

Cooking time 35 minutes

1. Preheat the oven to 230°C. Place the butterflied chicken, skin side down, in a 37,5cm x 26,5cm baking tin.

2. In a small bowl, mix the origanum, thyme, rosemary, salt and pepper. Whisk in the oil, lemon juice and Worcestershire sauce. Drizzle half of the mixture over the chicken. Bake the chicken for 20 minutes.

3. Drain the excess fat from the chicken. Turn the chicken over and brush on the remaining origanum-oil mixture. Continue baking for approximately 15 minutes more until the chicken thighs are tender and the juices run clear. Serve.

CHICKEN IN RED WINE *Serves 4*

1 chicken (about 1,5kg), cut into serving portions

Pinch each of salt and ground black pepper

⅓ cup flour

3 tablespoons sunflower oil

2 cups (about 250g) small mushrooms

8 small (about 125g) white onions, peeled

2 cloves garlic, finely chopped

1½ cups dry red wine

1 teaspoon dried thyme

1 bay leaf

1 tablespoon (15g) butter or margarine, softened

2 tablespoons chopped parsley

Preparation time 11 minutes

Cooking time 34 minutes

1. Sprinkle the chicken pieces with the salt and pepper. Place ¼ cup of the flour in a pie plate. Dip the chicken in the flour until well coated, shaking off the excess.

2. In a 5-litre flameproof casserole dish, heat 2 tablespoons of the oil over moderately high heat. Arrange the chicken portions, skin side down, so that they cover the bottom of the dish without crowding. Sauté for 5 to 7 minutes until the skin side is lightly browned. Transfer the chicken portions to a bowl and set aside. Discard the drippings.

3. In the same casserole dish, heat the remaining 1 tablespoon of oil over moderately high heat. Add the mushrooms and onions, and sauté for about 3 minutes until the vegetables are lightly browned. Stir in the garlic. Add the wine, thyme and bay leaf.

4. Return the chicken and any accumulated juices to the dish. Bring the mixture to the boil. Reduce the heat to low, cover, and cook the chicken for 15 to 20 minutes until tender. Meanwhile, in a cup, mix the butter and the reserved flour into a paste.

5. Using a slotted spoon, transfer the chicken, mushrooms and onions to a serving platter. Discard the bay leaf. Increase the heat to high and stir the flour paste into the remaining liquid. Bring the mixture to the boil, stirring constantly, and cook until slightly thickened. Pour some of the sauce over the chicken and sprinkle it with the parsley. Serve, passing the extra sauce separately.

STIR-FRIED CHICKEN WITH ALMONDS

STIR-FRIED CHICKEN WITH ALMONDS *Serves 4*

4 large (about 500g) skinless chicken-breast fillets

1½ cups chicken stock

2 tablespoons soy sauce

4 teaspoons cornflour

1 teaspoon Oriental sesame oil

3 tablespoons sunflower oil

⅓ cup blanched whole almonds

2 cloves garlic, finely chopped

250g green beans, cut into 5cm lengths

4 large carrots, peeled and sliced diagonally

 Preparation time 15 minutes

 Cooking time 14 minutes

SERVING SUGGESTION Serve this exotic stir-fry with hot egg noodles tossed with a dash of soy sauce and Oriental sesame oil.

1. Slice the chicken into 1cm-wide strips. In a cup, combine ½ cup of the stock, the soy sauce, cornflour and sesame oil and set aside. In a wok or large frying pan, heat the sunflower oil over high heat. Add the almonds and sauté for 1 to 2 minutes until lightly browned. Using a slotted spoon, transfer the almonds to a medium-sized bowl and set aside.

2. Add the chicken strips to the wok and stir-fry until lightly browned. Using a slotted spoon, add the chicken to the almonds.

3. Reduce the heat to moderate. Add the garlic to the wok and stir-fry for 10 seconds. Stir in the green beans, carrots and remaining 1 cup of stock. Cover and cook the vegetables for approximately 5 minutes until crisp-tender.

4. Stir the cornflour mixture and add it to the vegetables. Cook gently for about 1 minute until the sauce is thickened and bubbly. Stir in the chicken and almonds. Cook until just heated through and serve immediately.

VARIATIONS ON THE CHICKEN BREAST

A flavourful sauce turns the everyday chicken breast into an elegant main dish. Start with the basic recipe for grilled chicken breasts, below, taking special care not to overcook them – they should be tender and juicy. Top them with a sweet or savoury sauce from the group at the right. Add a salad and rice or potatoes, and you have the makings of a memorable dinner party. Each recipe makes four servings.

Basic grilled chicken breasts Preheat the grill. In a medium-sized bowl, place 4 *large skinless chicken-breast fillets* (about 160g each). Toss with 1 tablespoon (15g) *melted butter* or *margarine* and ¼ teaspoon each *salt* and *ground black pepper*. Arrange the chicken on the rack over a grill pan.

Grill the chicken 10cm from the heat for 7 to 8 minutes until lightly browned. While the chicken is grilling, prepare one of the sauces. Turn the chicken and continue grilling for a further 4 to 7 minutes until tender and lightly browned. Place the chicken on a warmed serving platter and pour the sauce over it. Serve immediately.

▶ **Cheese sauce** In a saucepan, melt 2 *tablespoons (30g) butter*. Stir in ¼ *cup chopped spring onions* and cook for 1 minute. Stir in 2 *tablespoons flour;* and gradually stir in 1¼ *cups milk*. Cook, stirring, until sauce thickens. Stir in ¾ *cup grated mature Cheddar cheese,* ½ *teaspoon Dijon mustard* and ½ *teaspoon paprika*. Cook until cheese is just melted and smooth.

▶ **Mushroom sauce** In a saucepan, melt 2 *tablespoons (30g) butter*. Add *100g sliced mushrooms* and sauté until tender. Stir in 2 *tablespoons flour*. Gradually stir in 1 *cup chicken stock*. Cook, stirring, until sauce thickens. Stir in 1 *teaspoon dried thyme* and season with *salt* and *pepper*.

▶ **Spiced cranberry sauce** In a saucepan, combine 1 *cup cranberry sauce, 1 teaspoon dry mustard,* ½ *teaspoon Worcestershire sauce,* ⅛ *teaspoon ground ginger* and *3 or 4 drops Tabasco sauce*. Bring to the boil over moderate heat. In a cup, mix 1 *tablespoon cornflour* with 2 *tablespoons water*. Stir the mixture into the sauce and boil for 1 minute.

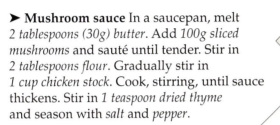

◀ **Honey mustard sauce** In a blender, combine ¼ *cup coarse-grained prepared mustard* with ¼ *cup honey,* 2 *tablespoons tomato sauce* or *ketchup* and 6 *tablespoons olive oil* until well blended. Season the sauce with *salt* and *pepper* to taste.

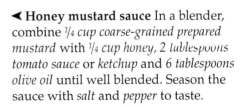

◀ **Curry sauce** In a saucepan, melt 2 *tablespoons (30g) butter* or *margarine* over moderate heat. Add 1 *small onion, sliced,* and sauté until soft. Stir in 2 *tablespoons flour* and 1 *teaspoon curry powder*. Gradually stir in 1 *cup chicken stock* and ¼ *cup cream*. Cook, stirring, until sauce thickens. Season the sauce with *salt* and *pepper* to taste.

POULTRY

Chicken schnitzels with mushrooms *Serves 4*

4 large (about 500g) skinless chicken-breast fillets

¼ cup flour

½ teaspoon salt

¼ teaspoon ground black pepper

3 tablespoons sunflower oil

2 tablespoons (30g) butter or margarine

2 cups (about 250g) sliced mushrooms

1 clove garlic, finely chopped

¼ cup chicken stock

1 tablespoon chopped parsley

 Preparation time 9 minutes

 Cooking time 15 minutes

Serving suggestion For an easy side dish, prepare a packaged stuffing mixture according to the manufacturer's directions. Roll the cooked stuffing into 5cm balls, brush with oil and bake at 200°C for about 10 minutes until browned.

1 Place the chicken-breast fillets between two sheets of plastic wrap or in a large food storage bag. Using a mallet, pound each piece until it is about 5mm thick.

2 Mix the flour, salt and black pepper in a pie plate. Dip the chicken schnitzels into the flour mixture until they are well coated, shaking off the excess.

3 In a large frying pan, heat 2 tablespoons of the sunflower oil over moderately high heat. Add enough of the schnitzels to cover the bottom of the frying pan without crowding or overlapping. Sauté for approximately 2 to 3 minutes on each side until they are golden brown. Transfer the schnitzels to a warmed serving platter and keep warm.

4 Add the third tablespoon of oil to the frying pan, cook the remaining schnitzels and transfer them to the platter.

5 In the same frying pan, melt the butter over moderate heat. Add the mushrooms and garlic and sauté for 5 minutes. Add the chicken stock to the mushrooms and bring the mixture to the boil, stirring and scraping the bottom of the frying pan to loosen any fragments that may have stuck to the base. Spoon the mushroom mixture over the schnitzels, sprinkle with the chopped parsley and serve immediately.

Sliced smoked chicken is quite delicious, and has the added advantage of being low in fat. Use it to make this quick and tasty microwave supper.

Chicken and rice casserole

In a 1½-litre microwave-safe casserole dish, place ½ *cup chopped sweet green pepper*. Add a little water, cover and microwave on high power until the pepper is softened. Drain. Stir in *one 375g jar ready-made tomato pasta sauce, 1 cup quick-cooking rice, one 225g tin butter beans, drained, 125g slivered smoked chicken* and ¼ *cup water*. Cook on high, covered, for 5 to 8 minutes until the rice is tender, stirring once. Sprinkle with ½ *cup grated mild Cheddar cheese*. Serves 4

POULTRY

Chicken breasts with guacamole *Serves 2 to 4*

4 large (about 500g) skinless chicken-breast fillets
2 tablespooons olive oil
2 tablespoons lemon juice
½ teaspoon cumin
Salt to taste
1 ripe avocado pear
1 tomato, chopped
2 spring onions, chopped
1 fresh red chilli, chopped
Fresh coriander leaves to garnish
1 head crisp lettuce, finely chopped

 Preparation time
12 minutes

 Cooking time
9 minutes

SERVING SUGGESTION *Serve this piquant chicken dish with tortillas or fried rice for an authentic Mexican flavour.*

1 Preheat the oven to 200°C. Rinse and pat the chicken-breast fillets dry with paper towels and brush with 1 tablespoon of the oil.

2 On the top of the stove, heat a flameproof casserole dish over high heat. Add the chicken-breast fillets and sear for about 1 minute on each side to seal in the juices. Transfer the dish to the oven and bake for 5 minutes or until the chicken is springy to the touch, just cooked and still moist.

3 Meanwhile, mix together half the lemon juice, the remaining oil and the cumin. Season to taste with the salt. To make the guacamole, peel the avocado pear and remove the pip. In a small bowl, mash the flesh. Add the remaining lemon juice, the tomato, spring onions, chilli and salt to taste. Mix well.

4 Remove the chicken from the oven, pour the lemon juice and olive oil mixture over it and garnish with the coriander leaves. Serve immediately with the guacamole, the chopped lettuce and accompanied with tortillas or fried rice, if desired.

Chicken breasts with gremolata *Serves 2 to 4*

4 medium (about 450g) skinless chicken-breast fillets
1 tablespoon lemon juice
2 tablespoons olive oil
Salt and freshly ground black pepper to taste
1 tablespoon chopped parsley
1 clove garlic, crushed
Grated rind of 1 lemon

 Preparation time
5 minutes

 Cooking time
9 minutes

SERVING SUGGESTION *The delicate flavour of freshly cooked pasta or steamed baby potatoes would be the perfect foil for the garlic-lemon gremolata topping.*

1 Preheat the oven to 200°C. Rinse the chicken-breast fillets and pat dry using paper towels. Mix together the lemon juice and oil and season with salt and pepper to taste. Moisten the chicken with the lemon juice mixture.

2 On the top of the stove, heat a flameproof casserole dish over high heat. Add the chicken-breast fillets and sear for about 1 minute on each side to seal in the juices. Transfer the dish to the oven and cook the chicken for 5 minutes or until springy to the touch, just cooked and still moist.

3 Meanwhile, mix together the parsley, garlic and lemon rind. Spread over the cooked chicken and serve immediately.

SPICED CHICKEN BURGERS

SPICED CHICKEN BURGERS *Serves 4*

600g minced chicken

2 tablespoons finely chopped onion

2 tablespoons chopped parsley

¼ teaspoon each salt and ground black pepper

¼ teaspoon each ground coriander, ground cumin and curry powder

1 tablespoon sunflower oil

4 hamburger rolls

1 cup alfalfa sprouts or finely chopped lettuce

1 ripe tomato, sliced

 Preparation time 10 minutes

 Cooking time 6 minutes

SERVING SUGGESTION Add crunch to these burgers with a basket of potato or corn chips, or a crisp salad.

1. In a medium-sized bowl, combine the chicken, onion, parsley, salt, pepper, coriander, cumin and curry powder. Shape the mixture into four patties, each about 1cm thick.

2. In a large frying pan, heat the oil over moderately high heat. Add the chicken patties and cook for about 3 minutes on each side until browned on both sides and cooked through.

3. Meanwhile, toast the hamburger rolls. Place a chicken patty in each roll. Top each with some of the alfalfa sprouts or lettuce and slices of tomato. Serve immediately, with mustard and tomato sauce or ketchup, if desired.

POULTRY

CHICKEN PICCATA *Serves 4*

2 large eggs

1 tablespoon water

2 cups (120g) fresh bread crumbs

4 large (about 500g) skinless chicken-breast fillets

2 tablespoons (30g) butter or margarine

1 tablespoon sunflower oil

¾ cup chicken stock

2 tablespoons lemon juice

4 lemon slices

 Preparation time
15 minutes

 Cooking time
10 minutes

Food note The tangy lemon-flavoured sauce gives a mouthwatering lift to this Italian-inspired dish. Tender chicken breasts are used here, but you may substitute veal if you prefer.

1 In a pie plate, beat the eggs with the water. Place the bread crumbs on a plate. Dip the chicken fillets first into the egg mixture, then into the crumbs, coating them evenly.

2 In a large frying pan, heat the butter and oil over moderate heat. Add the chicken and sauté for 2 to 3 minutes on each side until golden brown. Transfer the chicken to a plate.

3 Stir the stock and lemon juice into the drippings in the frying pan, stirring and scraping the bottom of the pan. Bring the mixture to the boil and simmer, stirring constantly, for about 1 minute until it is slightly thickened.

4 Return the chicken to the frying pan and continue cooking until the slices are heated through. Arrange the chicken and sauce on a warmed platter, garnish with the lemon slices and serve.

CHICKEN SAUSAGE WITH CHILLI *Serves 4*

500g chicken sausage

1 tablespoon sunflower oil

1 medium onion, thinly sliced

1 clove garlic, crushed

1 fresh chilli, thinly sliced

1 tin (410g) chopped tomatoes

Salt and freshly ground black pepper to taste

Chopped parsley or coriander leaves to garnish

 Preparation time
5 minutes

 Cooking time
32 minutes

Serving suggestion A serving of creamy mashed sweet potatoes would be the ideal accompaniment for this tantalizingly spicy combination of chicken and chillies.

1 Prick the sausage all over. In a nonstick frying pan, cook the sausage for about 5 minutes on each side until just cooked through and browned all over. Remove the sausage from the pan and set aside.

2 Pour the oil into the pan. Add the onion and sauté gently for about 10 minutes or until it is softened and just starting to brown. Stir in the garlic and the chilli and mix well. Add the chopped tomatoes and season the mixture with salt and black pepper to taste. Simmer, uncovered, for 10 minutes or until the mixture is slightly thickened.

3 Cut the sausage into 2 or 3 pieces and add to the tomato mixture. Allow to heat through. Check the seasoning. Garnish with parsley or coriander leaves and serve immediately.

SESAME CHICKEN AND ASPARAGUS

Sesame chicken and asparagus Serves 4

2 tablespoons Oriental sesame oil

1 tablespoon soy sauce

1 teaspoon honey

¼ teaspoon ground cumin

4 large (about 500g) skinless chicken-breast fillets, cut into strips

500 slim green asparagus

1 tablespoon sesame seeds

2 tablespoons sunflower oil

Salt and ground black pepper to taste

 Preparation time 18 minutes

 Cooking time 9 minutes

Serving suggestion Chicken acquires an Asian character in this easily-prepared stir-fry dish. Serve it with herbed or fried rice.

1. In a large bowl, combine the sesame oil, soy sauce, honey and cumin. Add the chicken, turn to coat evenly and leave for 15 minutes to marinate. Trim the lower ends of the asparagus and discard. Slice the asparagus diagonally into 5cm lengths.

2. In a wok or large frying pan, heat the sesame seeds over moderate heat until browned, stirring constantly. Transfer to a bowl and set aside.

3. Increase the heat to high. Pour the sunflower oil into the wok, add the chicken and stir-fry for 5 minutes. Add the asparagus and cook, stirring constantly, for 2 to 4 minutes until it is crisp-tender. Season with the salt and pepper. Transfer to a serving dish, sprinkle with the sesame seeds and serve.

PAN-FRIED CHICKEN MILANO

PAN-FRIED CHICKEN MILANO *Serves 4*

2 tablespoons flour

¼ teaspoon each salt and ground black pepper

4 large (about 500g) skinless chicken-breast fillets

4 tablespoons olive or sunflower oil

1 small onion, chopped

¼ cup dry white wine

1 tin (400g) artichoke hearts, drained

1 cup chopped fresh or tinned crushed tomatoes, well-drained

½ teaspoon dried origanum

Fresh basil leaves for garnishing, if desired

 Preparation time
6 minutes

 Cooking time
20 minutes

SERVING SUGGESTION For an authentic Italian taste, team these chicken breasts with pasta tossed with butter and chopped fresh herbs.

1 Combine the flour, salt and pepper in a pie plate. Dip the chicken-breast fillets into the flour mixture until well coated, shaking off the excess.

2 In a large frying pan, heat 2 tablespoons of the oil over moderately high heat. Sauté two of the chicken breasts for 2 to 3 minutes on each side until golden brown. Transfer to a warmed serving platter. Add another tablespoon of oil to the frying pan, sauté the remaining fillets and transfer them to the platter.

3 In the same frying pan, heat the last 1 tablespoon of oil over moderate heat. Add the onion and sauté for about 5 minutes until soft. Add the wine and bring the mixture to the boil, stirring and scraping the bottom of the frying pan. Stir in the artichokes, tomatoes and origanum and bring to the boil. Pour the sauce over the chicken, garnish with basil leaves, if desired, and serve.

POULTRY

CHEESE-STUFFED CHICKEN ROLLS Serves 4

100g soft garlic-and-herb cheese

¼ cup (30g) coarsely grated mozzarella cheese

4 large (about 500g) skinless chicken-breast fillets

2 tablespoons (30g) butter or margarine

⅓ cup (40g) packaged bread crumbs

1 clove garlic, finely chopped

1 cup ready-made tomato pasta sauce

1 teaspoon dried origanum

Salt and ground black pepper to taste

 Preparation time
12 minutes

 Cooking time
30 minutes

1 Preheat the oven to 190°C. Lightly grease a 20cm square baking tin. In a medium-sized bowl, combine the cheeses.

2 Place the chicken-breast fillets between two sheets of plastic wrap. Using a mallet, pound the fillets until they are about 5mm thick. Spread an equal amount of the cheese mixture along the centre of each flattened chicken fillet. Roll each portion, Swiss-roll style, and secure with a wooden toothpick.

3 In a small saucepan, melt the butter over low heat. Remove the saucepan from the heat. Place the bread crumbs on a plate. Dip the chicken rolls into the melted butter, then coat them with the crumbs. Set the saucepan with the remaining butter aside.

4 Arrange the breaded chicken rolls 2,5cm apart in the prepared baking tin. Bake, uncovered, for 25 to 30 minutes until they are just golden brown.

5 In the saucepan with the remaining butter, sauté the garlic gently for 10 seconds. Stir in the pasta sauce and the origanum, season with the salt and pepper and bring to the boil. Place the chicken rolls on a serving platter, top with the sauce and serve.

HERBED CHICKEN MARSALA Serves 4

¼ cup flour

½ teaspoon dried sage

½ teaspoon salt

¼ teaspoon ground black pepper

4 large (about 500g) skinless chicken-breast fillets

2 tablespoons sunflower oil

1 tablespoon (15g) butter or margarine

1 medium onion, sliced

1 cup (about 125g) quartered mushrooms

¼ cup Marsala

¼ cup water

 Preparation time
10 minutes

 Cooking time
15 minutes

FOOD NOTE Chicken-breast fillets are an excellent alternative to veal and are more economical. Here they are covered with a simple sauce of onions, mushrooms and Marsala wine.

1 Combine the flour, sage, salt and pepper in a pie plate. Dip the chicken-breast fillets into the flour mixture until they are well coated, shaking off the excess flour.

2 In a large frying pan, heat the oil over moderately high heat. Add the chicken and sauté for 2 to 3 minutes on each side until they are golden brown. Transfer the chicken to a plate and set aside.

3 In the same frying pan, melt the butter over moderate heat. Add the onion and mushrooms, and sauté for about 5 minutes. Add the Marsala and water and bring to the boil, stirring and scraping the bottom of the pan. Return the chicken to the pan, cover and cook until the chicken is heated through. Serve immediately.

POULTRY

BRAISED BABY CHICKENS WITH VEGETABLES *Serves 4*

2 baby chickens (500g to 600g each)

2 tablespoons (30g) butter or margarine

4 medium carrots

1 medium onion, thinly sliced

1 bay leaf

½ teaspoon dried rosemary

1¼ cups chicken stock

100g baby green beans

2 tablespoons flour

Salt and ground black pepper to taste

 Preparation time
3 minutes

 Cooking time
40 minutes

1. Cut each chicken in half lengthwise. In a 5-litre flameproof, casserole dish or large, deep frying pan, melt the butter over moderate heat. Place the chickens, skin side down, in the dish and cook for 10 to 15 minutes until they are lightly browned on both sides. Meanwhile, peel the carrots and slice them into 2,5cm lengths.

2. Drain the fat from the dish, if desired. Add the carrots, onion, bay leaf, rosemary and 1 cup of the stock to the dish. Bring the mixture to the boil over high heat. Reduce the heat to moderately low, cover, and simmer the chickens and vegetables for about 5 minutes. Meanwhile, blanch the baby green beans by placing them in boiling water for 1 minute.

3. Stir the baby green beans into the casserole dish and continue cooking the chickens for about 15 minutes until they are tender and cooked through. In a small bowl or cup, combine the flour and the remaining ¼ cup of chicken stock until the mixture is completely smooth.

4. Transfer the chickens to a serving platter and keep them warm. Gradually stir the flour mixture into the liquid in the dish. Cook, stirring constantly, until the sauce boils and thickens. Discard the bay leaf and season the sauce with salt and pepper. Spoon the sauce over the chickens and serve immediately.

GRILLED BABY CHICKENS *Serves 4*

2 baby chickens (about 500g each)

2 tablespoons (30g) butter or margarine

1 tablespoon lemon juice

1 tablespoon Worcestershire sauce

½ teaspoon dried tarragon

½ teaspoon dried thyme

¼ teaspoon salt

 Preparation time
5 minutes

 Cooking time
35 minutes

1. Preheat the grill. Cut each chicken in half lengthwise. Place the chickens, skin side down, on the rack over a grill pan. Grill the chickens 12,5cm from the heat for about 20 minutes until they are lightly browned on one side and almost tender.

2. Meanwhile, in a small saucepan, melt the butter over moderate heat. Remove the saucepan from the heat and stir in the lemon juice, Worcestershire sauce, tarragon, thyme and salt.

3. Brush the chickens with some of the butter mixture. Turn them over and grill for 5 minutes. Brush them with more of the butter mixture and continue grilling them for approximately 10 minutes more until they are tender. Place the chickens on a warmed platter, pour the drippings over them and serve immediately.

BAKED BABY CHICKENS WITH RICE PILAFF

BAKED BABY CHICKENS WITH RICE PILAFF *Serves 4*

2 tablespoons (30g) butter or margarine

1 tablespoon lemon juice

2 baby chickens (500g to 600g each)

½ teaspoon paprika

½ teaspoon salt

¼ teaspoon ground black pepper

For the rice pilaff:

1 tablespoon sunflower oil

1 small onion, chopped

1 cup long-grain white rice

¼ cup seedless raisins

2 cups chicken stock

1 tablespoon chopped parsley

 Preparation time 3 minutes

 Cooking time 40 minutes

1. Preheat the oven to 190°C. Place the butter and lemon juice in a 37,5cm x 26,5cm baking tin and melt the butter in the oven while it is preheating. Meanwhile, cut each chicken in half lengthwise. In a cup, mix the paprika, salt and pepper, and rub the mixture over the chickens.

2. Remove the baking tin from the oven and place the chickens, skin side down, in the tin. Bake the chickens for 20 minutes.

3. Meanwhile, prepare the rice pilaff. Heat the oil over moderate heat in a medium-sized saucepan. Add the onion and sauté for about 5 minutes until soft. Stir in the rice and raisins until well mixed, then add the stock. Increase the heat to high and bring the mixture to the boil. Reduce the heat to low, cover and simmer the rice mixture for about 15 minutes until tender. Using a fork, stir in the parsley.

4. Brush the chickens with the pan drippings and turn the pieces over. Continue baking the chickens for 15 to 20 more minutes until they are golden brown and tender. Place the chickens with the pan drippings and rice pilaff on a warmed serving platter. Serve immediately.

POULTRY

BRAISED TURKEY WITH WATERBLOMMETJIES *Serves 4*

1,5kg turkey drumsticks
500g waterblommetjies
4 tablespoons sunflower oil
Salt and freshly ground black pepper
2 medium onions, thinly sliced
2 stalks celery, thinly sliced
2 cloves garlic, crushed
3 cups chicken stock
3 medium potatoes, peeled and cubed
1 bay leaf
2 tablespoons chopped fresh dill or dried dill
Juice of 2 lemons
Dill sprigs for garnishing

 Preparation time 30 minutes

 Cooking time 1 hour 12 minutes

FOOD NOTE Turkey gets a traditional Cape treatment with the addition of waterblommetjies. This freshwater plant is available in spring, but tinned waterblommetjies may be substituted. Serve with steamed rice.

1. Wash and dry the turkey drumsticks. Remove and discard the stems of the waterblommetjies and soak the blommetjies (flowers) in a large bowl of lightly salted water.

2. Heat the oil in a large heavy-based saucepan. Add the turkey drumsticks and sauté until browned all over. Remove with a slotted spoon, set aside and season with the salt and pepper.

3. In the same saucepan, sauté the onions and celery for about 4 minutes until soft. Stir in the garlic and a little more seasoning.

4. Return the turkey to the saucepan. Add the stock, the drained and well rinsed waterblommetjies, the potatoes, bay leaf, dill and lemon juice. Bring to a simmer, then reduce the heat and cook, covered, for about 1 hour until the turkey and vegetables are very tender. Adjust the seasoning according to taste and add more lemon juice if necessary. If there is too much liquid, remove the turkey and vegetables with a slotted spoon and keep warm. Boil the liquid briskly, stirring regularly, until reduced. Garnish with dill sprigs and serve on a bed of steamed rice.

SHELF MAGIC

Chicken portions are easily available and a breeze to prepare. Arrange them in an oven dish, top them with one of these delicious sauces and bake in the oven for a simple but sumptuous meal.

APRICOT-GINGER CHICKEN

Preheat the oven to 180°C. Place *8 chicken portions* in a single layer in a casserole dish. Sprinkle generously with *ground ginger* and season lightly with *salt* and *pepper*, if desired. Mix *1 packet of mushroom soup* with *250ml apricot nectar* and *½ cup water*. Pour over the chicken portions. Bake, uncovered, for 1 to 1½ hours, basting occasionally. Serve with rice. Serves 4

SHERRIED-MUSHROOM CHICKEN

Preheat the oven to 180°C. Place *8 chicken portions* in a single layer in a casserole dish. Season lightly with *salt* and *pepper*. Add *250g sliced and sautéed mushrooms*. Mix together *1 tin (410g) mushroom soup*, *1½ tablespoons water* and *1½ tablespoons sherry*. Pour over the chicken. Bake, uncovered, for about 1 hour, basting occasionally, until chicken is tender. Serves 4

Meat

Beef steak Cajun style (page 172)

BEEF

A favourite with most meat-eating South Africans, beef forms the basis of a robust array of nourishing dishes, ranging from the sophisticated steak and the formal Sunday roast to the ever-popular hamburger, and many more.

BARBECUED SHORT RIBS *Serves 4*

- 2kg beef short ribs, cut into individual portions
- 1 tablespoon sunflower oil
- 1 medium onion, chopped
- 1½ cups tomato sauce
- ¼ cup firmly packed light brown sugar
- 2 tablespoons ready-made white horseradish
- 1 teaspoon Worcestershire sauce
- ½ teaspoon salt
- 1 tablespoon chopped parsley

 Preparation time
6 minutes

 Cooking time
30 minutes

SERVING SUGGESTION Enhance this lip-smacking dish by serving it with piping hot corn on the cob and a refreshing green salad. Save preparation time by asking your butcher to separate the ribs into individual serving portions for you.

1. Preheat the grill. Place the ribs on the rack over a grill pan. Grill the ribs 12,5cm from the heat for about 20 minutes, turning occasionally, until they are browned and tender when pierced with a fork.

2. Meanwhile, in a small saucepan, heat the oil over moderate heat. Add the onion and sauté for about 5 minutes until soft. Stir in the tomato sauce, brown sugar, horseradish, Worcestershire sauce and salt. Bring the mixture to the boil, stirring occasionally. Reduce the heat to low, cover the saucepan and simmer the barbecue sauce for 10 minutes.

3. Brush the ribs with some of the barbecue sauce. Continue grilling for approximately 10 more minutes, turning the ribs over and brushing them once more during grilling to coat them well. Transfer the ribs to a warmed platter, sprinkle with the chopped parsley and serve immediately.

SHELF MAGIC

Marinated vegetables may be found at Italian delicatessens or speciality food shops. If they're not available, use finely chopped lettuce.

DELICATESSEN-BEEF SANDWICH

Cut a thin slice off the top of each of *four 15cm-long crisp rolls*. Hollow out the bottoms, leaving about 1cm shell. Spread the cavity of each roll with a teaspoonful of *Dijon mustard*. Divide *250g thinly sliced cooked beef* among the rolls, tucking the meat inside each cavity. Drain *2 cups marinated vegetables*. Fill each roll with one-quarter of the vegetables. Cover with the tops of the rolls and serve. Serves 4

MEAT

Beef steak Cajun style Serves 4 (Picture page 169)

1x2,5cm-thick (about 750g) beef steak

2 tablespoons olive oil

2 cloves garlic, finely chopped

1 teaspoon chilli powder

½ teaspoon ground cumin

½ teaspoon dried thyme

¼ teaspoon cayenne pepper

2 tablespoons (30g) butter or margarine, cut into pieces

1 tablespoon finely chopped parsley

 Preparation time
25 minutes

 Cooking time
15 minutes

1. Trim and discard any excess fat from the steak. Place the steak in a shallow glass dish. In a small bowl, combine the oil, garlic, chilli powder, cumin, thyme and cayenne pepper. Brush both sides of the steak with the oil mixture. Leave it to stand at room temperature for about 15 minutes to marinate. Meanwhile, preheat the grill.

2. Place the marinated steak on the rack over a grill pan. Grill the steak 10cm from the heat for 10 minutes. Turn the steak over and continue grilling until it is done according to taste, about 5 minutes for rare.

3. Transfer the steak to a carving board with a well to catch the juices. Dot the steak with the pieces of butter and leave it to stand for several minutes to allow the juices to settle. Slice the steak across the grain into thin strips. Transfer it to a warmed serving platter. Pour any accumulated juices over the steak, sprinkle with the parsley and serve.

Beef stroganoff Serves 4

750g boneless beef sirloin steak

1 tablespoon (15g) butter or margarine

1 tablespoon sunflower oil

1 medium onion, sliced

2 cups (about 250g) small mushrooms, halved

1 teaspoon cornflour

1 cup beef stock

¼ cup sour cream

Salt and ground black pepper to taste

1 tablespoon chopped parsley

Hot cooked noodles (optional)

 Preparation time
10 minutes

 Cooking time
20 minutes

1. Trim and discard any excess fat from the steak. Cut the steak into strips about 5cm long and 1cm wide. Heat the butter and oil over high heat in a large, heavy frying pan. Add the steak and brown it quickly on all sides. Using a slotted spoon, transfer the strips to a bowl, cover and keep them warm.

2. Reduce the heat to moderately low. Add the onion slices to the remaining drippings in the frying pan and sauté for about 5 minutes until soft. Add the mushrooms to the frying pan and cook for about 5 minutes until they are just tender.

3. In a cup or small bowl, combine the cornflour with some of the stock. Stir it into the mushroom mixture until well mixed. Gradually stir in the remaining stock. Bring the mixture to the boil, stirring constantly. Simmer for about 2 minutes until the sauce is slightly thickened.

4. Stir the sour cream into the sauce and season it with salt and pepper. Remove the pan from the heat. Stir the steak and any accumulated juices into the sauce. Sprinkle with the parsley. Serve immediately, over noodles, if desired.

BROCCOLI-GINGER BEEF

BROCCOLI-GINGER BEEF *Serves 4*

- ⅓ cup plus 1 tablespoon soy sauce
- 1½ tablespoons cornflour
- 4½ tablespoons honey
- 1½ tablespoons dry sherry
- 1x1cm-thick (about 500g) boneless beef sirloin steak
- 3 tablespoons sunflower oil
- 1 tablespoon slivered fresh ginger
- 4 cups (600g) broccoli florets
- ½ cup water
- 1 tin (230g) sliced water chestnuts or bamboo shoots, drained
- ⅓ cup sliced spring onions
- Salt to taste

 Preparation time 11 minutes

 Cooking time 10 minutes

FOOD NOTE A heady combination of ginger and water chestnuts gives this beef stir-fry an exotic flavour. Serve it with rice or Chinese noodles.

1. In a cup, combine the soy sauce, cornflour, honey and sherry. Trim and discard any excess fat from the steak. Cut the beef lengthwise into 2 strips, then crosswise into 1cm-thick slices.

2. Heat the oil over high heat in a wok or large, heavy-based frying pan. Add the ginger and stir-fry for 1 minute. Add the beef and stir-fry for about 3 minutes until well browned. Using a slotted spoon, transfer the beef and ginger to a bowl and set aside.

3. Reduce the heat to moderate. Add the broccoli and water to the wok. Cover and cook for about 3 minutes until the broccoli is crisp-tender. Add the water chestnuts, spring onions and the soy-sauce mixture to the broccoli. Bring to the boil. Simmer, stirring constantly, for about 2 minutes until the mixture is thickened.

4. Return the beef and any accumulated juices to the broccoli mixture. Stir until well mixed. Season with salt, if desired, and serve immediately.

MEAT

GINGERED BEEF KEBABS *Serves 4* (Picture page 2)

1x3cm-thick (about 750g) boneless beef sirloin
¼ cup lemon juice
1 tablespoon honey
1 tablespoon soy sauce
1 teaspoon ground ginger
2 cloves garlic, finely chopped
1 large sweet green pepper
1 large sweet red pepper
1 medium onion
2 tablespoons sunflower oil

 Preparation time
25 minutes

 Cooking time
8 minutes

1. Trim and discard any excess fat from the sirloin. Cut the beef into 3cm cubes. In a large bowl, mix the lemon juice, honey, soy sauce, ginger and chopped garlic, stirring to blend thoroughly. Add the beef cubes and toss to coat evenly. Let them stand at room temperature for 5 minutes to marinate.

2. Meanwhile, core, seed and cut the green and red peppers into 3cm pieces. Slice the onion into 8 wedges.

3. Preheat the grill. On four metal skewers, alternately thread the beef cubes and the vegetable pieces, reserving the marinade. Place the skewers on the rack over a grill pan. Brush the kebabs on all sides with the oil.

4. Grill the kebabs 10cm from the heat for 5 minutes. Turn the kebabs and brush them with some of the reserved marinade. Continue grilling the kebabs until the beef is cooked according to taste, about 3 minutes for medium-rare. Transfer the kebabs to a warmed platter and serve.

BATTER-FRIED STEAK WITH GRAVY *Serves 4*

2 large eggs
2 tablespoons water
⅓ cup flour
½ teaspoon salt
¼ teaspoon ground black pepper
4 tenderized beef steaks (about 125g each)
4 tablespoons (60g) butter or margarine
1 cup milk

 Preparation time
3 minutes

 Cooking time
22 minutes

1. Beat the eggs and water together in a pie plate until well mixed. Sift together the flour, salt and black pepper on a plate. Dip the steaks first into the egg mixture, then into the flour mixture, shaking them gently to remove the excess flour. Reserve the remaining flour mixture.

2. In a large frying pan, melt 2 tablespoons of the butter over moderate heat. Add two of the steaks and fry for 3 to 4 minutes on each side until they are golden brown. Transfer the steaks to a warmed serving platter, cover and keep them warm.

3. Add another tablespoon of butter to the frying pan and cook the remaining two steaks. Transfer them to the serving platter, cover and keep them warm.

4. Add the remaining butter to the pan. Stir in the reserved flour mixture, blending until smooth. Gradually add the milk. Bring the mixture to the boil, stirring constantly. Simmer for about 5 minutes until the gravy thickens. Pour the gravy over the steaks and serve immediately.

BEEF IN RED-WINE SAUCE

BEEF IN RED-WINE SAUCE *Serves 4*

4 small 1cm-thick (about 180g each) beef steaks

1 tablespoon (15g) butter or margarine

1 tablespoon sunflower oil

1 medium onion, sliced

1 tablespoon flour

²⁄₃ cup dry red wine

²⁄₃ cup beef stock

1 teaspoon sugar

½ teaspoon ground black pepper

 Preparation time 10 minutes

 Cooking time 20 minutes

SERVING SUGGESTION A baked potato topped with sour cream and crumbled bacon offsets the hearty flavour of the steaks. Garnish with watercress, if desired.

1 Trim and discard any excess fat from the steaks. In a large frying pan, heat the butter and oil over moderately high heat. Add the steaks and sauté until they are well browned on both sides and cooked according to taste, about 5 minutes on each side for medium-rare. Transfer to a serving platter, cover and keep warm.

2 Add the onion to the remaining drippings in the frying pan. Sauté for about 5 minutes until soft. Add the flour and stir until well blended.

3 Add the wine, stock, sugar and pepper to the onions. Bring to the boil, stirring constantly. Continue cooking for 2 to 3 minutes until thickened. Spoon the sauce over the steaks and serve.

MEAT

Beef Fajitas *Serves 4*

- 500g beef steak, in one piece
- ¼ cup lemon or lime juice
- ½ teaspoon salt
- 1 clove garlic, crushed
- ½ teaspoon ground black pepper
- 1 large sweet red pepper
- 1 medium sweet green pepper
- 8 flour tortillas
- 2 tablespoons sunflower oil
- 1 medium onion, sliced
- ½ cup sour cream
- Ready-made tomato salsa (optional)

 Preparation time 25 minutes

 Cooking time 16 minutes

Food note This tasty Tex-Mex combination of beef and peppers, flavoured with garlic and lemon and served in a tortilla shell, forms a robust sandwich, filling enough to satisfy the most urgent of hunger pangs, and easily held in the hand.

1. Preheat the oven to 180°C. Trim and discard any excess fat from the steak. Place the steak in a shallow glass dish. Sprinkle on both sides with the lemon juice, salt, garlic and black pepper. Leave the steak to stand at room temperature for 15 to 20 minutes to marinate.

2. Meanwhile, core, seed and slice the red and green peppers into strips. Wrap the tortillas in aluminium foil and heat them in the oven for about 15 minutes until warmed.

3. In a large, heavy frying pan, heat the oil over moderately high heat. Add the marinated beef and sauté it for about 5 minutes on one side until well browned. Turn the steak over and continue cooking until done according to taste, about 5 more minutes for medium-rare. Transfer the steak to a carving board, cover with aluminium foil to keep it warm and set aside.

4. Reduce the heat to moderate. Add the onion and red and green peppers to the frying pan. Cook the vegetables, stirring occasionally, for about 5 minutes until they are tender but still firm to the bite. Remove the pan from the heat and cover it to keep warm.

5. Slice the steak thinly across the grain. Place an equal amount of the slices of beef and vegetables on each tortilla. Top each filling with a tablespoonful of the sour cream and salsa, if desired. Roll the tortillas and place them on serving plates. Serve immediately.

Time Savers

Make-ahead hamburgers With a little pre-planning, you can produce a platter of hamburgers in minutes.

- Shape lean minced beef into 1cm-thick patties (about 125g each). Stack the patties, placing two sheets of wax paper between each patty. Place the patties in a freezer container or sealed plastic bag and freeze.
- To serve the burgers, remove the number of patties you need (the wax paper makes it easy to separate them). Place the patties in a preheated frying pan. Cook, covered, over medium-low heat, for about 6 minutes on each side or until done according to taste. Season with salt and black pepper.

MEAT

Steak with watercress sauce Serves 4

1 bunch watercress

1 tablespoon (15g) butter or margarine

1 tablespoon sunflower oil

1 small onion, chopped

1 clove garlic, chopped

1 tablespoon flour

3/4 cup beef stock

2 teaspoons Worcestershire sauce

650g lean beef steak, in one piece

Salt and ground black pepper to taste

 Preparation time
10 minutes

 Cooking time
25 minutes

1. Preheat the grill. Setting aside 8 sprigs of watercress for garnishing, chop the remaining stems and leaves. Heat the butter and oil over moderate heat in a medium-sized saucepan. Add the onion and sauté for about 5 minutes until soft. Stir in the garlic and cook for 10 seconds. Add the flour and stir until well mixed. Simmer for 1 more minute.

2. Gradually stir the stock into the onions. Bring the mixture to the boil, stirring constantly. Cook for 2 to 3 minutes until slightly thickened. Remove the saucepan from the heat. Stir in the chopped watercress and Worcestershire sauce. If desired, purée the watercress sauce in a blender or food processor until the mixture is fairly smooth. Cover the sauce and set it aside.

3. Using a sharp knife, lightly score both sides of the steak in a diamond pattern. Place the steak on the rack over a grill pan. Grill the steak 7,5cm from the heat for 5 minutes. Turn the steak and continue grilling it until done according to taste, about 5 minutes for rare.

4. Transfer the steak to a carving board with a well to catch the juices, and leave it to stand for several minutes to let the juices settle. Sprinkle the steak with salt and pepper and slice thinly across the grain.

5. Transfer the steak to warmed serving plates and top with any accumulated juices and the watercress sauce. Garnish with the reserved watercress, if desired, and serve immediately.

Herbed beef rib steaks Serves 4

4x1cm-thick (about 180g each) beef rib steaks

2 tablespoons sunflower oil

2 tablespoons chopped mixed herbs (thyme, tarragon and origanum)

1 tablespoon Worcestershire sauce

1/2 teaspoon ground black pepper

2 cloves garlic, finely chopped

Fresh herb sprigs (optional)

 Preparation time
20 minutes

 Cooking time
10 minutes

1. Trim and discard any excess fat from the steaks. In a shallow glass dish, combine the oil, mixed herbs, Worcestershire sauce, pepper and garlic. Add the steaks and rub the herb mixture onto both sides of each. Let the steaks stand at room temperature for 15 minutes to marinate. Meanwhile, preheat the grill.

2. Place the steaks on the rack over a grill pan and grill them 10cm from the heat for 5 minutes. Turn the steaks over and continue grilling until done according to taste, about 5 more minutes for medium-rare. Place the steaks on a warmed serving platter, top with sprigs of fresh herbs, if desired, and serve immediately.

CURRIED BEEF STEAK WITH HONEY

CURRIED BEEF STEAK WITH HONEY *Serves 4*

4x2cm-thick (about 600g) beef fillet steaks

¼ cup soy sauce

1 tablespoon curry powder

1 tablespoon sunflower oil

2 tablespoons honey

⅛ teaspoon ground black pepper

Fresh watercress sprigs (optional)

Hot cooked rice (optional)

 Preparation time
25 minutes

 Cooking time
8 minutes

SERVING SUGGESTION To colour the rice, add some chopped sweet red and green pepper and a small pinch of saffron while cooking.

1. Trim and discard any excess fat from the steaks. In a shallow dish, combine the soy sauce, curry powder, oil, honey and pepper. Add the steaks to the soy-sauce mixture, turning to coat them evenly. Let the steaks stand at room temperature for 20 to 25 minutes to marinate, turning them occasionally. Meanwhile, preheat the grill.

2. Reserving the marinade, place the steaks on the rack over a grill pan and grill them 7,5cm from the heat for 5 minutes. Turn the steaks over and brush them with some of the marinade. Continue grilling until done according to taste, about 2 minutes for rare.

3. Transfer the steaks to warmed serving plates. Garnish with watercress and serve immediately, with rice, if desired.

MEAT

SPICY BEEF SIRLOIN WITH ARTICHOKES *Serves 4*

4 spring onions
1 large sweet red pepper
1x2,5cm-thick (about 600g) boneless sirloin steak
¼ cup water
2 tablespoons tomato sauce
1 tablespoon ready-made barbecue sauce
1 teaspoon cornflour
½ teaspoon Worcestershire sauce
3 tablespoons olive oil
½ tin (180g) marinated artichoke hearts, drained

 Preparation time
7 minutes

 Cooking time
10 minutes

1. Slice the spring onions into 2,5cm lengths. Seed the red pepper and chop the flesh into 2,5cm squares. Slice the steak thinly across the grain. In a cup, mix the water, tomato sauce, barbecue sauce, cornflour and Worcestershire sauce.

2. Pour 2 tablespoons of the oil into a large frying pan and heat it over moderately high heat. Add the red pepper and sauté, stirring occasionally, for about 2 minutes until it is crisp-tender. Stir in the spring onions and cook for 1 minute. Using a slotted spoon, transfer the pepper and onions to a bowl and set it aside.

3. Pour the remaining oil into the frying pan and heat it. Add the sliced steak and sauté until lightly browned. Transfer the steak to the bowl with the vegetables.

4. Stir the tomato sauce mixture into the frying pan. Bring the mixture to the boil, stirring constantly. Add the artichoke hearts, steak, vegetables and any accumulated juices to the frying pan. Cook until just heated through. Transfer to a warmed platter and serve immediately.

STIR-FRIED BEEF AND GREEN BEANS *Serves 4*

500g lean beef steak
250g green beans
3 tablespoons sunflower oil
1 clove garlic, finely chopped
1 large onion, sliced
½ cup beef stock
1 tablespoon cornflour
1 tablespoon soy sauce
1 tablespoon dry sherry
1 teaspoon ground ginger
Salt and ground white pepper to taste

 Preparation time
13 minutes

 Cooking time
15 minutes

1. Cut the steak in half along its length and then into thin slices across the grain. Trim and slice the beans into 5cm lengths.

2. In a wok or large, heavy-based saucepan, heat 2 tablespoons of the oil over high heat. Add the beef and garlic and stir-fry for about 4 minutes until the beef is browned. Using a slotted spoon, transfer the beef to a bowl and set it aside.

3. Add the remaining 1 tablespoon of oil to the wok and heat it until hot. Add the onion and stir-fry for 2 minutes. Add the green beans and stock. Reduce the heat to moderately high, cover the wok and cook the beans for about 5 to 7 minutes until they are tender but still firm to the bite. Meanwhile, in a cup, combine the cornflour, soy sauce, sherry and ginger.

4. Stir the cornflour mixture into the beans. Cook for approximately 30 seconds until thickened. Return the beef and any juices to the wok and simmer until the beef is just heated through. Remove from the heat, season with the salt and pepper and serve.

PEPPER STEAK

PEPPER STEAK *Serves 4*

2 tablespoons black peppercorns

1x2,5cm-thick (about 500g) lean beef steak

1 tablespoon (15g) butter or margarine

1 tablespoon sunflower oil

1 small onion, chopped

1 cup cream

Salt to taste

 Preparation time
5 minutes

 Cooking time
18 minutes

SERVING SUGGESTION A green salad and steamed asparagus or baby spinach leaves are the ideal accompaniments for this traditional piquant steak dish.

1 Place the peppercorns on a cutting board, cover with a paper towel and, with a rolling pin, crush them into coarse pieces. Press the crushed peppercorns onto both sides of the steak.

2 In a large frying pan, heat the butter and oil over moderately high heat. Add the steak and sauté for 5 minutes. Turn the steak over and continue sautéing until done according to taste, about 5 minutes for rare. Transfer to a carving board with a well to catch the juices. Cover with aluminium foil and keep warm.

3 Reduce the heat to moderate. Add the onion to the remaining drippings in the frying pan. Sauté the onion for about 5 minutes until soft. Gradually stir in the cream. Cook the sauce, stirring constantly, for 2 to 3 minutes until it thickens slightly (do not boil). Season the sauce with salt.

4 Cut the steak crosswise into thin slices and transfer it to a warmed serving platter. Pour any accumulated juices and the onion sauce over the steak and serve immediately.

VARIATIONS ON THE BASIC HAMBURGER

A hearty hamburger is one of the quickest and most versatile meals you can prepare. Purists prefer the simplest of burgers, adding only mustard, a slice of tomato and a lettuce leaf to adorn the robust beefy flavour. But, once you've made the basic meat mixture, you can add any combination of ingredients to create an appetizing variety of flavours. Prepare the basic hamburger mixture given below, then look to the right to give it an international lift out of the ordinary. Each recipe makes enough to serve four.

Basic hamburger In a medium-sized bowl, combine *750g lean minced beef* with *1 tablespoon Worcestershire sauce* and *¼ teaspoon each salt* and *ground black pepper.* Shape the beef mixture into four patties. In a large frying pan, heat *1 tablespoon sunflower oil* over high heat. Add the beef patties and sauté for 2 minutes. Turn the patties over and continue cooking until done according to taste, about 3 minutes for medium-rare. Serve with the topping and bread of your choice.

▶ **Pita burger** Prepare the basic hamburger patties and cook as directed. Halve each patty across its width. Slice *4 pita breads* in half crosswise. Stuff the pocket of each pita with half a patty, *alfalfa sprouts, sliced avocado pear* and *diced tomato*. Combine ½ *cup mayonnaise* with *3 tablespoons thick plain yoghurt*. Place a spoonful on each burger.

◀ **Tex-Mex burger** Omitting the Worcestershire sauce from the ingredients, prepare the basic hamburger mixture and add *1 teaspoon chilli powder*. Cook the patties as directed. Meanwhile, warm *4 tortillas* in the oven. Place a hamburger patty on each tortilla, top with some *finely chopped lettuce, coarsely grated Cheddar cheese, sliced black olives* and a generous spoonful of *ready-made tomato salsa*.

▶ **Caraway burger** Prepare the basic hamburger patties, adding *1 teaspoon caraway seeds* to the meat mixture. Cook as directed. Meanwhile, mix *2 cups shredded green cabbage, 3 tablespoons mayonnaise* and *1 teaspoon milk*. Spoon onto the bottom halves of *4 halved, toasted whole-wheat rolls*. Top with the patties, garnish with *red pepper strips* and *pickled gherkins* and cover with the tops of the rolls.

◀ **Italian burger** Prepare the basic hamburger patties. Sauté for 3 minutes, turn, then top each with a *slice of provolone cheese*. Cover the pan and cook for 2 minutes more or until the cheese melts. Place the burgers on *4 slices toasted French bread*. Top each with *onion rings* and *chopped sweet green pepper* and some heated *Italian-style tomato sauce*.

HAMBURGER STEAKS WITH WINE SAUCE

HAMBURGER STEAKS WITH WINE SAUCE *Serves 4*

4 rashers bacon

1 medium sweet red pepper

2 cups (about 250g) mushrooms, sliced

1 large onion, sliced

750g lean minced beef

½ teaspoon salt

½ teaspoon coarsely ground black pepper

⅓ cup dry red wine

¼ teaspoon dried thyme

 Preparation time 15 minutes

 Cooking time 16 minutes

FOOD NOTE This economical minced-beef dish is dressed up with a red-wine sauce and topped with crumbled bacon.

1. In a large frying pan, sauté the bacon over moderately high heat for about 5 minutes until crisp. Transfer the bacon to paper towels to drain and set it aside. Reserve the drippings in the pan.

2. Core and seed the red pepper and slice it into strips. Add the mushrooms, onion and the red pepper to the drippings in the frying pan. Cook, stirring frequently, for about 4 minutes until softened but still firm to the bite.

3. Meanwhile, shape the minced beef into four oval steaks about 2cm thick. Season both sides with the salt and pepper.

4. Transfer the vegetables to a serving platter, cover and keep them warm. In the same frying pan, sauté the steaks until they are well browned, about 3 minutes on each side for medium. Place them on top of the vegetable mixture, cover and keep them warm.

5. Add the wine and thyme to the pan and bring the mixture to the boil, stirring and scraping the bottom of the pan. Pour the wine sauce over the steaks. Top with the crumbled bacon and serve.

MEAT

CHILLI BEEF WITH BEANS Serves 4

500g extra-lean minced beef
1 large onion, chopped
2 cloves garlic, chopped
3 to 4 teaspoons chilli powder
¾ teaspoon salt
½ teaspoon dried origanum
¾ teaspoon ground cumin
1 tin (410g) tomato and onion mixture
1 tin (400g) red kidney beans, drained and rinsed
1 cup (280g) tomato pasta sauce
2 spring onions, chopped

 Preparation time
7 minutes

 Cooking time
30 minutes

1. In a large saucepan (preferably with nonstick coating), sauté the minced beef, onion and garlic over moderate heat, stirring occasionally, for about 7 minutes until the meat is well browned. Drain off the fat.

2. Stir the chilli powder, salt, origanum and cumin into the beef mixture until well mixed.

3. Add the tomato and onion mixture, the beans and pasta sauce to the meat. Bring the mixture to the boil. Reduce the heat to low, cover and simmer for 20 minutes. Spoon the meat into bowls, sprinkle each serving with some of the spring onions and serve.

CHILLI BEEF WITH RICE

Add *1 cup long-grain white rice* and *1½ cups beef stock* to the list of ingredients. Omit the salt, red kidney beans and tomato pasta sauce. Brown the beef with the onion and garlic as in Step 1 above. Stir the rice, chilli powder, origanum and cumin into the beef mixture. Stir in the tomato and onion mixture and the beef stock. Bring the mixture to the boil.

Reduce the heat to low, cover and simmer for 25 to 30 minutes until the rice is cooked and all of the liquid has been absorbed. Spoon the chilli beef into bowls, sprinkle each serving with some of the spring onions and serve.

RUSSIAN-STYLE BEEF PATTIES Serves 4

750g lean minced beef
1 tablespoon (15g) butter or margarine
2 spring onions, finely chopped
2 tablespoons brandy
1 cup sour cream
1 tin (410g) mixed vegetables, drained
Salt and ground black pepper to taste
Chopped dill

 Preparation time
5 minutes

 Cooking time
11 minutes

1. Shape the minced beef into four patties, each about 2cm thick. In a large frying pan, melt the butter over moderate heat. Add the beef patties and sauté gently until they are well browned, about 3 minutes on each side for medium. Using a spatula, transfer the patties to a warmed serving platter, cover and keep them warm.

2. Add the spring onions to the remaining drippings in the frying pan. Sauté for about 2 minutes until soft. Add the brandy and cook for 1 minute. Reduce the heat to moderately low. Add the sour cream and mixed vegetables. Cook, stirring constantly, until the mixture is heated through (do not boil).

3. Season the sauce with salt and pepper. Spoon the sauce over the beef patties, garnish with the dill and serve immediately.

MEAT

TEX-MEX CHILLI CASSEROLE *Serves 4*

500g lean minced beef

1 medium onion, chopped

2 to 3 teaspoons chilli powder

1 tin (410g) chopped tomatoes, drained

1 green chilli, seeded and chopped

1 tin (410g) corn kernels, drained

4 flour tortillas

1 cup (120g) coarsely grated Cheddar cheese

Fresh coriander sprigs (optional)

 Preparation time
9 minutes

 Cooking time
34 minutes

SERVING SUGGESTION *A salad of sliced tomatoes and chopped spring onions will complement the 'bite' of this chilli dish.*

1. Preheat the oven to 190°C. Lightly grease a 1½-litre casserole dish. In a large frying pan, brown the minced beef and onion over moderate heat, stirring occasionally, for 6 to 7 minutes. Drain fat, if necessary.

2. Stir the chilli powder into the meat and continue cooking for 1 more minute. Add the tomatoes, green chilli and corn kernels, and bring the mixture to the boil. Remove the pan from the heat.

3. Line the bottom of the prepared casserole dish with one tortilla. Spoon one-quarter of the meat mixture, then one-quarter of the cheese over the tortilla. Repeat the layering, ending with meat and reserving the last portion of the cheese. Cover the dish and bake for 20 to 25 minutes in the oven until hot and bubbling.

4. Remove the cover from the casserole dish, top the meat with the reserved cheese and continue baking for approximately 2 more minutes until the cheese is melted. Garnish with coriander, if desired, and cut into wedges before serving.

INDIVIDUAL MEAT LOAVES *Serves 4*

500g lean minced beef

½ cup (60g) packaged bread crumbs

1 small onion, finely chopped

1 large egg

2 tablespoons chopped parsley

½ teaspoon salt

½ teaspoon dried origanum

¼ teaspoon ground black pepper

¼ cup tomato sauce or ketchup

2 tablespoons water

Parsley sprigs (optional)

 Preparation time
10 minutes

 Cooking time
35 minutes

FOOD NOTE *This version of the meat loaf cooks a lot more quickly than its traditional counterpart. Use leftovers, if any, to make delicious sandwiches for school or the office.*

1. Preheat the oven to 190°C. Grease a 30cm x 20cm baking tin. In a large bowl, use a fork to mix the minced beef, bread crumbs, onion, egg, parsley, salt, origanum and pepper. Shape the mixture into four 10cm-long loaves. Place the loaves in the prepared baking tin. Bake them for 25 minutes.

2. In a cup, combine the tomato sauce and water. Brush the mixture over the meat loaves. Continue baking them for about 10 minutes more until the juices run clear, brushing them occasionally with more of the tomato sauce mixture. Transfer the loaves to a warmed serving platter. Garnish with sprigs of fresh parsley, if desired, and serve.

MEAT

SAUTÉED CALF'S LIVER *Serves 4*

250g baby marrows
3 tablespoons flour
½ teaspoon salt
¼ teaspoon ground black pepper
4x1cm-thick slices (about 125g each) calf's liver
4 tablespoons (60g) butter or margarine
2 large onions, sliced
⅓ cup dry red wine

 Preparation time
5 minutes

 Cooking time
25 minutes

1. Chop the baby marrows into 3cm x 1cm strips and set aside. Combine the flour, salt and pepper in a pie plate. Coat the slices of liver with the flour mixture, shaking off the excess.

2. In a large frying pan, melt 2 tablespoons of the butter over moderate heat. Add the baby marrows and onions. Sauté for about 10 minutes until both are softened. Transfer the onion mixture to a warmed serving platter, cover and keep it warm.

3. In the same frying pan, melt the remaining butter over moderately high heat. Add the liver and sauté until lightly browned, about 5 minutes on each side for medium-rare.

4. Transfer the liver to the platter with the baby marrows, cover and keep warm. Add the wine to the frying pan and bring it to the boil, stirring and scraping the bottom of the frying pan. Pour the wine sauce over the liver and baby marrows and serve.

VEAL PARMIGIANA *Serves 4*

8 veal schnitzels (about 600g)
1 large egg
3 tablespoons water
¼ cup flour
¾ cup (90g) packaged bread crumbs
4 tablespoons olive oil
2 cloves garlic, finely chopped
¼ cup dry white wine
2 cups tomato pasta sauce
8 slices (about 120g) mozzarella cheese
¼ cup (about 35g) grated Parmesan cheese
1 tablespoon finely chopped parsley

 Preparation time
13 minutes

 Cooking time
17 minutes

1. Place the schnitzels between two sheets of plastic wrap and, with a mallet, pound each schnitzel until it is about 3mm thick. In a pie plate, mix the egg and the water. Place the flour and bread crumbs on two separate plates. Coat the schnitzels first with the flour, then with the egg mixture, then dip into the crumbs.

2. In a large frying pan, heat 2 tablespoons of the oil over moderately high heat. Add enough veal schnitzels to cover the bottom of the frying pan in a single layer. Sauté for about 1½ minutes on each side until they are lightly browned.

3. Transfer the cooked veal to a plate and keep warm. Add the remaining 2 tablespoons of oil to the frying pan, sauté the remaining veal schnitzels and transfer them to the plate.

4. Add the garlic to the frying pan and sauté for 10 seconds. Add the wine, stirring and scraping the frying pan. Add the pasta sauce and bring to the boil. Return the veal and any accumulated juices to the pan. Top each schnitzel with a slice of the mozzarella cheese and a sprinkling of the Parmesan cheese. Reduce the heat to low, cover and cook for about 5 minutes until the cheeses are melted. Sprinkle the schnitzels with the parsley and serve.

HERBED VEAL CHOPS

HERBED VEAL CHOPS *Serves 4*

2 tablespoons olive oil

1 tablespoon (15g) butter or margarine

2 spring onions, finely chopped

1 tablespoon Dijon mustard

1 tablespoon chopped parsley

1 teaspoon dried tarragon

4x2cm-thick (about 180g each) veal chops

12 large mushrooms

Salt and ground black pepper to taste

 Preparation time
15 minutes

 Cooking time
14 minutes

Serving suggestion Serve this full-flavoured veal dish with steamed and glazed baby carrots.

1. Preheat the grill. In a small saucepan, heat the oil and butter over moderate heat. Add the spring onions and sauté for about 3 minutes until soft. Remove the saucepan from the heat. Add the mustard, parsley and tarragon and stir until well mixed.

2. Place the chops on the rack over a grill pan. Brush them with some of the herb mixture. Grill 10cm from the heat for 5 minutes.

3. Turn the chops over and arrange the mushrooms, stem side down, around them on the grill rack. Brush the chops and the mushrooms with more of the herb mixture. Continue grilling for about 3 minutes until the mushrooms are softened. Transfer the mushrooms to a warmed serving platter.

4. Brush the chops with more of the herb mixture. Continue grilling until the centres are light pink when pierced near the bone, or until they are done according to taste. Transfer the chops to the platter with the mushrooms, season with the salt and pepper and serve immediately.

LAMB

Aromatic and succulent, lamb combines with the flavours of herbs, vegetables and fruits to create a variety of full-bodied meals, suitable for both formal and quick family dinners.

GRILLED LAMB CHOPS WITH MINT *Serves 4*

8x1cm-thick (about 1kg) lamb rib chops

2 large ripe tomatoes, halved

3 tablespoons olive oil

2 cloves garlic, chopped

1 tablespoon finely chopped fresh mint (or 1 teaspoon dried mint)

1/4 teaspoon ground black pepper

Mint sprigs (optional)

Salt to taste

 Preparation time 20 minutes

 Cooking time 10 minutes

FOOD NOTE *The sweet taste of mint is the traditional partner for tender lamb, which is best served slightly rare.*

1 Trim and discard any excess fat from the chops. Place the chops and tomatoes in a shallow glass dish. In a small bowl, combine the oil, garlic, mint and black pepper.

2 Brush the oil mixture over the sliced surfaces of the tomatoes and on both sides of the lamb chops. Leave the tomatoes and chops to stand at room temperature for at least 15 minutes to marinate. Meanwhile, preheat the grill.

3 Place the chops on the rack over a grill pan and grill them 7,5cm from the heat for 5 minutes. Turn them over and add the tomatoes to the grill rack.

4 Continue grilling the chops until done according to taste, about 5 minutes for rare. (If the tomatoes begin to overcook before the chops are ready, transfer them to a serving platter, cover and keep them warm.)

5 Transfer the chops and tomatoes to a warmed serving platter. Garnish with mint sprigs, if desired, season with salt and serve.

TIME SAVERS

LAMB

■ Add cooked minced lamb to a ready-made tomato-based pasta sauce to turn it into a quick main dish. Drain the meat well before you add it to the sauce. Mix well, then heat the sauce thoroughly and serve it over your choice of pasta.

■ When cooking leftover meat, don't overcook it. As the meat has already been cooked, all you have to do is reheat it thoroughly so that any bacteria that may have formed is destroyed. This is best done in the microwave oven or by stir-frying. Add diced vegetables and herbs.

■ Save preparation time by asking your butcher to slice the lamb or other meat into the cuts you need.

■ Make a quick sauce for lamb by combining crushed garlic and chopped origanum with a small carton of plain yoghurt. Pass it around separately.

BROCHETTES OF LAMB

BROCHETTES OF LAMB *Serves 4*

750g leg of lamb

2 tablespoons sunflower oil

1 tablespoon red wine vinegar

2 cloves garlic, finely chopped

½ teaspoon ground ginger

½ teaspoon turmeric

½ teaspoon ground cumin

¼ teaspoon cayenne pepper

¼ teaspoon salt

Hot cooked rice (optional)

Lemon wedges (optional)

 Preparation time 30 minutes

 Cooking time 15 minutes

FOOD NOTE Turmeric, cumin and cayenne pepper give these brochettes their exotic flavour. Serve them drizzled with a squeeze of lemon juice.

1 Trim and discard the bones and any excess fat from the lamb and cut it into 3cm cubes. In a large bowl, combine the oil, vinegar, garlic, ginger, turmeric, cumin, cayenne pepper and salt. Add the lamb and toss to coat. Leave to stand at room temperature for 15 minutes to marinate.

2 Preheat the grill. Thread the lamb cubes on four short metal skewers. Place the skewers on the rack over a grill pan. Grill the lamb 10cm from the heat for 5 minutes. Turn the brochettes over and continue grilling them until done according to taste, about 10 minutes for medium-rare.

3 Transfer the brochettes to a warmed serving platter, adding rice, if desired. Garnish with lemon wedges, if desired, and serve.

MEAT

GLAZED LAMB SHOULDER CHOPS Serves 4

4x2cm-thick (about 250g each) lamb shoulder chops

¼ cup apple jelly

2 tablespoons dry white wine

1 clove garlic, finely chopped

½ teaspoon salt

¼ teaspoon ground black pepper

 Preparation time
3 minutes

 Cooking time
15 minutes

1 Preheat the grill. Trim and discard any excess fat from the chops and place them on the rack over a grill pan. Grill the chops 10cm from the heat for 5 minutes.

2 Meanwhile, in a small saucepan, mix the apple jelly, wine, garlic, salt and pepper. Bring the mixture to the boil over moderate heat, stirring occasionally. When the jelly melts, remove the pan from the heat.

3 Brush both sides of the lamb chops with the warm jelly mixture. Continue grilling the chops, occasionally brushing them with more of the jelly mixture, until they are done according to taste, about 10 minutes for medium. Transfer to a warmed platter and serve immediately.

LAMB-STUFFED PITA Serves 4

500g minced lamb

½ cup (30g) fresh bread crumbs

1 clove garlic, finely chopped

1 teaspoon ground cumin

½ teaspoon salt

2 tablespoons chopped parsley

½ cup plain low-fat yoghurt

½ teaspoon dried dill

4 pita breads

½ cucumber, peeled and thinly sliced

2 small tomatoes, thinly sliced

 Preparation time
20 minutes

 Cooking time
8 minutes

COOK'S TIP Make your own fresh bread crumbs in the blender or – even quicker – use packaged bread crumbs. Either way, enjoy the Middle Eastern flavour of these easy sandwiches.

1 Preheat the grill. In a large bowl, using an electric mixer, beat the lamb, bread crumbs, garlic, cumin and salt until the mixture has a paste-like consistency. Beat in the parsley. (Alternatively, using a food processor, break up a slice of bread into the container. Add a whole clove of garlic and the parsley and process until finely chopped. Add the lamb, cumin and salt and process until well blended.)

2 Shape the lamb mixture into 4 patties, each about 2,5cm thick. Lightly grease the rack over a grill pan. Place the patties on the rack and grill them 10cm from the heat for 5 minutes. Turn them over and continue grilling until done according to taste, about 3 minutes for medium. (The patties should not be served rare.)

3 Transfer the patties to a carving board and leave to stand for 5 minutes. In a small bowl, mix the yoghurt and dill. Cut the pita breads in half across their width and open each pocket.

4 Slice each lamb patty into 6mm-thick strips. Fill each pita-bread pocket with an equal amount of the cucumber, tomato and lamb. Top each with a spoonful of the yoghurt sauce and serve.

Pork, sausage and ostrich

These pork, sausage and ostrich recipes include all-time favourites such as chops and casseroles, plus a few fragrant dishes from the cuisines of Europe and the Far East to tempt your palate.

Pork à l'Orange Serves 4

4x1cm-thick (about 180g each) pork rib chops

1 tablespoon (15g) butter or margarine

1 tablespoon sunflower oil

2 medium navel oranges

½ cup chicken stock

2 tablespoons tomato sauce

3 spring onions, coarsely chopped

Salt and ground black pepper to taste

 Preparation time 5 minutes

 Cooking time 15 minutes

SERVING SUGGESTION *Serve the chops with steamed new potatoes tossed in butter and sprinkled with lemon zest and chives.*

1. Trim and discard any excess fat from the chops. In a large frying pan, heat the butter and oil over moderate heat. Add the chops and sauté for about 8 minutes until they are browned.

2. Meanwhile, finely grate the orange part of the rind (the zest) of one orange and set aside. Slice both ends off each orange, remove the peel and pith, and cut each orange crosswise into six slices.

3. Continue cooking the chops for approximately 4 more minutes until the juices run clear. Meanwhile, combine the stock and tomato sauce in a cup or small bowl. Transfer the chops to a serving platter, cover and keep them warm.

4. Add the spring onions to the remaining drippings in the frying pan and sauté for about 1 minute until they are just softened. Add the stock mixture and bring it to the boil, stirring constantly.

5. Add the orange slices and any accumulated meat juices to the sauce. Season with salt and pepper. Spoon the sauce over the chops, garnish with the reserved orange zest and serve immediately.

SHELF MAGIC

Pork sausages are deliciously versatile, whether they are served sizzling at the breakfast table or combined with other ingredients to make a fine supper. Try this easy one-dish meal.

Tex-Mex rice and sausage

In a large frying pan, brown *500g pork sausage*. Drain the fat. Stir in *one 410g tin Mexican-style tomatoes*, undrained, *one 410g tin whole-kernel corn*, drained, *½ cup water* and *1 tablespoon chilli powder*. Bring to the boil. Stir in *3 cups cooked rice*. Remove from the heat. Top with *¼ cup (30g) grated Cheddar cheese*. Let stand, covered, for about 2 minutes until the cheese is softened and warmed. Serves 4

MEAT

Glazed pork spareribs *Serves 4*

2kg small pork spareribs, cut into 2-rib portions
½ cup apricot jam
2 tablespoons lemon juice
1 teaspoon prepared mustard
½ teaspoon ground ginger
¼ teaspoon salt

 Preparation time
4 minutes

 Cooking time
27 minutes

1. Place the spareribs in a large saucepan and add enough water to cover the meat. Cover the saucepan and bring the water to the boil over high heat. Remove the lid and continue boiling for 5 minutes.

2. Meanwhile, in a small saucepan, mix the apricot jam, lemon juice, mustard, ginger and salt. Bring the mixture to the boil, stirring constantly. Remove the saucepan from the heat.

3. Preheat the grill. Drain the ribs thoroughly and place them on the rack over a grill pan. Grill the ribs 10cm from the heat for 5 minutes. Brush them with some of the apricot jam mixture and continue grilling 1 more minute.

4. Turn the ribs over, brush them with more of the mixture and continue grilling them for a further 9 to 10 minutes until they are well glazed. Serve immediately.

Pork chops with apples *Serves 4*

4x1cm-thick (about 180g each) loin or centre-cut pork chops
2 tablespoons olive oil
1 tablespoon finely chopped fresh thyme (or 1 teaspoon dried thyme)
¼ teaspoon salt
¼ teaspoon ground black pepper
1 large Granny Smith apple, unpeeled
1 tablespoon (15g) butter or margarine
1 teaspoon cornflour
½ cup apple juice
⅓ cup cream

 Preparation time
15 minutes

 Cooking time
12 minutes

1. Trim and discard any excess fat from the chops. Mix the oil, thyme, salt and pepper in a shallow glass dish. Place the chops in the dish, brush them with the oil mixture and leave them to stand at room temperature for 15 minutes to marinate. Meanwhile, quarter and core the apple and slice it thinly.

2. In a large frying pan, sauté the chops for approximately 3 minutes over moderately high heat until they are browned on one side. Turn the chops over and continue cooking for 3 more minutes until the juices run clear. Transfer the chops to a warmed serving platter, cover and keep warm.

3. Reduce the heat to moderate. Add the butter to the frying pan. Add the apple slices and cook for about 2 minutes until they are golden, turning once. Using a slotted spoon, transfer the apple slices to the serving platter, cover and keep warm.

4. Mix the cornflour, apple juice and cream in a cup or small bowl, blending until smooth. Stir the mixture into the remaining drippings in the frying pan and bring to the boil. Simmer, stirring constantly, for 2 to 3 minutes until the sauce thickens slightly. Pour the sauce over the pork chops and serve immediately.

PORK WITH CUMBERLAND SAUCE

PORK WITH CUMBERLAND SAUCE *Serves 4*

4x1cm-thick (about 180g each) rib or loin pork chops

1 tablespoon sunflower oil

¼ cup redcurrant jelly

2 tablespoons ruby port

1 teaspoon cornflour

1 teaspoon finely grated lemon peel

2 teaspoons lemon juice

Lemon slices (optional)

 Preparation time
5 minutes

 Cooking time
15 minutes

SERVING SUGGESTION Add an elegant touch with lightly steamed slivers of carrot and baby marrow tossed with butter and parsley.

1 Trim and discard any excess fat from the chops. In a large frying pan, heat the oil over moderate heat. Sauté the chops, turning occasionally, for about 6 minutes or until the juices run clear.

2 Meanwhile, in a small saucepan, melt the jelly over moderate heat. In a cup, mix the port and cornflour until smooth. Stir the mixture into the melted jelly. Cook for about 5 minutes until thickened and bubbling, stirring constantly. Stir in the lemon peel and lemon juice.

3 Transfer the chops to a warmed serving platter. Pour the sauce over the chops, garnish with lemon slices, if desired, and serve.

Start with Smoked Ham

If you keep a package of smoked ham in the refrigerator, you can make any of these sumptuous dishes in a trice. The ham is fully cooked already, so you can use it in cold salads and sandwiches as well as in hot dishes. Its smoky flavour is complemented by both fruits as well as crunchy vegetables. Try some of these new ideas for a quick, satisfying meal.

You may prefer to substitute the smoked ham with cooked ham for a more delicate flavour. Each of the following recipes makes four servings.

▶ **Ham penne** Cook *350g dried penne* according to the directions on the package. In a large frying pan, melt *4 tablespoons (60g) butter* over moderate heat. Add *1 large onion*, sliced, and *1½ cups broccoli florets* and sauté until crisp-tender. Stir in *3 tablespoons flour*. Gradually stir in *1¼ cups chicken stock* and bring to the boil. Add *2 cups smoked ham*, sliced into strips, and thin the sauce slightly with *a little milk*. Top the pasta with the ham sauce.

◀ **Ham and spanspek salad** In a large bowl, mix *2 cups diced smoked ham*, *¼ cup chopped walnuts*, *¼ cup sliced celery* and *¼ cup mayonnaise*. Slice *2 medium spanspek* in half across their width and scoop out the seeds. Place ¼ of the ham mixture into the cavity of each melon half and serve.

▶ **Wild rice and ham salad** Prepare *one package (175g) wild rice* according to the directions on the package. Set aside to cool slightly. In a large bowl, combine *2 cups diced smoked ham*, *1 cup chopped onion*, *1 cup sliced water chestnuts* and *¾ cup Italian dressing*. Add the rice and toss to coat evenly. Serve warm or cold.

➤ **Ham and citrus slaw** Mix *2 cups shredded red cabbage*, *2 cups shredded green cabbage* and *1 bunch spring onions*, thinly sliced. For the citrus dressing, blend together *2 tablespoons lemon juice*, *1 tablespoon orange juice*, *1 tablespoon wine vinegar*, *⅓ cup sunflower oil* and *salt* and *pepper* to taste. Add *125g thinly sliced smoked ham*, cut into strips. Serve garnished with thin slices of *peeled ruby grapefruit*, if desired.

◀ **Ham and Brie sandwiches** Thinly slice *2 small pears* and brush them with *lemon juice*. Place *8 slices pumpernickel bread* on four serving plates. Divide *250g Brie cheese*, sliced, and *2 cups finely chopped ham* equally among the bread slices. Top each with *2 or 3 slices of pear*. Garnish with *chopped parsley*, if desired.

➤ **Creamy potatoes and ham** Peel *2 large potatoes* and cut them into 3mm-thick slices. Boil the potatoes for about 5 minutes until tender. In a medium-sized saucepan, melt *3 tablespoons (45g) butter* over moderate heat. Add *2 cups diced smoked ham* and *1 small sweet green pepper*, diced. Sauté for about 6 minutes until lightly browned. Stir in *3 tablespoons flour*. Gradually stir in *1½ cups milk* and simmer until the sauce is thickened and bubbling. Drain potatoes and stir in ham mixture. Sprinkle with *2 tablespoons toasted bread crumbs*.

MEAT

STIR-FRIED PORK *Serves 4*

500g deboned pork shoulder or loin
¼ cup firmly packed light brown sugar
¼ cup soy sauce
2 tablespoons cornflour
4 medium carrots, peeled
125g mange-tout, trimmed
¼ cup sunflower oil
¾ cup chicken stock
¼ cup dry-roasted peanuts

 Preparation time 25 minutes

 Cooking time 25 minutes

SERVING SUGGESTION Succulent pork and crispy vegetables combine with the crunch of peanuts for an Oriental dish your family will relish.

1. Trim and discard any excess fat from the pork and cut it into 2,5cm cubes. In a large bowl, combine the brown sugar, soy sauce and cornflour. Add the pork cubes and toss to coat evenly. Leave them to marinate in the mixture at room temperature for about 15 to 20 minutes.

2. Meanwhile, chop the carrots diagonally into 1cm slices. Remove the strings and tips from the mange-tout.

3. In a wok or large frying pan, heat the oil over moderately high heat. Using a slotted spoon, add the pork cubes (reserve the marinade). Sauté the pork, stirring occasionally, for about 4 minutes until it is well browned.

4. Add the carrots and stock to the wok. Reduce the heat to moderately low, cover the wok and simmer for about 15 minutes until the pork and carrots are tender.

5. Add the mange-tout to the pork mixture and cook for about 2 minutes until slightly softened but still firm to the bite. Increase the heat to moderate, stir in the reserved marinade and cook, uncovered, for about 2 minutes until the sauce is thickened. Transfer the mixture to a warmed serving dish, sprinkle with the peanuts and serve.

PORK CHOPS WITH MUSHROOM SAUCE *Serves 4*

4x1cm-thick (about 180g each) rib or shoulder chops
1 tablespoon sunflower oil
1 medium onion, sliced
1 tin (295g) condensed cream of mushroom soup
1 cup water
½ teaspoon dried thyme
1 teaspoon Worcestershire sauce
1 cup frozen green peas

 Preparation time 5 minutes

 Cooking time 35 minutes

1. Trim and discard any excess fat from the chops. In a large frying pan, heat the oil over moderately high heat. Sauté the chops for about 3 minutes on each side until browned. Transfer to a plate and set aside. Drain all but 1 tablespoon of the fat from the pan.

2. Add the onion to the pan and sauté for about 5 minutes until soft. Reduce the heat to moderate, stir in the undiluted soup, the water, thyme, Worcestershire sauce and peas. Bring to the boil.

3. Return the chops and any accumulated juices to the sauce in the pan. Cover and cook, stirring occasionally, for 15 minutes until the chops are tender. Transfer to a serving dish and serve.

MEAT

Sweet and Sour Pork Serves 4

2 tablespoons olive oil
2 tablespoons cider vinegar
2 teaspoons chilli powder
2 cloves garlic, crushed
1 teaspoon ground cumin
1 teaspoon dry mustard
1 teaspoon honey
½ teaspoon ground black pepper
8x3mm-thick (about 500g) boneless pork loin slices
Salt to taste

 Preparation time
20 minutes

 Cooking time
9 minutes

Food note Grilled pork is complemented perfectly by the sweet-and-sour sauce. Serve it with a chilled, crunchy coleslaw.

1 In a 37,5cm x 26,5cm dish, combine the oil, vinegar, chilli powder, garlic, cumin, mustard, honey and pepper. Coat the pork slices thoroughly with the mixture and leave to stand at room temperature for 15 to 20 minutes to marinate. Meanwhile, preheat the grill.

2 Using a fork, transfer the pork to the rack over a grill pan. Reserve the marinade. Grill the pork 7,5cm from the heat for 5 minutes. Turn the pork over and brush with the marinade.

3 Continue grilling the pork for 3 to 4 more minutes until it is cooked through. Transfer the pork to serving plates, season with salt and serve.

Pork Sauté with Asparagus Serves 4

3 tablespoons (45g) butter or margarine
500g boneless pork fillet, trimmed and sliced diagonally into 1cm strips
500g asparagus
1 medium onion, thinly sliced
2 cups (about 250g) thinly sliced mushrooms
⅓ cup chicken stock
1 teaspoon cornflour
½ teaspoon dried tarragon or thyme
¼ teaspoon ground black pepper

 Preparation time
5 minutes

 Cooking time
15 minutes

1 In a large frying pan, melt 2 tablespoons of the butter over moderate heat. Sauté the pork slices for about 2 minutes on each side until browned. Remove and discard the top 10cm of the asparagus. Half fill a saucepan with water and bring it to the boil.

2 Using a slotted spoon, transfer the pork slices to a warmed serving platter, cover and keep them warm. Add the remaining 1 tablespoon of butter to the frying pan. Add the onion and sauté for about 3 minutes until it begins to soften. Add the mushrooms and sauté for a further 2 minutes until the mushrooms and onions are just softened.

3 Add the asparagus tips to the boiling water. Return to the boil, cover the saucepan, remove from the heat and set aside.

4 In a cup, combine the stock and cornflour. Add the stock, tarragon and pepper to the frying pan. Bring the mixture to the boil. Cook, stirring constantly, for about 1 minute until the stock is slightly thickened.

5 Return the pork slices with any accumulated juices to the frying pan. Stir to mix well and transfer to the serving platter. Drain the asparagus, add it to the platter and serve immediately.

PORK ESCALOPES DIJON

Pork escalopes Dijon *Serves 4*

4x1cm-thick (about 125g each) boneless pork loin chops

2 tablespoons (30g) butter or margarine, softened

1 tablespoon Dijon mustard

1 clove garlic, finely chopped

1½ teaspoons chopped dill (or ½ teaspoon dried dill)

Salt and ground black pepper to taste

Fresh dill sprigs (optional)

 Preparation time
15 minutes

 Cooking time
5 minutes

Serving suggestion This low-kilojoule dish is perfect for slimmers, especially when served with a green salad topped with croutons and shaved Parmesan cheese.

1. Preheat the grill. Place the chops between two sheets of wax paper and pound them with a mallet until about 3mm thick.

2. In a small bowl, mix the butter, mustard, garlic and dill. Spread a thin layer of the mustard mixture on one side of each chop. Place the pork, mustard side up, on the rack over a grill pan. Grill 7,5cm from the heat for about 5 minutes until lightly browned.

3. Transfer the pork to a warmed serving platter and pour any accumulated juices over it. Sprinkle the pork with salt and pepper, garnish it with fresh dill sprigs, if desired, and serve.

MEAT

PAN-FRIED BARBECUED PORK *Serves 4*

1 tablespoon sunflower oil

4x1cm-thick (about 250g each) pork steaks from the loin or neck

1 small onion, chopped

1 cup ready-made barbecue sauce

1 large sweet green pepper

4 lemon slices

 Preparation time
3 minutes

 Cooking time
42 minutes

FOOD NOTE Savour the spice of the braai from the convenience of your kitchen. Use your favourite ready-made barbecue sauce to re-create the unmistakeable flavour of meat grilled on the summertime braai fire.

1. In a large frying pan, heat the oil over moderately high heat. Sauté the steaks for 2 to 3 minutes on each side until they are lightly browned. Reduce the heat. Move the pork to one side of the pan. Add the onion and sauté for about 5 minutes until soft.

2. Add the barbecue sauce to the pork and onion in the pan. Cover the pan and simmer for 10 minutes. Reduce the heat to low, and continue cooking for approximately 15 minutes more until the meat is tender when pierced with a fork.

3. Meanwhile, core, seed and slice the pepper into thin strips. Stir the pepper into the pork mixture, cover and cook for about 6 minutes until softened but still firm to the bite.

4. Transfer the pork steaks and sauce to warmed serving plates, top each with a slice of the lemon and serve.

PORK WITH RHUBARB-ORANGE SAUCE *Serves 4*

4x1cm-thick (about 180g each) rib or loin pork chops

1 teaspoon dried rosemary

½ teaspoon salt

¼ teaspoon ground black pepper

2 tablespoons flour

2 tablespoons sunflower oil

1½ cups sliced rhubarb

⅓ cup sugar

¼ cup orange juice

1 tablespoon cornflour

 Preparation time
7 minutes

 Cooking time
21 minutes

1. Trim and discard any excess fat from the chops. Sprinkle both sides of the chops with some of the rosemary, salt and pepper. Dust them with flour, shaking off the excess.

2. In a large frying pan, heat the sunflower oil over moderately high heat. Add the chops and sauté for 6 to 7 minutes on one side until well browned. Turn them over and reduce the heat to moderate. Sauté for a further 6 to 7 minutes until the chops are cooked through. Transfer to a warmed serving platter, cover and keep them warm.

3. Add the rhubarb and sugar to the same frying pan. Cook over moderate heat for about 6 minutes, stirring constantly, until soft. In a cup, combine the orange juice and cornflour until smooth.

4. Stir the cornflour mixture into the rhubarb and bring to the boil, stirring constantly. Continue cooking the rhubarb sauce for about 30 seconds until thickened. Pour the sauce over the chops and serve immediately.

PORK FILLET WITH PINEAPPLE SALSA

PORK FILLET WITH PINEAPPLE SALSA *Serves 4*

500g pork fillet

2 tablespoons olive oil

1 teaspoon dried thyme

½ teaspoon salt

¼ teaspoon cayenne pepper

250g finely chopped fresh pineapple

¼ cup finely chopped red onion

1 small tomato, finely chopped

1 small chilli, seeded and finely chopped

¼ cup chopped coriander leaves

¾ teaspoon ground cumin

 Preparation time 20 minutes

 Cooking time 8 minutes

FOOD NOTE Pork gets the Hawaiian treatment with the addition of a tangy pineapple salsa. Try cooking it over the braai coals in summer.

1. Preheat the grill. Trim and discard any excess fat from the pork. To butterfly the pork, place a sharp knife along one long side of the fillet and slice it horizontally almost through to the opposite side. Open the meat like a book and press it flat.

2. Place the pork on the rack over a grill pan. In a small bowl, combine the oil, thyme, salt and cayenne pepper. Brush both sides of the pork with the mixture and grill 10cm from the heat for 5 minutes. Turn the meat over and continue grilling for about 3 more minutes until it is just cooked but still moist.

3. Meanwhile, in a small bowl, combine the pineapple, onion, tomato, chilli, coriander and cumin.

4. Transfer the pork to a carving board, allow it to stand for several minutes, then slice it across the grain. Place the slices on a serving platter and serve, passing the pineapple salsa separately.

MEAT

SMOKED SAUSAGE STEW *Serves 4*

500g smoked sausage (e.g. kielbasa or knackwurst), cut into 3cm chunks

8 small pickling onions, peeled

8 small potatoes, quartered

4 medium carrots, cut into 1cm-thick slices

1 teaspoon dried marjoram or thyme

1 bay leaf

2 cups water

1 teaspoon cornflour

1 cup frozen green peas or frozen cut green beans

Salt and ground black pepper to taste

 Preparation time 10 minutes

 Cooking time 38 minutes

SERVING SUGGESTION This smoked-sausage stew needs only a basket of warmed bread to take the chill out of a cold winter's day.

1. In a 5-litre flameproof casserole dish or large saucepan, sauté the sausage over moderate heat until browned on all sides, turning frequently. Line a plate with paper towels. Using a slotted spoon, transfer the sausage to the plate and set aside.

2. Add the onions, potatoes and carrots to the remaining drippings in the casserole dish. Sauté, stirring occasionally, for about 10 minutes until the vegetables are lightly browned.

3. Return the sausage to the casserole dish. Add the marjoram, bay leaf and all but 1 tablespoon of the water. Increase the heat to high and bring the mixture to the boil. Reduce the heat to low, cover and cook for about 20 minutes until the potatoes and carrots are tender. Meanwhile, in a cup, mix the remaining 1 tablespoon of water and the cornflour until smooth.

4. Stir the cornflour mixture and the frozen peas into the stew. Increase the heat to high and bring to the boil, stirring constantly. Continue cooking for 5 more minutes or until the peas are tender. Season with the salt and pepper, discard the bay leaf and serve.

PORK SAUSAGE STEW *Serves 4*

500g pork sausage

1 medium onion, sliced

1 tin (410g) chopped tomatoes

250g frozen or fresh corn kernels

1 cup tomato sauce

1 cup water

2 cups (about 125g) elbow macaroni

2 cups thinly sliced green cabbage

Salt and ground black pepper to taste

 Preparation time 4 minutes

 Cooking time 21 minutes

COOK'S TIP The recipe calls for elbow macaroni, but you may prefer to use any one of the wide variety of smaller pasta shapes available.

1. In a 5-litre flameproof casserole dish or large saucepan, sauté the sausage and onion over moderately high heat for about 7 minutes until the pork is well browned and the onion is soft. Drain the excess fat.

2. Add the tomatoes with their juice, the corn kernels, tomato sauce and water to the pork mixture and bring to the boil. Stir in the macaroni and cabbage. Return the mixture to the boil.

3. Reduce the heat to low, cover the dish and simmer the mixture for 8 to 10 minutes until the macaroni is tender and most of the liquid has been absorbed. Season the stew with the salt and pepper and serve.

KIDNEY BEANS AND SAUSAGE

KIDNEY BEANS AND SAUSAGE *Serves 4*

1 tablespoon sunflower oil

1 medium onion, halved and sliced

1 stalk celery, sliced

500 smoked sausage (e.g. kielbasa or knackwurst)

1 tin (410g) chopped tomatoes

1 tin (410g) butter beans, drained and rinsed

1 tablespoon firmly packed light brown sugar

2 tablespoons dry white wine

½ cup chicken stock

1 teaspoon dried origanum

¼ teaspoon each salt and ground black pepper

 Preparation time
15 minutes

 Cooking time
27 minutes

FOOD NOTE This economical stove-top casserole will satisfy the most hearty of appetites on a chilly winter evening. Serve it with a crunchy salad for an interesting contrast of texture.

1 In a 5-litre flameproof casserole dish or large saucepan, heat the oil over moderate heat. Add the onion and celery and sauté for about 5 minutes until soft.

2 Meanwhile, slice the sausage diagonally into 2,5cm slices. In a large dry frying pan, sauté the sausage for approximately 5 minutes until it is lightly browned. Line a plate with paper towels. Transfer the sausage to the plate and set aside.

3 Add the tomatoes with their juice, the beans, sugar, wine, stock, origanum, salt and pepper to the onion mixture. Increase the heat to high and bring the mixture to the boil.

4 Add the sausage to the tomato mixture and reduce the heat to low. Cover the casserole dish and let the mixture simmer for 10 minutes. Remove the lid and continue cooking for 5 more minutes. Spoon the beans and sausage into bowls and serve.

MEAT

Smoked sausage with creamy vegetables *Serves 4*

4 cups water

500g smoked sausage (eg kielbasa or knackwurst)

4 medium potatoes, peeled

1 cup frozen green peas

4 tablespoons (60g) butter or margarine

1 medium onion, chopped

¼ cup flour

1 cup milk

Salt and ground black pepper to taste

 Preparation time
7 minutes

 Cooking time
32 minutes

1. Pour the water into a large saucepan or flameproof casserole dish and bring it to the boil over high heat. Meanwhile, slice the sausage into 4 pieces and make diagonal slashes about 3mm deep on each slice. Add the sausage to the boiling water, cover the saucepan and simmer for 5 minutes. Meanwhile, chop the potatoes into 1cm-thick slices.

2. Using a slotted spoon, transfer the sausage to a bowl, cover and keep it warm. Add the potatoes to the water in the saucepan and return it to the boil. Reduce the heat to moderate, cover the saucepan and cook the potatoes for about 8 minutes until they are almost tender.

3. Add the frozen green peas to the potatoes and cook for 1 to 2 minutes until the peas are thawed. Drain the potatoes and peas, reserving 1 cup of the cooking liquid. Transfer the cooked vegetables to a second bowl and set them aside.

4. In the same saucepan, melt the butter over moderate heat. Add the chopped onion and sauté for approximately 5 minutes until soft. Add the flour and stir until well mixed. Gradually add the reserved water in which the potatoes were cooked. Cook, stirring constantly, for about 10 seconds until the mixture is thickened and smooth.

5. Stir the milk into the onion mixture. Gently add the potatoes and peas. Season the creamed vegetables with the salt and pepper. Transfer to a serving dish, top with the sausage and serve.

SHELF MAGIC

Sausage and lentils make a tempting combination. Serve with creamy mashed or sautéed potatoes.

Bockwurst and lentils

Cut *4 bockwurst* into chunks. In a large saucepan, heat *1 tablespoon sunflower oil* and sauté *1 large onion*, thinly sliced, until softened but still pale in colour. Add *1 clove garlic*, crushed and stir to combine. Season lightly to taste with *salt* and *freshly ground black pepper* and cook the mixture for 1 minute, stirring constantly. Add the chunks of sausage and sauté until browned all over. Add *one 400g tin of lentils* (or *one 410g tin of baked beans*, if preferred) and allow to heat through. Spoon onto warmed individual plates, garnish with *chopped parsley*, if desired, and serve. Serves 3

MEAT

ROASTED BOEREWORS AND SWEET POTATO *Serves 4*

500g boerewors

4 medium slim (about 600g) sweet potatoes, unpeeled

2 tablespoons sunflower oil

Salt and freshly ground black pepper

Ready-made tomato salsa

Finely chopped lettuce (optional)

 Preparation time 15 minutes

 Cooking time 30 minutes

Food note Sweet potato is an unusual but delicious partner for boerewors, a traditional South African favourite. Substitute boerewors with spicy German bratwurst for an equally satisfying dish.

1. Preheat the oven to 200°C. Cover the base of a roasting pan with approximately 1cm water. Coat a grill rack with non-stick cooking spray and set it over the roasting pan. Prick the boerewors all over and place it on the rack.

2. Scrub the sweet potatoes well. Slice very thinly and place in a medium-sized bowl. Add the oil, salt and pepper and toss to coat well. Coat a second baking tray with non-stick spray and arrange the sweet potatoes on the tray in a single layer.

3. Roast the boerewors and the sweet potatoes for 20 to 30 minutes or until the sausage is browned, cooked through and still moist, and the sweet potatoes are tender and just starting to brown. Place on a warmed serving platter and garnish with the tomato salsa and finely chopped lettuce, if desired. Serve immediately.

PEPPERED OSTRICH FILLET STEAKS *Serves 4*

1 tablespoon (15g) butter or margarine

2 teaspoon sunflower oil

350g ostrich fillet steaks

Salt and freshly ground black pepper

¼ cup cream

½ teaspoon green peppercorns, crushed

⅓ teaspoon mustard powder

 Preparation time 10 minutes

 Cooking time 5 minutes

Serving suggestion A cool green salad comprising a variety of lettuce leaves tossed in a light salad dressing would be the perfect foil for this full-flavoured dish.

1. Heat a large, cast-iron frying pan (preferably with grooves to allow air circulation) over moderately high heat. Add the butter and oil and fry the steaks in a single layer for about 30 to 45 seconds on each side until browned. Remove from the pan and place on a warmed serving platter.

2. Repeat with the remaining steaks. Season to taste with the salt and black pepper and set aside, keeping them warm.

3. Allow the pan to cool slightly. Add the cream, green peppercorns and mustard powder. (If you have used a grooved pan, heat the sauce ingredients in a clean pan, scraping the meaty residue from the grid into the second pan.) Stir to mix well and heat through, taking care not to let the mixture boil. Pour the sauce over the steaks and serve immediately.

Pasta and Grains

Spaghettini alla puttanesca (page 220)

PASTA

Economy, versatility and convenience are the three keys to the popularity of pasta, one of the staple foods of Italy. Adorn it with a simple sauce for everyday family fare, or dress it up with exotic ingredients to grace the most glamorous of dinner parties.

PENNE PRIMAVERA Serves 4

500g penne or other short tubular pasta

125g green beans, cut into 5cm lengths

1 bunch (about 350g) broccoli, cut into 5cm lengths

250g asparagus, trimmed to use tips only

125g mange-tout, tips and strings removed

2 large carrots, sliced into thin strips

2 tablespoons chopped fresh basil or origanum (or 2 teaspoons dried)

For the vinaigrette:

½ cup olive oil

3 tablespoons wine vinegar

2 teaspoons prepared mustard

1 clove garlic, finely chopped

Salt and ground black pepper to taste

 Preparation time 20 minutes

 Cooking time 25 minutes

SERVING SUGGESTION *This springtime favourite is delicious served either hot or cold. Substitute any fresh vegetables in season – try using fresh green peas, cauliflower, sweet red peppers or baby marrows. For a fitting finale, serve fresh orange slices steeped in a sweet caramel sauce.*

1 Bring 4 litres of water to the boil in a large saucepan. Cook the penne in the boiling water according to the directions on the package or until they are tender but still firm to the bite.

2 Meanwhile, pour 2,5cm of water into another saucepan fitted with a steaming rack and bring it to the boil.

3 Set a heatproof plate on the rack, place the green beans on it and steam them for 2 minutes. Add the remaining vegetables and steam for 3 to 4 more minutes or until they are tender but still firm to the bite. (Alternatively, cook the vegetables directly in boiling water, cooking each separately.) Drain the vegetables thoroughly and place them in a large bowl with the herbs.

4 To make the vinaigrette: Use a fork to beat all the ingredients together in a cup. Pour the mixture over the vegetables and herbs. Drain the pasta thoroughly. Add the pasta to the vegetables and toss gently. Serve immediately.

TIME SAVERS

PERFECT PASTA
Keep these handy tips in mind to create platefuls of perfectly prepared pasta:
■ Be sure that the water is at a good rolling boil before adding the pasta. Once added, stir to separate the pieces. Stir occasionally during cooking and drain immediately once cooked.
■ Take care not to overcook. The pasta must be `al dente', that is, it must be tender but still firm to the bite. As a general rule, dried pasta cooks in about 12 minutes, and fresh pasta takes about 3 to 4 minutes.
■ Don't drain away all the water. Leave a little to moisten the pasta so that the sauce and seasonings coat the pasta evenly.

PASTA AND GRAINS

Orzo with Garden Vegetables *Serves 4*

500g orzo (rice-shaped pasta)

4 tablespoons (60g) butter or margarine

1 large onion, chopped

1 medium sweet red pepper, cored, seeded and slivered

1 cup (about 125g) sliced mushrooms

1 teaspoon dried origanum

½ cup (60g) grated Parmesan cheese

Salt and ground white pepper to taste

 Preparation time 8 minutes

 Cooking time 25 minutes

Serving suggestion This light main course also makes an excellent dish to serve as an accompaniment to beef or chicken. As a side dish it will make 6 to 8 servings.

1. Bring 4 litres of water to the boil in a large saucepan. Cook the orzo in the boiling water according to the directions on the package or until it is tender but still firm to the bite.

2. Meanwhile, in a large frying pan, melt the butter over moderate heat. Add the onion and sauté for about 5 minutes until soft. Add the red pepper, mushrooms and origanum and continue sautéing for a further 5 minutes.

3. Drain the pasta and transfer it to a serving bowl. Toss gently with the onion mixture and Parmesan cheese. Season with the salt and pepper and serve immediately.

Rigatoni with Beans and Vegetables *Serves 4*

350g broccoli

250g rigatoni (large tube-shaped pasta)

2 medium carrots, thinly sliced

3 tablespoons olive oil

1 large bunch (about 8 cups) coarsely chopped Swiss chard

2 cloves garlic, finely chopped

1 small tin (225g) butter beans, drained and rinsed

⅓ cup (40g) grated Parmesan cheese

Salt and ground white pepper to taste

 Preparation time 6 minutes

 Cooking time 28 minutes

Diet note Broccoli, carrots, Swiss chard and butter beans combine with pasta and cheese to create a delicious vegetarian meal that is rich in vitamins and minerals. To reduce the kilojoules, the amount of olive oil can be reduced to 2 tablespoons.

1. Bring 4 litres of water to the boil in a large pot. Chop the broccoli into 5cm lengths. Cook the rigatoni and carrots in the boiling water for 9 minutes.

2. Stir in the broccoli and continue cooking for about 2 to 3 minutes until the rigatoni, carrots and broccoli are just tender but still firm to the bite.

3. Meanwhile, in a large frying pan, heat the oil over moderate heat. Add the Swiss chard and garlic and sauté for approximately 2 minutes until the Swiss chard is just softened. Stir in the butter beans and cook gently for about 3 minutes until they are heated through.

4. Drain the pasta, carrots and broccoli and transfer the mixture to a serving bowl. Toss gently with the Swiss chard-bean mixture and Parmesan cheese. Season the rigatoni with the salt and pepper and serve immediately.

ANGEL-HAIR PASTA WITH BABY MARROWS

ANGEL-HAIR PASTA WITH BABY MARROWS *Serves 4*

- 3 medium baby marrows
- 2 spring onions
- ¼ cup olive oil
- 1 clove garlic, finely chopped
- 2 cups chicken stock
- 350g capelli d'angelo (angel-hair pasta)
- ½ cup (60g) feta cheese, crumbled
- 1 large tomato, halved, seeded and diced
- Salt and ground black pepper to taste

 Preparation time 10 minutes

 Cooking time 20 minutes

COOK'S TIP The fine strands of angel-hair pasta cook very quickly – start testing it after only one minute to avoid overcooking.

1 Bring 4 litres of water to the boil in a large saucepan. Slice the baby marrows into 5cm x 1cm strips, and slice the spring onions into 2,5cm lengths. In a large frying pan, heat the oil over moderately high heat. Add the baby marrows and sauté gently for about 10 minutes until lightly browned. Stir in the spring onions and garlic and sauté for 1 more minute. Add the stock to the baby marrows and bring the mixture to the boil. Remove the frying pan from the heat and keep it warm.

2 Cook the pasta in the boiling water according to the directions on the package or until it is tender but still firm to the bite. Drain the pasta and transfer it to a serving bowl.

3 Gently toss the baby marrow mixture into the pasta. Add the feta cheese, tomato, salt and pepper and mix well. Serve immediately.

PASTA AND GRAINS

PASTA VERDE *Serves 4*

500g rotelle or fusilli (wheel-shaped or corkscrew-shaped) pasta

2 cloves garlic, halved

¼ cup shelled pistachio or pine nuts

1 cup fresh basil (do not use dried)

½ cup parsley

½ cup olive oil

⅓ cup (40g) grated Parmesan cheese

Salt and ground black pepper to taste

Additional shaved Parmesan cheese for garnishing (optional)

 Preparation time
5 minutes

 Cooking time
15 minutes

SERVING SUGGESTION *This classic pesto-covered pasta dish would be perfectly rounded off with a simple bruschetta: French or Italian bread covered with chopped tomatoes lightly tossed with basil, vinegar and olive oil (see page 53).*

1 Bring 4 litres of water to the boil in a large saucepan. Add the pasta and boil according to the directions on the package or until tender but still firm to the bite.

2 Meanwhile, in a food processor or electric blender, finely chop the garlic and nuts together. Add the basil, parsley and oil and process until the herbs are puréed. Add the cheese and process until just mixed. Season with the salt and pepper.

3 Drain the pasta thoroughly and transfer it to a serving bowl. Toss gently with the sauce until well mixed. Sprinkle with additional Parmesan cheese, if desired, and serve immediately.

CHEESY-BAKED SHELLS *Serves 6*

1 package (about 450g) soft ricotta cheese

2 cups (250g) coarsely grated mozzarella cheese

1 large egg

2 tablespoons chopped fresh parsley, origanum or basil

¼ teaspoon salt

1 bottle (475g) ready-made tomato spaghetti sauce

250g medium (2,5cm) pasta shells

Additional herb sprigs (optional)

 Preparation time
5 minutes

 Cooking time
40 minutes

COOK'S TIP *To avoid overcooking pasta that is going to be baked, drain it when partially cooked and run cold water over it.*

1 Preheat the oven to 190°C. Lightly grease a 37,5cm x 26,5cm baking dish. Bring 4 litres of water to the boil in a large saucepan. Meanwhile, in a medium-sized bowl, combine the ricotta cheese, 1 cup of the mozzarella cheese, the egg, herbs and salt until well mixed. In a medium-sized saucepan, heat the spaghetti sauce over moderately high heat.

2 Partially cook the pasta shells in the boiling water for half the time given in the package directions. Drain the pasta thoroughly and rinse with cold water. Return the pasta to the saucepan and toss it gently with the ricotta mixture.

3 Pour about half of the spaghetti sauce into the bottom of the prepared dish. Spoon the pasta and cheese mixture over the sauce. Spoon the remaining spaghetti sauce over the pasta. Sprinkle with the remaining mozzarella cheese.

4 Bake the pasta for 20 to 25 minutes until it is hot and bubbling. Garnish with herb sprigs, if desired, and serve.

FETTUCCINE WITH SALMON

FETTUCCINE WITH SALMON *Serves 4*

2 cups cream

2 tablespoons (30g) butter or margarine

1 teaspoon grated lemon peel

350g dried or 500g fresh spinach fettuccine

125g sliced smoked salmon, cut into thin strips

¼ cup (about 30g) grated Parmesan cheese

1 tablespoon finely chopped fresh dill

Ground black pepper to taste

 Preparation time
10 minutes

 Cooking time
28 minutes

FOOD NOTE Elevate everyday pasta to heavenly heights by teaming it with cream and delicately-flavoured smoked salmon. An ideal dish for a special occasion.

1 Bring 4 litres of water to the boil in a large saucepan. In a second large saucepan, heat the cream, butter and lemon peel over moderate heat until just hot, but not boiling. Reduce the heat to low and cook for about 10 minutes until slightly thickened.

2 Cook the fettuccine in the boiling water according to the directions on the package or until tender but still firm to the bite.

3 Meanwhile, remove the cream mixture from the heat. Stir in the salmon, cheese and dill, and season with the black pepper.

4 Drain the pasta thoroughly and transfer it to a serving bowl. Add the salmon mixture and toss gently. Serve immediately.

PASTA AND GRAINS

ROTELLE WITH CHEESE AND WALNUTS *Serves 4 (Picture page 2)*

500g rotelle or fusilli (wheel-shaped or corkscrew-shaped pasta)

1 tablespoon (15g) butter or margarine

1 cup chopped walnuts

½ cup cream

½ cup chicken stock

½ tub (125g) mascarpone or cream cheese, softened

Ground black pepper to taste

2 tablespoons chopped parsley

 Preparation time 3 minutes

 Cooking time 23 minutes

Diet note Walnuts provide a good source of protein, B-group vitamins and minerals. Here the crunchy texture of the sautéed nuts contrasts deliciously with the creamy sauce.

1. In a large saucepan, bring 4 litres of water to the boil. Cook the pasta in the boiling water according to the directions on the package or until it is tender but still firm to the bite.

2. Meanwhile, in a small saucepan, melt the butter over low heat. Add the chopped walnuts and sauté them for approximately 1 minute until they are lightly toasted. Add the cream and stock. Increase the heat to moderately high and gently bring the mixture to the boil.

3. Reduce the heat. Add the marscapone cheese to the cream mixture and whisk until the liquid is smooth. Season with the pepper and stir in the parsley.

4. Drain the pasta thoroughly and transfer it to a serving bowl. Pour the sauce over the pasta and toss gently. Serve immediately.

LINGUINE WITH CLAM SAUCE *Serves 4*

500g dried or 600g fresh linguine

¼ cup olive oil

2 cloves garlic, finely chopped

2 tablespoons flour

¼ teaspoon ground white pepper

2 cups fish or chicken stock

3 tablespoons dry white wine (optional)

2 tins (200g each) baby clams, drained

3 tablespoons chopped parsley

 Preparation time 6 minutes

 Cooking time 28 minutes

Cook's tip This delicate combination of clams, white wine and parsley creates a sublime dish fit for a king. To prevent the clams from becoming tough, cook them briefly.

1. Bring 4 litres of water to the boil in a large saucepan. Cook the linguine in the boiling water according to the directions on the package or until it is tender but still firm to the bite.

2. Meanwhile, in a large saucepan, heat the oil over moderate heat. Add the garlic and sauté for 15 seconds. Stir in the flour and pepper. Stir in the stock and white wine, if desired, and bring the mixture to the boil, stirring occasionally.

3. Stir the clams into the stock mixture and continue cooking gently until they are just heated through.

4. Drain the pasta thoroughly and transfer it to a warmed serving bowl. Add the clam sauce and the chopped parsley and toss it gently. Serve immediately.

PASTA AND GRAINS

SPAGHETTINI ALLA PUTTANESCA Serves 4 (PICTURE PAGE 211)

500g spaghettini (thin spaghetti) or vermicelli

2 tablespoons olive oil

4 cloves garlic, finely chopped

4 anchovy fillets, coarsely chopped

2 tins (400g each) whole, peeled tomatoes, chopped, liquid reserved

½ cup pitted black olives, cut in half

¼ cup drained capers

1 teaspoon dried origanum

⅛ teaspoon crushed chillies, or to taste

2 tablespoons chopped parsley

 Preparation time
8 minutes

 Cooking time
25 minutes

FOOD NOTE *This traditional dish, named for Italy's ladies of the night, has deep peasant roots, as do most quick and economical Italian pastas. Serve it with a hearty red wine to complement its robust flavour.*

1 In a large saucepan, bring 4 litres of water to the boil. Cook the spaghettini in the boiling water according to the directions on the package or until it is tender but still firm to the bite.

2 Meanwhile, in a large saucepan, heat the oil over moderate heat. Add the garlic and anchovies and cook gently for about 3 minutes until the anchovies are very soft. Stir in the tomatoes with their liquid, the olives, capers, origanum and chilli. Cook for 5 minutes, stirring occasionally.

3 Drain the pasta thoroughly and transfer it to warmed individual serving plates. Pour the anchovy sauce over the hot spaghettini and garnish each serving with a little of the chopped parsley. Serve immediately.

TUNA NOODLE CASSEROLE Serves 6

250g farfalle (bow-tie-shaped pasta) or medium-width egg noodles

1 container (227g) cream cheese, softened

1 cup sour cream

½ cup milk

1 tin (185g) tuna packed in water, drained and flaked

¼ cup chopped spring onions

2 tablespoons finely chopped sweet red pepper

Salt and ground black pepper to taste

½ cup (60g) grated Cheddar cheese

 Preparation time
5 minutes

 Cooking time
40 minutes

FOOD NOTE *The combination of succulent flakes of tuna and tender pasta, livened up here with a touch of spring onions and zesty red pepper, never fails to provide a tasty and healthy family meal. Use top grade pasta – we have used bow-tie pasta – for the best results, although egg noodles may be substituted if you prefer them.*

1 Preheat the oven to 190°C. In a large saucepan, bring 4 litres of water to the boil. Partially cook the pasta in the boiling water for half the time recommended on the package.

2 Meanwhile, butter a 6-cup casserole dish. In a large bowl, combine the cream cheese, sour cream and milk until smooth and creamy. Stir in the tuna, spring onions and red pepper. Season with the salt and black pepper.

3 Drain the noodles and stir them into the tuna mixture. Place the noodles into the prepared casserole dish and sprinkle them with the grated cheese. Bake the casserole for about 25 minutes until the mixture is bubbling and the topping is lightly browned. Serve immediately.

SHELLS WITH SHRIMP SAUCE

SHELLS WITH SHRIMP SAUCE *Serves 4*

500g medium (2,5cm) pasta shells

1 tablespoon olive oil

2 cloves garlic, finely chopped

¼ teaspoon crushed chillies, or to taste

2 tins (400g each) whole, peeled tomatoes, chopped, liquid reserved

1 cup dry white wine

1 teaspoon dried basil

300g shrimps, cooked, shelled and deveined

1 cup frozen green peas

Salt to taste

 Preparation time 5 minutes

 Cooking time 30 minutes

SERVING SUGGESTION Serve this pasta dish, bathed in a fragrant, low-kilojoule tomato and shrimp sauce, with steamed broccoli florets and a glass of crisp white wine.

1 In a large saucepan, bring 4 litres of water to the boil. Cook the pasta shells in the boiling water according to the directions on the package or until it is tender but still firm to the bite.

2 Meanwhile, in a large saucepan, heat the oil over moderate heat. Add the garlic and chilli and sauté for 1 minute. Add the tomatoes with their liquid, the wine and basil. Bring to the boil over high heat. Reduce the heat to low, partially cover the saucepan and simmer for 10 minutes.

3 Add the shrimps and peas to the sauce and cook over high heat until both are just heated through. Season with the salt.

4 Drain the pasta and transfer it to a warmed serving dish. Toss the shrimp sauce gently into the pasta and serve immediately.

Start with a Portion of Pasta

Records show that the Chinese were eating pasta some 3500 years ago and murals in Italy show that it is no newcomer to Italian cuisine. It's popularity has stood the test of time and today pasta is still the perfect staple to have on hand for a quick dinner for family or guests. Serve it with one of these tasty sauces, each of which requires only a few ingredients and very little time. When you're choosing which shape of pasta to use, a general rule is that thinner sauces suit longer, finer pastas and thicker sauces are best served with smaller shapes. Estimate about 500g of dried pasta to make four main-course servings.

◄ **Meat sauce** In a large saucepan, heat 1 tablespoon olive oil. Add *500g lean minced beef*, *1 large onion*, chopped, and *2 cloves garlic*, chopped. Cook until the beef is well browned. Pour off any excess fat. Add *one 400g tin chopped tomatoes*, *½ cup red wine* or *beef stock*, *2 tablespoons chopped parsley* and *1 teaspoon dried origanum*. Bring the sauce to the boil. Reduce the heat to low, cover and simmer for 15 minutes. Season with *salt* and *pepper*.

► **Cheese sauce** Using a food processor or electric blender, purée *1 cup ricotta cheese*, *¼ cup grated Parmesan cheese*, *2 cloves garlic* and *¼ cup cream* until smooth. In a large saucepan, heat *2 tablespoons olive oil*. Add *1 small sweet red pepper*, cored, seeded and slivered, and *4 spring onions* chopped into 1cm slices (white and green parts). Sauté for 3 minutes. Add the cheese mixture to the pepper mixture and heat through (do not boil). Season with *salt* and *pepper*.

▼ **Creamy clam sauce** In a large saucepan, heat *2 tablespoons olive oil*. Add *2 spring onions*, chopped, and *3 cloves garlic*, chopped. Sauté for about 3 minutes until the onions are soft. Whisk in *one 227g package cream cheese*, softened, *one 200g tin baby clams*, chopped, and *½ cup dry white wine* or *water*. Cook until heated.

▲ **Olive-marinara sauce** Heat *2 tablespoons olive oil*. Add *1 onion*, sliced, and *2 cloves garlic*, chopped. Sauté for about 3 minutes. Stir in *one 400g tin chopped tomatoes* and *one 115g tin tomato paste*. Add *1 cup red wine*, *½ cup pitted black olives*, halved, and *1 teaspoon dried origanum*. Bring to the boil, reduce heat, cover and simmer for 15 minutes. Add a *pinch of cayenne pepper* and *sugar* to taste.

▼ **Broccoli pesto sauce** Using a food processor or electric blender, finely chop *¼ cup pecan nuts* and *3 cloves garlic*. Add *1 cup olive oil*, *300g frozen chopped broccoli*, thawed, and *1 cup parsley*. Process until fairly smooth. Transfer to a medium-sized bowl. Stir in *½ cup grated Parmesan cheese*. Season the sauce with *salt* and *pepper*.

▲ **Mushroom-baby marrow sauce** Chop *250g mushrooms* into quarters and slice *200g baby marrows* into 5cm x 1cm sticks. In a large frying pan, melt *3 tablespoons (45g) butter*. Sauté baby marrows for 2 minutes. Add the mushrooms and cook until tender. Stir in *1 tablespoon flour*. Stir in *1 cup chicken stock*, *½ cup cream*, *2 tablespoons chopped parsley* and *¼ teaspoon pepper*. Bring sauce to the boil over moderately high heat, stirring constantly.

PASTA AND GRAINS

CREAMY PESTO CHICKEN PASTA *Serves 4*

3 tablespoons (45g) butter or margarine

250g skinless chicken-breast fillets, sliced into strips

2 cloves garlic, chopped

¼ cup flour

⅛ teaspoon ground black pepper

500g fusilli (corkscrew-shaped pasta) or spaghetti

1 cup chicken stock

½ cup milk

1 cup lightly packed chopped parsley

1 cup lightly packed fresh basil (do not use dried)

⅓ cup (40g) grated Parmesan cheese

Additional fresh basil (optional)

 Preparation time 10 minutes

 Cooking time 25 minutes

1. Bring 4 litres of water to the boil in a large pot. Meanwhile, in a large frying pan, melt the butter over moderate heat. Add the chicken-breast fillets and sauté for about 7 minutes until lightly browned. With a slotted spoon, transfer the chicken to a bowl, keeping it warm.

2. Add the garlic to the frying pan and sauté for a few seconds. Stir in the flour and black pepper. Keep stirring and cook until the mixture starts to bubble. Remove the frying pan from the heat. Cook the fusilli or spaghetti in the boiling water according to the instructions on the package or until tender but still firm to the bite.

3. Meanwhile, with a wire whisk, gradually stir the stock into the flour mixture until blended. Gradually stir in the milk. Return the frying pan to moderate heat. Cook the mixture for 2 to 3 minutes until it is thickened, stirring constantly.

4. Purée the sauce in a food processor or electric blender. Add the parsley and basil and continue puréeing the sauce until it turns green, stopping frequently to scrape the sides of the container.

5. Drain the pasta and transfer it to a serving bowl. Add the creamy pesto sauce, the chicken and cheese, and toss gently until it is well mixed. Garnish with additional basil, if desired, and serve immediately.

SHELF MAGIC

These two simple, meatless pasta sauces require no cooking – the heat of the pasta will warm them sufficiently. With 500g of dried, cooked fusilli, penne or spaghetti, you'll have a substantial side dish or a light main course.

ARTICHOKE-OLIVE SAUCE

Drain *one 400g tin artichoke hearts*. Chop the artichokes and place them in a medium-sized bowl. Add *1 tablespoon chopped parsley, 75g pitted and sliced black olives, 2 tablespoons olive oil, salt* and *black pepper*. Mix gently until well combined. Drain the cooked pasta, add it to the sauce and toss until thoroughly coated. Serves 4

BASIL AND PINE-NUT SAUCE

Heat *1 tablespoon olive oil* in a small frying pan. Lightly sauté *2 tablespoons pine nuts*. Drain the cooked pasta and toss it gently with *1 tablespoon (15g) butter* or *margarine, 1 tablespoon chopped fresh basil* or *parsley* and the pine nuts. Sprinkle a little *paprika* over the top of each serving. Serves 4

SPICY SESAME NOODLES WITH CHICKEN

SPICY SESAME NOODLES WITH CHICKEN *Serves 4*

350g dried or 500g fresh linguine

1 tablespoon sesame seeds

2 tablespoons sunflower or peanut oil

250g skinless chicken-breast fillets, thinly sliced

1/3 cup smooth peanut butter

1/2 cup hot water

1 tablespoon soy sauce

1 tablespoon white vinegar

1 tablespoon honey

1 tablespoon Oriental sesame oil

1/4 teaspoon crushed chillies

1 spring onion, sliced diagonally

 Preparation time
4 minutes

 Cooking time
26 minutes

DIET NOTE Dress up linguine with an exotically nutty sauce combining everyday peanut butter with honey, sesame oil and a hint of chilli.

1 Bring 4 litres of water to the boil in a large saucepan. Cook the linguine in the boiling water according to the directions on the package or until it is tender but still firm to the bite.

2 Meanwhile, in a large frying pan, toast the sesame seeds over moderate heat until golden, shaking the pan constantly. Place the seeds in a small bowl and set aside. In the same frying pan, heat the oil. Add the chicken and stir-fry for about 2 to 3 minutes until cooked through. Remove the frying pan from the heat.

3 In a medium-sized bowl, blend the peanut butter and water. Stir in the soy sauce, vinegar, honey, sesame oil and chilli. Drain the pasta and transfer it to a serving bowl.

4 Stir the peanut-butter mixture into the linguine until well mixed. Toss the linguine with the chicken and its juices. Sprinkle with the sesame seeds and spring onion and serve immediately.

PASTA AND GRAINS

CHICKEN CACCIATORE WITH PASTA *Serves 4*

3 tablespoons flour

¼ teaspoon salt

¼ teaspoon ground black pepper

500g skinless chicken-breast fillets, cut into 1cm pieces

3 tablespoons olive oil

1 large onion, sliced

1 tin (410g) Italian-style tomatoes, crushed

½ cup dry red wine

350g dried or 500g fresh fettuccine

1 large sweet green pepper, chopped

 Preparation time
5 minutes

 Cooking time
40 minutes

1. Bring 4 litres of water to the boil in a large saucepan. Meanwhile, in a plastic food-storage bag, combine the flour, salt and pepper. Add the chicken pieces and shake to coat with the flour mixture.

2. In a large frying pan, heat the oil over moderate heat. Add the chicken and sauté for about 5 minutes until browned on all sides.

3. Stir the onion into the chicken. Cook for about 3 minutes until the onion is slightly soft. Stir the tomatoes and wine into the chicken mixture. Increase the heat to high and bring the mixture to the boil. Reduce the heat to low, cover the frying pan and simmer for 15 minutes, stirring occasionally.

4. Meanwhile, cook the fettuccine according to the directions on the package or until tender but still firm to the bite.

5. Add the green pepper to the chicken and continue cooking for approximately 5 more minutes until the chicken is tender when pierced with a fork. Drain the pasta thoroughly and transfer it to a serving bowl. Pour the chicken and sauce over the pasta. Serve immediately.

SPAGHETTI WITH BACON AND VEGETABLES *Serves 4 (COVER PICTURE)*

250g sliced lean bacon, cut into 5cm lengths

500g spaghetti

3 tablespoons sunflower oil

1 sweet red pepper, cored, seeded and cut into strips

1 sweet green pepper, cored, seeded and cut into strips

1 small brinjal, unpeeled, quartered lengthwise then sliced

½ cup (60g) grated Parmesan cheese

½ cup cream

Salt and pepper to taste

 Preparation time
10 minutes

 Cooking time
24 minutes

1. In a large saucepan, bring 4 litres of water to the boil. Meanwhile, in a large frying pan (preferably with nonstick coating), cook the bacon over moderate heat until lightly browned and crisp.

2. Remove the bacon and drain it on paper towels. Discard the bacon fat. Using paper towels, clean the frying pan.

3. Cook the spaghetti according to the directions on the package or until it is tender but still firm to the bite.

4. Meanwhile, in the frying pan, heat 2 tablespoons of the oil over moderate heat. Add the red and green peppers and brinjal. Sauté for about 5 minutes until softened. (Add 1 more tablespoon of oil if necessary.)

5. Drain the pasta and return it to the saucepan. Stir in the cheese and cream. Season with the salt and pepper. Transfer the spaghetti to a serving bowl. Top with the vegetables and the bacon. Toss gently and serve immediately.

HAM AND SPINACH-FETTUCCINE ALFREDO

Ham and spinach-fettuccine Alfredo *Serves 4*

500g dried or 625g fresh spinach fettuccine

2 tablespoons (30g) butter or margarine

250g smoked ham, sliced into strips

2 tablespoons flour

1 3/4 cups milk

3/4 cup cream

1/2 cup (60g) grated Parmesan cheese

Salt and ground white pepper to taste

Additional grated Parmesan cheese (optional)

 Preparation time 4 minutes

 Cooking time 26 minutes

Serving suggestion When you want a pasta splurge, this is it. Serve with a salad of radicchio or red oak leaf lettuce and feta cheese tossed with chives and a vinaigrette dressing.

1. Bring 4 litres of water to the boil in a large saucepan. Cook the fettuccine in the boiling water according to the instructions on the package or until it is tender but still firm to the bite.

2. Meanwhile, in a large frying pan, melt the butter over moderate heat. Sauté the ham for about 2 to 3 minutes until lightly browned. Stir in the flour until well mixed. Gradually stir in the milk until well blended. Bring to the boil, stirring constantly. Reduce the heat to low and stir in the cream. Heat the sauce for about 1 minute until just hot (do not boil). Add the cheese and mix until smooth. Season the sauce with salt and pepper.

3. Drain the pasta and transfer it to a serving dish. Top with the ham sauce and additional Parmesan cheese, if desired, and toss gently. Serve immediately.

PASTA AND GRAINS

THAI PORK AND NOODLES *Serves 4*

250g 1cm-thick boneless pork sirloin cutlets

2 tablespoons soy sauce

3 cloves garlic, finely chopped

1 teaspoon finely chopped fresh ginger (or ¼ teaspoon ground ginger)

Pinch of cayenne pepper

350g dried or 500g fresh linguine

2 medium carrots, peeled and sliced

2 tablespoons sunflower oil

2 large eggs, beaten

250g bean sprouts

1 tablespoon chopped coriander leaves (or chopped parsley)

 Preparation time
10 minutes

 Cooking time
26 minutes

SERVING SUGGESTION End this Asian-inspired meal with slices of tart star fruit and juicy oranges.

1 In a large saucepan, bring 4 litres of water to the boil. Meanwhile, trim the fat from the pork. Slice the pork into 6mm-wide strips. In a medium-sized bowl, combine the pork, soy sauce, garlic, ginger and cayenne pepper. Leave to stand for 20 minutes to marinate.

2 Cook the linguine and carrots together in the boiling water for 9 to 11 minutes until crisp-tender. (If using fresh linguine, cook the carrots for 4 minutes before adding the pasta.)

3 In a large frying pan, heat 1 tablespoon of the oil over moderate heat. Pour the eggs into the pan and fry until the underside is set, then turn them over and cook the other side. Transfer the eggs to a plate and cut them into 1cm strips. Set aside.

4 In the same frying pan, heat the remaining oil over high heat. Add the pork strips and stir-fry for 3 to 4 minutes until they are lightly browned. Add the bean sprouts and cook for about 1 more minute until they are slightly softened.

5 Drain the linguine and carrots. Transfer them to a serving bowl. Add the pork mixture, the egg and coriander leaves. Toss gently and serve immediately.

ZITI AL FORNO *Serves 4*

350g ziti or other short tubular pasta

125g pepper salami

125g Fontina or mozzarella cheese, sliced

2 cups ready-made spaghetti sauce (or Italian-style tomatoes, crushed)

¼ cup (30g) grated Parmesan cheese

2 tablespoons sliced black olives

 Preparation time
5 minutes

 Cooking time
38 minutes

1 Preheat the oven to 200°C. In a large saucepan, bring 4 litres of water to the boil. Partially cook the ziti in the boiling water for half the time recommended on the package.

2 Meanwhile, lightly grease 4 small individual oval baking dishes or one 30cm x 20cm shallow baking dish. Cut the salami into 1cm cubes and the Fontina cheese slices into narrow strips.

3 Drain the pasta and return it to the saucepan. Add the spaghetti sauce and the salami to the ziti and toss gently. Divide the ziti among the prepared small baking dishes or place it in the large baking dish. Top with the Fontina and Parmesan cheeses.

4 Bake for 15 to 20 minutes until the cheese is melted and golden. Garnish with the sliced olives and serve.

PASTA AND GRAINS

SPAGHETTI TUSCAN STYLE Serves 4

250g mild Italian sausage (available from Italian delicatessens)

1 small onion, finely chopped

2½ cups ready-made spaghetti sauce, or Italian-style tomatoes, crushed

1 teaspoon dried origanum

350g spaghetti

1 tablespoon (15g) butter or margarine

250g baby spinach leaves

1 tablespoon milk

⅓ cup (40g) grated Parmesan cheese

Preparation time 10 minutes

Cooking time 25 minutes

SERVING SUGGESTION A basket of bread and some extra Parmesan cheese are the only accompaniments needed to enjoy this hearty pasta dish.

1 Bring 4 litres of water to the boil in a large saucepan. Meanwhile, remove the casing from the sausage and, in a large frying pan (preferably with nonstick coating), cook the sausage over moderate heat until well browned, stirring occasionally. Drain off the excess fat. Stir in the onion and cook for 2 minutes.

2 Increase the heat to high, add the spaghetti sauce and origanum to the sausage and onion mixture and bring it to the boil. Reduce the heat to low, cover the saucepan and simmer the sauce for 15 minutes.

3 Cook the spaghetti in the boiling water according to the directions on the package or until tender but still firm to the bite.

4 Meanwhile, in a medium-sized saucepan, melt the butter over moderate heat. Add the spinach, cover and cook for about 2 minutes until it is softened, stirring occasionally. Remove the saucepan from the heat. Stir in the milk and half of the cheese.

5 Drain the pasta and transfer it to a serving bowl. Cover it first with the sausage sauce, then with the spinach mixture. Sprinkle with the remaining cheese. Serve immediately.

SHELF MAGIC

With a tin or two of Italian-style tomatoes in the cupboard and a few extra simple ingredients, the possibilities for a delicious pasta sauce are endless. Cook 500g of dried spaghetti or penne while you're making the sauce.

SPICY TOMATO-BACON SAUCE

Crush the contents of *2 tins of Italian-style tomatoes* in a medium-sized saucepan and heat. Meanwhile, slice *125g lean bacon* into short strips. In a small frying pan, heat *1 teaspoon olive oil* and sauté the bacon. Add the bacon and *½ teaspoon crushed chillies* to the sauce. Serve over *cooked pasta*. Serves 4

BABY MARROW-TOMATO SAUCE

In a medium-sized saucepan, crush the contents of *2 tins of Italian-style tomatoes* and heat. Meanwhile, slice *125g baby marrows* and finely chop *1 small onion*. In a small frying pan, heat *1 tablespoon olive oil* and sauté the baby marrows and onion. Add the mixture to the sauce. Serve over *cooked pasta*. Serves 4

PASTA AND GRAINS

PENNE WITH SHRIMPS AND PEPPERS *Serves 4*

500g penne (quill-shaped pasta)

250g baby marrows

2 tablespoons olive oil

300g large uncooked, shelled and deveined shrimps (thawed if frozen)

1 clove garlic, finely chopped

1 large sweet red pepper, coarsely chopped

2 tablespoons chopped fresh basil (or 2 teaspoons dried basil)

Salt and ground black pepper to taste

1/3 cup (40g) grated Parmesan cheese

Additional basil sprigs (optional)

 Preparation time 10 minutes

 Cooking time 30 minutes

COVER RECIPE This light, pretty main-dish pasta is perfectly partnered by the classic accompaniments – mixed salad and a loaf of crispy French bread.

1 Bring 4 litres of water to the boil in a large pot. Cook the penne in the boiling water according to the package directions or until tender but still firm to the bite.

2 Meanwhile, slice the baby marrows in half lengthwise, then chop them roughly crosswise.

3 Heat the oil in a large frying pan. Sauté the shrimps for 3 to 5 minutes until they turn pink. Add the garlic and red pepper to the frying pan. Cook for approximately 3 minutes until the pepper is softened. Add the baby marrows and basil. Cook for about 3 more minutes until the baby marrows are tender.

4 Drain the pasta and transfer it to a warmed serving platter. Add the shrimp mixture, season with the salt and pepper and toss gently. Sprinkle with the Parmesan cheese, garnish with basil sprigs, if desired, and serve.

CHILLI SPAGHETTI *Serves 6*

1 tablespoon sunflower oil

1 medium onion, chopped

1 small sweet green pepper, halved, cored and diced

500g lean minced beef

2 tablespoons chilli powder or to taste

1/2 teaspoon ground cumin

2 tins (410g each) Italian-style tomatoes, crushed

1 tin (425g) red kidney beans, drained

Salt to taste

350g spaghetti

Additional chopped onion and sweet green pepper (optional)

Grated Cheddar cheese (optional)

 Preparation time 5 minutes

 Cooking time 40 minutes

1 Bring 4 litres of water to the boil in a large pot. Meanwhile, in a large frying pan, heat the oil over moderate heat. Sauté the onion and green pepper for 5 minutes. Stir in the minced beef and cook for about 3 minutes until browned. Add the chilli powder and cumin, stir until well mixed and cook for 1 more minute.

2 Add the tomatoes to the meat mixture and bring to the boil over high heat. Reduce the heat to low, cover and simmer the sauce for 15 minutes. Add the kidney beans and simmer for a further 5 minutes. Season the sauce with salt.

3 Meanwhile, cook the pasta in the boiling water according to the directions on the package or until tender but still firm to the bite.

4 Drain the pasta thoroughly and transfer it to individual serving plates. Pour an equal amount of the chilli sauce over each serving and garnish with additional onion, green pepper and cheese, if desired. Serve immediately.

LASAGNE-STYLE BOW-TIE PASTA

Lasagne-style bow-tie pasta *Serves 4*

250g farfalle (bow-tie-shaped pasta)

1 tablespoon sunflower oil

1 small onion, chopped

250g lean minced beef

1 bottle (475g) ready-made tomato spaghetti sauce

1 cup soft ricotta or low-fat cottage cheese

1 large egg

⅓ cup (40g) grated Parmesan cheese

1 cup (125g) grated mozzarella cheese

 Preparation time
7 minutes

 Cooking time
38 minutes

FOOD NOTE Enjoy the earthy flavours of lasagne in only a fraction of the time it takes to create the traditional version.

1. Preheat the oven to 220°C. Grease a 20cm square baking dish. Bring 4 litres of water to the boil in a large pot. Partially cook the farfalle in the boiling water for half the time given in the directions on the package.

2. Meanwhile, in a large frying pan, heat the oil over moderate heat. Add the onion and sauté for 1 minute. Stir in the minced beef and sauté for about 3 minutes until it is lightly browned. Add the spaghetti sauce and bring to the boil. Reduce the heat to low, partially cover the pan and simmer the sauce for 5 minutes.

3. In a small bowl, combine the ricotta cheese, egg and Parmesan cheese. Drain the pasta and place half of it in the baking dish. Spoon the cheese mixture over the pasta, top with half of the meat sauce and sprinkle with half of the mozzarella cheese. Layer the remaining pasta, sauce and mozzarella.

4. Cover with aluminium foil and bake for 15 minutes. Uncover the dish and bake for a further 5 to 8 minutes until heated through. Serve immediately.

GRAINS

Grains have sustained human life for thousands of years and today they make up a large and delicious part of many meals across the world.

CRUNCHY GRANOLA *Serves 10*

4 tablespoons (60g) butter or margarine

¼ cup honey

1 teaspoon ground cinnamon

2 cups rolled oats

2 cups wheat cereal squares (eg Weeties, Shreddies or 4 Weetbix broken into small chunks)

1 cup shelled sunflower seeds

⅔ cup raisins

 Preparation time 5 minutes

 Cooking time 25 minutes

SERVING SUGGESTION Served with milk or yoghurt and followed with a glass of orange juice, this healthy cereal makes a delicious special occasion breakfast. For a quick dessert, serve it over ice cream.

1. Preheat the oven to 180°C. In a small saucepan, melt the butter over moderate heat. Stir in the honey and cinnamon and set the mixture aside.

2. Line a large Swiss roll or roasting tin with aluminium foil. Coat the foil with nonstick vegetable spray. In a large bowl, carefully toss the oats, cereal squares and sunflower seeds with the honey mixture. Spread the mixture into the prepared tin.

3. Bake the granola, stirring it several times during baking, for about 25 minutes until it is golden and dry. Remove the granola from the oven, stir in the raisins and leave to cool before serving or placing in a storage container.

FRUITY THREE-GRAIN CEREAL *Serves 4*

2 cups water

1 cup apple juice

1 cup rolled oats

½ cup yellow maize (mealie) meal

¼ cup wheat germ

½ cup coarsely chopped dried apple

½ teaspoon ground cinnamon

1 to 1½ cups skimmed milk

Brown sugar to taste

 Preparation time 5 minutes

 Cooking time 12 minutes

DIET NOTE Protein-rich oats also contain polyunsaturated fats and soluble fibre, which slows down the body's absorption of sugars. Here they combine with apple juice and maize meal for a hearty breakfast.

1. In a large saucepan, mix the water, apple juice, oats, maize meal, wheat germ, dried apple and cinnamon. Bring the mixture to the boil, stirring constantly. Reduce the heat, cover and cook for 5 minutes, stirring occasionally. (The cereal should be the consistency of stiff mashed potatoes. If it is too stiff, stir in more water or juice.)

2. Add 1 cup of the milk to the cereal and stir until it reaches a creamy consistency, adding more milk if necessary. Spoon into serving bowls, sprinkle with brown sugar to taste and serve.

PASTA AND GRAINS

RICE PILAFF *Serves 6*

2 tablespoons (30g) butter or margarine

½ cup (60g) vermicelli or spaghettini (very thin spaghetti), broken into small pieces

1 small onion, chopped

1 cup long-grain white rice

3 cups chicken stock

1 tablespoon sunflower oil

2 tablespoons pine nuts

1 small sweet red pepper, cored, seeded and sliced into strips

 Preparation time
8 minutes

 Cooking time
30 minutes

1. In a medium-sized saucepan, melt the butter over moderate heat. Add the vermicelli and sauté, stirring constantly, for about 2 minutes until it is lightly browned. Stir in the onion and rice and sauté for 1 minute. Add the stock and bring the mixture to the boil over moderately high heat.

2. Reduce the heat to low, cover and simmer the mixture for about 20 minutes until the rice is tender and the liquid is absorbed.

3. Meanwhile, in a small frying pan, heat the oil over moderate heat. Add the pine nuts and sauté until golden. Using a slotted spoon, remove the nuts and set aside. Add the red pepper to the frying pan and sauté for about 3 minutes until it is tender but still firm to the bite. Remove the frying pan from the heat.

4. With a fork, toss the rice mixture with the red pepper. Spoon into a warmed serving dish, sprinkle with the pine nuts and serve.

HAM FRIED RICE *Serves 6*

1 tablespoon (15g) butter or margarine

1⅔ cups water

1 cup long-grain white rice

3 tablespoons sunflower oil

2 large eggs, beaten

125g cooked ham, cubed

1 small onion, chopped

1 cup frozen green peas, thawed under warm running water

1 tablespoon soy sauce

1 tablespoon Oriental sesame oil

 Preparation time
5 minutes

 Cooking time
28 minutes

1. In a medium-sized saucepan, bring the butter and water to the boil over high heat. Stir in the rice. Reduce the heat to moderately low, partially cover the saucepan and simmer for about 5 minutes until most of the liquid is absorbed. Stir the rice with a fork. Reduce the heat to low, cover and continue cooking for about 15 minutes until the rice is tender and the liquid is absorbed.

2. Meanwhile, in a large frying pan, heat 1 tablespoon of the sunflower oil over moderately high heat, swirling the pan to coat evenly. Add the eggs to the frying pan and fry until they are set, turning them once with a spatula. Transfer the cooked eggs to a plate and cut them into 5cm x 1cm strips. Set the eggs aside.

3. In the same frying pan, heat another 1 tablespoon of the sunflower oil. Add the ham cubes and cook until they are lightly browned. Transfer to the plate with the eggs and set aside.

4. Heat the remaining 1 tablespoon of sunflower oil in the frying pan. Add the onion and stir-fry for 1 minute. Stir in the peas, cover and cook for 2 to 3 minutes until the peas are tender. Gently stir in the rice, eggs, ham, soy sauce and sesame oil. Cook until heated through. Serve immediately.

FESTIVE MEXICAN RICE

FESTIVE MEXICAN RICE *Serves 4*

2 tablespoons sunflower oil

1 cup long-grain white rice

1 small onion, chopped

2 cloves garlic, chopped

1 cup tinned or fresh tomatoes, peeled and chopped

1¼ cups chicken stock

1 large carrot, cut into short strips

1 fresh green chilli, chopped

½ cup frozen green peas

 Preparation time
5 minutes

 Cooking time
22 minutes

SERVING SUGGESTION Dress up rice with a vibrant combination of tomatoes, carrots, chilli and peas. Served with flour tortillas, the dish will soon become a firm family favourite.

1 In a large frying pan, heat the oil over moderately high heat. Add the rice and sauté for about 3 minutes until it is golden, stirring constantly. Add the onion and cook for 2 minutes, stirring occasionally. Stir in the garlic and tomatoes with their juice until well mixed. Add the stock, carrot and chilli, increase the heat to high and bring to the boil. Reduce the heat to low, cover and simmer for 10 minutes.

2 Add the peas, cover and cook for a further 5 minutes until the rice is tender and the liquid is absorbed. Serve immediately.

PASTA AND GRAINS

JAMBALAYA *Serves 4*

2 tablespoons sunflower oil

250g large, uncooked, peeled and deveined shrimps, thawed if frozen

1 large onion, chopped

1 small sweet green pepper, cored, deseeded and chopped

1 medium stalk celery, chopped

1 clove garlic, crushed

250g smoked pork sausage, thinly sliced

1 cup long-grain white rice

1½ cups chicken stock

1 tin (410g) whole, peeled tomatoes, drained and chopped

1 teaspoon dried thyme

½ teaspoon Tabasco sauce

1 bay leaf

Salt and ground black pepper to taste

 Preparation time
15 minutes

 Cooking time
34 minutes

FOOD NOTE This traditional New Orleans fish and rice dish is a meal in itself. A culinary cousin of the Spanish paella, jambalaya was adapted by Creole cooks making use of their local ingredients.

1. In a large saucepan, heat the oil over moderate heat. Add the shrimps and sauté for about 1 minute until they are firm and pink. Using a slotted spoon, remove the shrimps from the saucepan and set them aside.

2. Add the onion, green pepper, celery, garlic and sausage to the saucepan. Cook, stirring frequently, for 2 minutes. Add the rice and stir to coat.

3. Stir the stock, tomatoes, thyme, Tabasco sauce and bay leaf into the mixture. Increase the heat to high and bring the mixture to the boil. Reduce the heat to low, cover the saucepan and simmer for about 20 minutes until the rice is almost tender and the liquid is absorbed.

4. With a fork, stir the shrimps into the rice mixture. Cover and simmer gently for 5 more minutes, stirring occasionally, until the shrimps are reheated. Discard the bay leaf and season the jambalaya with salt and pepper. Transfer it to a warmed serving bowl and serve immediately.

TIME SAVERS

RICE

- Add a delicious, nutty flavour to plain long-grain white rice by browning it in a frying pan (without oil) over moderate heat. Once it is toasted, cook the rice as directed on the package.
- Another quick way of adding extra flavour to plain white rice is to simmer the rice in chicken or beef stock or a combination of stock and water, rather than using water alone.
- Save time on meals by cooking rice dishes a couple of days before you need them. Many grain dishes (excluding risotto) can be cooked in advance and frozen, then thawed and gently reheated.
- For a perfect risotto, be sure to use short-grain rice such as the Italian arborio. Do not rinse the rice – the starch that coats each grain is essential for making the rice creamy.
- Remember to use a large enough saucepan when cooking rice – it swells to three or four times its size during the cooking process.
- Prevent the grains of white rice from sticking together by adding a tablespoon of oil or butter to the water before cooking.
- Rice cooks best in a heavy-based saucepan – the bottom layer is less likely to scorch and it makes cleaning much easier.

Paella

Paella *Serves 4*

2 tablespoons olive oil

4 large (about 750g) chicken thighs

1 medium sweet green pepper

1 small onion, chopped

2 cloves garlic, chopped

1 cup long-grain white rice

1 teaspoon turmeric

$1/8$ teaspoon saffron threads (optional)

1 cup tinned tomato and onion mixture

$1^{1}/_{2}$ cups water

250g cooked smoked pork sausage (eg kielbasa or chorizo), sliced

Salt and ground black pepper to taste

Parsley sprigs

 Preparation time 5 minutes

 Cooking time 40 minutes

Cook's tip Emphasize the Spanish flavour of this paella by adding three or four tablespoons of red wine during the last minutes of cooking. Use a broad shallow pan to ensure that all the liquid evaporates.

1 In a 25cm heavy-based frying pan (preferably with nonstick coating), heat the oil over moderately high heat. Add the chicken thighs and sauté for about 10 minutes until browned all over.

2 Meanwhile, slice the green pepper into 1cm wide strips. When the chicken is browned, remove it from the pan and set aside. Add the green pepper to the pan and sauté for 1 minute. Using a slotted spoon, remove the pepper and set aside. Add the onion, garlic and rice to the pan and sauté for 5 minutes. Stir in the turmeric and saffron, if desired. Add the tomato and onion mixture and the water, increase the heat to high and bring to the boil. Continue boiling for 2 minutes, stirring occasionally.

3 Place the chicken on the rice. Reduce the heat, cover and simmer for 15 minutes until the chicken and rice are almost tender. Add the sausage and green pepper. Cook for 5 more minutes until the rice is tender and the sausage is heated through. Season the paella with salt and pepper, garnish with the parsley and serve.

PASTA AND GRAINS

VEGETABLE CASSEROLE WITH COUSCOUS Serves 6

2 tablespoons olive oil

1 large onion, chopped

2 cups vegetable stock

2 large (about 500g) sweet potatoes, peeled and cut into 2,5cm cubes

200g baby marrows, thickly sliced

1 cup tinned chickpeas, drained

⅓ cup raisins

2 cloves garlic, chopped

2½ cups water

1 tablespoon (15g) butter or margarine

1½ cups (300g) quick-cooking couscous

1 cup tinned tomato and onion mixture

Salt and ground black pepper to taste

 Preparation time 13 minutes

 Cooking time 27 minutes

FOOD NOTE This North African speciality originated with the Berbers – who steamed it in a traditional pot over a stew, where it could best absorb the flavour of the spices. Serve, garnished with fresh coriander leaves, as the perfect accompaniment for a spicy lamb or chicken dish.

1 In a large saucepan, heat the oil over moderate heat. Add the onion and sauté for about 5 minutes until soft. Stir in the stock, sweet potatoes, baby marrows, chickpeas, raisins and garlic. Raise the heat to high and bring to the boil. Reduce the heat, cover and simmer for about 10 minutes until the potatoes are just tender when pricked with a fork.

2 Meanwhile, in a medium-sized saucepan, bring the water and butter to the boil. Add the couscous and boil for 1 minute, stirring frequently. Remove the saucepan from the heat, cover it tightly and leave to stand for 5 to 10 minutes until all of the water is absorbed. Stir the tomato and onion mixture into the vegetables and simmer for 5 more minutes. Season the vegetables with salt and pepper.

3 Fluff the couscous with a fork and spoon it into the centre of a shallow serving dish. Arrange the vegetables around the couscous to form a border and serve immediately.

NUTTY GROATS PILAFF Serves 4

2 tablespoons (30g) butter or margarine

1 large onion, chopped

2 medium stalks celery, sliced

1 large egg

1 cup groats

2 cups water

1 teaspoon dried sage

1 teaspoon dried thyme

1 cup raisins

½ cup coarsely chopped walnuts

Salt to taste

 Preparation time 5 minutes

 Cooking time 27 minutes

1 In a large frying pan, melt the butter over moderate heat. Add the onion and celery. Sauté for about 3 minutes until the vegetables begin to soften.

2 In a small bowl, mix the egg with the groats. Add the mixture to the vegetables in the frying pan and cook the groats for 1 minute, stirring constantly, until the grains are dry and separated.

3 Add the water, sage and thyme to the mixture. Increase the heat to high and bring to the boil. Reduce the heat to low, cover and cook for 10 to 15 minutes until the groats are almost tender.

4 Stir the raisins and walnuts into the groats mixture. Continue cooking for about 5 more minutes or until the groats are tender and all the liquid is absorbed. Season with salt and serve immediately.

◂ VEGETABLE CASSEROLE WITH COUSCOUS

PASTA AND GRAINS

POLENTA WITH FONTINA CHEESE SAUCE *Serves 4*

1½ cups (180g) coarsely grated Fontina cheese

½ cup milk

4½ cups water

1½ cups yellow maize (mealie) meal

2 tablespoons (30g) butter or margarine

3 large egg yolks

Pinch of ground white pepper

Thinly sliced mushrooms (optional)

 Preparation time 5 minutes

 Cooking time 25 minutes

FOOD NOTE Polenta – a smooth, warming maize meal mixture – is a northern Italian classic that comes in many guises. Combined as it is here with Fontina cheese, it creates what the Italians call fonduta. *It makes a nourishing vegetarian dish.*

1. Mix the cheese and milk together in a medium-sized bowl and set the mixture aside. To make the polenta, in a medium-sized saucepan, bring 3½ cups of the water to the boil. In a small bowl, combine the remaining 1 cup of water and the maize meal. Add the maize meal mixture to the boiling water and cook, stirring constantly, for about 5 minutes until thickened.

2. Reduce the heat to low, cover and continue cooking the maize meal for 5 more minutes. Remove the saucepan from the heat and set it aside, keeping the mixture warm.

3. Meanwhile, partially fill the lower part of a double boiler with water and bring it to the boil. Reduce the heat to very low. In the upper part of the double boiler, melt the butter over hot, not simmering, water. Add the cheese mixture and stir until the cheese melts. Add the egg yolks and continue stirring until the mixture is smooth. Stir in the white pepper.

4. Spoon the polenta to form individual mounds on warmed serving plates. Using the back of a spoon, make an indentation in each mound. Pour an equal amount of the cheese sauce into each indentation. Garnish each serving with some of the mushrooms, if desired, and serve.

SHELF MAGIC

Brighten your meals with these tasty side dishes using quick-cooking rice.

ORANGE RICE

Cook *one packet quick-cooking rice* according to the instructions on the package for 9 to 10 minutes. In a medium-sized saucepan, combine *½ cup orange juice, 1 tablespoon (15g) butter* or *margarine* and *1 teaspoon grated orange peel*. Bring to the boil and simmer gently for 5 minutes. Stir in the cooked rice and *½ cup chopped pecan nuts*. Serves 4

CURRIED RICE

Cook *one packet quick-cooking rice* according to the directions on the package for 9 to 10 minutes. In a medium-sized saucepan, combine *½ cup chicken stock, ⅓ cup raisins, 1 tablespoon curry powder* and *1 tablespoon (15g) butter*. Bring to the boil and leave to stand for 5 minutes. Stir in the cooked rice and *⅓ cup chopped peanuts*. Serves 4

POLENTA PIZZA

POLENTA PIZZA *Serves 4*

3 cups water

1½ cups yellow maize (mealie) meal

¼ teaspoon salt

2 tablespoons olive oil

1 medium onion, sliced

1 cup (about 125g) sliced mushrooms

1 cup ready-made tomato pasta sauce

125g thinly sliced pepper salami

¼ cup sliced black olives

1 cup (125g) grated mozzarella cheese

 Preparation time 10 minutes

 Cooking time 38 minutes

SERVING SUGGESTION Serve a simple leafy salad with this easy variation on the much-loved pizza – a maize meal base superbly topped with traditional Italian ingredients.

1. Preheat the oven to 200°C. Lightly grease a 30cm pizza tin or large baking sheet. To make the polenta base: In a medium-sized saucepan, bring 1½ cups of the water to the boil. Meanwhile, combine the remaining 1½ cups of water, the maize meal and salt in a medium-sized bowl. Using a wire whisk, stir the maize meal mixture into the boiling water and cook, stirring occasionally, for about 2 minutes until it thickens. Spread it in an even layer on the pizza tin, or form a 30cm circle on the baking sheet, making a slight rim around the edge. Bake for 15 minutes.

2. In a large frying pan, heat the oil over moderate heat. Add the onion and sauté for 3 minutes. Add the mushrooms and sauté for 3 minutes until softened. Remove from the heat.

3. Remove the base from the oven and spread it with the pasta sauce. Arrange the onions, mushrooms, salami and olives over the sauce. Sprinkle with the cheese. Bake for about 15 minutes until the topping is bubbly. Cut into wedges and serve at once.

PASTA AND GRAINS

Vegetable risotto Serves 4

2 cups chicken stock

2 cups water

2 tablespoons (30g) butter or margarine

1 tablespoon olive oil

1 small onion, finely chopped

1 clove garlic, finely chopped

1½ cups arborio or other short-grain white rice

125g baby marrows, sliced

1 cup (125g) small broccoli florets

½ cup frozen green peas, thawed under warm running water

⅓ cup (40g) grated Parmesan cheese

Additional grated Parmesan cheese (optional)

 Preparation time
8 minutes

 Cooking time
22 minutes

COOK'S TIP To produce a classic, creamy Italian risotto, add the stock and water mixture to the rice in small amounts, stirring frequently. Use any vegetables in season, as long as they are chopped into small pieces.

1 In a medium-sized saucepan, bring the stock and water to the boil over moderate heat. Meanwhile, in a large saucepan, melt the butter and oil over moderate heat. Add the onion and garlic to the butter and sauté for 1 minute. Add the rice to the onion mixture and cook, stirring constantly, for 2 minutes.

2 Add 2 cups of the hot stock and water to the rice mixture, ½ cup at a time, stirring frequently. Allow all of the stock to be absorbed before adding more.

3 Add the baby marrows, broccoli and 1 more cup of the stock and water. Cook for 5 more minutes, uncovered, stirring occasionally. Continue to add the stock and water until the mixture is creamy and the rice is cooked but still firm to the bite. (Not all of the stock may be needed.) Stir the peas and cheese into the rice mixture and continue cooking for about 1 minute until the peas are heated through. Serve the risotto immediately, passing additional Parmesan cheese separately, if desired.

Cheese-topped barley with mushrooms Serves 4

3 cups water

1 cup pearl barley

½ teaspoon salt

2 tablespoons (30g) butter or margarine

1 medium onion, sliced

2 cups (about 250g) halved small mushrooms

1 clove garlic, chopped

1 bay leaf

2 cups chicken stock

¼ cup (30g) coarsely grated Cheddar cheese

1 spring onion, finely chopped

 Preparation time
6 minutes

 Cooking time
45 minutes

FOOD NOTE Barley is high in B vitamins and soluble fibre and is commonly used in South Africa to make soups. Try it topped with cheese as a tasty alternative to rice or potatoes.

1 In a large saucepan, add the barley and the salt to the water, bring to the boil and simmer, covered, for about 30 minutes. Remove from the heat. Meanwhile, in a second saucepan, melt the butter. Sauté the onion gently for about 3 minutes until softened. Add the mushrooms, garlic and bay leaf and sauté for 2 more minutes until the mushrooms are softened.

2 Add the stock and barley. Increase the heat to high and bring to the boil. Reduce the heat, cover and simmer for about 10 minutes until the barley is tender and the liquid is absorbed. Discard the bay leaf. Spoon into a warmed serving dish, top with the cheese and onion and serve immediately.

Eggs and Cheese

Baked eggs Florentine (page 257)

EGGS AND CHEESE

Brimming with proteins, minerals and vitamins, eggs and cheese are universally popular in the everyday diet. Choose one of our easy-to-prepare dishes for a light, nutritious meal.

CORN SOUFFLÉ-STUFFED PEPPERS *Serves 4*

4 large (about 250g each) flat-bottomed red or green sweet peppers

²⁄₃ cup milk

²⁄₃ cup yellow maize (mealie) meal

¼ cup water

1 tablespoon (15g) butter or margarine

¼ teaspoon salt

Pinch of ground black pepper

4 large eggs, separated, at room temperature

½ cup tinned corn kernels (or frozen corn kernels, thawed)

1 tablespoon chopped spring onion top (green part only)

 Preparation time 15 minutes

 Cooking time 30 minutes

SERVING SUGGESTION *Serve this colourful meal in a sweet pepper 'cup' with a green salad and lightly sautéed baby marrow slivers.*

1. Preheat the oven to 200°C and grease a 23cm round baking dish. Slice the tops off the peppers and reserve. Core and seed the pepper cups. Stand the peppers upright in the prepared dish (trim a thin slice off the bottom of any peppers that will not stand erect). Place the reserved tops in the dish alongside the cups.

2. In a medium-sized saucepan, heat the milk over moderate heat until almost boiling. Meanwhile, mix the maize meal with the water in a small bowl until well blended and stir it into the hot milk. Cook the mixture for about 2 minutes until thickened, stirring constantly. Stir in the butter, salt and black pepper. Remove the saucepan from the heat and beat in the egg yolks, corn kernels and spring onion.

3. In a medium-sized bowl, beat the egg whites with an electric mixer until they are stiff but not dry. Stir a heaped spoonful of the egg whites into the maize meal mixture. Fold the maize meal mixture into the remaining egg whites. Spoon an equal amount into each pepper. Bake for 25 to 30 minutes until they are puffed and golden brown. Serve each stuffed pepper with its lid.

TIME SAVERS

EGG WHITES

- To get the greatest volume from beaten egg whites, use eggs that have been brought to room temperature. If you have forgotten to remove them from the refrigerator, place them in warm water for a few minutes before beating. A small pinch of salt added when you begin beating will help the whites to stiffen.
- Use a beaten egg white to glaze pastries. Paint the egg white onto uncooked pastry before baking to prevent the moisture in the filling from penetrating the dough. This also gives a professional sheen to the baked pastry.
- Folding in egg whites is easier if you first stir a quarter of the whites into the mixture to lighten it. Add the remaining whites with a rubber spatula.

SPANISH POTATO OMELETTE *Serves 6*

6 tablespoons olive oil

4 large (about 1kg) potatoes, peeled and thinly sliced

1 large onion, thinly sliced

½ cup water

½ teaspoon salt

1 clove garlic

1 tin (410g) chopped tomatoes, drained

½ cup chicken stock

⅛ teaspoon saffron threads, crumbled

6 large eggs

 Preparation time
20 minutes

 Cooking time
28 minutes

1. Heat 4 tablespoons of the oil in a large frying pan or heavy-based saucepan over low heat. Add the potatoes and onion, stirring carefully to coat them with the oil. Add the water and salt. Cover and cook, stirring occasionally, for about 15 minutes until the potatoes are tender but not browned.

2. Meanwhile, prepare the sauce: Heat 1 tablespoon of the oil in a medium-sized saucepan over moderately high heat. Add the garlic and sauté for 15 seconds. Stir in the tomatoes, stock and saffron, cover and bring to the boil. Reduce the heat to low and simmer for 15 minutes. If desired, press the sauce through a strainer into a bowl to extract the pulp and to remove the seeds.

3. Beat the eggs in a large bowl. Stir the cooked potato mixture into the eggs. In a 25cm frying pan or omelette pan (preferably with nonstick coating), heat the remaining 1 tablespoon of oil over moderately low heat. Add the egg mixture, tilting the pan to spread evenly. Cover and cook for about 8 minutes until the underside of the eggs begins to brown and the top begins to set. Place a greased baking sheet upside-down over the pan and carefully invert the omelette onto the baking sheet. Slide the omelette, upside-down, back into the frying pan and continue cooking for about 3 minutes until it is browned on the other side.

4. Transfer the omelette to a platter and slice it into wedges. Serve the omelette immediately, passing the sauce separately.

MIXED VEGETABLE EGG SCRAMBLE *Serves 4*

2 tablespoons (30g) butter or margarine

100g baby marrows, quartered lengthwise and sliced

1 medium carrot, very thinly sliced

1 small onion, sliced

½ cup frozen green peas

6 large eggs

⅓ cup water

¼ teaspoon salt

¼ teaspoon dried origanum

 Preparation time
7 minutes

 Cooking time
17 minutes

1. In a large frying pan (preferably with nonstick coating), melt the butter over moderate heat. Add the baby marrows, carrot and onion and sauté for 5 to 7 minutes. Reduce the heat to low. Stir in the peas, cover the frying pan and continue cooking for about 5 minutes until the vegetables are tender.

2. Meanwhile, in a medium-sized bowl, beat the eggs, water, salt and origanum. When the vegetables are cooked, pour the egg mixture into the frying pan. Cook, stirring gently from the edge toward the centre of the frying pan for 2 to 3 minutes until the eggs begin to set. Cover and cook for a few more minutes, until the eggs are just set. Serve immediately.

SPINACH SOUFFLÉ

SPINACH SOUFFLÉ *Serves 4*

4 tablespoons (60g) butter or margarine

1 small onion, finely chopped

1 package (250g) frozen creamed spinach

¹/₁ cup flour

1 cup milk

¹/₂ teaspoon salt

6 large eggs, separated, at room temperature

 Preparation time 8 minutes

 Cooking time 36 minutes

COOK'S TIP Fold the spinach mixture into the beaten egg whites very gradually to create a puffy, golden brown soufflé.

1. Preheat the oven to 160°C. In a medium-sized saucepan, melt the butter over moderate heat. Add the onion and sauté for about 5 minutes until soft. Add the frozen spinach, cover and cook for about 3 minutes until thawed, shaking the saucepan occasionally. Remove the lid and cook for 1 more minute until all of the liquid is evaporated. Stir the flour into the spinach until well mixed. Gradually stir in the milk and salt. Cook for about 1 minute until the mixture thickens, stirring constantly. Remove from the heat and stir in the lightly beaten egg yolks.

2. In a large bowl, beat the egg whites with an electric mixer until stiff. Gently fold in the spinach. Spoon into a 2-litre soufflé dish. Bake for 25 to 30 minutes until the soufflé is puffy and golden (do not open the oven during baking). Serve immediately.

BASQUE EGGS

BASQUE EGGS *Serves 4*

2 tablespoons olive oil

1 medium onion, thinly sliced

1 small sweet red pepper, sliced into thin strips

180g cooked ham, sliced into thin strips

225g tinned or fresh tomatoes, chopped

2 large garlic cloves, crushed

1 teaspoon dried origanum (or 1 tablespoon chopped fresh basil)

8 large eggs

1/4 teaspoon salt

1/8 teaspoon ground black pepper

1 tablespoon (15g) butter or margarine

 Preparation time 15 minutes

 Cooking time 12 minutes

SERVING SUGGESTION *Known in Spain as a* piperade, *this substantial dish teams well with sliced, sautéed potatoes. Precook the potatoes slightly in boiling water before sautéeing.*

1 Heat the oil in a large saucepan over moderate heat. Add the onion and red pepper and sauté for 2 to 3 minutes. Stir in the ham, tomatoes, garlic and origanum. Continue cooking, stirring occasionally, for 3 minutes. Remove the saucepan from the heat, cover and set aside.

2 In a medium-sized bowl, beat the eggs, salt and black pepper. In a large frying pan (preferably with nonstick coating), melt the butter over low heat, swirling the pan to coat evenly.

3 Pour the egg mixture into the frying pan and cook for about 1 minute until the edges begin to set. Using a wooden spoon or spatula, gently scrape the cooked egg toward the centre, allowing the uncooked egg to run to the bottom of the frying pan. Repeat until only a thin layer of uncooked egg remains on top.

4 Spoon the ham and tomato mixture evenly over the eggs. Cook, uncovered, until the eggs are just set. Serve immediately.

EGGS AND CHEESE

HAM AND CHEESE SOUFFLÉ OMELETTE *Serves 4*

6 large eggs, separated, at room temperature

2 tablespoons water

½ teaspoon salt

2 tablespoons (30g) butter or margarine

180g cooked ham, cut into thin strips

2 tablespoons (30g) grated Gruyère cheese

Parsley for garnishing

 Preparation time 15 minutes

 Cooking time 15 minutes

1. Preheat the oven to 200°C. In a large bowl, using an electric mixer, beat the egg whites until stiff but not dry. In a small bowl, again using the electric mixer, beat the yolks, water and salt for about 5 minutes until the mixture is thickened and has turned a pale yellow. Fold the yolk mixture into the beaten egg whites.

2. In an ovenproof 30cm frying pan, melt 1 tablespoon of the butter over moderately low heat, swirling the pan to coat evenly. Add the egg mixture and cook for about 5 minutes until golden underneath. Place the pan in the oven and bake for 5 to 10 minutes until the top of the omelette is golden and springs back when touched lightly. Meanwhile, in a medium-sized saucepan, heat the remaining 1 tablespoon of butter. Add the ham and sauté for 4 to 5 minutes. Remove from the heat.

3. To serve, loosen the omelette from the frying pan. Spoon the ham onto half of the omelette, fold it over the filling and slide onto a warmed serving platter. Sprinkle with grated Gruyère cheese and garnish with parsley. Serve immediately.

CHEESE AND VEGETABLE SOUFFLÉ OMELETTE

Preheat the oven to 200°C. Melt *2 tablespoons (30g) of butter* in a medium-sized frying pan over moderate heat. Add *1 small sweet green pepper,* chopped, *2 baby marrows,* chopped, and *1 small onion,* chopped. Sauté the vegetables for about 5 minutes until soft. Add *1 tin (410g) tomatoes,* drained and chopped, *¼ cup sliced black olives, 1 teaspoon dried origanum* and *¼ teaspoon ground black pepper.* Cook for about 2 minutes until heated through, stirring occasionally. Cover the frying pan and keep the vegetables warm. Prepare the omelette as directed in Steps 2 and 3 above. To serve, loosen the baked omelette from the frying pan and transfer it to a large serving platter. Spoon the vegetable mixture on top of the omelette and sprinkle with *½ cup grated Cheddar cheese.* Slice the omelette into wedges and serve immediately.

APPLE AND CINNAMON SOUFFLÉ OMELETTE

Preheat the oven to 200°C. Melt *2 tablespoons (30g) of butter* in a medium-sized frying pan. Add *2 tablespoons sugar* and stir until well mixed. Add *2 peeled and thinly sliced apples* and sauté until softened and caramelized. Add *1 teaspoon ground cinnamon* and stir to mix well. Prepare the omelette as directed and spoon the apple mixture on top. Fold over and serve immediately.

EGGS AND CHEESE

CHINESE EGG FRITTERS *Serves 4*

For the Oriental sauce:
1 cup chicken stock
1 tablespoon cornflour
1 teaspoon soy sauce
¼ teaspoon sugar
½ teaspoon Oriental sesame oil

For the fritters:
4 large eggs
1½ cups (250g) frozen shrimps, cooked
3 cups (about 250g) chopped bean sprouts
¼ cup chopped spring onion
2 to 3 tablespoons sunflower or peanut oil

 Preparation time 10 minutes

 Cooking time 18 minutes

1. To prepare the sauce: Mix the stock, cornflour, soy sauce and sugar in a small saucepan. Bring to the boil over high heat, stirring constantly. Stir in the sesame oil. Remove from the heat and keep warm.

2. To make the fritters: Beat the eggs in a large bowl. Add the shrimps, bean sprouts and spring onion. Heat a large frying pan (preferably with nonstick coating) over moderate heat until hot. Add 1 tablespoon of the sunflower oil, swirling to coat the pan.

3. Spoon about ⅓ cup of the egg mixture into the frying pan for each fritter. Fry the fritters, 2 or 3 at a time, for about 1 minute until the underside is golden brown and set. Using a spatula, turn each fritter and cook the other side. Transfer the fritters to a serving platter and keep them warm.

4. Repeat with the remaining egg mixture, adding more sunflower oil as necessary. Place two fritters on each plate and pour an equal amount of the sauce over each serving. Serve immediately.

EGGS BENEDICT *Serves 4*

For the Hollandaise sauce:
3 large egg yolks
2 tablespoons lemon juice
⅛ teaspoon salt
Pinch of cayenne pepper
5 tablespoons (75g) butter or margarine, softened

4 large eggs
4 slices rindless back bacon
2 crumpets or soft round rolls, halved
Paprika for garnishing

 Preparation time 5 minutes

 Cooking time 12 minutes

1. To make the sauce: Half fill the lower part of a double boiler with water and bring it to the boil. Lightly beat the egg yolks in the upper part of the double boiler. Stir in the lemon juice, salt and cayenne pepper and place over the boiling water (the upper pan should not touch the water). Stirring constantly, add the butter, one teaspoon at a time. Stir for about 5 minutes until the mixture is thickened and all of the butter has been added. Remove the pan from the heat, cover and set aside.

2. To prepare the eggs: In a small frying pan, bring 2,5cm of water to the boil. Keeping the water at a gentle boil, break the eggs, one at a time, into a saucer and slide each one into the water. Poach until cooked. (Alternatively, use a poaching pan, if available.)

3. Meanwhile, in a large frying pan, sauté the bacon until lightly browned. Toast the crumpets. Place a slice of bacon on each halved crumpet and, with a slotted spoon, top each with a poached egg. Thin the sauce with a little hot water, if necessary, and spoon it over each egg. Garnish with paprika and serve immediately.

PAN-FRIED CORNED BEEF HASH WITH EGGS

PAN-FRIED CORNED BEEF HASH WITH EGGS *Serves 4*

3 large (about 500g) potatoes, cooked, peeled and sliced into 1cm cubes

250g cooked corned beef, sliced into 1cm cubes

2 medium onions, chopped

1 sweet green pepper, chopped

¼ cup milk

2 tablespoons flour

2 tablespoons chopped parsley

3 tablespoons sunflower oil

4 large eggs

Additional chopped parsley (optional)

 Preparation time 18 minutes

 Cooking time 27 minutes

SERVING SUGGESTION Serve this meal-in-a-pan breakfast with whole-wheat toast for a balanced, nutritious start to the day.

1. In a large bowl, mix the potatoes, corned beef, onions, green pepper, milk, flour and parsley. In a large frying pan (preferably with nonstick coating), heat the oil over moderate heat. Add the corned beef mixture and, using a spatula, pack it down firmly to form a solid cake. Cook the hash for about 10 minutes until the underside begins to brown.

2. Reduce the heat to low. Continue cooking, shaking the frying pan occasionally to prevent it from sticking, for about 10 more minutes until the underside is crusty and well browned.

3. Using the back of a spoon, make four indentations in the hash. Break the eggs into a saucer, one at a time, and slip them into the indentations. Increase the heat to moderate, cover the pan and cook for about 6 minutes until the eggs are just set. Slice into wedges, garnish with chopped parsley, if desired, and serve.

Sausage and Broccoli Custard *Serves 6*

1 tablespoon (15g) butter or margarine

500g pork sausage

1 small onion, chopped

1 package (250g) frozen broccoli

4 large eggs

1 teaspoon prepared mustard

2 cups milk

Pinch of ground black pepper

Pinch of ground nutmeg

Sweet red pepper slivers (optional)

 Preparation time
4 minutes

 Cooking time
45 minutes

1. Preheat the oven to 180°C. In a large frying pan, melt the butter over moderately high heat. Add the sausage and onion. Cook for about 10 minutes until the sausage is well browned, stirring occasionally to break it into pieces.

2. Meanwhile, prepare the frozen broccoli according to the directions on the package. Drain thoroughly. Stir the cooked broccoli into the cooked sausage mixture.

3. Grease a 23cm square baking dish. In a large bowl, beat the eggs and mustard until well mixed. Beat in the milk, pepper and nutmeg. Stir the broccoli and sausage mixture into the egg mixture and pour it into the prepared baking dish.

4. Bake for 30 to 35 minutes until the custard is set and a knife inserted in the centre comes out clean. Slice the custard into rectangles. Sprinkle each serving with slivers of red pepper, if desired, and serve immediately.

Mexican Eggs *Serves 4*

4 tortillas

½ cup ready-made mild tomato salsa

1 tablespoon sunflower oil

8 eggs

½ cup (60g) coarsely grated mild Cheddar cheese

Coriander leaves (optional)

 Preparation time
5 minutes

 Cooking time
12 minutes

1. Preheat the oven to 180°C. Wrap the tortillas tightly in aluminium foil and warm them in the oven for 10 to 15 minutes. Maintain the oven temperature. Place the salsa in a small saucepan, cover and heat over low heat.

2. Meanwhile, in a 30cm frying pan (preferably with nonstick coating), heat the sunflower oil over moderate heat. Carefully break the eggs, one at a time, into the frying pan. When the edges of the egg whites are firm, reduce the heat to low. Cover the frying pan and cook for approximately 3 minutes until the egg yolks are just set.

3. Place the warmed tortillas on individual serving plates. Top each tortilla with two fried eggs and sprinkle with some of the grated cheese. Spoon an equal amount of the warmed salsa over each serving and top with the remaining cheese.

4. Place the plates in the preheated oven for 2 minutes (or in the microwave oven for a few seconds) to melt the cheese. Garnish each serving with coriander leaves, if desired, and serve immediately.

EGGS WITH CREAM CHEESE AND SMOKED SALMON

EGGS WITH CREAM CHEESE AND SMOKED SALMON *Serves 4*

8 large eggs

2 tablespoons sour cream

Pinch of ground black pepper

1 tablespoon (15g) butter or margarine

1 package (100g) cream cheese, cut into 1cm cubes

60g smoked salmon, cut into narrow strips

Chopped dill for garnishing

 Preparation time
5 minutes

 Cooking time
7 minutes

SERVING SUGGESTION Serve warmed croissants with this unashamedly self-indulgent combination of eggs, smooth cream cheese and elegant smoked salmon.

1. In a large bowl, beat the eggs and sour cream. Stir in the black pepper. In a large frying pan (preferably with nonstick coating), melt the butter over moderately low heat, swirling the pan to coat evenly. Add the egg mixture and cook, stirring lightly, for about 4 minutes until the eggs begin to set.

2. Sprinkle the cheese and salmon over the scrambled eggs. Reduce the heat to low, cover and cook for 1 to 2 minutes until the cream cheese just begins to soften. Garnish with the dill and serve.

BAKED EGGS PROVENÇALE

BAKED EGGS PROVENÇALE *Serves 4*

1 tablespoon olive oil

1 tablespoon (15g) butter or margarine

6 large eggs

½ cup (60g) coarsely grated Gruyère cheese

2 spring onions, chopped

½ teaspoon dried thyme

¼ teaspoon salt

¼ teaspoon ground black pepper

2 medium tomatoes, sliced

 Preparation time 10 minutes

 Cooking time 15 minutes

DIET NOTE Enjoy this easy-to-make main dish, filled with the sunny flavours of the south of France, without overloading on kilojoules.

1 Preheat the oven to 200°C. Place the oil and butter in a shallow 20cm round baking dish. Place in the oven to melt the butter.

2 In a large bowl, beat the eggs lightly and stir in the cheese, spring onions, thyme, salt and pepper.

3 Remove the dish from the oven and swirl to coat it evenly with the oil and butter. Pour in the egg mixture and arrange the tomato slices on top. Bake for about 15 minutes until the eggs are just set. Serve immediately.

EGGS AND CHEESE

CREAMED EGGS AND LEEKS *Serves 4*

4 large eggs

500g small leeks, trimmed, cleaned and thinly sliced

2 medium potatoes, peeled and thinly sliced

2 tablespoons (30g) unsalted butter or margarine

2 tablespoons flour

½ teaspoon mustard powder

1 cup milk

1 cup (120g) coarsely grated Cheddar cheese

¼ teaspoon salt

Pinch of ground black pepper

1 tablespoon chopped fresh chives or parsley

 Preparation time 15 minutes

 Cooking time 20 minutes

1. Place the eggs in a medium-sized saucepan and cover them with cold water. Bring to the boil over high heat. Remove the saucepan from the heat and leave it to stand, covered, for 15 minutes.

2. Meanwhile, half fill a large saucepan with water and bring it to the boil. Add the leeks and potatoes. Reduce the heat to low, partially cover the saucepan and simmer for about 10 minutes until the potatoes are tender when pierced with a fork. Drain the vegetables. Drain the eggs and rinse them with cold water. Shell the eggs, cut them in half lengthwise and set aside.

3. In a medium-sized saucepan, melt the butter over moderate heat. Add the flour and mustard and stir until well mixed. Gradually stir in the milk and cook the mixture, stirring constantly, for about 2 minutes until it is smooth and thick. Stir in half of the cheese, the salt and pepper. Continue stirring until the cheese begins to melt. Remove from the heat.

4. Preheat the grill. Place the potatoes and leeks in a shallow 25cm x 20cm baking dish. Place the eggs, yolks down, on top of the vegetables. Pour the sauce over the eggs and sprinkle with the remaining cheese. Grill for a few seconds until the cheese is lightly browned. Sprinkle with the chives and serve immediately.

BAKED EGGS FLORENTINE *Serves 4* (PICTURE PAGE 245)

3 tablespoons (45g) butter or margarine

1 cup (about 125g) sliced mushrooms

3 tablespoons flour

¼ teaspoon black pepper

⅛ teaspoon ground nutmeg

⅛ teaspoon salt

1 cup milk

1 package (250g) frozen spinach, thawed, drained and squeezed dry

½ cup (60g) grated Parmesan cheese

4 large eggs

 Preparation time 10 minutes

 Cooking time 28 minutes

1. Preheat the oven to 180°C. Grease four shallow 1-cup (250ml) individual baking dishes. In a medium-sized saucepan, melt the butter over moderate heat. Add the mushrooms and sauté for about 3 minutes until they are soft. Stir in the flour, pepper, nutmeg and salt until well mixed. Add the milk gradually and cook, stirring constantly, for about 5 minutes until the mixture thickens. Add the spinach and mix well.

2. Spoon the mushroom-spinach mixture evenly into the prepared baking dishes, making a shallow depression in the centre of each dish. Sprinkle each serving with 1 tablespoon of the grated Parmesan cheese.

3. Break 1 egg into each depression and sprinkle each with some of the remaining cheese. Bake for 13 to 18 minutes until the eggs are just set. Serve immediately.

CRUSTLESS HAM AND TOMATO QUICHE Serves 4

4 large eggs

½ cup full cream milk or cream

1 cup smooth cottage cheese

2 tablespoons flour

100g cooked ham, finely chopped

1 tin (410g) Italian-style tomatoes, chopped

¼ cup (about 30g) sliced mushrooms

1 cup (120g) coarsely grated Gruyère or Emmenthal cheese

 Preparation time
10 minutes

 Cooking time
30 minutes

COOK'S TIP You only need one mixing bowl to prepare this simple, filling brunch or supper main dish. While it's in the oven, make a crisp green lettuce salad garnished with fresh herbs to accompany it.

1 Preheat the oven to 190°C. Grease a 23cm pie dish or a 24cm x 16cm baking dish. In a large bowl, whisk the eggs, milk, cottage cheese and flour until well blended. Stir in the ham, tomatoes, mushrooms and ¾ cup of the cheese.

2 Spoon the mixture into the prepared dish and sprinkle it with the remaining ¼ cup of cheese. Bake for 30 minutes until the quiche is golden brown and a knife inserted in the centre comes out clean. Slice into wedges or squares and serve either warm or at room temperature.

ITALIAN-STYLE FRITTATA Serves 4

250g potatoes, unpeeled

6 large eggs

½ teaspoon dried origanum

¼ teaspoon salt

2 tablespoons olive oil

1 tin (400g) artichoke hearts, drained and chopped

½ cup (60g) coarsely grated mozzarella cheese

1 tablespoon (20g) grated Parmesan cheese

Chopped parsley (optional)

 Preparation time
6 minutes

 Cooking time
28 minutes

FOOD NOTE A frittata is the Italian version of a flat omelette – crisp on the bottom and fluffy on the inside. Serve it with a crusty French loaf and a scrumptious garden salad.

1 Fill a large saucepan with 5cm of water, cover and bring to the boil. Meanwhile, scrub the potatoes and cut them into 5mm-thick slices.

2 Add the potatoes to the boiling water, cover and cook for about 10 minutes until they are almost tender when pricked with a fork. Drain the potatoes and pat them dry.

3 Preheat the grill. In a medium-sized bowl, beat the eggs, origanum and salt until well mixed. In an ovenproof 25cm frying pan or omelette pan, heat the oil over moderately high heat, swirling to coat the pan. Add the potatoes and artichokes and cook for about 5 minutes until lightly browned, stirring gently.

4 Reduce the heat to moderately low. Add the egg mixture, cover and cook for 7 to 8 minutes until the eggs are almost set.

5 Sprinkle the eggs with both cheeses. Place the frying pan under the grill for 1 to 2 minutes until the eggs are set and the cheese melts and begins to brown. Sprinkle with parsley, if desired. Slice the frittata into wedges and serve immediately.

SMOKED SALMON AND DILL FRITTATA

SMOKED SALMON AND DILL FRITTATA *Serves 4*

7 large eggs

¼ cup sour cream

1 tablespoon chopped fresh dill (or ½ teaspoon dried dill)

¼ teaspoon salt

¼ teaspoon ground white pepper

125g sliced smoked salmon, cut into narrow strips

2 tablespoons (30g) butter or margarine

1 cup (120g) grated Gruyère or Emmenthal cheese

Additional sour cream, lumpfish roe or caviar and dill sprigs (optional)

Preparation time 5 minutes

Cooking time 12 minutes

SERVING SUGGESTION Serve this light special occasion lunch with a glass of white wine, or slice it into squares to serve as an appetizer.

1. Preheat the grill. In a medium-sized bowl, beat the eggs, sour cream, dill, salt and pepper until well mixed. Stir in the salmon.

2. Melt the butter over moderate heat in an ovenproof 25cm frying pan or omelette pan, swirling to coat the pan evenly. Pour in the egg mixture. Reduce the heat to moderately low, cover and cook for about 10 minutes until almost set. Sprinkle the frittata with the cheese.

3. Place the frying pan under the grill for about 1 minute until the eggs are set and the cheese melts and begins to brown. Slice the frittata into wedges and garnish each serving with additional sour cream, lumpfish roe and dill, if desired. Serve immediately.

EGGS AND CHEESE

HAM AND CHEESE ROULADE Serves 6

⅓ cup (80g) butter or margarine

½ cup flour

2 cups milk

⅛ teaspoon ground black pepper

6 large eggs, separated, at room temperature

12 thin slices (about 250g) Cheddar cheese

¼ cup watercress leaves

6 thin slices (about 180g) ham

Watercress sprigs (optional)

 Preparation time 11 minutes

 Cooking time 38 minutes

SERVING SUGGESTION *Don't be daunted by the glamorous appearance of this roulade – it's easier to make than it looks. Serve it with a cucumber and celery salad.*

1. In a medium-sized saucepan, melt the butter over moderate heat. Stir in the flour and cook for about 1 minute until bubbly. Remove the saucepan from the heat and, using a wire whisk, gradually stir in the milk. Return to moderate heat and cook, stirring constantly, for about 4 minutes until thickened (do not boil). Remove the saucepan from the heat and stir in the pepper.

2. Preheat the oven to 200°C. In a small bowl, beat the egg yolks lightly. Beat in a small amount of the hot milk mixture. Slowly stir the yolk mixture into the remaining hot milk and set it aside.

3. Line the base of a Swiss roll tin with wax paper and coat it with nonstick cooking spray. In a large bowl, using an electric mixer, beat the egg whites until stiff but not dry. Fold the yolk mixture gently into the beaten egg whites. Spread into the prepared tin and bake for 20 to 25 minutes until the surface is firm. Do not switch the oven off.

4. Cover the roulade with aluminium foil and invert it onto a large baking sheet. Peel off the wax paper. Arrange the cheese slices evenly over the surface, sprinkle with the watercress and top with the sliced ham.

5. Starting from a short edge, roll up the roulade, using the foil to help lift it as it is rolled. Transfer it, seam side down, to an oven-safe platter and place in the oven for 3 to 4 minutes until heated through. Garnish with watercress, if desired, and serve at once.

SHELF MAGIC

This quick lunch takes less than 10 minutes to prepare. Although this recipe calls for a microwave oven, it can easily be prepared on the stove.

MEXICAN CHEESE MELTS

Cut *125g processed cheese* into cubes. In a 1-litre microwave-safe casserole dish, mix the cheese with *2 tablespoons milk* and *1 fresh green chilli*, chopped. Cover and cook on high power for 1 to 2 minutes or until the cheese is melted, stirring once. On each of *two halved, toasted bread rolls*, place *a slice of tomato* and *two slices of avocado pear*. Top each with an equal amount of the cheese. Serves 2

Variations on the basic Omelette

Once you've mastered the art of making an omelette, you have at your fingertips the means to create innumerable delicious and rapidly prepared meals. The fluffy envelope can contain any combination of meat, cheese and vegetables, or it may ooze with a delectable savoury or sweet sauce.

If you're going to fill the omelette, prepare the filling first as the eggs cook very quickly and require your undivided attention. These fillings are enough to fill four omelettes, but they can easily be reduced for fewer servings.

Basic omelette In a large bowl, beat *2 eggs, 2 tablespoons water* and *a pinch of salt* and *pepper*. In a medium-sized frying pan or omelette pan, melt *1 teaspoon (5g) butter* or *margarine* over moderately high heat, swirling to coat the pan evenly. Add the egg mixture and cook, without stirring, for about 20 seconds until it starts to bubble around the edge. As the bottom begins to set, slide a spatula underneath and lift the cooked egg to allow the uncooked mixture to flow under it. Cook for 2 to 3 minutes until the bottom is lightly browned. Spoon the filling across half of the omelette, fold over and serve.

◀ **Primavera filling** In a large frying pan, heat *¼ cup olive oil* over moderate heat. Add *2 medium sweet red peppers*, cut into thin strips and sauté for 2 minutes. Add *2 baby marrows*, cut into 5cm sticks, *2 small onions*, sliced and *1 teaspoon dried origanum*. Sauté for 6 to 7 minutes until the vegetables are crisp-tender. Season the filling with *salt* and *pepper* to taste.

◀ **Broccoli cheese filling** In a large saucepan, cook *500g frozen broccoli florets* according to the directions on the package. Drain and set aside. In the same saucepan, melt *2 tablespoons (30g) butter* or *margarine* over moderate heat. Stir in *2 tablespoons flour* and *2 drops Tabasco sauce*. Stir in *1 cup milk* and cook until thickened, stirring constantly. Stir in *1 cup (about 120g) grated Cheddar cheese* until just melted. Fold in the cooked broccoli and season with *salt* and *pepper*.

▶ **Walnut and goat's cheese filling** Preheat the oven to 200°C. Spread *4 tablespoons chopped walnuts* into a baking dish. Toast the walnuts for about 5 minutes until lightly browned, shaking the dish halfway through cooking. Remove from the oven and let the walnuts cool slightly. In a small bowl, crumble *¼ to ½ cup (30g to 60g) goat's cheese*. Stir in *1 tablespoon sour cream* and the toasted walnuts.

▶ **Oriental asparagus filling** Slice *600g fresh green asparagus* diagonally. In a large frying pan, heat *2 tablespoons sunflower* or *peanut oil* over moderately high heat. Add *1 large onion*, sliced and sauté for 5 minutes. Stir in the asparagus and sauté for about 5 minutes until crisp-tender. Add *1½ teaspoons soy sauce, 1½ teaspoons Oriental sesame oil* and *1½ teaspoons sesame seeds* and mix well.

▶ **Mexican avocado filling** In a medium-sized bowl, combine *1 peeled and cubed avocado pear, 2 chopped plum tomatoes, ¼ cup ready-made tomato salsa, 1 tablespoon chopped spring onion* and *a pinch each of salt* and *pepper*. Prepare the omelette as directed. Just before folding the omelette, sprinkle the filling with a small handful of *grated Gouda cheese*. Top each omelette with a dollop of *sour cream* just before serving.

THREE-CHEESE SAVOURY BREAD PUDDING

THREE-CHEESE SAVOURY BREAD PUDDING *Serves 4*

1²/₃ cups milk

1 tablespoon (15g) butter or margarine

6 slices day-old or lightly toasted whole-wheat bread

4 large eggs, separated, at room temperature

1 tin (170g) evaporated milk

½ cup (60g) coarsely grated Gouda cheese

½ cup (60g) coarsely grated Emmenthal cheese

¼ cup (30g) crumbled blue cheese

⅛ teaspoon ground white pepper

Pinch of ground nutmeg

 Preparation time 10 minutes

 Cooking time 34 minutes

FOOD NOTE This tasty, full-flavoured bake transforms an old nursery favourite into a filling family meal.

1. Preheat the oven to 180°C. In a medium-sized saucepan, heat the milk over moderate heat until almost boiling, stirring frequently. Grease a shallow oval 30cm x 20cm baking dish with the butter.

2. Slice four slices of the bread in half diagonally and cut the remaining two slices into small cubes. Using a spatula, briefly dip the halved slices into the hot milk and line the side of the baking dish with them, overlapping the edges. Add the bread cubes to the remaining milk and leave them to stand to absorb as much of the milk as possible.

3. In a large bowl, beat the egg yolks, evaporated milk, remaining bread and milk and the cheeses. Add the pepper and nutmeg.

4. In a medium-sized bowl, using an electric mixer, beat the egg whites until stiff and fold them into the cheese mixture. Pour the mixture over the bread. Bake for 25 to 30 minutes until golden and a knife inserted in the centre comes out clean. Serve at once.

EGGS AND CHEESE

INDIVIDUAL CHEDDAR SOUFFLÉS Serves 4

3 tablespoons (45g) butter or margarine

3 tablespoons flour

¼ teaspoon salt

⅛ teaspoon cayenne pepper

1¼ cups milk

1 cup (120g) coarsely grated mild Cheddar cheese

4 large eggs, separated, at room temperature

 Preparation time
10 minutes

 Cooking time
37 minutes

COOK'S TIP Check the flavour of the soufflé base – it should be well seasoned to counteract the blandness of the egg whites.

1. Preheat the oven to 160°C. In a medium-sized saucepan, melt the butter over moderate heat. Add the flour, salt and cayenne pepper and stir until well mixed. Gradually stir in the milk. Cook for about 4 to 5 minutes until the mixture thickens, stirring constantly. Remove the saucepan from the heat. Stir in the cheese until just melted.

2. In a small bowl, beat the egg yolks lightly. Beat in a small amount of the hot cheese mixture. Slowly stir the yolk mixture into the remaining cheese mixture and set it aside.

3. Place four 1-cup ramekins or soufflé dishes on a rimmed baking sheet for easier handling. In a medium-sized bowl, using an electric mixer, beat the egg whites until they are stiff but not dry. Fold in the cheese mixture (the mixture should be just liquid enough to fall from a spoon) and spoon it into the dishes. With the back of a spoon, make an indentation around each soufflé about 2,5cm from the rim to create a top-hat effect after baking.

4. Bake for 25 to 30 minutes until they are puffy and lightly browned (do not open the oven during baking). Serve at once.

MOZZARELLA RAMEKINS Serves 4

1 tablespoon olive oil

600g (about 4 cups) sliced baby marrows

1 clove garlic, finely chopped

4 large eggs

1 cup (120g) coarsely grated mozzarella cheese

¼ cup (30g) packaged bread crumbs

1 tablespoon chopped parsley

¼ teaspoon salt

⅛ teaspoon crushed chillies

 Preparation time
10 minutes

 Cooking time
26 minutes

SERVING SUGGESTION This light meal can be made more substantial by serving it with a loaf of crusty garlic bread and a freshly chopped tomato and basil salad.

1. Preheat the oven to 200°C. Grease four individual 8,5cm ramekins or small shallow oval baking dishes. In a large frying pan, heat the oil over moderate heat. Add the baby marrows and garlic and sauté for about 5 minutes until they are tender. Remove the pan from the heat.

2. In a large bowl, combine the eggs, cheese, bread crumbs, parsley, salt and chillies. Stir the baby marrows into the egg mixture.

3. Spoon the mixture into ramekins or dishes and bake for 15 to 20 minutes until set. Serve immediately.

EGGS AND CHEESE

Herbed goat's-cheese tart *Serves 4*

1 package ready-rolled pastry

2 tablespoons (30g) butter or margarine

2 cloves garlic, finely chopped

2 tablespoons flour

1 teaspoon dried origanum

½ teaspoon dried thyme

¾ cup milk

2 large eggs, separated, at room temperature

2 cups (250g) crumbled goat's cheese

 Preparation time 8 minutes

 Cooking time 40 minutes

1. Preheat the oven to 200°C. Roll out the pastry and press it into a greased 23cm or 25cm baking tin with a removable base, trimming it evenly around the edge of the tin. With a fork, pierce the base and sides of the pastry to prevent it from puffing up during baking. Set the baking tin in a roasting pan for easier handling and place it in the oven for about 10 minutes until the crust is partially done.

2. Meanwhile, in a medium-sized saucepan, melt the butter over moderate heat. Add the garlic and sauté for 15 seconds. Stir in the flour, origanum and thyme, and gradually stir in the milk. Cook for 1 to 2 minutes until the mixture thickens, stirring constantly. Remove the saucepan from the heat.

3. In a small bowl, beat the egg yolks lightly. Beat in a small amount of the hot milk, herbs and flour. Slowly stir the yolks into the remaining milk and flour mixture and set aside. In a small bowl, using an electric mixer, beat the egg whites until they are stiff but not dry. Fold into the yolk mixture.

4. When the pastry shell is partially baked, remove it from the oven and reduce the temperature to 190°C. Sprinkle the cheese into the crust and gently spoon the egg mixture over it. Bake for 25 to 30 minutes until the filling is golden brown and a knife inserted in the centre comes out clean. Remove the rim of the pan and serve the tart immediately.

SHELF MAGIC

This spicy dip is ideal for parties – serve it with a plate of savoury biscuits and sliced fresh vegetables or with a basket of chips.

Easy cheese dip

In a 1-litre microwave-safe casserole dish, combine *⅓ cup beer* or *apple juice* and *several dashes of Tabasco sauce*. Cook, uncovered, on high power for appoximately 1 to 2 minutes until the mixture is very hot. Meanwhile, toss together *1 cup (about 125g) grated Cheddar cheese, 1 tablespoon flour* and *½ teaspoon mustard powder*.

Stir the cheese into the beer mixture. Cook, uncovered, on high for 2 to 4 minutes until the cheese melts and the mixture is hot, stirring once every minute. Stir in *2 to 3 tablespoons milk* to make the mixture of a dipping consistency. Serve the dip with a basket or plate of *savoury biscuits, chips* or *vegetable sticks*. Makes ¾ cup

SPINACH CHEESE PIE

SPINACH CHEESE PIE *Serves 6*

250g frozen creamed spinach

1 cup flour

½ cup whole-wheat flour

¼ teaspoon salt

⅓ cup plus 1 tablespoon canola or olive oil

3 tablespoons cold water

½ cup (125g) cottage cheese

½ cup cream

4 large eggs

¼ cup (30g) grated Parmesan cheese

1 teaspoon dried thyme

 Preparation time 15 minutes

 Cooking time 30 minutes

SERVING SUGGESTION *Sautéed baby onions and strips of red and yellow pepper make a cheerful accompaniment to this easy supper or brunch dish. Garnish with sprigs of parsley.*

1. Thaw the spinach in the microwave oven or in a colander under warm running water. Drain the spinach and squeeze it dry.

2. Meanwhile, to make the pie crust: Combine the flours with the salt in a medium-sized bowl. Stir in the oil and add the water, a tablespoon at a time, until the pastry just holds together when pressed into a ball. Between two sheets of wax paper, roll the pastry into a 25cm round. Fit it into a 23cm pie plate.

3. Preheat the oven to 200°C. With a food processor or electric blender, process the cottage cheese and cream until smooth. (Alternatively, press the cheese through a fine strainer into a bowl, then stir in the cream.) In a medium-sized bowl, beat the eggs lightly. Stir in the cottage-cheese mixture, the Parmesan cheese, thyme and, finally, the spinach. Pour the mixture into the pie crust. Bake for 25 to 30 minutes until a knife inserted in the centre comes out clean. Serve warm or at room temperature.

EGGS AND CHEESE

CHEESE FONDUE *Serves 4*

4 cups (500g) coarsely grated Gruyère or Emmenthal cheese

2 tablespoons flour

¼ teaspoon ground black pepper

⅛ teaspoon ground nutmeg

1¼ cups dry white wine

2 tablespoons kirsch or brandy

1 clove garlic, quartered

Any combination of cubed French bread, breadsticks, small mushrooms, broccoli florets, julienned carrots, baby marrows or sweet peppers for dipping

 Preparation time 5 minutes

 Cooking time 18 minutes

FOOD NOTE A Swiss peasant dish, fondue remains a favourite for entertaining – everyone loves dipping into the pot. Serve with platters of crusty bread and delectable dew-fresh vegetables.

1. In a medium-sized bowl, mix the cheese with the flour, black pepper and nutmeg. In a medium-sized saucepan or fondue pot that can be used on top of the stove, heat the wine, kirsch and garlic over moderately high heat for about 3 minutes until almost boiling. Remove and discard the garlic.

2. Reduce the heat to low. Gradually add the floured cheese to the wine mixture, a handful at a time, stirring constantly until the cheese melts. Arrange the bread, breadsticks and/or vegetables on a serving platter.

3. If using a saucepan, place the fondue over a table-top burner or place the fondue pot on its stand. (Keep the temperature low to prevent the cheese from becoming hard and sticking to the pan.) To serve, let each person spear the bread and vegetables with long-handled forks and dip the food into the fondue.

CHEESE-STUFFED BUTTERNUT SQUASH *Serves 4*

2 butternut squash (about 1kg)

Salt and freshly ground black pepper to taste

A sprinkling of nutmeg

4 to 8 fresh sage leaves (optional)

2 tablespoons (30g) butter or margarine

3 tablespoons flour

1 cup milk, warmed

1 cup (120g) grated Cheddar cheese

¼ teaspoon Dijon mustard

2 eggs, separated, at room temperature

1 package brown and wild rice mixture, cooked

 Preparation time 15 minutes

 Cooking time 50 minutes

1. Preheat the oven to 200°C. In a large saucepan, bring 2,5 cm of water to the boil. Halve each squash lengthwise and scoop out the seeds. Season lightly with salt and pepper, sprinkle with the nutmeg and dot with the sage leaves, if desired. Place on a trivet over the boiling water and steam for 20 to 30 minutes or until tender. Remove from the heat. Grease a baking dish with nonstick cooking spray.

2. Meanwhile, melt the butter in a small saucepan and add the flour, stirring until smooth. Gradually add the milk and, stirring constantly, cook until thickened. Remove from the heat. Stir in ¾ cup of the cheese and the mustard. Season to taste.

3. In a small bowl, beat the egg whites until stiff. Beat a little of the cheese mixture into the egg yolks, then beat the egg yolks into the cheese mixture. Fold in the egg whites. Spoon the mixture into the squash. Sprinkle with the remaining cheese and bake for 15 to 20 minutes until golden. Serve with the rice mixture.

EGGS AND CHEESE

WELSH RAREBIT *Serves 4*

3 tablespoons (45g) butter or margarine

3 tablespoons flour

¼ teaspoon salt

¼ teaspoon mustard powder

3 to 4 drops of Tabasco sauce

1⅓ cups milk

⅓ cup beer

1 teaspoon Worcestershire sauce

1½ cups (180g) coarsely grated mature Cheddar cheese

8 slices white or whole-wheat bread, toasted and kept warm

 Preparation time
6 minutes

 Cooking time
7 minutes

COOK'S TIP You may prefer to use halved, toasted white rolls instead of bread. For an authentic British flavour, garnish each serving with pickled onions or gherkins. It's the ideal solution when you have to prepare a quick late supper.

1. Preheat the grill. In a medium-sized saucepan, melt the butter over moderate heat. Add the flour, salt, mustard and Tabasco sauce and stir until well mixed. Gradually stir in the milk, beer and Worcestershire sauce. Cook, stirring constantly, for about 5 minutes until the mixture thickens. Stir in the cheese until it is just melted.

2. Arrange the toast on a baking sheet. Pour the hot cheese mixture over it. Grill for a few seconds until the cheese begins to brown. Serve immediately.

BAKED CHEESE AND SAUSAGE *Serves 4*

500g baby potatoes

250g kielbasa (or other cooked smoked garlic sausage)

250g Gruyère cheese, sliced into 6mm-thick slices

Pinch of ground black pepper

Gherkins or cocktail-size pickled onions (optional)

 Preparation time
4 minutes

 Cooking time
25 minutes

COOK'S TIP You need only three readily available ingredients to create this filling winter warmer – a hearty combination of potatoes, garlic sausage and cheese to ward off the icy chills.

1. In a large saucepan, bring 5cm of water to the boil over high heat. Reduce the heat to low, add the potatoes, cover the saucepan and cook for about 10 minutes until they are just tender when pricked with a fork.

2. Meanwhile, remove the casing from the sausage and slice it diagonally into 1cm-thick slices.

3. Preheat the oven to 190°C. Arrange the cooked potatoes around the edge of a 23cm or 25cm shallow baking dish. Place the sausage in the centre of the dish. Arrange the cheese slices over the potatoes, overlapping them if necessary.

4. Place the dish in the oven and bake for approximately 10 to 15 minutes until the cheese is completely melted and the sausage is heated through.

5. Sprinkle a pinch of black pepper over the melted cheese and garnish the dish with gherkins or small pickled onions, if desired. Serve immediately.

Vegetables

Ratatouille (page 282)

Vegetable accompaniments

Crisply fresh and brimming with nutrients and flavour, creatively prepared vegetables make perfect first courses and accompaniment dishes.

Asparagus Dijonnaise Serves 4

600g asparagus

¼ cup olive oil

1 tablespoon white wine vinegar

1 tablespoon Dijon mustard

1 teaspoon dried tarragon

2 tablespoons sour cream

Salt and ground black pepper to taste

2 tablespoons finely chopped onion

 Preparation time
15 minutes

 Cooking time
10 minutes

Cook's tip When the asparagus is cooked, remove the spears from the heat and plunge quickly into cold water to prevent overcooking.

1 In a large frying pan, bring 1cm of water to the boil over high heat. Meanwhile, cut or break off the tough ends of the asparagus. Using a vegetable peeler, peel the lower half of each asparagus spear.

2 Add the asparagus spears to the boiling water. Reduce the heat to low, cover and cook for 8 to 10 minutes until they are tender but still firm to the bite. Drain and rinse with cold water. Pat dry with paper towels and place them on a serving platter. Place in the refrigerator while preparing the sauce.

3 In a small bowl, using a wire whisk, beat the oil with the vinegar, mustard and tarragon until well blended. Add the sour cream and beat until smooth. Season the mixture with salt and pepper.

4 Spoon the mustard mixture over the asparagus, sprinkle it with the chopped onion and serve immediately.

French-style Peas Serves 4

1½ cups finely chopped crisp lettuce, eg Iceberg

500g frozen green peas, partially thawed in hot water

2 spring onions, chopped

1 teaspoon sugar

2 tablespoons (30g) butter or margarine, chopped into small pieces

Salt and ground white pepper to taste

 Preparation time
10 minutes

 Cooking time
5 minutes

Food note This traditional French method of cooking peas uses steam created by the moisture in the lettuce. Garnish with fresh mint.

1 Place ¾ cup of the lettuce in a medium-sized saucepan. Cover the lettuce with the peas and the spring onions. Sprinkle with the sugar and dot with the butter. Cover with the remaining lettuce.

2 Cover the saucepan and cook the lettuce and peas over moderately low heat for 4 to 5 minutes until the peas are tender, shaking the saucepan occasionally. Season with salt and pepper. Transfer the vegetables to a bowl and serve immediately.

VEGETABLES

CREOLE GREEN BEANS *Serves 4*

350g green beans, trimmed and sliced into 5cm lengths

2 slices bacon

1 medium onion, chopped

¼ cup chopped sweet green pepper

1 tin (410g) chopped tomatoes, drained

1 teaspoon sugar or to taste

Salt and ground black pepper to taste

 Preparation time
13 minutes

 Cooking time
23 minutes

Serving suggestion For an unusual combination of textures and colours, serve this mélange of tomatoes, beans and green peppers with grilled chicken or pork.

1. In a large saucepan, bring 2,5cm of water to the boil over high heat. Add the beans and return to the boil. Reduce the heat to low, cover and cook for about 8 minutes, stirring once, until the beans are tender but still firm to the bite.

2. Meanwhile, in a large frying pan, cook the bacon over moderate heat until crisp. Leaving the bacon drippings in the frying pan, drain the bacon on paper towels. Drain the cooked beans and set them aside.

3. Add the onion and green pepper to the drippings in the frying pan and cook for about 4 minutes until soft but not brown. Stir in the tomatoes and sugar. Cook for about 15 minutes, stirring occasionally.

4. Stir the beans into the tomato mixture. Season with salt and pepper and transfer them to a serving dish. Crumble the bacon over the beans and serve immediately.

SAUTÉED BROCCOLI ITALIANO *Serves 4*

750g broccoli

3 tablespoons olive oil

1 clove garlic, finely chopped

½ cup water

1 plum tomato, seeded and chopped

1 tablespoon red wine vinegar

¼ teaspoon crushed red chillies

Salt to taste

 Preparation time
9 minutes

 Cooking time
13 minutes

Diet note Broccoli is highly nutritious, being rich in fibre, calcium and vitamins A, C, E and K, so be sure to include it in your diet regularly.

1. Trim and set aside the woody ends of the broccoli stalks and separate the tops into florets. With a vegetable peeler, peel the stalks and cut them diagonally into 6mm-thick slices.

2. In a 5-litre flameproof casserole dish or stockpot, heat the oil over moderate heat. Add the sliced broccoli stalks and sauté for 5 minutes. Stir in the garlic, water and the broccoli florets. Cover and cook for about 5 more minutes until the florets are tender but still firm to the bite. Remove the casserole dish from the heat.

3. Using a slotted spoon, transfer the broccoli to a serving bowl, leaving any liquid in the dish. Add the tomato, vinegar and chillies to the liquid. Cook over low heat until hot. Season with salt. Pour the tomato mixture over the broccoli and serve.

STIR-FRIED BABY MARROWS AND WATER CHESTNUTS

STIR-FRIED BABY MARROWS AND WATER CHESTNUTS *Serves 4*

¼ cup chicken stock

1 tablespoon soy sauce

½ teaspoon cornflour

½ teaspoon sugar

⅛ teaspoon crushed chillies

500g baby marrows

2 tablespoons sunflower oil

3 spring onions, sliced into 5cm lengths

1 tin (230g) sliced water chestnuts, drained

Salt to taste

 Preparation time 6 minutes

 Cooking time 5 minutes

COOK'S TIP Choose baby marrows that are firm with no soft patches. With their mild-flavoured flesh, these small members of the squash family are tender enough to be eaten raw.

1. In a bowl, mix the stock, soy sauce, cornflour, sugar and chillies, and set aside. Slice the baby marrows into 5cm x 1cm lengths.

2. Heat the oil in a wok or large frying pan over high heat. Add the baby marrows and stir-fry for about 3 minutes until just crisp-tender. Add the spring onions and water chestnuts and stir-fry for 1 more minute. Stir the stock mixture into the baby marrow mixture and bring to the boil, stirring constantly. Season with salt and serve immediately.

SWEET-AND-SOUR RED CABBAGE (LEFT) AND FRESH MEALIES WITH PEPPERS

FRESH MEALIES WITH PEPPERS *Serves 4*

4 mealies

2 spring onions

2 tablespoons (30g) butter or margarine

½ cup diced sweet red pepper

¼ cup water

Salt and ground black pepper to taste

 Preparation time 15 minutes

 Cooking time 8 minutes

COOK'S TIP Rub the husked mealies (or ears of corn) lightly with a clean damp cloth to remove the silky threads, known as corn silk, easily.

1. Clean the mealies and remove the corn silk. Using a sharp knife, cut the kernels from the cobs. Break up any kernels that are stuck together. Cut the spring onions into 6mm-thick slices.

2. Melt the butter in a large saucepan. Add the kernels, spring onions, red pepper and water and bring to the boil. Continue cooking, uncovered, for about 5 minutes until the kernels are tender and the water has evaporated, stirring occasionally. Season with salt and pepper, transfer to a bowl and serve.

VEGETABLES

Sweet-and-sour red cabbage *Serves 4*

1 small head (about 500g) red cabbage

2 tablespoons (30g) butter or margarine

1 small onion, chopped

1 tablespoon cider vinegar

2 teaspoons light or dark brown sugar

Salt and ground black pepper to taste

 Preparation time
5 minutes

 Cooking time
16 minutes

COOK'S TIP Reduce preparation time even further by chopping the cabbage in a food processor, if one is available.

1. Discard any tough outer leaves from the cabbage. Cut the cabbage in half through the core, then remove and discard the core. Slice the cabbage crosswise into thin slices or shreds.

2. In a large saucepan, melt the butter over moderate heat. Add the onion and sauté for about 5 minutes until soft. Add the vinegar, sugar and the cabbage, tossing to coat with the onion mixture.

3. Cover the saucepan and cook the cabbage for 8 to 10 minutes, stirring occasionally, until it is tender but still firm to the bite. Season the cabbage mixture with salt and pepper, spoon into a bowl and serve immediately.

Roasted baby potatoes *Serves 4*

700g baby potatoes, unpeeled and scrubbed

1 medium onion

2 tablespoons olive oil

2 teaspoons chopped fresh rosemary (or 1 teaspoon dried rosemary)

1 clove garlic, chopped

Salt and ground black pepper to taste

 Preparation time
10 minutes

 Cooking time
25 minutes

1. Preheat the oven to 180°C. Dry the potatoes on paper towels. Cut each potato into quarters and slice the onion into 6mm rings.

2. Combine the potatoes and onion in a 37,5cm x 26,5cm baking tray. Add the oil, rosemary and garlic, tossing until well mixed. Bake the potatoes for 20 to 25 minutes until tender and browned, stirring occasionally. Season with salt and pepper and serve.

TIME SAVERS

VEGETABLES
Many supermarkets now have salad bars that stock a variety of cleaned and prepared vegetables. Make use of these when you are short of preparation time. Look for broccoli florets, red and green peppers and mushrooms.

Broccoli stalks will cook faster if you peel and discard the outer fibrous layer first.

Frozen baby peas do not need cooking for use in salads. Place them in a colander and rinse under hot running water until defrosted.

To ripen tomatoes quickly, pierce a few holes in a brown paper packet and keep the tomatoes in it, at room temperature, until they are ready to use. The same works for avocado pears, which will ripen even faster if you put an apple in the packet with them.

VEGETABLES

LOW-FAT MASHED POTATOES *Serves 4*

700g potatoes

⅓ cup plain low-fat yoghurt

⅓ cup ricotta or low-fat cottage cheese

Salt and ground black pepper to taste

2 tablespoons chopped fresh herbs (parsley, basil or chives)

 Preparation time 15 minutes

 Cooking time 15 minutes

DIET NOTE This low-fat version of mashed potatoes provides a rich source of proteins and calcium without filling you with extra kilojoules. Preserve the extra nutrients by leaving the potatoes unpeeled.

1. Peel the potatoes, if desired, and slice them into 2,5cm cubes. Place the potatoes in a large saucepan and cover them with cold water. Cover the saucepan and bring the potatoes to the boil over high heat. Reduce the heat to moderate and continue cooking for about 15 minutes until tender.

2. Meanwhile, using an electric blender or a food processor fitted with the chopping blade, process the yoghurt and ricotta cheese until the mixture is completely smooth.

3. Drain the potatoes and return them to the saucepan. Heat the potatoes over moderate heat for approximately 30 seconds to 1 minute until the excess moisture has evaporated. Remove the saucepan from the heat.

4. Using a potato masher or a hand-held electric mixer, beat the yoghurt mixture into the boiled potatoes until smooth. Season with salt and pepper. Stir in the chopped herbs, transfer the potatoes to a bowl and serve immediately.

POTATO FRITTERS *Serves 4*

4 large (about 1kg) potatoes

1 small onion

1 large egg

2 tablespoons flour (or matzo meal)

1 teaspoon salt

¼ teaspoon ground black pepper

Sunflower oil for frying

Sour cream (optional)

 Preparation time 10 minutes

 Cooking time 12 minutes

1. Preheat the oven to 100°C. Peel and coarsely grate the potatoes and onion into a large bowl. Stir in the egg, flour, salt and ground black pepper. Line a baking sheet with a double layer of paper towels.

2. In a large frying pan, heat 6mm of the oil over moderately high heat. Drop the potato mixture into the hot oil, 1 heaped tablespoonful at a time, flattening each one slightly with a spatula. Fry three or four fritters at a time for about 4 minutes until the edges are brown and crispy. Turn them over and continue cooking for approximately 1 more minute until they are golden brown.

3. Drain the fritters on the prepared baking sheet and keep them warm in the oven while cooking the remaining fritters. Place on a warmed platter and serve with sour cream, if desired.

BAKED POTATO CAKES

BAKED POTATO CAKES *Serves 4*

3 tablespoons olive oil

1 clove garlic, finely chopped

2 large (about 500g) potatoes, preferably round in shape

1 tablespoon chopped fresh thyme (or 1 teaspoon dried thyme)

1 tablespoon (about 20g) grated Parmesan cheese

Ground black pepper

Thyme sprigs (optional)

 Preparation time 13 minutes

 Cooking time 20 minutes

SERVING SUGGESTION This simple dish can be baked in the oven when you are roasting a chicken or a joint of beef or lamb. Serve with a tempting salad of spinach, carrot and baby marrows.

1 Preheat the oven to 230°C. Brush a large baking sheet with 1½ tablespoons of the oil. In a small saucepan, heat the remaining 1½ tablespoons of oil over moderate heat. Add the garlic and sauté for about 1 minute until just golden. Remove from the heat.

2 Peel the potatoes and cut them into very thin (3mm) slices. Divide into 8 equal portions. For each potato cake, arrange the slices overlapping in a circular pattern on the baking sheet, making a total of 8 cakes, each about 10cm in diameter. Brush with the garlic oil and sprinkle with the thyme, Parmesan cheese and pepper. Bake for 15 to 20 minutes until cooked and browned, pressing several times during baking with a spatula so that the slices stick together. Garnish with thyme, if desired, and serve.

VEGETABLES

GINGERED SWEET POTATOES *Serves 4*

4 medium (about 1kg) sweet potatoes

2 tablespoons (30g) butter or margarine

1 tablespoon finely chopped fresh ginger (or 1 teaspoon ground ginger)

1/8 teaspoon ground cinnamon

1/4 cup firmly packed light brown sugar

Salt and ground black pepper to taste

 Preparation time 10 minutes

 Cooking time 18 minutes

SERVING SUGGESTION Sweet potatoes are lifted to heavenly heights with the addition of ginger and a touch of cinnamon. Serve with cooked ham or a crisply roasted chicken.

1 In a large saucepan, bring 5cm of water to the boil over high heat. Meanwhile, peel the sweet potatoes and cut them into 1cm-thick slices. Add the sweet-potato slices to the boiling water, cover the saucepan and return to the boil. Reduce the heat to low and cook the potatoes for about 8 minutes until tender.

2 Meanwhile, in a large frying pan, melt the butter over moderate heat. If using chopped fresh ginger, add the ginger and cinnamon and cook for 1 minute. Add the brown sugar and heat, stirring constantly until the sugar dissolves. (If using ground ginger, add the ginger and cinnamon at the same time as the brown sugar.)

3 Drain the sweet potatoes, add them to the sugar mixture in the frying pan and cook, stirring gently, until they are thoroughly coated with the sugar mixture. Season with salt and pepper, transfer to a warmed bowl and serve.

ORANGE-GLAZED PARSNIPS *Serves 4*

700g parsnips

1 cup water

1 large or 2 medium oranges

2 tablespoons (30g) butter or margarine

2 tablespoons light or dark brown sugar

2 teaspoons lemon juice

Salt and ground white pepper to taste

1 tablespoon chopped parsley

 Preparation time 17 minutes

 Cooking time 20 minutes

1 Peel the parsnips and cut them into 7,5cm x 1cm sticks. In a large frying pan, bring the parsnips and the water to the boil over moderate heat. Reduce the heat to low, cover the frying pan and cook for about 8 minutes until the parsnips are tender but still firm to the bite.

2 Meanwhile, finely grate the orange part of the orange peel (the zest) to make 1 tablespoon of grated zest. Cut the orange in half and squeeze enough juice to make 1/4 cup.

3 Remove the lid from the frying pan and increase the heat to moderately high. Add the orange juice, orange zest, butter, brown sugar and lemon juice to the parsnips and stir to blend thoroughly. Continue cooking for about 7 minutes, stirring occasionally, until the liquid is reduced to a syrupy consistency and the parsnips are glazed.

4 Season the parsnips with salt and pepper. Transfer to a serving dish, sprinkle with the parsley and serve.

SPINACH-FILLED TOMATOES

SPINACH-FILLED TOMATOES *Serves 4*

4 large tomatoes

750g fresh spinach

2 tablespoons (30g) butter or margarine

1 small onion, sliced

2 tablespoons flour

1 cup milk

2 tablespoons whipping cream

¼ teaspoon ground nutmeg

Salt and ground black pepper to taste

 Preparation time 10 minutes

 Cooking time 15 minutes

SERVING SUGGESTION Serve this colourful dish with whole-wheat rolls for a perfect starter or light summer lunch. Use firm-fleshed tomatoes.

1. Preheat the oven to 200°C. Using a sharp knife, remove and discard a 5mm slice from the stem end of the tomatoes. Scoop out and discard the seeds and pulp. Place the tomatoes upside-down on paper towels to drain.

2. Meanwhile, rinse and drain the spinach and discard any large stems. Place the spinach and a little water in a large saucepan. Cover and cook over high heat for about 3 minutes until the leaves are wilted, stirring occasionally. Drain in a colander, pressing the leaves to extract the water. Chop and set aside.

3. In the same saucepan, melt the butter over moderate heat. Add the onion and sauté for about 5 minutes until soft. Add the flour and stir until well mixed. Gradually stir in the milk and bring to the boil. Add the spinach, cream and nutmeg and cook until the spinach is heated through. Season with salt and pepper. Fill each tomato with an equal amount of the spinach mixture. Place in an ungreased baking dish and bake for 3 to 5 minutes until the tomatoes are heated through. Serve immediately.

VEGETABLES

RATATOUILLE *Serves 4* (PICTURE PAGE 271)

1 small (about 250g) brinjal

1 medium sweet green pepper

¼ cup olive or sunflower oil

1 medium onion, chopped

1 medium baby marrow, sliced

1 clove garlic, chopped

1 tin (410g) chopped tomatoes

2 teaspoons dried basil or origanum

Salt and ground black pepper to taste

 Preparation time
9 minutes

 Cooking time
36 minutes

1. Discard the ends of the brinjal and slice it into 2,5cm cubes. Core and seed the green pepper and chop it into 2,5cm pieces.

2. In a 5-litre, heavy-based saucepan or casserole dish, heat the oil over moderate heat. Add the onion and sauté for about 5 minutes until soft. Add the brinjal, green pepper, baby marrow and garlic and cook for 5 minutes, stirring occasionally.

3. Add the undrained tinned tomatoes and basil to the saucepan and bring the mixture to the boil. Reduce the heat to low and partially cover the saucepan. Simmer the vegetables for about 25 minutes until they are tender, stirring occasionally.

4. Season the ratatouille with salt and black pepper to taste. Spoon it into a serving bowl and serve immediately, or cover and refrigerate to serve chilled later.

MICROWAVE OVEN VERSION

Place the oil and onion in a large microwave-safe bowl or casserole dish. Cover and cook on high power for 3 to 4 minutes until the onion softens, stirring halfway through the cooking time. Stir the brinjal, green pepper, baby marrow, garlic and basil into the onion. Replace the cover and cook on high for 10 minutes, stirring twice during cooking.

Drain the tomatoes and stir them into the brinjal mixture. Continue cooking, uncovered, on high power, for about 15 minutes until the vegetables are tender, stirring twice during cooking. Season with salt and pepper and serve.

Add interest to mealies, whether fresh from the cob or out of a tin, with a touch of spice.

SPICED CORN KERNELS

Drain *one 410g tin whole kernel corn* and place the kernels in a medium-sized saucepan. Add *one 410g tin Indian-style chopped tomatoes* and mix well. Heat thoroughly. Serve with grilled chicken, hamburger patties or fish, and brown rice. Serves 4

CHILLI CORN ON THE COB

Wrap *4 fresh, cleaned mealies* in wax paper. Microwave on full power until just tender (about 9 to 11 minutes). Melt *3 tablespoons (45g) of butter*, stir in ¼ *teaspoon chilli powder* and cook for 1 minute. Brush the chilli butter over the mealies and serve. Serves 4

STUFFED BABY MARROWS

STUFFED BABY MARROWS *Serves 4*

- 4 large (about 700g) baby marrows
- 2 tablespoons (30g) butter or margarine
- 1 small onion, chopped
- 1½ cups (90g) fresh bread crumbs
- ¼ cup chopped parsley
- 1 teaspoon dried origanum
- Salt and ground black pepper to taste
- 1 large egg
- 2 tablespoons (40g) grated Parmesan cheese

 Preparation time 10 minutes

 Cooking time 25 minutes

COOK'S TIP This dish, which never fails to please, can easily be doubled to become a main course, making a light, low-kilojoule meal.

1. Preheat the oven to 200°C. Grease a 37,5cm x 26,5cm baking tin. Halve each baby marrow along its length. Scoop out and reserve the flesh, leaving a 6mm-thick shell. Place the baby marrow shells, cut side down, into the baking tin. Bake for about 10 minutes until tender but still firm to the bite.

2. Meanwhile, dice the baby marrow pulp. In a medium-sized saucepan, melt the butter over moderate heat. Add the onion and the diced baby marrow and sauté for about 5 minutes until soft. Stir in the bread crumbs, parsley and origanum. Season with salt and pepper. Remove the saucepan from the heat.

3. Beat the egg lightly, add it to the bread-crumb mixture and stir until well mixed. Remove the baby marrow shells from the oven, turn them over and season lightly with salt and black pepper. Fill with the crumb mixture and sprinkle with the cheese. Bake for about 15 minutes until the crumbs are lightly browned and serve.

VARIATIONS ON THE BASIC BAKED POTATO

By making use of your microwave oven, you can have four piping hot baked potatoes in less than half the time they would take in a conventional oven. Once the potatoes are ready to eat, you can create any number of delectable meals by topping them with one of these easy sauces. Each recipe makes four servings.

▶ **Basic microwave baked potatoes** Scrub *four 225g potatoes* well and pierce them all over with a fork. Arrange them, evenly spaced, on a microwave-safe plate. Place the potatoes in the microwave oven and cook on high power for 20 to 25 minutes until they are tender, turning them over and rearranging them halfway through the cooking time. Fill or top the hot potatoes with the topping of your choice.

➤ **Chilli topping** In a medium-sized saucepan, heat *one 400g tin chilli con carne* over moderate heat until hot and bubbling. Remove from the heat. Cut an X in the top of each of *4 baked potatoes*. Fluff up the potato pulp with a fork. Top each potato with ¼ of the chilli con carne, a handful each of *coarsely grated mild Cheddar cheese* and *finely chopped lettuce* and a spoonful of *ready-made tomato salsa*.

◀ **Cream-cheese topping** In a small bowl, combine ½ *cup softened cream cheese* with *2 tablespoons garlic-flavoured salad dressing*, *2 tablespoons chopped sweet red pepper* and *2 tablespoons finely chopped pine nuts* until well mixed. Cut an X in the top of each of *4 baked potatoes*. Fluff up the potato pulp with a fork. Top each with some of the cheese mixture.

➤ **Vegetable-salami topping** In a large frying pan, heat *1 tablespoon olive oil* over moderate heat. Add *1 small onion, sliced* and *¼ cup julienned sweet green pepper*. Sauté for 5 minutes until soft. Add *1 clove garlic, chopped* and *½ teaspoon dried origanum*. Sauté for 10 seconds. Remove from the heat. Stir in *60g pepper salami*, cut into half rounds. Cut an X in the top of each of *4 baked potatoes*. Fluff up the potato pulp. Top each with some of the vegetable-salami mixture. Sprinkle with *grated Parmesan cheese*.

◀ **Cheese and herb topping** Halve *4 baked potatoes* horizontally. Scoop the potato pulp into a bowl leaving 5mm-thick potato shells. Add *60g coarsely grated mature Cheddar cheese*, *¼ cup plain low-fat yoghurt*, *2 tablespoons chopped parsley* and *1 tablespoon chopped chives* to the potato pulp and mix well. Season with *salt* and *pepper* to taste. Spoon the mixture back into the potato shells and reheat in the microwave oven for about 4 minutes until hot. Sprinkle with *paprika*, if desired.

Main-course vegetables

These healthy vegetable-based dishes – some with meat and some vegetarian – are brimming with goodness and are satisfying enough to make a complete meal.

Tofu with stir-fried vegetables *Serves 4*

½ cup plus 1½ tablespoons cornflour

1½ tablespoons soy sauce

500g extra-firm tofu

⅓ cup sunflower or peanut oil

300g green beans

1 large sweet red pepper

2 cups (about 250g) sliced mushrooms

3 cloves garlic, finely chopped

1 cup vegetable or chicken stock

 Preparation time 18 minutes

 Cooking time 27 minutes

Diet note Derived from the soy bean, tofu is rich in vegetable proteins and contains no cholesterol. Serve with rice.

1. In a cup, combine 1½ tablespoons of the cornflour with the soy sauce and set aside. Drain the tofu and cut it crosswise into four slices. Pat the slices with a paper towel to remove excess moisture. Cut each slice in half diagonally to form a triangle. Place the remaining cornflour in a pie plate. Dip the tofu in the cornflour, coating thoroughly. Set aside. In a wok or large frying pan, heat the oil over moderately high heat.

2. Add the tofu and cook, turning carefully, for 10 to 12 minutes until golden brown. Meanwhile, slice the green beans diagonally into 4cm lengths. Core and seed the red pepper and cut it into strips. Transfer the tofu to a plate. Add the mushrooms and garlic to the wok and stir-fry for 2 minutes. Add the green beans and stock and bring to the boil. Reduce the heat to low, cover and cook for about 7 minutes until the beans are crisp-tender.

3. Increase the heat to moderately high. Add the red pepper and the soy-sauce mixture to the vegetables and cook for about 2 minutes until thickened and bubbling. Add the tofu and stir gently. Cook for about 2 more minutes until heated through and serve.

Time Savers

Baked potatoes

When you're baking potatoes in a conventional oven, there are two simple ways to speed up the cooking time. You'll save about 15 minutes by using either method.

The first method: Cut the scrubbed potatoes in half lengthwise. Place the halves, cut sides down, on a greased baking sheet, then bake.

The second method: Stick a metal prong through the centre of the whole potato, then bake. The metal conducts the heat so that the potato bakes on both the inside and the outside.

Using either method, bake the potatoes in the oven at 220°C for about 35 minutes until they are soft.

HAM-STUFFED ACORN SQUASH

HAM-STUFFED ACORN SQUASH *Serves 4*

2 large (about 500g each) acorn squash

3 tablespoons (45g) butter or margarine

1 spring onion, chopped

1 cup slivered or finely cubed smoked ham

½ teaspoon dried thyme

¼ teaspoon salt

¾ cup water

½ cup quick-cooking couscous

¼ cup raisins

2 tablespoons honey

Salt and ground black pepper to taste

 Preparation time 12 minutes

 Cooking time 24 minutes

Serving suggestion This low-kilojoule, satisfying main dish goes well with a salad of endive, radicchio and succulent artichoke hearts.

1 Cut each acorn squash in half along its length. Scoop out and discard the seeds. Partially fill a large saucepan with 2,5cm of water. Add the squash and bring to the boil over high heat. Reduce the heat to low, cover and cook for 15 to 20 minutes until the squash is tender when pierced with a fork.

2 Meanwhile, in a large saucepan, melt 1 tablespoon of the butter over moderate heat. Add the spring onion and sauté gently until soft. Stir in the ham, thyme, salt and water and bring to the boil. Stir in the couscous and raisins. Remove from the heat, cover and leave to stand for about 15 minutes until the couscous softens.

3 Preheat the grill. Drain the squash and place the halves, cut side up, on the rack over a grill pan. Place ½ tablespoon each butter and honey into each cavity. Sprinkle with salt and pepper. Grill 10cm from the heat until the butter melts. Brush the open surfaces of the squash with the butter mixture. Continue grilling for 3 to 4 minutes until lightly browned. Spoon the ham mixture into the squash cavities and serve.

VEGETABLES

LENTILS AND PEAS WITH RICE Serves 4

250g green lentils
2 tablespoons sunflower oil
1 medium onion, chopped
1 clove garlic, crushed
1 cup white rice
3 cups water
1 fresh chilli, split
Salt and ground black pepper to taste
250g frozen peas
3 tablespoons chopped coriander leaves
Coriander leaves for garnishing

 Preparation time
20 minutes

 Cooking time
30 minutes

1. Soak the lentils in cold water for 20 minutes. In a medium-sized saucepan, heat the oil over moderate heat. Add the onion and sauté for about 5 minutes until soft. Add the garlic and rice and stir until well mixed. Add the water, increase the heat to high and bring the mixture to the boil.

2. Drain the lentils and add them to the rice mixture. Stir in the chilli and season to taste with salt and pepper. Reduce the heat, cover and cook for 20 minutes. Add the frozen peas, stirring to break up the chunks. Cover and cook for a further 5 minutes until the peas are cooked and the rice and lentils are tender.

3. Stir the coriander into the rice and lentil mixture and check the seasoning. Turn the mixture into a large dish, garnish with coriander leaves and serve immediately.

VEGETABLE GRATIN ON TOAST Serves 4

250g baby marrows
250g yellow pattypan squash
¼ cup olive oil
2 cloves garlic, finely chopped
4x1cm-thick slices Italian bread
1 large onion, sliced
½ teaspoon dried thyme
½ teaspoon salt
125g Provolone cheese, sliced
1 large ripe tomato, sliced
2 tablespoons (about 20g) grated Parmesan cheese

 Preparation time
15 minutes

 Cooking time
25 minutes

FOOD NOTE This simple, economical vegetable and cheese supper dish is crammed with the rich mellow flavours of Italy.

1. Preheat the oven to 200°C. Lightly grease a 2-litre shallow baking or gratin dish. Chop the baby marrows and pattypan squash diagonally into 5mm-thick slices.

2. Heat the oil over moderate heat in a large frying pan. Add the garlic and sauté for 1 minute. Remove the pan from the heat.

3. Brush both sides of the bread slices with half of the garlic oil. Set the frying pan with the remaining oil aside. Place the bread in the prepared dish and bake for about 8 minutes until golden, turning once halfway through the baking time.

4. Meanwhile, sauté the onion in the pan with the remaining garlic oil over moderate heat for 3 minutes. Add the baby marrows, squash, thyme and salt. Sauté for about 5 minutes until soft.

5. Spoon half of the vegetable mixture over the toasted bread and top each with an equal amount of the Provolone cheese slices. Spoon the remaining vegetable mixture over the cheese, top with the slices of tomato and sprinkle with the Parmesan cheese. Bake for about 10 minutes until the mixture is heated through. Serve.

VEGETABLES

VEGETARIAN CHILLI *Serves 4*

1 medium sweet green pepper
1 tin (425g) red kidney beans
1 tablespoon sunflower oil
1 medium onion, chopped
2 to 3 teaspoons chilli powder
1 teaspoon ground cumin
½ teaspoon salt
125g baby marrows, diced
2 tins (410g each) chopped tomatoes, undrained
250g frozen corn kernels
½ cup (60g) coarsely grated Cheddar cheese

 Preparation time
8 minutes

 Cooking time
25 minutes

COOK'S TIP *If you prefer your chilli very mild or fire-alarm hot, adjust the amount of chilli powder accordingly.*

1 Core, seed and chop the green pepper. Drain and rinse the red kidney beans and set them aside. In a 5-litre, heavy-based saucepan or flameproof casserole dish, heat the oil over moderate heat. Add the onion and green pepper and sauté for about 5 minutes until soft. Stir in the chilli powder, cumin and salt and cook for 1 minute.

2 Stir the beans, baby marrows, tomatoes and corn kernels into the onion mixture. Increase the heat to moderately high and bring the mixture to the boil. Partially cover the saucepan, reduce the heat to low and simmer the mixture for approximately 15 minutes, stirring occasionally.

3 Ladle the chilli mixture into serving bowls, top each with an equal amount of the Cheddar cheese and serve.

VEGETARIAN STUFFED PEPPERS *Serves 4*

4 large (about 225g each) sweet green, red or yellow peppers
1 tablespoon sunflower oil
1 medium onion, chopped
125g baby marrows, diced
1 clove garlic, finely chopped
1 tin (425g) red kidney beans, drained and rinsed
1 teaspoon dried origanum
250g mozzarella cheese, diced
2 cups ready-made Italian tomato pasta sauce

 Preparation time
9 minutes

 Cooking time
35 minutes

1 Cut each pepper in half along its length and remove the seeds. In a 30cm frying pan, bring 1cm of water to the boil over high heat. Add the pepper halves, cover and cook for about 5 minutes until the peppers are tender but still firm to the bite.

2 Drain the peppers, remove them from the frying pan and set aside. In a medium-sized saucepan, heat the oil over moderate heat. Add the onion and baby marrows and sauté for about 5 minutes until soft. Stir in the garlic and sauté for 10 seconds. Remove the saucepan from the heat.

3 Stir the beans, origanum and cheese into the onion mixture. Fill each pepper half with an equal amount of the mixture. Pour the pasta sauce into the frying pan.

4 Arrange the peppers, filled sides up, in the frying pan. Cover and bring the sauce to the boil over high heat. Reduce the heat to low and simmer for approximately 15 minutes until the vegetables are heated through and the cheese is melted. Transfer the cooked peppers to a platter, spoon the pasta sauce over them and serve immediately.

MUSHROOM AND ONION PIE

MUSHROOM AND ONION PIE *Serves 4*

4 tablespoons (60g) butter or margarine

6 cups (about 750g) sliced mushrooms

1 large onion, sliced

⅓ cup flour

½ cup dry white wine

1 container (250g) cottage cheese

¼ cup chopped parsley

½ teaspoon salt

¼ teaspoon ground white pepper

½ package (200g) ready-rolled pastry

1 egg yolk

2 tablespoons water

 Preparation time 15 minutes

 Cooking time 30 minutes

DIET NOTE This traditional tummy warmer has a pastry lid only, keeping the kilojoule count to a minimum. Serve with a bowl of steamed baby potatoes.

1. Preheat the oven to 220°C. Melt the butter in a large frying pan over moderately high heat. Add the mushrooms and onion and sauté for about 10 minutes until soft. Add the flour, stirring until well mixed. Add the wine and simmer for about 1 minute until thickened. Remove the pan from the heat. Stir the cottage cheese, parsley, salt and white pepper into the mixture and pour it into an ungreased 23cm pie plate.

2. Roll out the pastry, place it over the filling and trim to neaten the edges. Press down around the rim to seal it onto the plate. Flute the edge decoratively, if desired. In a cup, mix the egg yolk with water and brush over the pastry. Cut slits into the crust to allow the steam to escape during baking. Bake for 15 to 20 minutes until the crust is golden brown. Serve immediately.

VEGETABLES

BRINJAL PARMIGIANA *Serves 4*

1 large (about 500g) brinjal
1 large egg
2 tablespoons water
⅓ cup flour
½ teaspoon dried origanum
4 tablespoons olive or sunflower oil
⅓ cup (45g) grated Parmesan cheese
1 cup ready-made Italian tomato pasta sauce
1 cup (120g) coarsely grated mozzarella cheese

 Preparation time 15 minutes

 Cooking time 22 minutes

Serving suggestion Serve this Italian favourite as a starter for a dinner party for eight, or as an accompaniment for chicken or veal.

1. Peel the brinjal and cut it crosswise into 1cm-thick slices. Beat the egg with the water in a pie plate. Combine the flour and origanum in a second pie plate. Dip the brinjal slices first into the egg mixture and then into the flour mixture, shaking off the excess flour.

2. In a large frying pan, heat 2 tablespoons of the oil over moderately high heat. Add enough of the brinjal slices to cover the bottom of the frying pan without overlapping and sauté for about 3 minutes on each side until golden brown. Drain on paper towels. Add the remaining 2 tablespoons of oil to the frying pan and sauté the remaining brinjal slices until golden. Drain.

3. Wipe the frying pan with paper towels. Return the brinjal slices to the pan, overlapping them, if necessary, to fit into the base. Sprinkle with the Parmesan cheese. Top with the pasta sauce and mozzarella cheese. Cover and cook for 5 to 7 minutes over moderately low heat until heated through. Spoon the brinjal onto plates and serve immediately.

MIXED VEGETABLE STEW *Serves 4*

250g Swiss chard
12 baby carrots (about 250g)
125g mange-tout
4 spring onions
250g frozen baby green beans, thawed under hot running water
2 tablespoons (30g) butter or margarine
1 tablespoon olive oil
1 cup (about 125g) halved mushrooms
1 clove garlic, chopped
1 cup hot water
Salt and ground black pepper to taste
1 tablespoon chopped parsley

 Preparation time 15 minutes

 Cooking time 15 minutes

1. Cut the stems of the chard into 2,5cm lengths and the leaves into 1cm-wide ribbons. Slice the carrots in half lengthwise, trim the mange-tout and chop the onions and beans into 1cm lengths.

2. In a 5-litre, heavy-based saucepan, heat the butter with the oil over moderately high heat. Add the spring onions and sauté for 30 seconds. Stir in the chard stems, carrots, green beans, mushrooms, garlic and water. Bring to the boil. Reduce the heat to low, cover and cook for 8 to 10 minutes until the carrots are almost tender.

3. Add the chard leaves and the mange-tout to the vegetable mixture. Continue cooking for about 4 more minutes until the vegetables are tender but still firm to the bite. Season with salt and pepper. Spoon the mixture into a warmed serving dish, sprinkle with the parsley and serve immediately.

SALADS

Seafood salad (page 314)

Salad accompaniments

Liven up your meals by serving them with salads – combining subtle flavours and interesting textures with all the nutrients your family needs.

Spinach salad with oranges Serves 4

¼ cup slivered almonds

3 navel or Valencia oranges

½ small red onion, thinly sliced

4 cups torn fresh spinach leaves or whole baby spinach leaves

For the red wine vinegar dressing:

¼ cup sunflower oil

¼ cup red wine vinegar

1 tablespoon sugar

½ teaspoon salt

¼ teaspoon ground black pepper

 Preparation time 14 minutes

 Cooking time 4 minutes

SERVING SUGGESTION *This eye-catching salad marries the sweet and tart flavours of fruit and spinach – it's an excellent braai accompaniment.*

1 In a large frying pan, heat the oil for the dressing over moderate heat. Add the almonds and sauté for 2 to 3 minutes until golden. Remove the frying pan from the heat. Using a slotted spoon, transfer the almonds to a small bowl, leaving the oil in the pan.

2 To make the dressing: Add the vinegar, sugar, salt and pepper to the sunflower oil in the frying pan and stir until the sugar dissolves. Set aside.

3 Peel the oranges and slice across their width. In a salad bowl, combine the oranges, onion slices and spinach leaves. Sprinkle with the almonds. Add the dressing, toss gently and serve.

SHELF MAGIC

Here are two easy salads – one with the exotic Moroccan flavours of bulgur or cracked wheat and pine nuts, and the other a potato salad with a tangy lemon-garlic dressing. Either makes an unusual accompaniment for a braai or picnic.

Warm tabbouleh salad

In a large saucepan, bring *3 cups water* to the boil. Stir in *1½ cups bulgur* or *cracked wheat*. Remove from the heat, cover and leave for 15 to 20 minutes until soft. Dice *1 large tomato*. Chop *3 spring onions* and *¼ cup shelled pistachio nuts*. In a large bowl, combine the tomato, onion, nuts, *½ cup sliced pitted dates*, *1 tablespoon each chopped parsley* and *chopped mint*. Stir in *½ cup prepared salad dressing, 1 tablespoon lemon juice* and the bulgur. Serves 6

Potato bean salad

Boil *one packet of ready-peeled baby potatoes* (available from supermarkets) for about 10 to 15 minutes until tender. Drain, place in a large bowl and, while still warm, toss with *lemon and garlic salad dressing* (see recipe on page 305). Add *1 tin (400g) butter beans, 2 tablespoons chopped parsley* and *2 tablespoons chopped spring onion*. Toss gently until well mixed. Refrigerate until needed. Just before serving, garnish with *1 cup cherry tomatoes*, halved. Serves 6

SALADS

ORIENTAL SALAD Serves 4

250g mange-tout, trimmed

1 cup bean sprouts, rinsed and drained

1 large carrot, cut into matchstick strips

12 thin slices cucumber, halved

For the Oriental dressing:

¼ cup peanut or sunflower oil

1 tablespoon Oriental sesame oil

1 tablespoon rice vinegar or white vinegar

1 tablespoon soy sauce

½ teaspoon ground ginger

½ teaspoon sugar

Pinch of crushed red chillies

 Preparation time
11 minutes

 Cooking time
5 minutes

1. In a medium-sized saucepan, bring 5cm of water to the boil over high heat. Drop the mange-tout into the saucepan of boiling water. When the water returns to the boil, drain the mange-tout into a colander, rinse them under cold running water and drain thoroughly.

2. Transfer the mange-tout to a large bowl and add the sprouts, carrot and cucumber slices.

3. To make the dressing: In a small jar or cruet, blend the peanut oil and sesame oil. Add the vinegar, soy sauce, ginger, sugar and crushed chillies. Cover and shake until well mixed. Pour the dressing over the vegetables. Toss to mix well and serve immediately.

ORIENTAL CHICKEN SALAD

Add *2 tablespoons peanut* or *sunflower oil* and *two 180g skinless chicken-breast fillets* to the list of ingredients above. In a medium-sized frying pan, heat the extra *2 tablespoons of oil* over moderate heat. Sauté the chicken for about 3 minutes on each side until the juices run clear. Remove the chicken and slice it into 5mm-thick strips. Prepare the salad as in Steps 1 and 2 above, adding the chicken just before the dressing.

RED AND GREEN COLESLAW Serves 4

1 small head green cabbage

½ small head red cabbage

1 large carrot

1 medium red-skinned apple

Salt and ground black pepper to taste

For the yoghurt dressing:

½ cup mayonnaise

⅓ cup low-fat yoghurt

2 tablespoons apple juice

1 tablespoon cider vinegar

1 teaspoon celery seeds

 Preparation time
18 minutes

 Cooking time
0 minutes

1. Cut the green cabbage in half, remove the tough core and coarsely grate the leaves. Repeat with the red cabbage. Peel and coarsely grate the carrot. Core the unpeeled apple and chop the flesh finely.

2. In a large bowl, lightly toss the green and red cabbage with the carrot and apple until well mixed.

3. To make the dressing: In a small bowl, whisk together the mayonnaise, low-fat yoghurt, apple juice, cider vinegar and celery seeds.

4. Add the dressing to the vegetables and apple and toss until coated. Season the salad with salt and pepper. Serve immediately, or cover and refrigerate until ready to serve.

ARTICHOKE AND AVOCADO PEAR SALAD

ARTICHOKE AND AVOCADO PEAR SALAD *Serves 4*

2 cups alfalfa sprouts

1 tin (400g) artichoke hearts in water, drained

3 plum tomatoes

1 avocado pear

2 tablespoons (20g) grated Parmesan cheese

½ cup lemon and garlic salad dressing (see page 305)

 Preparation time
15 minutes

 Cooking time
0 minutes

SERVING SUGGESTION If you prefer, substitute finely chopped lettuce for the alfalfa sprouts. Serve the salad on individual plates as a starter.

1. Spread an even layer of the sprouts on a serving platter. Slice the artichoke hearts in half (or in quarters if they are large). Slice the tomatoes. Arrange the artichokes and tomatoes on the sprouts.

2. Halve the avocado pear, remove the pip, then peel it and slice the flesh. Arrange the avocado pear slices on the platter with the sprouts. Sprinkle with the cheese, drizzle the dressing over the top and serve immediately.

SALADS

Mushroom Asparagus Salad *Serves 4*

3 cups water
500g fresh asparagus
½ cup white wine vinegar
½ teaspoon salt
½ teaspoon dried thyme
16 mushroom caps
8 cos lettuce leaves
2 tablespoons slivered fresh or roasted sweet red pepper
2 tablespoons extra-virgin olive oil

 Preparation time
15 minutes

 Cooking time
12 minutes

Serving suggestion This spring salad is pretty enough to serve as a first course for a special dinner party. It's ideal before lamb or fish.

1. In a large saucepan, bring the water to the boil over high heat. Meanwhile, snap the tough ends off the asparagus and discard. If desired, peel the lower half of each asparagus spear. Add the asparagus to the boiling water, reduce the heat to moderate and cook for 8 to 10 minutes until just crisp-tender.

2. Using a slotted spoon, transfer the asparagus to a plate lined with paper towels and set aside to cool. Meanwhile, add the white wine vinegar, salt and thyme to the water in the saucepan. Bring the mixture to the boil, add the mushroom caps and return to the boil. Remove the mushroom mixture from the heat and leave it to cool.

3. To serve, line each of four individual salad plates with two cos lettuce leaves, overlapping them to form a fan shape. Pat the asparagus dry and arrange it in a fan shape over the cos.

4. Drain the mushroom caps and toss with the red pepper slivers. Arrange the mushroom mixture at the base of the asparagus stems. Drizzle the oil over the asparagus and mushroom mixture and serve immediately.

Tomato and Mozzarella Salad *Serves 4*

3 large ripe tomatoes
500g mozzarella cheese
1 cup cherry tomatoes
¼ cup fresh basil

For the olive oil dressing:
½ cup olive oil
3 tablespoons red wine vinegar
¼ teaspoon salt
⅛ teaspoon ground black pepper

 Preparation time
15 minutes

 Cooking/chilling time
30 minutes

1. Cut the large tomatoes and the mozzarella cheese into 6mm-thick slices. Halve the cherry tomatoes.

2. On a serving platter, arrange alternating slices of the tomatoes and mozzarella cheese around the edge of the platter. Place the cherry tomatoes in the centre. Cover and refrigerate the salad for at least 30 minutes or until ready to serve.

3. Meanwhile, prepare the dressing: In a small jar or cruet, combine the oil, vinegar, salt and pepper. Cover and shake the dressing until well mixed.

4. Just before serving, tear or cut the basil leaves into slivers and sprinkle them over the tomato salad. Shake the dressing, drizzle it over the top and serve immediately.

SALADS

CREAMY CUCUMBER SALAD *Serves 4*

For the sour cream dressing:
½ cup sour cream
1 teaspoon dried dill
1 tablespoon cider vinegar
1 teaspoon sugar
½ teaspoon salt
¼ teaspoon white pepper

2 large cucumbers, chilled
½ small onion, thinly sliced

 Preparation time
10 minutes

 Cooking time
0 minutes

1. To make the dressing: Combine the sour cream, dried dill, cider vinegar, sugar, salt and white pepper in a large bowl and stir thoroughly until well mixed. Place in the refrigerator until the salad is ready to serve.

2. Peel the cucumbers, halve them lengthwise, remove the seeds and slice the flesh thinly. Fold the cucumber and onion into the dressing. Spoon the salad into a serving dish and serve immediately.

GRATED CARROT AND BEETROOT SALAD *Serves 4*

300g carrots, peeled
¼ cup raisins
300g medium beetroot, peeled

For the sweet and sour dressing:
½ cup sunflower oil
2 tablespoons red wine vinegar
1 teaspoon sugar
½ teaspoon mustard powder
¼ teaspoon salt

 Preparation time
15 minutes

 Cooking/chilling time
15 minutes

1. Using a hand grater or a food processor, grate the carrots and place them in a small bowl. Add the raisins. Grate the beetroot and place it in a second small bowl.

2. To make the dressing: In a small jar or cruet, combine the oil, vinegar, sugar, mustard powder and salt. Cover and shake until well mixed. Pour half of the dressing over each bowl of vegetables. Toss each until coated. Cover and refrigerate for about 15 minutes or until ready to serve.

3. To serve, spoon the beetroot into the centre of a platter and arrange the grated carrots around it. Serve immediately.

MARINATED CHICKPEA SALAD *Serves 4*

1 small cucumber
1 small sweet green pepper
6 red radishes
1 tin (425g) chickpeas, drained
½ cup pitted black olives (preferably Greek), halved
¼ cup Italian-style salad dressing
Lettuce leaves, rinsed and dried, for serving
4 cherry tomatoes, halved

 Preparation time
10 minutes

 Cooking/chilling time
30 minutes

1. Peel the cucumber, remove the seeds and cut the flesh into chunks. Core and seed the green pepper and cut it into strips. Trim and slice the radishes.

2. In a medium-sized bowl, combine the cucumber, green pepper, radishes, chickpeas and olives. Pour the dressing over the salad and toss lightly. Cover and refrigerate for at least 30 minutes.

3. Line a serving platter with the lettuce leaves. Spoon the marinated salad over the leaves, garnish with the cherry tomatoes and serve immediately.

BROCCOLI-ORANGE SALAD

BROCCOLI-ORANGE SALAD *Serves 6*

For the orange dressing:

2 tablespoons sunflower or canola oil

1 small onion, sliced

2 teaspoons cornflour

½ cup orange juice

2 cups broccoli florets

2 cups cauliflower florets

Salt and ground black pepper to taste

2 cups thinly sliced red cabbage

Red cabbage leaves, rinsed and dried (optional)

 Preparation time 8 minutes

 Cooking time 26 minutes

COOK'S TIP To cool the broccoli and cauliflower quickly, plunge the cooked vegetables into a large bowl of iced water.

1. To make the dressing: In a medium-sized saucepan, heat the oil over moderate heat. Add the onion and sauté for 5 minutes until soft. Add the cornflour and mix, then stir in the orange juice and bring to the boil. Cook until slightly thickened. Remove from the heat, pour the mixture into a bowl and refrigerate to cool quickly.

2. Meanwhile, in a large saucepan, bring 5cm of water to the boil over high heat. Add the broccoli and cauliflower and cook for about 7 minutes until just crisp-tender. Drain the vegetables and rinse with cold water. Add the vegetables to the orange dressing and toss until coated. Season with salt and pepper. Cover and refrigerate until ready to serve.

3. To serve, add the sliced red cabbage to the vegetable mixture and toss until well mixed. Line a serving platter with red cabbage leaves, if desired, top with the salad and serve immediately.

SALADS

CORN AND BEAN SALAD *Serves 8*

For the cumin dressing:
6 tablespoons sunflower oil
3 tablespoons cider vinegar
1½ teaspoons Dijon mustard
¾ teaspoon salt
¾ teaspoon ground cumin
¼ teaspoon sugar

3 cups cooked corn kernels
1 tin (400g) red kidney beans, drained and rinsed
100g sliced pitted black olives
1 small sweet red pepper
Curly endive leaves, rinsed and dried

 Preparation time
10 minutes

 Cooking/chilling time
30 minutes

1. To make the dressing: In a medium-sized bowl, whisk together the oil, cider vinegar, Dijon mustard, salt, cumin and sugar until well mixed.

2. Stir the corn kernels, kidney beans and olives into the bowl with the cumin dressing and toss to coat thoroughly. Cover and refrigerate for at least 30 minutes.

3. Keeping the red pepper whole, remove the core and seeds. Cut the pepper across its width into 6mm-wide rings.

4. To serve, line a platter with the endive leaves. Spoon the corn mixture over the endive, top with the red pepper rings and serve immediately.

THREE-BEAN SALAD

Omit the corn kernels and sweet red pepper from the list of ingredients above. Add *one 400g tin cut green beans*, drained, *one 400g tin butter beans*, drained and *⅓ cup chopped onion* to the list of ingredients. Prepare the dressing as in Step 1, above. Add all of the beans and the onion, then cover and refrigerate for at least 30 minutes. Line a platter with the *endive leaves*. Spoon the bean mixture over the leaves and serve.

WARM RICE SALAD *Serves 4*

3 tablespoons sunflower oil
1 small onion, sliced
1 cup long-grain white rice
2½ cups water
1 cup frozen green peas
1 cup sliced celery
1 tablespoon red wine vinegar
½ teaspoon salt
½ teaspoon dried tarragon
¼ teaspoon ground black pepper

 Preparation time
5 minutes

 Cooking time
35 minutes

1. Heat 1 tablespoon of the oil over moderate heat in a large saucepan. Add the onion and sauté for about 5 minutes until soft. Add the rice and the water and bring the mixture to the boil. Reduce the heat to low, cover and cook for about 10 minutes.

2. Using a fork, gently stir the frozen peas into the rice mixture. Cover and continue to cook the rice and peas for about 5 minutes until they are tender and all the liquid is absorbed. Remove the saucepan from the heat and leave the rice to stand, covered, for 5 minutes.

3. Meanwhile, in a large bowl, combine the celery, the remaining 2 tablespoons of oil, the vinegar, salt, tarragon and pepper. Add the cooked rice and toss until coated. Serve the salad warm or at room temperature.

WARM WINTER SALAD

WARM WINTER SALAD *Serves 4*

8 baby potatoes, unpeeled and halved

2 cups Brussels sprouts, trimmed, or 250g frozen Brussels sprouts

250g carrots, peeled and sliced diagonally

1 tablespoon chopped parsley or chives

For the creamy mustard dressing:

¾ cup mayonnaise

1 tablespoon Dijon mustard

1 tablespoon cider vinegar

2 teaspoons celery seeds

Salt and ground black pepper to taste

 Preparation time 15 minutes

 Cooking time 20 minutes

SERVING SUGGESTION *This simple, well-tempered salad with its sharp mustard dressing partners roast beef or chicken perfectly. It can also serve two as a robust vegetarian lunch.*

1 Cook the potatoes in a saucepan of boiling water for about 15 minutes until they are tender. In another saucepan of boiling water, cook the Brussels sprouts and carrots for about 10 minutes until they are tender but still firm to the bite.

2 Meanwhile, make the dressing: In a small bowl, using a wire whisk, blend the mayonnaise, mustard, vinegar and celery seeds. Season to taste with salt and pepper.

3 Drain the vegetables and arrange them on a serving platter, allowing them to cool slightly. Spoon some of the mayonnaise dressing over the vegetables and sprinkle with the parsley. Serve immediately, passing the remaining dressing separately.

VARIATIONS ON THE BASIC GREEN SALAD

When making a salad, don't restrict yourself to the tired old lettuce-and-tomato cliché. With very little extra effort – perhaps adding a variety of crisp garden vegetables or a drizzle of tantalizing dressing – they can really lift a meal out of the ordinary. Below is a recipe for a basic salad using a fresh combination of salad vegetables. Once you've tossed them together, refer to the suggestions on the right for dressings and toppings that will really add zest to the salad. Each dressing makes ½ cup. The basic salad and toppings are all sufficient to serve four.

➤ **Basic green salad** Wash and dry *1 bunch rocket, 1 small head cos lettuce, 1 small head butter lettuce, 1 small head radicchio* and *250g baby spinach leaves*. Into a large salad bowl, tear the leaves into bite-size pieces.

Prepare the dressing and additional ingredients from one of the recipes on the right and serve immediately.

◄ **Tomato basil dressing** In a food processor or blender, combine *2 medium tomatoes, skinned and seeded, 3 tablespoons olive oil, 1 tablespoon white wine vinegar, 1 teaspoon tomato paste, 1 teaspoon sugar, 4 to 6 fresh basil leaves* or *½ teaspoon dried origanum*. Blend until smooth. Season to taste with *salt* and *ground black pepper*. Prepare the *basic green salad*, top with *one chopped hard-boiled egg, chopped cucumber* and *prepared croutons*. Toss with the dressing and serve.

◄ **Curried yoghurt dressing** In a food processor or blender, combine *½ cup plain yoghurt, 2 tablespoons mango chutney, 1 teaspoon curry powder, 1 teaspoon lemon* or *lime juice, 6 to 8 fresh mint leaves* or *½ teaspoon dried mint*. Blend until smooth. Season with *salt* and *ground black pepper*. Prepare the *basic green salad*, top with *orange segments* or *sliced apple* and sprinkle with *chopped peanuts*. Toss with the dressing and serve.

► **Tangy cocktail dressing** In a bowl, combine *¼ cup mayonnaise, 2 tablespoons tomato sauce* or *ketchup, 1 tablespoon chopped parsley, 1 spring onion, finely chopped, 1 tablespoon chopped stuffed olives, 1 tablespoon lemon juice* and *1 teaspoon paprika*. Prepare the *basic green salad* and top with *125g cooked small prawns* or *shrimps*. Toss with the dressing and serve.

► **Horseradish cream dressing** In a bowl, combine *⅔ cup sour cream, 1 tablespoon creamed horseradish, 2 tablespoons lemon juice, salt* and *ground black pepper* to taste. Prepare the *basic green salad*, top with *125g finely chopped roast beef, 1 medium chopped tomato* and *½ cup grated baby marrows*. Toss with the dressing and serve.

► **Lemon and garlic dressing** In a small jar or cruet, combine *3 tablespoons olive oil, 3 tablespoons sunflower oil, 2 tablespoons fresh lemon juice, 1 clove garlic, crushed* and *½ teaspoon dried origanum*. Shake to mix well. Season to taste with *salt* and *ground black pepper*. Prepare the *basic green salad* and top with *100g to 125g sliced goat's cheese*. Toss with the dressing and serve with *whole-wheat toast triangles*.

MACARONI VEGETABLE CHEESE SALAD

MACARONI VEGETABLE CHEESE SALAD *Serves 6*

125g Cheddar cheese
125g baby marrows
1 carrot
250g elbow macaroni
¾ cup mayonnaise
¼ cup plain low-fat yoghurt
¼ cup Italian-style salad dressing
Salt and ground black pepper to taste
Carrot curls (optional)

 Preparation time
8 minutes

 Cooking time
20 minutes

SERVING SUGGESTION This nutritious version of the old noodle salad standby is ideal with cold meats for an informal buffet supper.

1. In a large saucepan, bring 3 litres of water to the boil over high heat. Meanwhile, coarsely grate the cheese, baby marrows and carrot into a large bowl, and set aside.

2. Add the macaroni to the boiling water and cook according to the package directions or until it is tender but still firm to the bite. Stir the mayonnaise, yoghurt and salad dressing into the cheese and vegetables.

3. Drain the macaroni in a colander and rinse under cold running water for 1 to 2 minutes until it is cold. Stir the well-drained macaroni into the cheese mixture. Season with salt and pepper.

4. Transfer the macaroni salad to a serving bowl and garnish with carrot curls, if desired. Serve immediately, or cover and refrigerate until ready to serve.

TWO-POTATO SALAD *Serves 6*

2 sweet potatoes (about 180g each)

500g baby potatoes, unpeeled

⅓ cup Italian-style or oil-and-vinegar salad dressing

½ cup mayonnaise

¼ cup water

1½ tablespoons prepared mustard

2 spring onions, chopped

¼ cup chopped fresh basil, tarragon or parsley

Salt and ground black pepper to taste

 Preparation time
9 minutes

 Cooking/chilling time
25 minutes

1. Bring 5cm water to the boil over high heat in a large, heavy-based saucepan. Meanwhile, peel the sweet potatoes and cut them into 2,5cm cubes. Halve the unpeeled baby potatoes. Drop the baby potatoes into the boiling water. Cover and return the water to the boil and cook the potatoes for 5 minutes.

2. Add the sweet potatoes to the saucepan and continue cooking for about 7 minutes more until tender. Drain them in a colander and rinse with cold water to cool. Transfer the potatoes to a large bowl and drizzle with the Italian-style dressing, tossing to coat them well. Cover and refrigerate for at least 5 minutes.

3. In a small bowl, mix the mayonnaise, water and mustard until smooth. Add the spring onions and basil. Fold the mayonnaise mixture into the potatoes and season to taste with salt and pepper. Serve immediately or cover and refrigerate until ready to serve.

CREAMY PASTA SALAD *Serves 4*

1 large sweet red pepper

180g penne (quill-shaped pasta)

3 tablespoons olive or sunflower oil

1 small onion, sliced

1 cup broccoli florets

1 clove garlic, chopped

1 tablespoon red wine vinegar

1 cup fresh basil (or 1 cup watercress)

1 cup sour cream

Salt and ground black pepper to taste

 Preparation time
10 minutes

 Cooking time
25 minutes

1. In a large saucepan, bring 3 litres of water to the boil over high heat. Core and seed the red pepper and slice it thinly.

2. Add the penne to the boiling water and cook according to the directions on the package or until it is tender but still firm to the bite.

3. Meanwhile, in a large frying pan, heat the oil over moderate heat. Add the onion and sauté for about 5 minutes until soft. Add the red pepper, broccoli florets and garlic. Cook for about 4 minutes until crisp-tender. Remove the pan from the heat and stir in the vinegar.

4. Drain the pasta and rinse it well with cold water to cool quickly. Return the pasta to the large saucepan. Using a blender or food processor, purée the basil with the sour cream until the mixture is smooth.

5. Add the creamy basil dressing to the cooked pasta and toss gently until coated. Season with salt and pepper to taste. Transfer the pasta salad to a large serving bowl, top it with the sautéed vegetables and serve immediately.

SALADS

MINTY FRUIT SALAD *Serves 4*

1 spanspek
1 medium peach
2 red plums
1 cup green seedless grapes

For the honey-mint dressing:
3 tablespoons natural yoghurt
1 tablespoon chopped mint
1 tablespoon lemon juice
1 teaspoon honey

 Preparation time
15 minutes

 Cooking time
0 minutes

1 Cut the spanspek in half along its length and scoop out the seeds. Slice the flesh thinly and peel each slice. Halve the peach and the plums, discard the pips and slice thinly. On a serving platter, arrange the grapes with the sliced fruits.

2 To make the dressing: In a small jar or cruet, combine the yoghurt, mint, lemon juice and honey. Cover and shake until well mixed. Drizzle the dressing evenly over the fruit and serve immediately.

APPLE GRAPE SALAD *Serves 4*

2 stalks celery
1 large Granny Smith apple
1 cup red or green seedless grapes
¼ cup pecan nuts, chopped
½ cup mayonnaise
2 tablespoons apple juice or cider
Salt and ground white pepper to taste
Lettuce leaves, rinsed and dried

 Preparation time
12 minutes

 Cooking time
3 minutes

1 Cut the celery stalks into 6mm slices. Core the apple and cut the flesh into 2cm cubes. Halve the grapes. Place the pecan nuts in a small frying pan and toast them over moderate heat, stirring frequently, for 2 to 3 minutes until lightly browned. Set the toasted nuts aside.

2 In a medium-sized bowl, combine the celery slices, apple cubes and grapes. Add the mayonnaise and apple juice and stir to mix well. Season to taste with salt and pepper. Cover and refrigerate until ready to serve.

3 To serve, line a serving dish with the lettuce leaves. Spoon the apple mixture into the centre and sprinkle with the toasted pecan nuts. Serve immediately.

TIME SAVERS

SALADS

■ Use scissors to snip fresh herbs and salad leaves directly into the serving bowl rather than taking the time to chop them with a knife. If exact measurements are required, snip the ingredients into a measuring cup. Dried fruit and cooked meats can also be cut with a pair of scissors.

■ For the speediest salads, make use of the wide variety of prewashed and packaged salad vegetables available from your local supermarket.

■ When making salads in which precision is not essential, don't waste preparation time by measuring each ingredient to exact specifications. The amounts given are approximate. Be guided by your eyes and taste buds!

WATERCRESS PEAR SALAD

WATERCRESS PEAR SALAD *Serves 4*

1 bunch watercress

2 pears

½ cup (about 60g) crumbled blue cheese

⅓ cup sliced pitted prunes (optional)

¼ cup chopped walnuts

For the raspberry vinegar dressing:

⅓ cup sunflower oil

2 tablespoons raspberry vinegar

Salt and ground black pepper to taste

 Preparation time 21 minutes

 Cooking time 0 minutes

COOK'S TIP Red wine vinegar may be used in place of the raspberry vinegar to create this sophisticated starter.

1 Discard the thick stems of the watercress. Halve the pears along their length, remove the cores and slice the flesh lengthwise.

2 On four individual serving plates, arrange an equal amount of the watercress, pears, cheese and prunes, if desired, and sprinkle with the walnuts.

3 To make the dressing: In a small jar or cruet, combine the oil, vinegar, salt and pepper. Cover and shake until well mixed. Drizzle the dressing over each serving and serve immediately.

Main-course salads

Bursting with fresh flavours and filling enough to make a complete meal, these easy salads can be made in a flash.

Mediterranean salad Serves 4

2 ripe tomatoes

1 cucumber

125g sliced salami

6 tablespoons olive oil

1 small red onion, thinly sliced

1 cup (about 125g) thinly sliced mushrooms

2 cloves garlic, chopped

2 cups 1cm cubes of Italian bread

2 tablespoons red wine vinegar

Salt and ground black pepper to taste

4 cups torn firm salad greens such as cos lettuce or curly endive

½ cup fresh basil (optional)

1 cup (about 125g) crumbled feta cheese

 Preparation time 15 minutes

 Cooking time 10 minutes

Cook's tip Create another Mediterranean-inspired favourite by substituting a tin of tuna, drained and flaked, for the salami.

1 Cut the tomatoes into 2,5cm chunks. Peel the cucumber and cut it into 5mm-thick slices. Cut the sliced salami into strips.

2 In a 4-litre saucepan, heat 2 tablespoons of the olive oil over moderate heat. Add the onion and sauté for about 5 minutes until soft and slightly transparent. Add the mushrooms and garlic and sauté for approximately 3 minutes until softened. Remove the saucepan from the heat. Stir in the bread cubes and set aside to cool.

3 Meanwhile, in a small jar or cruet, combine the remaining 4 tablespoons of olive oil, the vinegar, salt and pepper. Cover and shake the dressing until well mixed.

4 To serve, in a salad bowl, toss the tomatoes, cucumber, salad greens and basil, if desired. Top with the salami, cheese and the bread mixture. Drizzle the dressing over the salad. Toss gently and serve.

SHELF MAGIC

Pack this wholesome and well-balanced salad if you don't have the time to stop for lunch. Finish off with an apple or a slice of melon.

Butter beans with tuna

Drain *one 400g tin butter beans* and rinse with cold water. Drain *two 185g tins tuna packed in water*. Cut *3 ripe plum tomatoes* into 1cm cubes. Finely chop *1 spring onion*. In a large bowl, combine the beans, tomatoes, spring onion, *¼ cup olive oil*, *2 tablespoons lemon juice*, *1 clove garlic*, finely chopped, *½ teaspoon dried origanum* and *2 tablespoons chopped parsley*. Gently fold the tuna into the butter bean mixture and season to taste with *salt* and *freshly ground black pepper*. Serve the salad immediately or cover the bowl and refrigerate until ready to serve. Toss lightly before serving. Serves 4

SALADS

ANTIPASTO SALAD BOWL *Serves 4*

250g salami, in one piece

1 small sweet red pepper

180g large black olives, pitted and chilled

½ tin (200g) chickpeas, chilled

1 cup (about 250g) sliced mushrooms

½ tin (200g) marinated artichoke hearts, chilled

2 tablespoons olive oil

1 tablespoon red wine vinegar

½ teaspoon dried origanum

Lettuce leaves, rinsed and dried

 Preparation time
21 minutes

 Cooking time
0 minutes

SERVING SUGGESTION Serve this robust salad with a basket of warm Italian bread and garlic butter. Follow with a luscious dessert of creamy ice cream served with vanilla wafers or the crunchy Italian almond macaroons called amaretti.

1 Using a sharp knife, cut the salami into 2cm cubes. Core and seed the red pepper and cut it into 2,5cm pieces. Drain the olives. Drain and rinse the chickpeas.

2 In a large bowl, mix the salami, red pepper, olives, chickpeas, mushrooms and artichoke hearts with their marinade. Add the oil, vinegar and origanum.

3 To serve, line a shallow glass salad bowl with the lettuce. Spoon the salami mixture into the centre of the leaves and serve immediately or cover and refrigerate until ready to serve.

BROCCOLI AND LENTIL SALAD *Serves 4*

1 cup dried lentils

2 cups water

2 cups broccoli florets

1 spring onion, chopped

¼ cup Italian-style salad dressing

¼ cup mayonnaise

Salt and ground black pepper to taste

¼ cup toasted sunflower seeds

8 red radishes, sliced

Additional Italian-style salad dressing (optional)

 Preparation time
10 minutes

 Cooking/chilling time
30 minutes

1 Rinse and drain the dried lentils. In a medium-sized saucepan, bring the lentils and the water to the boil over high heat. Reduce the heat to low, cover and simmer the lentils for 15 to 20 minutes until they are tender but still firm.

2 Meanwhile, in a small saucepan, bring 2,5cm of water to the boil over high heat. Place the broccoli florets in the boiling water and return the water to the boil, uncovered. Cook for approximately 2 minutes until the broccoli is tender but still firm to the bite. Drain and rinse under cold running water. Arrange the broccoli florets around the outer edge of a shallow serving dish and refrigerate.

3 Drain the cooked lentils and rinse them under cold water. In a medium-sized bowl, mix the lentils with the chopped spring onion, salad dressing and mayonnaise. Season to taste with salt and black pepper. Refrigerate the lentils for at least 10 minutes until cool.

4 To serve, spoon the lentils in the centre of the broccoli florets on the serving dish and sprinkle with the toasted sunflower seeds. Garnish the salad with the radish slices. Serve immediately, passing additional dressing separately, if desired.

PINEAPPLE-COTTAGE CHEESE SALAD

Pineapple-cottage cheese salad *Serves 4*

500g low-fat cottage cheese

250g chopped fresh pineapple

2 tablespoons raisins

1 tablespoon chopped fresh mint

2 red-skinned apples, eg Red Delicious or Starking, chilled

1 head red oak leaf lettuce

2 tablespoons chopped walnuts

Mint sprigs (optional)

 Preparation time 10 minutes

 Cooking time 0 minutes

DIET NOTE Simplicity itself to prepare, this low-kilojoule lunch turns plain cottage cheese into a tasty treat. Serve it with whole-wheat rolls.

1 In a small bowl, combine the cottage cheese, pineapple, raisins and mint. Cover and refrigerate until ready to serve.

2 Just before serving, quarter and core the apples but do not peel. Cut the apples into thin wedge-shape slices. Rinse and dry the lettuce leaves.

3 Line four individual serving plates with the lettuce. Spoon an equal amount of the cheese mixture on top of the lettuce, surround with the apple slices and sprinkle with the walnuts. Garnish with mint sprigs, if desired, and serve immediately.

SALADS

SEAFOOD SALAD Serves 4 (PICTURE PAGE 293)

For the lemon-garlic dressing:

1/3 cup sunflower oil

2 tablespoons lemon juice

1 clove garlic, finely chopped

1 teaspoon Worcestershire sauce

1/4 teaspoon mustard powder

300g fresh fish fillets

1 small head cos lettuce

1 tin (66g) anchovy fillets

1 cup prepared croutons

2 tablespoons (40g) grated Parmesan cheese

Ground black pepper to taste

 Preparation time 25 minutes

 Cooking time 5 minutes

COOK'S TIP *You can create a simpler version of this salad by omitting the fish fillets altogether. Be sure to use fresh, crisp lettuce that has been rinsed and dried thoroughly.*

1 Preheat the grill. To prepare the dressing: In a small jar or cruet, combine the oil, lemon juice, garlic, Worcestershire sauce and mustard powder. Cover and shake until thoroughly blended.

2 Place the fish on a greased rack over the grill pan and drizzle the fillets with 1 tablespoon of the dressing. Grill the fish 10cm from the heat for about 5 minutes until it flakes easily when tested with a fork. Transfer to a plate and leave to cool for 10 minutes.

3 Meanwhile, rinse and dry the lettuce leaves. Tear the leaves into bite-sized pieces and place them in a salad bowl. Drain the anchovies and cut them in half across their width. Cut into small chunks and remove any bones. Add the fish, anchovies and croutons to the lettuce.

4 Shake the remaining dressing and drizzle it over the salad. Garnish with the cheese and pepper, toss gently and serve.

SMOKED SALMON TROUT AND ASPARAGUS SALAD Serves 4

500g slim fresh green asparagus

1 packet prepared baby salad greens

2 spring onions, thinly sliced

4 fillets (about 250g) hot-smoked salmon trout, skinned and flaked

Dill sprigs for garnishing

For the dill and lemon dressing:

2 tablespoons lemon juice

1 tablespoon chopped dill

1/2 teaspoon coarsely ground mustard

Salt and ground black pepper to taste

1/4 cup olive oil

 Preparation time 15 minutes

 Cooking time 7 minutes

COOK'S TIP *Substitute the asparagus with baby green beans, if desired.*

1 In a 4-litre saucepan, bring 10cm of water to the boil over high heat. Trim the asparagus, drop them into the boiling water and return the water to the boil. Cook for 2 to 3 minutes until tender but still firm to the bite. Drain and rinse with cold water. Pat dry. Place the asparagus in a bowl and refrigerate until ready to serve.

2 To make the dressing: In a large bowl, whisk together the lemon juice, dill and mustard, and season to taste with salt and black pepper. Gradually whisk in the olive oil and check the seasoning.

3 In a large bowl, mix the salad greens, the spring onion and some of the dressing and toss to coat. Using a slotted spoon, place the salad on four large plates. Add the asparagus to the remaining dressing, then remove with the slotted spoon and place on the salad. Top each with a salmon trout fillet and drizzle with a little of the remaining dressing. Garnish with dill sprigs and serve.

SHRIMP COUSCOUS SALAD

SHRIMP COUSCOUS SALAD *Serves 4*

 Preparation time
10 minutes

 Cooking time
15 minutes

4 tablespoons olive or sunflower oil

100g baby marrows, sliced

1 clove garlic, finely chopped

1 teaspoon curry powder

1½ cups vegetable stock or water

1½ cups quick-cooking couscous

300g medium uncooked, peeled and deveined shrimps, thawed

3 ripe plum tomatoes, diced

2 tablespoons chopped parsley

1 tablespoon red wine vinegar

Salt and ground black pepper to taste

COOK'S TIP This nutritious grain salad is delicious served warm or cold. Be sure to use quick-cooking couscous, available from health food shops and selected supermarkets.

1 In a large frying pan, heat 2 tablespoons of the oil over moderate heat. Add the baby marrows and sauté for 4 minutes until soft. Add the garlic and curry powder and cook for 1 minute.

2 Add the stock to the frying pan with the baby marrows and bring to the boil. Stir in the couscous, cover and remove the frying pan from the heat. Let the couscous stand for about 10 minutes until it softens and absorbs all of the liquid.

3 Meanwhile, in a large saucepan, bring 5cm of water to the boil over high heat. Drop the shrimps into the boiling water and cook for about 1 minute until they are pink and firm. Drain.

4 In a large bowl, combine the shrimps, tomatoes, parsley, vinegar and the remaining 2 tablespoons of oil. Stir in the couscous mixture, separating the grains with a fork. Season to taste with salt and pepper. Serve the salad warm or cover and refrigerate until ready to serve.

SALADS

TEX-MEX SALAD Serves 4

1 medium sweet green pepper
3 tablespoons sunflower oil
1 medium onion, chopped
1 clove garlic, chopped
500g lean minced beef
2 teaspoons chilli powder
1 teaspoon ground cumin
1 cup ready-made chunky tomato salsa
½ medium head crisp lettuce, eg Iceberg
1 cup (about 120g) coarsely grated Cheddar cheese
½ cup sliced pitted black olives
¼ cup sliced red radishes

 Preparation time 17 minutes

 Cooking time 10 minutes

Serving suggestion Serve with a basket of warmed flour tortillas – you may choose to make them into burritos by spooning the salad into the tortillas and rolling them up. They taste especially good with a dollop of sour cream.

1. Core and seed the sweet green pepper and cut the flesh into 2,5cm squares.

2. In a large frying pan, heat the oil over moderately high heat. Add the onion, garlic and minced beef and sauté until the meat is lightly browned. Add the chilli powder and cumin and continue cooking for 1 more minute.

3. Remove the frying pan from the heat. Stir the green pepper and tomato salsa into the meat mixture and set it aside.

4. Rinse and pat the lettuce dry, then chop the leaves finely and use them to line a serving platter. Spoon the meat mixture over the lettuce. Sprinkle the cheese, olives and radishes over the top and serve immediately.

LAYERED CHICKEN SALAD Serves 4

6 slices bacon
2 large (about 300g) skinless chicken-breast fillets
1 small head cos lettuce
3 large ripe tomatoes
2 small avocado pears
1 cup ready-made blue cheese salad dressing

 Preparation time 17 minutes

 Cooking time 13 minutes

1. In a large frying pan, cook the bacon over moderate heat until crisp. Leaving the drippings in the pan, remove the bacon and place on paper towels to drain. Crumble the bacon and set aside.

2. Using a sharp knife, cut each chicken-breast fillet into 3mm-thick slices across its width. Place the chicken in the pan with the drippings and sauté over moderately-high heat for about 5 minutes until tender. Set the chicken aside to cool slightly.

3. Cut the lettuce crosswise into 1cm-wide slices. Thinly slice the tomatoes. Halve the avocado pears, remove the pips and slice the flesh crosswise.

4. To arrange the salad, place the sliced lettuce in the bottom of a large glass salad bowl. Forming layers, add the chicken, then the tomatoes, then the avocado pear slices, spacing them evenly. Add the crumbled bacon and top with a generous spoonful of blue cheese dressing. Transfer the remaining dressing to a small bowl or pitcher. Serve the salad, passing the extra dressing separately.

SALADS

BEEF NOODLE SALAD *Serves 4*

2 packages (85g each) ramen noodle soup (any flavour)

2 spring onions

2 large carrots

300g rare roast beef, cut into strips

Lettuce leaves, rinsed and dried

For the peanut-sesame dressing:

²/₃ cup hot water

¹/₃ cup creamy peanut butter

2 tablespoons soy sauce

2 tablespoons Oriental sesame oil

1 tablespoon white vinegar

1 teaspoon sugar

Pinch of red pepper flakes or ¹/₄ teaspoon crushed red chillies

 Preparation time 20 minutes

 Cooking time 10 minutes

1. In a large saucepan, bring 5cm of water to the boil over high heat. Add the noodles (discard the seasoning packets), cover and reduce the heat to moderate. Cook the noodles for about 3 minutes until they are soft.

2. Meanwhile, slice the spring onions into thin strips along their length, then crosswise into 5cm lengths. Peel the carrots and slice them into 6mm-thick strips. Drain the cooked noodles in a colander, rinse well under cold running water and set them aside to cool slightly.

3. To make the dressing: In a large bowl, using a wire whisk, combine the hot water, peanut butter, soy sauce, sesame oil, vinegar, sugar and red pepper flakes.

4. Add the cooked noodles, spring onions, carrots and beef to the peanut-butter mixture and fold gently until well mixed.

5. Line a serving platter with the lettuce leaves and top with the beef noodle salad. Serve immediately or cover and refrigerate the salad until ready to serve.

HAM AND SMOKED CHEESE SALAD *Serves 4*

For the mustard dressing:

¹/₄ cup sunflower oil

1 tablespoon red wine vinegar

1 tablespoon Dijon mustard

1 tablespoon chopped chives or spring onion tops

Salt and ground black pepper to taste

250g smoked ham

250g smoked cheese

2 stalks celery

Baby spinach leaves

2 medium ripe tomatoes, cut into wedges

 Preparation time 18 minutes

 Cooking time 0 minutes

COOK'S TIP *Instead of ham and smoked cheese, try a combination of sliced cold chicken with Emmenthal cheese, or thin slices of salami with Edam. This makes an excellent salad to pack for an office lunch or a family picnic.*

1. To make the dressing: In a medium-sized bowl, whisk together the sunflower oil, vinegar, mustard and chopped chives until thoroughly blended. Season the dressing to taste with salt and ground black pepper.

2. Using a sharp knife, slice the ham, cheese and celery stalks into 6mm-thick strips. Add to the bowl with the salad dressing and toss gently until evenly coated. Rinse the spinach leaves and pat them dry.

3. Line a serving platter with the spinach leaves. Spoon the salad mixture over the leaves and arrange the tomato wedges around the salad. Serve immediately.

WARM SAUSAGE-ONION SALAD

WARM SAUSAGE-ONION SALAD *Serves 4*

300g smoked sausage, eg kielbasa

2 large red or white onions

2 cups (about 250g) quartered mushrooms

2 tablespoons olive oil

1 tablespoon red wine vinegar or balsamic vinegar

1 sprig fresh rosemary

1 clove garlic, finely chopped

4 cups rocket leaves

 Preparation time
10 minutes

 Cooking time
20 minutes

SERVING SUGGESTION A steaming baked potato, topped with melted Cheddar cheese, would be the perfect partner for this delicious cold-weather salad.

1. Preheat the oven to 220°C. Using a sharp knife, cut the sausage diagonally into 1cm-thick slices and the onions into 6mm-thick slices. In a large open roasting pan, toss the sausage, onions, mushrooms, oil, vinegar, rosemary and garlic until well mixed.

2. Place in the oven and roast the sausage and vegetables for 15 to 20 minutes until they are lightly browned, stirring halfway through the roasting time.

3. Meanwhile, rinse the rocket leaves and pat them dry. Line a serving platter or four individual serving plates with the rocket. Spoon the sausage and vegetable mixture, with their pan juices, over the leaves and serve immediately.

SALADS

SPINACH, BACON AND EGG SALAD Serves 4

4 thick rashers bacon

2 large eggs, beaten

8 cups baby spinach leaves, rinsed and dried

2 cups (about 250g) sliced mushrooms

2 spring onions, sliced

For the cider vinegar dressing:

¼ cup olive oil

1 tablespoon sugar

2 tablespoons cider vinegar

¼ teaspoon ground black pepper

 Preparation time 24 minutes

 Cooking time 12 minutes

COOK'S TIP Cooking the eggs in the bacon drippings adds extra flavour to this substantial salad.

1 Heat a large frying pan over moderate heat, add the bacon and sauté until crisp, turning occasionally. Remove the bacon and place it on paper towels to drain, leaving the drippings in the frying pan. Crumble the bacon and set it aside.

2 Add the beaten eggs to the frying pan and fry until set on the bottom. Turn the eggs over and continue to cook until set throughout. Transfer the eggs to a plate and cut into strips.

3 To make the dressing: In a small jar or cruet, combine the olive oil, sugar, vinegar and pepper. Cover and shake until the ingredients are mixed thoroughly.

4 In a large salad bowl, combine the baby spinach, mushrooms and spring onions. Top with the strips of egg and the bacon and toss gently to mix. Drizzle the dressing over the salad, toss until coated and serve.

TURKEY PASTA SALAD Serves 4

200g medium ripe tomatoes

125g shaved or thinly sliced smoked turkey, cut into strips

2 cloves garlic, crushed

50g rocket leaves, coarsely chopped or torn

¼ cup olive oil

2 tablespoons balsamic vinegar

Salt and coarsely ground black pepper to taste

400g fresh angel hair pasta

Rocket leaves for garnishing

 Preparation time 15 minutes

 Cooking time 15 minutes

DIET NOTE This light and refreshing summer pasta salad tastes best when served at room temperature.

1 In a large saucepan, bring 2 litres of water to the boil over high heat. Meanwhile, plunge the tomatoes in a bowl of boiling water for a few minutes, remove with a fork and peel off the skin. Chop the flesh finely and place in a large decorative serving bowl. Add the smoked turkey, garlic, chopped rocket leaves, olive oil and balsamic vinegar and mix well. Season to taste with salt and black pepper.

2 Place the pasta in the saucepan of boiling water and cook according to the directions on the package or for just a few minutes until tender but still firm to the bite (do not overcook). Drain and add to the smoked-turkey mixture, stirring gently until mixed thoroughly.

3 Check the seasoning and adjust if necessary. Garnish the salad with the rocket leaves and serve immediately.

Breads, Cakes and Biscuits

Apple bran muffins (page 331)

BREADS

This selection of sweet and savoury breads rises most impressively to the occasion, providing a warm and aromatic addition to any meal.

CHILLI CORN BREAD Serves 8

1 cup tinned or frozen corn kernels

1 cup yellow maize (mealie) meal

1 cup flour

¼ cup sugar

2½ teaspoons baking powder

½ teaspoon salt

⅔ cup milk

2 tablespoons sunflower oil

1 large egg

1 to 3 teaspoons chopped green chillies

 Preparation time 7 minutes

 Cooking time 25 minutes

COOK'S TIP *If you prefer the subtle flavour of plain corn bread, omit the chillies. If you like it hot, increase the chillies to 2 tablespoons.*

1 Preheat the oven to 220°C. Grease a 20cm round baking tin. Drain the tinned corn kernels or thaw the frozen kernels under warm water. In a large bowl, combine the maize meal, flour, sugar, baking powder and salt.

2 In a small bowl, combine the milk, oil and egg until well mixed. Stir the milk mixture into the dry ingredients until just moistened. Fold in the corn kernels and chillies. Spoon the maize meal batter into the prepared tin.

3 Bake the corn bread for about 25 minutes until a toothpick inserted in the centre comes out clean. Cut the bread into wedges and serve warm.

SAVOURY HERBED SCONES Serves 8

2 cups flour

2 teaspoons bicarbonate of soda

1 teaspoon cream of tartar

½ teaspoon salt

6 tablespoons (90g) butter or margarine, cut into pieces

¼ cup chopped fresh dill, basil or parsley

¾ cup (190ml) plain low-fat yoghurt

 Preparation time 15 minutes

 Cooking time 18 minutes

COOK'S TIP *To make scones that are easy to split, roll out the dough to a thickness of 5mm, then fold it in half and cut it into the desired shapes.*

1 Preheat the oven to 220°C. Mix the flour, bicarbonate of soda, cream of tartar and salt in a large bowl. Using a pastry blender or two knives held like a pair of scissors, cut in the butter until the mixture resembles coarse crumbs. Add the dill, stirring until well mixed. Add the yoghurt and stir to form a soft dough. Knead very briefly in the bowl until just combined.

2 On a lightly floured surface, roll out the dough to a thickness of 1cm. Cut out the scones with a floured 7,5cm round cookie cutter and place them on an ungreased baking sheet. Pat the dough scraps together, roll out again and cut out more scones. Bake for about 18 minutes until golden brown. Serve warm.

BREADS, CAKES AND BISCUITS

Garlic Toast *Serves 4*

8x2cm-thick slices Italian or French bread

2 tablespoons (30g) butter or margarine

1 tablespoon olive oil

2 cloves garlic, very finely chopped

1 teaspoon dried origanum

2 tablespoons (40g) grated Parmesan cheese

 Preparation time 4 minutes

 Cooking time 6 minutes

1. Preheat the grill. Arrange the slices of Italian bread on the grill rack over a grill pan and set aside.

2. In a small saucepan, heat the butter and oil over moderate heat. Add the garlic and origanum and sauté for 10 seconds. Remove the saucepan from the heat.

3. Grill the bread about 10cm from the heat until it is lightly toasted. Turn the slices over, brush with the garlic mixture and sprinkle with the Parmesan cheese. Continue grilling until the bread is golden brown. Serve immediately.

Popovers *Serves 6*

2 large eggs

1 cup milk

1 tablespoon sunflower oil

1 cup flour

½ teaspoon salt

 Preparation time 15 minutes

 Cooking time 30 minutes

Food note The popover is cousin to the English Yorkshire Pudding

1. Preheat the oven to 230°C. In a small bowl, using an electric mixer, beat the eggs until frothy. Beat in the milk and oil, then add the flour and salt, beating until well mixed. Leave the batter to stand for 10 minutes.

2. Grease one 6-cup muffin tin (or coat it with nonstick cooking spray) and place it in a roasting pan containing a little water. Pour the batter into the prepared muffin tin.

3. Bake the popovers for about 30 minutes until puffed and well browned. Remove immediately and serve hot.

SHELF MAGIC

Keep a few ready-to-use pizza bases in your freezer and use them to create these quick savoury pizza breads.

Pan-fried onion pizzas

Chop *4 to 6 spring onions*. In a large frying pan, heat *2 tablespoons olive oil* and sauté the onions until softened. Remove with a slotted spoon and set aside. Add *one pizza base* to the pan and cook over moderate heat for about 5 minutes on each side until crisp and golden brown. Remove from the heat and sprinkle with the softened onion. Slice into wedges and serve immediately. Serves 8

SPICY PARMESAN PUFFS

SPICY PARMESAN PUFFS *Serves 8*

¼ cup water

¼ cup milk

4 tablespoons (60g) butter or margarine

½ cup flour

1 spring onion

2 large eggs

⅓ cup (45g) grated Parmesan cheese

¼ teaspoon salt

¼ teaspoon cayenne pepper

Butter for spreading (optional)

 Preparation time 10 minutes

 Cooking time 30 minutes

SERVING SUGGESTION Serve these light, melt-in-the-mouth puffs with a freshly made salad or a bowl of hot soup.

1 Preheat the oven to 200°C. Place the water, milk and butter in a medium-sized saucepan and bring to the boil over moderate heat. Add the flour and, using a wooden spoon, beat the mixture until it leaves the side of the saucepan and forms a ball. Remove the saucepan from the heat and leave to cool slightly.

2 Meanwhile, lightly grease a baking sheet. Trim and finely chop the spring onion, including the green leaves.

3 Beat the eggs, one at a time, into the flour mixture until smooth. Stir in the cheese, onion, salt and cayenne pepper. Drop 8 heaped spoonfuls of the batter about 5cm apart on the prepared sheet. Bake for 25 to 30 minutes until the puffs are crisp and golden. Serve warm with butter, if desired.

BREADS, CAKES AND BISCUITS

PARMESAN ONION BREAD *Serves 8*

½ cup (120g) butter or margarine

1 medium onion, finely chopped

1 loaf (about 30cm) Italian or French bread

¼ cup (about 35g) grated Parmesan cheese

 Preparation time
6 minutes

 Cooking time
32 minutes

SERVING SUGGESTION *The rustic flavour of this crispy cheese-and-onion loaf would go well with a supper of soup or a light pasta dish.*

1 Preheat the oven to 190°C. In a large frying pan, melt 2 tablespoons of the butter over moderate heat. Add the onion and sauté for 5 to 7 minutes until soft and lightly golden. Remove the frying pan from the heat and allow the onion to cool slightly.

2 Meanwhile, using a serrated knife, slice the bread in half horizontally and place the halves side by side on a long sheet of aluminium foil. Stir the remaining butter into the sautéed onion until melted.

3 Spoon the onion butter over the sliced surfaces of the bread and sprinkle with the cheese. Keeping the halves open, wrap the bread loosely in the foil and bake for 10 minutes.

4 Open the foil and continue to bake for 10 to 15 more minutes until the onion bread is crisp and golden. Cut into generous slices and serve while still warm.

SWEET CREAM-CHEESE TOAST *Serves 4*

4x2,5cm-thick slices white bread

100g cream cheese, softened

1 tablespoon chopped pistachio nuts, almonds or pecan nuts

2 tablespoons apricot jam

2 large eggs

½ cup milk

½ teaspoon vanilla essence

¼ teaspoon ground cinnamon

1 tablespoon sunflower oil

1 tablespoon (15g) butter or margarine

Icing sugar (optional)

 Preparation time
5 minutes

 Cooking time
8 minutes

COOK'S TIP *It's better to buy an uncut loaf of bread and slice it yourself to ensure that the slices are thick enough to hold the cream-cheese filling without falling apart.*

1 Using a serrated knife, cut a pocket in each slice of bread from the upper to the lower crusts, taking care not to cut all the way through.

2 In a small bowl, combine the cream cheese, nuts and jam. Spoon about 2 tablespoons of the mixture into the pocket of each slice of bread. In a pie plate, whisk the eggs, milk, vanilla essence and cinnamon. Heat the oil and butter over moderate heat in a large frying pan.

3 Dip the stuffed bread slices, one at a time, into the egg mixture, turning to coat both sides and taking care not to squeeze out the cheese filling (use two spatulas, if necessary). Sauté the bread for about 1½ minutes on each side until golden brown. Dust with icing sugar, if desired, and serve immediately.

OVEN-BAKED FRENCH TOAST

OVEN-BAKED FRENCH TOAST *Serves 4*

1 loaf (about 40cm) French bread

4 large eggs

½ cup (125ml) cream

¼ cup honey

½ teaspoon ground nutmeg

½ teaspoon vanilla essence

Fresh strawberries (optional)

Warmed syrup (optional)

 Preparation time 20 minutes

 Cooking time 20 minutes

SERVING SUGGESTION Brighten a brunch with this delicious dish of crunchy toast and ripe, juicy strawberries.

1. Preheat the oven to 250°C. Grease two large baking sheets. Cut the French loaf diagonally across its width into 2,5cm slices. Place the slices of bread in a 37,5cm x 26,5cm baking dish.

2. In a medium-sized bowl, whisk together the eggs, cream, honey, nutmeg and vanilla essence. Pour the egg mixture over the bread and turn the slices to coat evenly. Let the bread soak for about 15 minutes until the egg mixture is absorbed.

3. Place the bread on the prepared baking sheets. Bake for 8 to 10 minutes on each side until golden brown. Transfer to serving dishes. Top each portion with strawberries and syrup, if desired, and serve immediately.

Start with a Crêpe

Tantalizingly light and endlessly adaptable, crêpes lend themselves to any number of elegant main courses or desserts. They are easy to make and store (see page 27) and ready-made ones are widely available. To warm chilled crêpes, preheat the oven to 160°C, wrap the crêpes in foil and place them in the oven for a few minutes. Meanwhile, prepare your filling. Each recipe will fill eight crêpes, enough for four servings.

◄ **Spinach and cheese crêpes** In a medium-sized saucepan, melt 4 *tablespoons (60g) butter* over low heat. Stir in *¼ cup flour* and *⅛ teaspoon pepper*. Gradually stir in *½ cup milk* and *½ cup (125ml) cream*. Cook over moderate heat, stirring constantly, until thickened. Add *two 250g packages frozen creamed spinach, cooked*, and *1 cup (about 120g) grated Gruyère cheese*. Cook, stirring, until the cheese melts. Spoon the mixture onto the crêpes and roll up. Place in a greased baking dish and grill for 5 minutes.

▼ **Chicken-filled crêpes** Scald *1 cup milk*. Melt *2 tablespoons (30g) butter* over low heat. Stirring constantly, add *2 tablespoons flour*. Add the milk slowly and cook, stirring, until thickened. Add *1 cup cooked, shredded chicken* and *½ cup sliced mushrooms*. Cook for 5 minutes. Fill the crêpes, fold over and place in a greased baking dish. Grill for 5 minutes.

▼ **Ratatouille-filled crêpes** Sauté *2 medium onions*, sliced, and *2 cloves garlic* in *¼ cup olive oil*. Add *one small brinjal*, cubed, *1 large sweet green pepper*, cut into strips, *4 baby marrows*, sliced, *3 tomatoes*, peeled and chopped, *2 tablespoons chopped parsley, 2 teaspoons salt, ½ teaspoon dried origanum* and *⅛ teaspoon pepper*. Cover and simmer for 10 to 15 minutes. Uncover and simmer until thickened. Spoon onto the crêpes and fold the ends under. Place in a greased baking dish. Grill for 5 minutes.

One-ingredient combinations

Savoury Fillings	Sweet Fillings	Toppings
Grated Cheddar cheese	Jam or preserves	Icing sugar
Soft cream cheese	Melted chocolate chips	Brandy or liqueur
Scrambled eggs	Chopped fresh fruit	Honey or syrup

▶ **Crêpes Suzette** Make the orange butter: Cream *4 tablespoons (60g) butter, 2 teaspoons icing sugar, 2 teaspoons strained orange juice, 2 teaspoons grated orange peel* and *1 teaspoon orange liqueur*. Spread on the crêpes. In a large frying pan, sauté each crêpe, butter side down, for 1 to 2 minutes until hot. Fold in a triangle and push to the side of pan until all are cooked. Spread the crêpes out and flame with *2 tablespoons each of brandy* and *Grand Marnier*.

◀ **Apple crêpes** Preheat oven to 190°C. Sauté *2 sliced apples* in *2 tablespoons (30g) butter*. Add *2 tablespoons sugar*. Stir to caramelize. Fill the crêpes, fold them over and place in a greased baking dish. Bake for 8 minutes. Flame with *¼ cup Calvados* or *brandy*. Serve with *cream*.

▶ **Peach crêpes** In a small saucepan, bring *2 cups water* and *¼ cup icing sugar* to the boil. Stir until mixture is clear. Add *4 peaches*, skinned and sliced. Cook for about 10 minutes until soft. Meanwhile, prepare orange butter as in Crêpes Suzette (above) and spread on the crêpes. In a large frying pan, sauté each crêpe, butter side down, for 1 to 2 minutes. Fill with the peaches, fold each one into a triangle and return to the pan, spreading them evenly. Flame with *2 tablespoons Grand Marnier*. Serve immediately.

BLUEBERRY PANCAKES

BLUEBERRY PANCAKES *Serves 4*

1¼ cups flour

2 tablespoons sugar

2 teaspoons baking powder

¼ teaspoon salt

1¼ cups milk

1 large egg

3 tablespoons (45g) butter or margarine, melted

⅔ cup blueberries

Warmed syrup (optional)

 Preparation time 5 minutes

 Cooking time 10 minutes

SERVING SUGGESTION Served with a jug of warmed syrup, blueberry pancakes will bring a taste of America to your Sunday breakfast table.

1. In a large bowl, sift together the flour, sugar, baking powder and salt. In a small bowl, combine the milk, egg and butter. Add the milk mixture to the dry ingredients and stir until just moistened (the batter may be somewhat lumpy). Gently fold the blueberries into the mixture.

2. Lightly grease a large frying pan and heat it over moderately high heat. For each pancake, pour about ⅓ cup of the batter into the hot pan, making a few at a time. Cook the pancakes for about 3 minutes until several bubbles burst on the surface and the bottom is lightly browned. Flip the pancakes over and cook the other side for about 2 more minutes until golden brown.

3. Transfer the pancakes to a platter and keep them warm. Cook the remaining batter, making a total of 8 pancakes. Serve with slightly warmed syrup, if desired.

BREADS, CAKES AND BISCUITS

CURRANT SCONES *Makes 12*

2 cups flour

2 tablespoons sugar

1 tablespoon baking powder

½ teaspoon salt

¼ teaspoon bicarbonate of soda

6 tablespoons (90g) butter or margarine, cut into pieces

½ cup dried currants or raisins

½ cup buttermilk

2 large eggs

 Preparation time 15 minutes

 Cooking time 15 minutes

SERVING SUGGESTION Recognized as a traditional English tea-time treat, these light and crumbly scones may be served with honey for breakfast.

1. Preheat the oven to 220°C. In a large bowl, combine the flour, sugar, baking powder, salt and bicarbonate of soda. Using a pastry blender or two knives held like a pair of scissors, cut in the butter until the mixture resembles coarse crumbs.

2. Stir the currants into the flour mixture until well mixed. In a small bowl, combine the buttermilk and eggs. Add the buttermilk mixture to the dry ingredients and stir gently to form a soft dough. With floured hands, gently knead the dough very briefly in the bowl until just blended. Divide the dough into two equal portions.

3. On a large ungreased baking sheet, carefully pat each piece of dough into a 15cm round. Using a large knife, cut each round into 6 equal wedges but do not separate the segments. Bake the scones for 12 to 15 minutes until they are golden brown. Separate the wedges and serve them warm.

APPLE BRAN MUFFINS *Makes 9* (PICTURE PAGE 321)

1 large apple

2½ cups bran flakes, crushed

1¼ cups flour

1½ teaspoons baking powder

½ teaspoon bicarbonate of soda

¼ teaspoon salt

¾ cup buttermilk

¼ cup syrup or honey

¼ cup sunflower oil

1 large egg

 Preparation time 7 minutes

 Cooking time 20 minutes

SERVING SUGGESTION These muffins are marvellous with apple butter. Blend a large spoonful of apple sauce into a little softened butter, scoop it into a small bowl and serve separately.

1. Preheat the oven to 190°C. With butter or paper cupcake liners, grease or line a 9-cup muffin tin. Grate the unpeeled apple coarsely with a food processor or hand grater.

2. In a large bowl, combine the crushed bran flakes, flour, baking powder, bicarbonate of soda and salt until well mixed. Add the grated apple and stir until well mixed. In a small bowl, combine the buttermilk, syrup, sunflower oil and egg. Stir the buttermilk mixture into the dry ingredients until the batter is just moistened (do not overmix).

3. Spoon the batter into the prepared muffin cups. Bake for about 20 minutes until lightly browned. Remove the muffins immediately and serve them warm.

BREADS, CAKES AND BISCUITS

Date Muffins *Makes 9*

3 tablespoons (45g) butter or margarine
1 cup flour
1 cup quick-cooking oats
¼ cup firmly packed light brown sugar
2 teaspoons baking powder
½ teaspoon salt
½ teaspoon ground cinnamon
½ cup chopped pitted dates
1 cup milk
1 large egg

 Preparation time 15 minutes

 Cooking time 25 minutes

COOK'S TIP *To prevent the dates from sticking to the knife when chopping, place the fruit on the chopping board and sprinkle a little flour over them. If there is enough time, chilling the dates before cutting them makes the job even easier.*

1 Preheat the oven to 200°C. With butter or paper cupcake liners, grease or line a 9-cup muffin tin.

2 In a small saucepan, melt the butter over moderate heat. In a large bowl, combine the flour, oats, brown sugar, baking powder, salt and ground cinnamon until thoroughly mixed. Add the dates and stir well.

3 Combine the milk, egg and melted butter in a small bowl. Using a wooden spoon, stir the milk mixture into the dry ingredients until just moistened (do not overmix).

4 Spoon the batter into the prepared muffin cups. Bake for 20 to 25 minutes until lightly browned. Remove the muffins from the cups immediately and serve them warm.

Savoury Baby Marrow Muffins *Makes 9*

125g baby marrows
1 cup cake flour
¾ cup whole-wheat flour
¼ cup sugar
1 tablespoon baking powder
1 teaspoon finely grated lemon peel
½ teaspoon salt
¼ teaspoon ground nutmeg
⅓ cup milk
⅓ cup (80g) butter or margarine, melted
1 large egg

 Preparation time 9 minutes

 Cooking time 20 minutes

COOK'S TIP *To store leftover muffins, wrap the cooled muffins tightly in aluminium foil and refrigerate. To reheat, loosen the foil and bake them at 120°C for ten minutes.*

1 Preheat the oven to 200°C. With butter or paper cupcake liners, grease or line a 9-cup muffin tin. Coarsely grate the baby marrows with a food processor or hand grater.

2 In a large bowl, combine the cake and whole-wheat flours, sugar, baking powder, lemon peel, salt and nutmeg until well mixed. Stir in the grated baby marrows.

3 In a small bowl, combine the milk, butter and egg. Stir the milk mixture into the dry ingredients until just moistened (do not overmix).

4 Spoon the batter into the prepared muffin cups. Bake for 18 to 20 minutes until the muffins are lightly browned. Remove from the cups and serve them warm.

RAISIN GRANOLA MUFFINS

Raisin Granola Muffins *Makes 8*

¼ cup seedless raisins
½ cup cake flour
½ cup whole-wheat flour
2 teaspoons baking powder
¼ teaspoon salt
2 tablespoons brown sugar
1 cup granola or toasted muesli
1 egg
½ cup buttermilk
2 tablespoons sunflower oil

 Preparation time
15 minutes

 Cooking time
20 minutes

Cook's tip Fill any empty cups in the muffin tin with a little water during baking. Serve with spanspek and yoghurt for breakfast.

1. Preheat the oven to 200°C. With butter or nonstick cooking spray, grease an 8-cup muffin tin. In a small bowl, soak the raisins in a little boiling water until softened. Drain and set aside.

2. In a medium-sized bowl, mix together the flours, baking powder, salt and sugar. Add ¾ cup of the granola and the raisins. In a small bowl, whisk the egg, buttermilk and oil. Add to the dry ingredients, stirring until just moistened (do not overmix).

3. Spoon the batter into the muffin tin. Sprinkle with the remaining ¼ cup granola and press it in lightly. Bake for 15 to 20 minutes until golden. Remove the muffins carefully and serve warm.

CAKES

A home-made cake, fresh from the oven and filled to bursting with the fragrant aromas of sugar and spices, is a real treat. Surprise your family with one of these easy-to-make bakes.

LEMON-GLAZED APRICOT CAKE *Serves 8*

1 tin (400g) apricots, drained

¾ cup flour

Pinch of salt

2 teaspoons baking powder

2 eggs

½ cup sugar

2 tablespoons (30g) butter or margarine, melted and slightly cooled

¾ cup buttermilk

2 tablespoons flaked almonds

For the glaze:

2 tablespoons (30g) butter

2 tablespoons icing sugar

1 tablespoon lemon juice

 Preparation time
15 minutes

 Cooking time
30 minutes

FOOD NOTE *This wonderful cake marries the sharp, fresh flavours of apricots and lemon. Simplicity itself to prepare, it is sure to become a family favourite.*

1 Preheat the oven to 180°C. Grease a 26cm x 16cm rectangular baking dish with a little butter or nonstick cooking spray. Place the drained apricots in the base of the dish.

2 In a medium-sized bowl, sift together the flour, salt and baking powder. In a second bowl, whisk together the eggs, sugar, butter and buttermilk. Add to the dry ingredients and stir until just combined.

3 Spoon the mixture over the apricots, sprinkle with the almonds and bake for 30 minutes or until golden brown and a toothpick inserted in the centre comes out clean.

4 Meanwhile, make the glaze: Melt the butter. Sift the icing sugar and add it to the butter. Stir until the sugar is dissolved. Add the lemon juice and stir until well blended.

5 When the cake is cooked, place it on a serving platter and drizzle with the glaze. Serve while still warm.

This easy chocolate sauce makes a tasty dessert topping for a chocolate or sponge cake. If rushed for time, purchase a fresh cake from your local bakery. Try using coffee-flavoured liqueur in place of the brandy.

CHOCOLATE-COFFEE SAUCE

In a small saucepan, melt *4 tablespoons (60g) butter or margarine*. Add *180g plain dark chocolate*, chopped, and *2 tablespoons water*. Stir over low heat until melted. Pour in *5 or 6 tablespoons strong black coffee* and *2 tablespoons brandy*. Sweeten with *1 to 3 tablespoons icing sugar*. Place *4 slices of cake* on individual serving plates and pour the sauce over each. Garnish with *strawberries*. Serves 4

BREADS, CAKES AND BISCUITS

CREAM CHEESE-FILLED COCOA COOKIES *Makes 12*

125g cream cheese, softened

1 large egg, separated

1 cup plus 1 tablespoon sugar

½ cup (about 90g) chocolate chips or chopped dark chocolate

1½ cups flour

¼ cup unsweetened cocoa powder

1½ teaspoons bicarbonate of soda

½ teaspoon salt

¾ cup water

⅓ cup sunflower oil

1 tablespoon white vinegar

1 teaspoon vanilla essence

 Preparation time
17 minutes

 Cooking time
25 minutes

1. Preheat the oven to 180°C. With butter, margarine or paper cupcake liners, grease or line a 12-cup muffin tin. Using an electric mixer, beat the cream cheese with the egg yolk and 1 tablespoon of the sugar. Stir in the chocolate chips and set the mixture aside.

2. In a large bowl, using an electric mixer, combine the remaining 1 cup of sugar, the flour, cocoa, bicarbonate of soda and salt. Add the egg white, water, oil, vinegar and vanilla essence and beat the mixture until smooth.

3. Pour the cocoa mixture into the prepared muffin cups and drop an equal amount of the cream-cheese mixture on top of each. Bake the cookies for about 25 minutes until a toothpick inserted in the centre comes out clean. Cool for 10 minutes in the tin, remove and serve. Store any leftover cookies in the refrigerator.

GINGER CAKE WITH LEMON SAUCE *Serves 9*

1¼ cups whole-wheat flour

1 cup cake flour

2 teaspoons ground ginger

1½ teaspoons baking powder

1 teaspoon cinnamon

¼ teaspoon bicarbonate of soda

¼ teaspoon salt

1 cup firmly packed dark brown sugar

½ cup (120g) butter or margarine, softened

2 large eggs

½ cup molasses

¾ cup hot water

For the lemon sauce:

1 large lemon

½ cup sugar

2 tablespoons cornflour

1 cup water

2 tablespoons (30g) butter

 Preparation time
10 minutes

 Cooking time
40 minutes

1. Preheat the oven to 180°C. Generously grease a 23cm square baking tin. In a medium-sized bowl, combine the flours, the ginger, baking powder, cinnamon, bicarbonate of soda and salt.

2. In a large bowl, using an electric mixer, beat the brown sugar and butter together until light and fluffy. Gradually beat in the eggs and molasses until well mixed. Add the flour mixture a little at a time, alternating with the hot water. Pour the batter into the prepared tin. Bake for 35 to 40 minutes until a toothpick inserted in the centre comes out clean.

3. Meanwhile, make the lemon sauce: Finely grate the lemon peel to make 1 teaspoon of lemon zest. Cut the lemon in half and squeeze to extract ¼ cup of lemon juice. Mix the sugar and cornflour in a small saucepan. Stir in the water. Bring the mixture to the boil over moderate heat, stirring constantly.

4. Stir the butter, lemon zest and lemon juice into the sauce mixture. Remove the saucepan from the heat and pour the sauce into a small heatproof jug.

5. Let the cake cool in the tin for 5 minutes. Cut it into squares and serve it warm, passing the lemon sauce separately.

APPLE-RAISIN UPSIDE-DOWN CAKE

Apple-raisin upside-down cake *Serves 8*

6 tablespoons (90g) butter or margarine

2 large red-skinned apples, unpeeled

⅓ cup firmly packed light brown sugar

½ teaspoon ground cinnamon

¼ cup raisins

1⅓ cups cake flour

⅔ cup white sugar

2 teaspoons baking powder

¼ teaspoon salt

½ cup milk

1 large egg

1 teaspoon vanilla essence

 Preparation time 15 minutes

 Cooking time 30 minutes

Cook's tip Place a large, shallow baking tin on the rack under the springform tin to catch any drippings during baking.

1. Preheat the oven to 190°C. Grease the sides of a 23cm springform tin. In a small saucepan, melt the butter over low heat. Meanwhile, quarter, core and thinly slice the apples.

2. Transfer 3 tablespoons of the melted butter to a small bowl and set it aside. Stir the brown sugar, cinnamon and raisins into the remaining butter in the saucepan. Pour the mixture into the prepared baking tin and spread the apple slices on top. Set aside.

3. In a large bowl, combine the flour, white sugar, baking powder and salt. Add the milk, egg, vanilla essence and the reserved melted butter. Using an electric mixer at low speed, beat the batter until just combined. Increase the mixer speed to high and continue beating for about 1 minute until the batter is smooth. Spoon the batter over the apples.

4. Bake the cake for about 30 minutes until a toothpick inserted in the centre comes out clean. Leave to cool for 5 minutes. Invert it onto a serving plate, leave for 1 minute, then remove the tin. Serve warm.

START WITH A BUTTER CAKE

Many delicious desserts are based on the simple and wholesome butter or plain sponge cake. Make your own (see our recipe on page 28) or buy a ready-made cake from your local bakery or supermarket.

This loaf cake is the best shape for these recipes as it is easy to slice horizontally with a serrated knife. Served with a scoop of your favourite ice cream, some fresh fruit or a drizzle of fruit or chocolate sauce, these desserts or teatime treats will have your family calling for second helpings!

▶ **Peanut brittle chocolate cake** In a medium-sized saucepan, melt *one cup (180g) chocolate chips* over very low heat, stirring often. Remove the saucepan from heat and stir in *⅔ cup sour cream* until smooth. Coarsely crush *one 50g slab peanut brittle* and set aside. Cut loaf cake in half horizontally. Place the lower layer on a serving plate, spread it with one-third of the icing and sprinkle it with one-third of the crushed peanut brittle. Top with second layer of cake. Ice with the remaining icing and sprinkle the remaining peanut brittle over the top. (Serves 8)

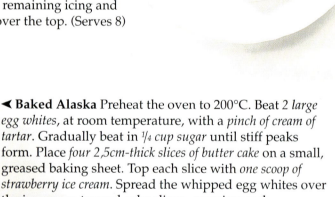

◀ **Baked Alaska** Preheat the oven to 200°C. Beat *2 large egg whites*, at room temperature, with a *pinch of cream of tartar*. Gradually beat in *¼ cup sugar* until stiff peaks form. Place *four 2,5cm-thick slices of butter cake* on a small, greased baking sheet. Top each slice with *one scoop of strawberry ice cream*. Spread the whipped egg whites over the ice cream-topped cake slices, covering each completely. Bake for 3 to 5 minutes until the meringue is golden brown. (Serves 4)

◀ **Raspberry trifles** Cut *four 2,5cm-thick slices of butter cake* into cubes and divide them among four individual glass serving dishes. Drizzle the cake with *4 tablespoons dry sherry* or *orange liqueur*. Spoon *250g fresh raspberries* over the cake cubes. Pour *1 cup instant vanilla pudding*, prepared according to the directions on the package, over the raspberries. Garnish each trifle with *a spoonful of whipped cream* and *mint sprigs*, if desired. (Serves 4)

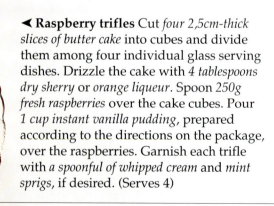

◄ **Cake and fruit with chocolate fondue** Place *one cup (180g) chocolate chips*, *¼ cup sour cream* and *½ cup cream* in a small saucepan. Cook over low heat, stirring constantly, until the mixture is smooth. Pour the chocolate into a small fondue pot and keep warm. On a serving platter, arrange *1½ cups cubed butter cake*, *1 apple*, cored and cut into cubes, *1 banana*, peeled and cut into chunks (dip the apple and banana slices in lemon juice to prevent discoloration) and *1 cup pineapple chunks*. Let your guests spear the cake and fruit with a fondue fork and dip it into chocolate fondue. If the fondue thickens, stir in some additional cream and reheat over low heat. (Serves 4)

► **Strawberry shortcake** In a medium-sized bowl, gently toss *2 cups strawberries*, sliced, with *2 tablespoons of sugar*. Leave to stand for 15 minutes, stirring occasionally. Beat *½ cup thick cream* with *1 teaspoon sugar* and *¼ teaspoon vanilla essence* until soft peaks form. Cut *eight 1cm-thick slices of butter cake*. Place a slice of the cake on each of four individual dessert plates. Spoon half of the strawberries with some of their juice and a dollop of whipped cream on each slice. Top with the remaining cake, the rest of the strawberries and the whipped cream. (Serves 4)

◄ **Peach torte** Cut *one butter cake* horizontally into three layers. Mix *1 cup chopped peaches* with *¼ teaspoon almond essence* and *½ cup vanilla custard* in a small bowl. On a serving plate, place the bottom layer of the cake and spread with half of the custard mixture. Cover with the second layer of cake, the remaining custard mixture and the top layer. Spread *¼ cup chocolate icing* over the top layer, or sprinkle with *sifted icing sugar*. Garnish with additional peach slices, if desired. (Serves 8)

GRILLED COCONUT CAKE

GRILLED COCONUT CAKE *Serves 9*

2 large eggs

1 cup white sugar

1 cup cake flour

1 teaspoon baking powder

½ cup milk

2 tablespoons (30g) butter or margarine

For the coconut topping:

½ cup firmly packed light brown sugar

4 tablespoons (60g) butter, softened

1 cup grated coconut

 Preparation time
11 minutes

 Cooking time
30 minutes

SERVING SUGGESTION When inviting guests for tea, enchant them with this delectable cake with its crunchy coconut topping.

1. Preheat the oven to 180°C. Grease a 23cm square baking tin. In a small bowl, using an electric mixer at high speed, beat the eggs until foamy. Gradually add the white sugar and beat at medium speed for about 5 minutes until the mixture is fluffy. Add the flour and baking powder. Mix at low speed until blended.

2. In a small saucepan, heat the milk and butter until the butter melts. Add to the batter and beat until smooth. Pour into the prepared tin and bake for 25 to 30 minutes until a toothpick inserted in the centre comes out clean. Remove the cake from the oven and preheat the grill.

3. Meanwhile, to make the topping: Mix the brown sugar and butter until smooth and creamy. Add the coconut and mix well. Spread over the cake and grill 10cm from the heat for 1 minute or until golden (watch closely to prevent burning). Cut into squares and serve warm.

BREADS, CAKES AND BISCUITS

SPICED PECAN CAKE *Serves 8*

1⅓ cups cake flour

⅔ cup sugar

2 teaspoons baking powder

½ teaspoon ground cinnamon

¼ teaspoon ground nutmeg or allspice

⅔ cup milk

4 tablespoons (60g) butter or margarine, softened

1 large egg

1 teaspoon vanilla essence

½ cup finely chopped pecan nuts

Icing sugar (optional)

Sweetened whipped cream (optional)

 Preparation time 10 minutes

 Cooking time 30 minutes

1 Preheat the oven to 180°C. Grease and flour a 20cm round baking tin. Mix the flour, sugar, baking powder, cinnamon and nutmeg in a large bowl.

2 Add the milk, butter, egg and vanilla essence to the flour mixture. Using an electric mixer at low speed, beat until just blended. Increase the speed to medium and continue beating for 1 minute. Stir in the nuts, then pour the batter into the baking tin.

3 Bake for 25 to 30 minutes until a toothpick inserted in the centre comes out clean. Leave the cake in the tin on a wire rack for 5 minutes to cool, then transfer it to a serving platter. Dust with icing sugar, if desired, and serve warm with whipped cream.

MICROWAVE OVEN VERSION

Increase the amount of butter to ⅓ cup (80g). Grease a microwave-safe 20cm round baking dish and line it with wax paper. Prepare the batter as described in Steps 1 and 2 above and pour it into the prepared dish. Place on a rack or an inverted saucer in the microwave oven and cook, uncovered, on high power for 10 minutes.

The cake may appear moist on top, but it is ready when a toothpick inserted in several places comes out clean. If not, continue cooking on high power for 30 seconds to 2 minutes longer until the surface of the cake is nearly dry. Cool in the dish on a wire rack for 5 minutes. Loosen the cake, invert it onto a serving platter and remove the wax paper. Dust with icing sugar, if desired, and serve.

TIME SAVERS

ALTITUDE VARIATIONS

To ensure the success of your baking, recipes made inland need to be adjusted slightly to compensate for the increase in altitude.

If you live at 1000 metres above sea level, decrease each teaspoon (5ml) of baking powder by ½ml and increase each cup (250ml) of liquid by 20ml. For those living at about 1600 metres above sea level (eg in Gauteng), decrease each teaspoon of baking powder by 1ml and increase each cup of liquid by 35ml. For those living over 2000 metres above sea level, decrease each teaspoon of baking powder by 2ml and increase each cup of liquid by 50ml. Also at this height, decrease each cup of sugar and shortening by 20ml, add ½ an egg for every 4 used and, when baking fruit cakes, decrease the baking time by as much as 20 per cent.

BISCUITS

Fill your biscuit tin with this crunchy selection of easy-to-make favourites, ranging from delicate tea-time treats to sturdy lunch box fillers.

SCOTTISH OAT WEDGES Makes 8

¾ cup (180g) butter, softened

⅔ cup firmly packed light brown sugar

1 teaspoon vanilla essence

¼ cup cake flour

3 cups oats

 Preparation time 15 minutes

 Cooking time 15 minutes

FOOD NOTE *In Scotland these are known as flapjacks, although their crunchy texture bears no resemblance to our South African version which is based on a pancake-like batter.*

1. Preheat the oven to 180°C. In a large bowl, using an electric mixer, beat the butter, sugar and vanilla essence until fluffy. Beat in the flour and half of the oats until well mixed. Using a wooden spoon or your hands, work in the additional oats until the dough just holds together.

2. Press the mixture into an ungreased 23cm round baking tin. Using a knife, divide the dough into 8 wedges without cutting all the way through to the bottom of the dough.

3. Bake for about 15 minutes until golden brown. Leave to cool in the tin, then cut into wedges and serve.

CINNAMON-SUGAR BISCUITS Makes 36

½ cup (120g) butter or margarine, softened

1 cup plus 2 tablespoons sugar

1 large egg

½ teaspoon vanilla essence

¼ teaspoon baking powder

¼ teaspoon bicarbonate of soda

1½ cups flour

1 teaspoon ground cinnamon

 Preparation time 15 minutes

 Cooking time 36 minutes

COOK'S TIP *This biscuit dough can be made ahead and frozen in an airtight container. Before baking, thaw it at room temperature.*

1. Preheat the oven to 190°C. In a large bowl, using an electric mixer, beat the butter and 1 cup of the sugar until well mixed. Beat in the egg and vanilla essence until the mixture is smooth. Add the baking powder, bicarbonate of soda and half of the flour and beat until smooth and fluffy. Beat in the remaining flour.

2. Drop rounded teaspoons of the dough, about 5cm apart, on an ungreased baking sheet. Combine the cinnamon with the remaining sugar and sprinkle some of the mixture over the dough. Bake for 10 to 12 minutes until lightly golden. Transfer to a wire rack. Repeat until all the mixture is used. When cool, store in an airtight container.

BREADS, CAKES AND BISCUITS

Lemon Tuiles *Makes 30*

²⁄₃ cup icing sugar

¹⁄₃ cup cake flour

2 large egg whites

1 teaspoon grated lemon peel

½ teaspoon lemon essence

½ cup (120g) butter or margarine, softened

1 cup sliced blanched almonds

 Preparation time
15 minutes

 Cooking time
40 minutes

SERVING SUGGESTION *These tuiles, or tiles, make a crispy accompaniment to ice cream or fruit for dessert. On their own they are low-kilojoule winners at tea-time. Be sure to shape the biscuits immediately after you take them out of the oven, while they are hot.*

1. Preheat the oven to 200°C. Lightly grease two baking sheets. In a large bowl, combine the icing sugar and flour. Make a well in the centre and add the egg whites, lemon peel and lemon essence. Mix thoroughly with a wooden spoon, then stir in the butter and add the sliced almonds.

2. Drop rounded teaspoons of the mixture onto the prepared baking sheets about 5cm apart (6 biscuits on each sheet). Using a fork dipped in cold water, flatten the biscuits slightly.

3. Bake the biscuits, one sheet at time, for 6 to 8 minutes until golden brown. Remove from the baking sheet immediately and drape them over a rolling pin. Allow to become firm on the rolling pin before transferring to a wire rack to cool. Repeat until all the mixture is used.

Golden Brownies *Makes 16*

5 tablespoons (75g) butter or margarine, softened

¾ cup firmly packed light brown sugar

2 large eggs

1 teaspoon vanilla essence

¾ cup flour

1 teaspoon baking powder

¾ cup chopped walnuts

 Preparation time
20 minutes

 Cooking time
25 minutes

COOK'S TIP *A quick way to soften butter that has been stored in the refrigerator is to grate it – it will soften in minutes. This batter can easily be beaten by hand if you'd prefer not to use a mixer.*

1. Preheat the oven to 180°C. Generously grease a 20cm square baking tin and dust it lightly with flour.

2. In a large bowl, using an electric mixer, beat the butter and the brown sugar until the mixture is smooth and fluffy. Add the eggs and the vanilla essence, beating the mixture until it is well blended. With the mixer at low speed, beat in the flour and baking powder. Using a rubber spatula, fold in the walnuts and spread the batter into the prepared tin.

3. Bake the brownies for 20 to 25 minutes until they are golden brown. Cool in the tin for about 10 minutes, then cut into 16 pieces and serve, or leave to cool completely and store in an airtight container.

LEMON TUILES (RIGHT) AND ALMOND-COCONUT MACAROONS

ALMOND-COCONUT MACAROONS *Makes 24*

1 cup blanched slivered almonds

2 large egg whites

²/₃ cup sugar

²/₃ cup grated coconut

½ teaspoon almond essence

 Preparation time 10 minutes

 Cooking time 25 minutes

COOK'S TIP For a smooth finish to the top of the biscuits, brush each with a pastry brush dipped in cold water before baking.

1. Preheat the oven to 160°C. Using an electric blender, chop the almonds until finely ground. Spread the almonds on a baking sheet and bake for 10 minutes to dry.

2. Meanwhile, in a small bowl, using an electric mixer, beat the egg whites until soft peaks form. Gradually add the sugar, beating constantly, until stiff, glossy peaks form.

3. Grease and flour two baking sheets or line them with nonstick baking paper. Using a rubber spatula, fold the coconut, almond essence and the ground almonds into the beaten egg whites.

4. Drop rounded tablespoons of the batter about 5cm apart onto the prepared baking sheets. Bake the macaroons for 15 to 20 minutes until the edges are lightly browned, switching the baking sheets around half way through the cooking time. Cool the biscuits on a wire rack.

BREADS, CAKES AND BISCUITS

Favourite fudge brownies *Makes 24*

2 cups chocolate chips

1 cup (240g) butter or margarine

4 large eggs

1 cup sugar

1 teaspoon vanilla essence

1 cup flour

¼ teaspoon baking powder

1 cup chopped walnuts (optional)

 Preparation time
15 minutes

 Cooking time
25 minutes

Serving suggestion Children will love these chewy, chocolaty biscuits in their school lunch boxes or with a glass of milk after school.

1. Preheat the oven to 180°C. Grease a 37,5cm x 26,5cm baking tin. In a medium-sized saucepan, melt the chocolate chips with the butter over low heat until smooth, stirring constantly. Remove the saucepan from the heat and let the chocolate mixture cool slightly.

2. Meanwhile, in a medium-sized bowl, using an electric mixer, beat the eggs until foamy. Gradually add the sugar, beating constantly for about 3 minutes until the mixture is thick and pale yellow. Add the vanilla essence.

3. Beat the chocolate mixture into the eggs until well mixed. At low speed, beat in the flour and baking powder. Stir in the walnuts, if desired. Pour the batter into the prepared tin.

4. Bake for 20 to 25 minutes until a toothpick inserted 5cm from the edge comes out clean (the centre will remain soft). Leave the brownies to cool slightly and cut them into squares.

Marbled brownies

Reduce the amount of chocolate chips to 1 cup. Melt the chocolate and butter separately. Proceed with Step 2 as above. Beat the butter, flour and baking powder into the egg-sugar mixture. Stir in the nuts, if desired.

Pour half of the batter into a second bowl. Stir the chocolate into one of the two bowls of batter. Alternately spoon dollops of the chocolate batter and the white batter into the tin, then run a knife through the batter to give it a marbled effect. Bake as described in Step 4 above.

Time Savers

Baking preparation
▪ A quick alternative to chopping walnuts is to put the nuts in a plastic bag, shaking them to the bottom. Roll lightly with a rolling pin to crush the nuts.

▪ To make measuring sticky liquids (such as honey) easier, either rinse the measuring cup or spoon in very hot water or spray it with nonstick cooking spray before measuring.

▪ Chocolate melts very easily in the microwave oven. Place it in a small microwave-safe bowl and heat it, uncovered, on high power for 1 to 2 minutes per 25g until shiny.

FAVOURITE FUDGE BROWNIES (FAR RIGHT) AND CARAMEL-PECAN SQUARES

CARAMEL-PECAN SQUARES *Makes 20*

2 cups cake flour

1½ cups firmly packed light brown sugar

1 cup (240g) butter or margarine, softened

1½ cups chopped pecan nuts

1 cup chocolate chips

 Preparation time
20 minutes

 Cooking time
20 minutes

COOK'S TIP Use a heavy-based saucepan, uncovered, to melt the chocolate chips. Alternatively, melt them in the microwave oven or in the top half of a double boiler.

1. Preheat the oven to 180°C. Grease a 37,5cm x 26,5cm baking tin. In a large bowl, combine the flour, 1 cup of the sugar and 120g of the butter until well mixed.

2. Press the flour mixture firmly and evenly into the baking tin to form a crust. Sprinkle with the pecan nuts. In a small saucepan, melt the remaining butter with the remaining sugar over moderate heat, stirring constantly, until the mixture begins to boil. Continue boiling for 1 minute, stirring constantly. Spoon the hot sugar mixture evenly over the pecan nuts. Bake for about 20 minutes until the top is bubbly and the crust is golden brown.

3. Meanwhile, in a small saucepan, melt the chocolate chips over low heat. Drizzle the melted chocolate over the top of the baked mixture. Leave to cool, then slice into 20 squares and serve.

BREADS, CAKES AND BISCUITS

CHOCOLATE-NUT BISCUITS Makes 24

½ cup (120g) butter or margarine, softened

½ cup white sugar

¼ cup firmly packed light brown sugar

1 large egg

1 teaspoon vanilla essence

1 cup plus 2 tablespoons cake flour

½ teaspoon bicarbonate of soda

1 cup chocolate chips

½ cup chopped walnuts

 Preparation time
7 minutes

 Cooking time
20 minutes

COOK'S TIP The biscuits will bake more evenly if they are done in two batches, rather than all at once.

1. Preheat the oven to 190°C. Lightly grease two baking sheets. In a large bowl, using an electric mixer, beat the butter and both sugars until well mixed. Beat in the egg, vanilla essence, flour and bicarbonate of soda to form a stiff dough. Stir in the chocolate chips and chopped walnuts.

2. Drop teaspoons of the dough about 5cm apart onto the prepared baking sheets.

3. Bake for 8 to 10 minutes until the edges of the biscuits are golden. Cool on the baking sheet for 1 minute, then transfer to a wire rack to cool completely. Repeat until all the mixture is used.

OAT-RAISIN BISCUITS

Delete the chocolate chips and chopped walnuts from the recipe, and reduce the amount of bicarbonate of soda to ¼ teaspoon. Prepare the dough as described in Step 1 above, adding *2 tablespoons of milk* with the white and brown sugar. Stir *1 cup quick-cooking oats* and *½ cup raisins* into the dough. Drop rounded tablespoons of the dough onto the baking sheet and bake for 10 to 12 minutes until golden.

APPLE-SPICE BISCUITS Makes 24

½ cup (120g) butter or margarine, softened

½ cup sugar

¼ cup firmly packed light brown sugar

1 teaspoon ground cinnamon

¼ teaspoon ground nutmeg

1 large egg

1 teaspoon vanilla essence

1 cup plus 2 tablespoons flour

¼ teaspoon bicarbonate of soda

1 cup diced dried apple

 Preparation time
8 minutes

 Cooking time
20 minutes

1. Preheat the oven to 190°C. In a large bowl, using an electric mixer, beat the butter, both sugars, the cinnamon and nutmeg until well mixed. Beat in the egg, vanilla essence, flour and bicarbonate of soda until the mixture is thoroughly combined and forms a stiff dough. Using a wooden spoon, stir the dried apples into the dough.

2. Drop rounded teaspoons of the dough about 5cm apart onto an ungreased baking sheet. Bake for 8 to 10 minutes until the edges of the biscuits are golden. Repeat until all the mixture is used.

3. Cool on the baking sheet for 1 minute, then, using a spatula, transfer the biscuits to a wire rack to cool completely. Store in an airtight container.

Desserts

Chocolate parfaits (page 367)

Fruit desserts

Use the first fresh fruits of the season to concoct these light desserts – a refreshing finale to any meal.

Chocolate-dipped strawberries Serves 4

100g dark chocolate, finely chopped

1 teaspoon butter or margarine

2 cups large fresh strawberries, stems intact

 Preparation time 15 minutes

 Cooking/chilling time 18 minutes

SERVING SUGGESTION *The contrast of smooth chocolate and succulent strawberries combine to make an ideal dessert for a champagne brunch.*

1 Partially fill the bottom half of a double boiler with water and bring to the boil over high heat. Reduce the heat to moderately low. Melt the chocolate and the butter in the top part of the double boiler over the hot, not boiling, water. (Alternatively, melt the chocolate and butter in the microwave oven, stopping frequently to check if the mixture is soft.)

2 Stir the chocolate until smooth. Remove the double boiler from the heat but keep the chocolate in the top part over the water.

3 Lightly grease a baking sheet. Rinse the strawberries and gently pat them dry. Pour the melted chocolate into a small bowl. Holding each strawberry by its stalk, dip the berry halfway into the chocolate. Let the excess chocolate drip off and place the strawberry on the prepared baking sheet.

4 Refrigerate the strawberries for approximately 15 minutes until the chocolate is firm. Arrange them in a single layer on a decorative platter and serve.

SHELF MAGIC

Two easy fruit desserts, one cool and the other warm, get a splash of spirits to boost their flavour. Serve with vanilla ice cream or plain yoghurt.

Mixed berries with liqueur

Gently toss *2 cups blackberries*, *2 cups raspberries* and *2 cups blueberries* together in a serving bowl. In a small bowl, combine *1 tablespoon Van der Hum liqueur* or *orange juice* and *1 tablespoon honey*. Pour over the berries, toss gently and serve. Serves 4

Spiced apricots and pears

Preheat the grill. Drain *one 410g tin apricot halves*, reserving *2 tablespoons syrup*, and *one 410g tin pear halves*. In a pie plate, mix the syrup with *2 tablespoons brandy*, *1 tablespoon honey* and *a pinch of cinnamon*. Add the fruit, stir to mix and grill until browned. Serves 4

GRAPE PARFAIT SUPREME

GRAPE PARFAIT SUPREME Serves 4

1 cup seedless green grapes (or seeded green grapes), halved

1 cup thick sour cream or plain yoghurt

3 tablespoons firmly packed light brown sugar

1 cup seedless red grapes (or seeded red grapes), halved

1 cup black grapes, seeded and halved

1 tablespoon chopped, shelled pistachio nuts

 Preparation time
20 minutes

 Cooking time
0 minutes

COOK'S TIP Simple yet elegant, this tempting dessert provides a fitting end to a festive dinner or summer picnic. Use a clear glass bowl to highlight the layers.

1. Place the green grapes in a 1-litre, funnel-shaped glass dish or medium-sized straight-sided glass bowl. Spread $1/3$ cup of the sour cream in a thin layer over the grapes. Sprinkle the sour cream with 1 tablespoon of the brown sugar.

2. Cover the sugar-cream layer with the red grapes, spread with $1/3$ cup of the sour cream and sprinkle with 1 tablespoon of the brown sugar. Top with the black grapes. Drop tablespoons of the remaining sour cream in the centre of the black grapes. Sprinkle with the remaining brown sugar and chopped pistachio nuts and serve immediately.

DESSERTS

FRESH FRUIT SALAD *Serves 4*

3 large nectarines

2 medium bananas

½ cup dark sweet cherries or strawberries

¼ cup orange juice

2 tablespoons Grand Marnier or orange juice

Mint leaves (optional)

 Preparation time
20 minutes

 Cooking time
0 minutes

1. Halve the nectarines, remove the pips and slice the flesh. Peel and slice the bananas. Halve the cherries and remove the stones (or hull the strawberries).

2. In a medium-sized bowl, toss the nectarines and bananas with the orange juice and Grand Marnier. Pour the fruit mixture into a glass bowl. Top with the cherries, garnish with mint leaves, if desired, and serve.

CARAMEL BANANAS *Serves 4*

⅓ cup (80g) butter

⅓ cup firmly packed light brown sugar

¼ cup water

4 large (about 600g) bananas

⅓ cup (40g) pecan nuts

Vanilla frozen yoghurt or ice cream (optional)

 Preparation time
2 minutes

 Cooking time
10 minutes

1. In a large frying pan, melt the butter over moderate heat. Stir in the brown sugar until it dissolves. Gradually add the water, stirring constantly. Bring the mixture to the boil, then reduce the heat to low and continue simmering the sauce.

2. Peel the bananas and cut them in half across their width. Add the bananas and pecan nuts to the caramel sauce in the frying pan and cook for 5 to 7 minutes until the bananas are just heated through, turning them gently in the sauce. Place the bananas and their sauce in small bowls, top them with frozen yoghurt or ice cream, if desired, and serve.

STRAWBERRIES IN BLUEBERRY SAUCE *Serves 4*

For the blueberry sauce:

1 cup fresh or bottled blueberries, drained

1 cup white sugar

1 teaspoon grated orange peel

2 tablespoons brandy

4 cups strawberries

1 cup sweetened whipped cream

Mint leaves (optional)

 Preparation time
12 minutes

 Cooking time
15 minutes

1. To make the sauce: Mix the blueberries, sugar and orange peel in a medium-sized saucepan. Cook over moderate heat, stirring gently, until the berries burst and the mixture begins to liquify. Simmer for 5 minutes, stirring occasionally.

2. Remove the saucepan from the heat and stir in the brandy. Leave the sauce to cool for at least 10 minutes or until ready to serve. Meanwhile, rinse and hull the strawberries and cut each in half.

3. To serve, pour the blueberry sauce into four dessert bowls and top each with an equal amount of the strawberries. Spoon the whipped cream on top and garnish with mint leaves, if desired.

DESSERTS

GLAZED PINEAPPLE *Serves 4*

1 tablespoon (15g) butter
6 tablespoons orange marmalade
1½ teaspoons lemon juice
1 large (840g) tin pineapple slices in unsweetened juice
3 tablespoons sliced almonds

 Preparation time
13 minutes

 Cooking time
16 minutes

COOK'S TIP *If you prefer, use fresh pineapple. Either slice your own or buy the prepared slices available at the salad bar section of your supermarket.*

1. Preheat the grill. In a small saucepan, melt the butter over moderate heat. Stir in the marmalade and cook until it is melted. Add the lemon juice and stir to mix. Remove the saucepan from the heat.

2. Drain the pineapple and arrange the slices on the rack over a grill pan. Brush the slices with half of the marmalade mixture. Grill 10cm from the heat for 3 to 6 minutes until lightly browned on one side.

3. Turn the pineapple slices over and brush them with the remaining marmalade mixture. Continue grilling for about 3 to 6 more minutes until lightly browned.

4. Sprinkle the pineapple with the almonds and continue grilling for 30 seconds to 1 minute until the nuts are golden brown. Place the warm pineapple slices on a plate and serve immediately.

TROPICAL FRUIT SKEWERS *Serves 4*

2 medium or 1 large mango
2 tablespoons white sugar
1 tablespoon lemon or lime juice
1 papaya
1 kiwi fruit
1 large banana

 Preparation time
25 minutes

 Cooking time
0 minutes

COOK'S TIP *You could prepare these a short while in advance if you brush the fruit pieces with a little lemon juice. Serve with a yoghurt dip, the acidic taste of which will highlight the flavours of the exotic fruit.*

1. Peel the mango, carefully cut the flesh away from the pip and place it in a food processor or electric blender. Add the sugar and the lemon juice and process the mixture until smooth. Pour the sauce into a small bowl and place in the refrigerator while preparing the fruit skewers.

2. Peel the papaya, cut it in half and discard the seeds. Chop the flesh into 2,5cm chunks. Peel the kiwi fruit, halve it and cut each half into four chunks. Peel the banana and cut it into 1cm slices.

3. Thread the fruit onto four wooden skewers, beginning and ending each with a chunk of kiwi fruit. To serve, pour a little of the mango sauce onto four individual serving plates. Top with a fruit skewer and serve immediately.

MELON COMPOTE

MELON COMPOTE *Serves 4*

750g watermelon
½ small spanspek
½ small honeydew melon
2 to 3 tablespoons finely chopped fresh mint leaves
2 tablespoons honey
Mint sprigs (optional)

 Preparation time
15 minutes

 Cooking/chilling time
30 minutes

DIET NOTE Perfect for those figure-conscious days of summer, this light, low-kilojoule dessert will give you your vitamin C for the day and satisfy your sweet tooth.

1 Using a melon-ball cutter, scoop out balls from the three melons. (Alternatively, cut the fruit into 2cm cubes.) Place in a large bowl, add the mint and honey and toss the mixture gently. Cover and refrigerate for at least 30 minutes to marinate the melon mixture.

2 Spoon the melon mixture and any accumulated juices into dessert dishes. Garnish each serving with a mint sprig, if desired, and serve immediately.

DESSERTS

STUFFED BAKED APPLES *Serves 4*

4 medium (about 500g) baking apples (eg Granny Smith)

2 tablespoons (30g) butter or margarine

½ cup (75g) digestive biscuit crumbs

3 tablespoons raisins

2 tablespoons firmly packed light brown sugar

½ teaspoon ground cinnamon

1 cup apple juice

¼ cup golden syrup or honey

Cream (optional)

 Preparation time 10 minutes

 Cooking time 35 minutes

SERVING SUGGESTION *This traditional and much-beloved winter warmer is wonderful when served hot and topped with a swirl of cream.*

1. Preheat the oven to 190°C. Halve the apples and core them, taking care not to cut all the way through to the bottom. Place the apple halves, cut side up, in a 37,5cm x 26,5cm baking dish.

2. In a small saucepan, melt the butter over moderate heat. Remove the saucepan from the heat and brush the apples lightly with some of the melted butter. Add the biscuit crumbs, the raisins, sugar and cinnamon to the remaining melted butter in the saucepan. Toss the crumb mixture until well mixed.

3. Fill the cavity of each apple half with some of the crumb mixture, creating a slight mound in the centre of each. In a cup, blend the apple juice and syrup. Pour a tablespoon of the juice mixture over each apple and pour the remaining mixture into the dish around the apples.

4. Bake the apples for 25 to 35 minutes until they are tender. Transfer them to dessert bowls, top with a spoonful of cream, if desired, and serve.

BRANDIED SPICED PEACHES *Serves 4*

1 cup white sugar

1 cup water

1 cinnamon stick (about 7,5cm long)

6 whole cloves

¼ teaspoon ground nutmeg

4 large (about 1kg) firm peaches

½ cup brandy

Sweetened whipped cream (optional)

 Preparation time 5 minutes

 Cooking time 6 minutes

1. In a large saucepan, bring 7,5cm of water to the boil over high heat. Meanwhile, in a medium-sized saucepan, combine the sugar, water, cinnamon stick, cloves and nutmeg, and bring the mixture to the boil over moderately high heat.

2. Place the peaches in the boiling water for 1 to 2 minutes to loosen their skins. Drain and rinse them under cold water, remove the skins, cut them in half and remove the pips.

3. Add the peach halves to the sugar mixture and cook gently for about 3 minutes until the flesh softens. Remove the saucepan from the heat and stir in the brandy. Set the peaches aside to cool slightly.

4. Spoon the warm peaches, with some of their cooking liquid, into small dessert bowls. Top each with a spoonful of whipped cream, if desired, and serve immediately.

DESSERTS

HONEY-BAKED PEARS *Serves 4*

4 firm (about 600g) pears
1 cup orange juice
¼ cup honey
¼ teaspoon ground ginger
1 tablespoon (15g) butter, cut into pieces
2 tablespoons chopped, shelled pistachio nuts or toasted almonds

 Preparation time
10 minutes

 Cooking time
30 minutes

1 Preheat the oven to 180°C. Peel the pears and halve them lengthwise. Remove the cores and the seeds.

2 Place the pears, cut sides down, in a single layer in a 30cm x 20cm baking dish. Combine the orange juice, honey and ginger in a small bowl until well mixed. Pour the mixture over the pears, dot with the butter and bake for 20 to 30 minutes until just tender.

3 Place the pears and their baking liquid in a dish or small bowls, sprinkle with the nuts and serve immediately.

GINGERED PEACHES WITH YOGHURT *Serves 4*

4 medium (about 500g) peaches
2 tablespoons (30g) butter
1 cup thick plain yoghurt
2 tablespoons finely chopped crystallized ginger
Mint sprigs (optional)

 Preparation time
7 minutes

 Cooking time
7 minutes

1 Halve the peaches, remove the pips and slice the flesh. In a large frying pan, melt the butter over moderate heat. Add the peach slices and sauté for approximately 5 minutes, stirring to prevent sticking, until they are tender.

2 Stir the yoghurt and 1 tablespoon of the crystallized ginger into the peaches until well mixed and just warmed. Remove the pan from the heat.

3 Place the warm peaches and yoghurt in small bowls and sprinkle each serving with an equal amount of the remaining crystallized ginger. Garnish with mint sprigs, if desired, and serve.

TIME SAVERS

FRUIT
■ For a snack that needs no cooking, make a batch of frozen grapes. Freeze individual seedless grapes on a baking sheet, transfer to a plastic food storage bag and seal tightly. They're good on their own or mixed into yoghurt for dessert.

■ Many supermarkets have salad bars, which can be used to save preparation time when making dishes containing fresh fruit. Look for cleaned strawberries, cubed spanspek and watermelon, and diced or sliced pineapple – well worth the slight extra cost.

■ Speed up the ripening process of fruit: Punch a few holes in a brown paper packet, place the fruit inside the packet and fold the top to close. Place in a cool, dark spot for a few days, checking every day to see whether the fruit is ripe and ready for eating.

CINNAMON POACHED PEARS

CINNAMON POACHED PEARS *Serves 4*

2½ cups apple juice
1 cup water
2 cinnamon sticks (each about 8cm long)
⅛ teaspoon ground nutmeg
4 firm (about 600g) pears with stems
Sour cream (optional)

 Preparation time
2 minutes

 Cooking time
30 minutes

COOK'S TIP These can also be served cold. Add a scoop of vanilla ice cream if you want a richer dessert.

1. In a large saucepan, combine the apple juice, water, cinnamon sticks and nutmeg and bring to the boil over moderately high heat.

2. Meanwhile, peel the pears, leaving the stems attached. Core the pears, starting at the lower end of each. Rinse and stand them upright in the saucepan with the apple-juice mixture. Cover and bring to the boil. Immediately reduce the heat to low and simmer the pears for about 25 minutes until they are just tender.

3. Remove the saucepan from the heat. Using a slotted spoon, lift the pears out of the saucepan and place them in a serving bowl. Strain the poaching liquid over the pears and allow them to cool slightly before serving. Serve with sour cream, if desired.

Frozen desserts

Cool and creamy frozen desserts are always popular, whatever the season. Try these easy recipes – they'll round off any meal with panache.

Chocolate ice cream pie *Serves 8*

19 cream-filled chocolate biscuits, finely crushed

4 tablespoons (60g) butter, melted

2 litres chocolate or coffee ice cream

1 cup whipping cream

180g dark chocolate, chopped

¼ teaspoon ground cinnamon

 Preparation time 15 minutes

 Cooking/chilling time 30 minutes

Cook's tip Children and adults alike will love this easy-to-make ice cream pie. Double the recipe and freeze one for later.

1. In a medium-sized bowl, use a fork to combine the crushed biscuits and butter. Set aside 1 tablespoon of the crumb mixture and press the remaining mixture into the bottom and sides of a deep 23cm pie plate. Place in the freezer for 10 minutes.

2. Scoop the ice cream into balls and place in the crumb crust. Using a rubber spatula, smooth the top of the ice cream. Sprinkle the surface with the remaining crumbs. Return the pie to the freezer.

3. Meanwhile, in a small bowl, use an electric mixer to beat ½ cup of the cream until it forms stiff peaks. Using a pastry bag fitted with a star tube, pipe the cream around the edge of the pie, and pipe any remaining cream in the centre of the pie. Freeze for at least 15 to 20 minutes.

4. Meanwhile, in a small saucepan, combine the chocolate with the remaining ½ cup of cream and the cinnamon. Cook over moderate heat, stirring constantly, until the chocolate melts and the mixture is smooth and bubbly (do not boil). Pour the mixture into a small jug. Slice the pie into wedges and serve, passing the chocolate sauce separately.

This refreshing ice-cream drink uses crumbed ginger biscuits for a spicy twist. Serve it in tall glasses with colourful straws.

Ginger-vanilla whip

In a food processor or blender, crush *6 ginger biscuits* until coarsely chopped. Using a large spoon, add *500ml vanilla ice cream*, slightly softened, to the processor bowl and blend until smooth. Pour the mixture into four goblets or glass dessert bowls, top each with *a pinch of nutmeg* and serve immediately. Serves 4

DESSERTS

QUICK BERRY ICE CREAM *Serves 4*

3½ cups (about 600g) strawberries, raspberries or sliced peaches

1 cup thick cream

⅓ cup white sugar

1 teaspoon vanilla essence

 Preparation time
6 minutes

 Cooking/chilling time
1 hour

Food note This soft ice cream tastes as if it were made in an ice-cream maker, but it takes only a few minutes to prepare. Make sure the fruit is well frozen when you add it to the cream.

1 Place the fruit on a baking tray, in a single layer, and freeze for 30 minutes to 1 hour until firm and frozen. Using a food processor with the chopping blade, process the cream, sugar and vanilla essence for about 1 minute until smooth.

2 Through the feed tube in the food processor, add the frozen fruit, a few pieces at a time and process until smooth. Spoon the ice cream into small bowls and serve immediately.

PINEAPPLE WITH LEMON SORBET *Serves 4*

2 fresh pineapples

¼ cup white sugar

1 tablespoon cornflour

1 tablespoon rum (optional)

1 large banana

2 cups lemon sorbet

Fresh mint sprigs

 Preparation time
15 minutes

 Cooking/chilling time
19 minutes

Cook's tip Fresh pineapple is worth the extra effort because this dessert looks so special served in bowls made from the rind. If you prefer not to buy a whole pineapple, buy pre-cut fresh pineapple from the supermarket and serve the dessert in small bowls.

1 Cut each pineapple in half along its length. Carefully cut the flesh away from the rind, leaving a shell about 1cm thick.

2 Remove the core from the pineapple pieces. Cut the pineapple flesh into 1cm-thick slices. Using an electric blender or food processor, process enough of the slices to yield 1 cup of finely chopped pineapple.

3 Fill the pineapple shells with the remaining pineapple slices. Wrap and refrigerate the pineapple shells until ready to serve.

4 In a medium-sized saucepan, combine the sugar, cornflour and rum, if desired. Add the chopped pineapple and stir until well mixed. Bring the pineapple mixture to the boil over moderate heat, stirring constantly, until thickened and bubbly. Remove the pineapple mixture from the heat and chill for 10 to 15 minutes.

5 Place a pineapple shell on each of four individual serving plates. Peel and slice the banana into approximately 16 slices and divide them among the shells. Scoop the lemon sorbet onto each shell. Top with the warm pineapple sauce, garnish with the sprigs of mint and serve immediately.

ICE CREAM TRIFLE

ICE CREAM TRIFLE *Serves 6*

1 small Swiss roll (about 20cm long), filled with strawberry jam

¼ cup cream sherry or orange juice

3 cups vanilla ice cream

1 cup (about 170g) fresh raspberries, rinsed and dried

½ cup sweetened whipped cream

2 tablespoons sliced almonds

 Preparation time 20 minutes

 Cooking time 0 minutes

SERVING SUGGESTION *Ring the changes by using sliced strawberries instead of raspberries. Whichever you choose, this summery dessert looks elegant and takes only minutes to prepare.*

1 Cut the Swiss roll into 1cm-thick slices. In a small shallow glass bowl or rimmed serving dish, line the bowl with the slices of cake. Sprinkle the cake with the sherry.

2 Fill with scoops of the ice cream and top with the raspberries, whipped cream and almonds. Serve immediately.

START WITH A SCOOP

Keep a container or two of your favourite ice cream or frozen yoghurt in the freezer. Start with a scoop, then add any combination of sauces, fresh fruit or liqueur for an irresistibly refreshing dessert treat. For a few ideas for single-ingredient additions, consult the box at the lower right. Each of these recipes serves four and may easily be halved or doubled.

◄ **Peach Melba** Crush *1½ cups (about 250g) fresh raspberries*. In a saucepan, combine *2 tablespoons castor sugar, 1 teaspoon cornflour* and *2 tablespoons lemon juice*. Push the berries through a strainer into the saucepan (discard the seeds). Gently bring to the boil and cook, stirring, until thickened. Remove from the heat. Peel, halve and remove the pips from *4 peaches*. Place 2 peach halves into each of four bowls. Scoop *2 cups vanilla ice cream* over them and top with the sauce.

► **Coconut snowballs** Scoop *2 cups vanilla ice cream* into four balls and roll the scoops in *1 cup (80g) desiccated coconut* until well coated, making four snowballs. Place the snowballs on a serving plate and refreeze until firm. Just before serving, pour *½ cup (90g) tinned crushed pineapple* over the four snowballs. Garnish with *sliced fresh strawberries*.

► **Amaretti chocolate ice cream** Place *1 cup (about 150g) crushed amaretti biscuits* or *almond macaroons* in a pie plate. Scoop *2 cups chocolate ice cream* into four balls and roll the balls in the crumbs. Place on a plate and refreeze until firm. To serve, spoon a thin coating of *ready-made chocolate sauce* or *topping* onto four small rimmed serving plates. Cut each ice cream ball into four wedges and arrange them on the plates. Garnish each serving with *a dollop of whipped cream* and *maraschino cherries*.

▶ **Lemon ice cream with raspberry sauce**
Using an electric blender or food processor, process *2 cups (about 300g) fresh raspberries* or *blackberries* until puréed. Press the purée through a fine sieve into a bowl (discard the seeds). Add *1 tablespoon crème de cassis* or *Grand Marnier* and *sugar* to taste. Scoop *2 cups lemon sorbet* into four serving bowls and top with the sauce.

◀ **Waffle à la mode** Lightly toast *4 frozen waffles*. In a small saucepan, heat *1 cup (260g) tinned pie apples*. Place a toasted waffle on each of four small dessert plates. Scoop *½ cup vanilla ice cream* on each waffle. Top with the warmed apple filling, sprinkle with *chopped pecan nuts* and *ground cinnamon*.

▶ **Tutti-frutti sundae** In a large bowl, combine *3 tablespoons sugar, 2 tablespoons brandy, 1 small diced nectarine, 1 small sliced banana* and *1 cup fresh* or *tinned cherries*, halved and pitted. Place *four 1cm thick slices loaf-shaped butter cake* into four dessert dishes. Place scoops from *2 cups lemon sorbet* on the slices of cake. Top with the fruit and garnish with *sliced almonds*.

ADD TO YOUR FAVOURITE ICE CREAM

Warmed apricot jam	Toasted slivered almonds	Brandied raisins
Sweetened instant chocolate powder	Crushed iced biscuits	Brandied peaches
Crème de Menthe liqueur	Toasted coconut	Chopped glacé cherries
Crushed peppermint crisp chocolate	Muesli	Chopped preserved orange peel
	Chocolate-covered raisins	Sliced strawberries

CAPPUCCINO ICE CREAM

CAPPUCCINO ICE CREAM *Serves 4*

2 cups coffee ice cream

½ cup cream

2 tablespoons icing sugar

1 tablespoon coffee liqueur

Flaked chocolate or ground cinnamon

 Preparation time
15 minutes

 Cooking/chilling time
30 minutes

FOOD NOTE *The flavours of coffee, ice cream and smooth coffee liqueur are fused here in a deliciously different dessert.*

1 Place half a cup of ice cream in each of four cappuccino cups or small dessert bowls.

2 Whip the cream until soft peaks form, then fold in the icing sugar and the liqueur. Spoon the cream mixture over each cup of ice cream to resemble the frothy topping on cappuccino.

3 Place the cups in the freezer and freeze for at least 30 minutes. Just before serving, sprinkle with chocolate flakes or ground cinnamon. Serve immediately.

DESSERTS

HOT APPLE PARFAIT *Serves 4*

3 large Golden Delicious apples

¼ cup raisins

¼ cup white sugar

¼ cup water

½ teaspoon ground cinnamon

200g shortbread biscuits or vanilla wafers

2 cups vanilla frozen yoghurt or ice cream

¼ cup (30g) chopped walnuts

 Preparation time
20 minutes

 Cooking time
20 minutes

1. Peel, core and coarsely chop the apples. In a medium-sized saucepan, combine the apples, raisins, sugar, water and cinnamon and bring the mixture to the boil over moderate heat.

2. Cover the saucepan and cook the apple mixture, stirring occasionally, for 15 minutes. If necessary, uncover the saucepan and continue cooking for a further 5 minutes until all of the liquid is evaporated. Meanwhile, place the biscuits in a plastic food-storage bag. With a rolling pin, crush the biscuits into crumbs, making about 2 cups.

3. Spoon half of the biscuit crumbs into four parfait glasses. Top with the warmed apple mixture and sprinkle with the remaining crumbs. Scoop the frozen yoghurt into each parfait glass and sprinkle with the walnuts. Serve immediately.

MICROWAVE OVEN VERSION

Chop the apples as in Step 1 above. Place the apples, raisins, sugar, water and ground cinnamon in a microwave-safe, 2-litre casserole dish. Toss gently to mix. Microwave on high power for 5 minutes, covered, stirring once during cooking. Uncover and continue cooking for 3 to 4 more minutes on high until the apples are very soft and almost all the liquid is evaporated, stirring once during cooking. Proceed with the recipe as described in Steps 2 and 3 above.

CHOCOLATE PARFAITS *Serves 4* (PICTURE PAGE 349)

½ cup (90g) chopped dark chocolate or chocolate chips

2 tablespoons (30g) butter or margarine

2 cups chocolate ice cream

1 cup (about 150g) crushed vanilla biscuits

½ cup sweetened whipped cream

2 tablespoons chopped walnuts

4 maraschino cherries with stems (optional)

 Preparation time
15 minutes

 Cooking time
3 minutes

1. In a small saucepan, melt the chocolate and the butter over low heat, stirring constantly. Remove the saucepan from the heat and set aside. (Alternatively, melt the chocolate and butter in the microwave oven.)

2. Divide half of the ice cream among four parfait glasses or stemmed goblets. Sprinkle each portion with half of the biscuit crumbs. Repeat with the remaining ice cream and biscuit crumbs.

3. Top the chocolate parfaits with the cream, walnuts and maraschino cherries, if desired. Pour the melted chocolate into a small jug. Serve the parfaits immediately, passing the melted chocolate separately.

ICE CREAM WITH BUTTERSCOTCH SAUCE

ICE CREAM WITH BUTTERSCOTCH SAUCE *Serves 4*

1 cup firmly packed light brown sugar

⅓ cup golden syrup

¼ cup water

4 tablespoons (60g) butter

⅓ cup cream, at room temperature

½ teaspoon rum essence

2 cups vanilla ice cream or frozen yoghurt

 Preparation time
14 minutes

 Cooking time
7 minutes

COOK'S TIP Toasted chopped almonds would add a crunchy texture – stir them directly into the sauce or sprinkle them on top.

1. In a small saucepan, combine the brown sugar, syrup, water and butter. Bring to the boil over moderate heat and continue boiling for about 4 minutes until the mixture reaches the soft ball stage on a sugar thermometer (112°C). Remove the saucepan from the heat and set the mixture aside for about 10 minutes to cool slightly.

2. Add the cream and rum essence to the mixture and stir until smooth. Pour the sauce into a small jug.

3. Scoop the ice cream into four individual dessert dishes and serve immediately, passing the sauce separately.

DESSERTS

Mini White Alaskas *Serves 4*

1 small loaf butter cake
2 cups strawberry ice cream
1 cup thick cream
2 tablespoons icing sugar
½ teaspoon vanilla essence
½ cup ready-made chocolate syrup

 Preparation time
10 minutes

 Cooking/chilling time
20 minutes

1. Cut 4 x 3cm-thick slices from the loaf cake (store any leftover cake for later use). Place the slices on a small baking sheet or freezer-safe plate. Scoop the ice cream into four balls and place one on each slice. Place in the freezer for 10 minutes.

2. Meanwhile, in a small bowl, using an electric mixer, beat the cream with the icing sugar and vanilla essence until the mixture forms stiff peaks. Remove the cake from the freezer and, using a rubber spatula, quickly cover the ice cream and cake with the whipped cream. Return the iced cakes to the freezer for a further 10 minutes or until ready to serve.

3. Just before serving, pour the chocolate syrup into four rimmed individual dessert plates. Using a spatula, place the mini alaskas on the sauce and serve immediately.

Tortoni *Serves 6*

1 cup (about 150g) crushed amaretti biscuits (or vanilla biscuits)
2 tablespoons dark rum (or 1½ tablespoons water with 1 teaspoon rum essence)
3 tablespoons coarsely chopped maraschino cherries
2 cups vanilla ice cream, slightly softened
3 tablespoons slivered blanched almonds
3 maraschino cherries, halved

 Preparation time
15 minutes

 Cooking/chilling time
30 minutes

1. Line a 6-cup muffin tin with fluted paper cupcake liners. In a medium-sized bowl, mix the biscuit crumbs, rum and chopped cherries. Quickly add the ice cream and fold in gently until just mixed. Spoon the mixture into the paper cups and freeze for about 30 minutes until the ice cream is firm.

2. Meanwhile, in a large frying pan, toast the almonds over moderate heat for about 3 minutes until lightly browned, stirring frequently. Remove from the heat and set aside to cool.

3. Transfer each paper cup from the freezer to a serving plate. Top each with some of the almonds and a halved cherry and serve.

Time Savers

Toasted Almonds
You can also use your microwave oven to toast almonds, making a nutty garnish for ice-cream. Place ½ *cup (about 60g) sliced almonds* in a 3-cup microwave-safe glass dish. Cook, uncovered, on high power for 2 to 3 minutes, stopping after each minute to stir. As soon as the almonds begin to brown, remove the dish from the oven and tip them onto a paper towel to cool. Chop, if desired, and sprinkle them over the ice cream.

Custards and soufflés

Velvety smooth and satisfying, these desserts are just the ticket when the end of the meal calls for something rich and creamy.

Rum chocolate mousse *Serves 4*

3 large eggs, at room temperature

¼ cup dark rum

100g dark chocolate, finely chopped

½ cup (120g) unsalted butter, cut into small pieces

¼ cup sugar

Sweetened whipped cream (optional)

Chocolate shavings (optional)

 Preparation time 10 minutes

 Cooking/chilling time 35 minutes

COOK'S TIP *Substitute the rum with Kahlua if you prefer the flavour of coffee. This dessert can be made in advance and refrigerated.*

1. Partially fill the bottom part of a double boiler with water and bring to the boil over high heat. Meanwhile, separate the eggs. In a small bowl, combine the egg yolks and rum until well blended and set aside.

2. Reduce the heat under the double boiler to moderately low. Place the chocolate in the top section of the double boiler and melt over the hot, not boiling, water. Add the butter and continue stirring until blended.

3. Remove the top part of the double boiler from the water. Gradually add the egg-yolk mixture and stir until thoroughly blended. Refrigerate the chocolate mixture briefly, while preparing the next step.

4. In a small bowl, using an electric mixer, beat the egg whites until foamy. Add the sugar, a little at a time, and continue beating until stiff peaks form. Using a rubber spatula, fold the egg whites into the chocolate mixture.

5. Spoon the mousse into four wine glasses or dessert bowls. Garnish with whipped cream and chocolate shavings, if desired. Refrigerate for at least 25 minutes before serving.

SHELF MAGIC

Use a package of instant pudding powder to whip up this creamy coffee-flavoured dessert. Tall parfait glasses will show off the layers best.

Mocha pudding

In a large bowl, using an electric mixer, beat *1 cup cream* with *2 tablespoons sugar* and *1 teaspoon instant coffee powder* until stiff peaks form. In a separate bowl, prepare one *90g package chocolate instant pudding* with *2 cups milk* according to the directions on the package. Spoon alternate layers of the two mixtures into four glasses. Refrigerate until ready to serve. Serves 4

DESSERTS

Strawberry Mousse Serves 4

1 envelope (10g) unflavoured gelatin
¼ cup orange juice
1½ cups (about 300g) strawberries, crushed
¼ cup castor sugar
1 teaspoon vanilla essence
1 cup cream
1 tablespoon icing sugar

 Preparation time
5 minutes

 Cooking/chilling time
30 minutes

SERVING SUGGESTION *This dewy-fresh fruit mousse makes a light dessert after a filling meal. Garnish it with sprigs of mint.*

1 In a medium-sized saucepan, sprinkle the gelatin evenly over the orange juice and let it stand for 1 minute to soften the gelatin slightly. Cook the mixture over low heat until the gelatin dissolves completely. Remove the saucepan from the heat and stir in the crushed strawberries, sugar and vanilla essence.

2 Place the mixture in the refrigerator for at least 10 minutes to cool. Meanwhile, in a small bowl, use an electric mixer to beat the cream and icing sugar together until the mixture forms stiff peaks (do not overbeat).

3 Using a rubber spatula, gently fold the chilled strawberry mixture into the whipped cream until it is well mixed. Spoon the mousse into a large serving bowl, individual glass dessert bowls or goblets. Refrigerate for approximately 15 minutes until the mousse is set, and serve.

Zabaglione Serves 4

2 cups fresh strawberries, hulled and sliced
6 large egg yolks
2 tablespoons sugar
⅓ cup Marsala

 Preparation time
15 minutes

 Cooking time
8 minutes

SERVING SUGGESTION *This rich Italian custard can also be served in wine glasses without the fruit. Garnish with finger biscuits or almond macaroons.*

1 Partially fill the bottom part of a double boiler with water and bring to the boil over high heat. Meanwhile, place the strawberries into four wine glasses and set aside.

2 In the top section of the double boiler (still separate from the bottom part), use an electric mixer to beat the egg yolks and the sugar together for about 4 minutes until thick and pale yellow. Gradually add the Marsala, beating until well combined.

3 Reduce the heat under the double boiler to moderately low. Place the top part of the double boiler over the hot, not boiling, water. Continue beating the egg-yolk mixture at medium speed for about 8 minutes until it begins to hold its shape. Spoon the zabaglione over the strawberries in the glasses and serve immediately (the zabaglione will separate if left to stand).

CHEESECAKE CUPS

CHEESECAKE CUPS *Serves 6*

6 small, plain round vanilla biscuits

1 package (227g) cream cheese, softened

¼ cup sugar

1 teaspoon vanilla essence

1 large egg

6 ripe strawberries

1 to 2 tablespoons redcurrant or quince jelly

 Preparation time
5 minutes

 Cooking/chilling time
40 minutes

SERVING SUGGESTION *These little melt-in-the-mouth cheesecakes make an excellent dessert for a buffet or a tea-time treat.*

1. Preheat the oven to 160°C. Line a 6-cup muffin tray with fluted foil cupcake liners. Place one biscuit in each cup. In a small bowl, using an electric mixer, beat the cream cheese, sugar and vanilla essence until smooth and fluffy. Add the egg and beat well.

2. Spoon the cream-cheese mixture into the cupcake liners. Bake for about 25 minutes until the cheesecake cups are just set. Refrigerate for at least 15 minutes or until ready to serve.

3. If desired, just before serving, make fanned strawberries: Make thin parallel cuts in each strawberry from the pointed to the stemmed end, taking care not to cut all the way through the berry. Ease the slices apart to form a fan and place one on top of each cheesecake cup.

4. In a small saucepan, heat the jelly over low heat, stirring until it is melted. Brush some of the glaze over each strawberry and serve immediately.

DESSERTS

BITTERSWEET CHOCOLATE SOUFFLÉS *Serves 4*

1 tablespoon (15g) butter or margarine

125g dark chocolate, finely chopped

½ cup sugar

3 tablespoons cherry-flavoured liqueur, brandy or orange juice

8 large eggs, separated, at room temperature

1 tablespoon icing sugar

 Preparation time 20 minutes

 Cooking time 15 minutes

COOK'S TIP Save time by melting the chocolate in the microwave oven, checking it frequently until it is soft and able to be stirred.

1 Preheat the oven to 220°C. Coat the bottom and sides of four 1½-cup individual soufflé dishes with the butter. Place the dishes on a rimmed baking sheet and set aside. Partially fill the bottom part of a double boiler with water and bring to the boil over high heat.

2 Reduce the heat under the double boiler to moderately low. Melt the chocolate in the top section of the double boiler. Stir in ¼ cup of the sugar and the liqueur until blended.

3 Remove the top part of the double boiler from the water. Add the egg yolks and stir until thoroughly blended. Refrigerate the chocolate mixture briefly (only while preparing the next step).

4 In a large bowl, using an electric mixer, beat the egg whites until foamy. Gradually add the remaining ¼ cup of sugar and beat until the mixture forms stiff peaks. Fold one-quarter of the beaten egg whites into the chocolate mixture until blended thoroughly, then fold the chocolate mixture into the remaining beaten egg whites.

5 Pour the mixture into the prepared soufflé dishes and bake for 12 to 15 minutes until puffed and risen (do not open the oven door during baking – they will collapse). Sift the icing sugar over the soufflés before serving.

PUMPKIN MOUSSE *Serves 4*

1 cup cooked, puréed pumpkin

⅓ cup firmly packed light brown sugar

½ teaspoon ground cinnamon

½ teaspoon ground ginger

¾ cup cream

2 tablespoons chopped crystallized ginger

 Preparation time 10 minutes

 Cooking time 0 minutes

1 In a medium-sized bowl, combine the pumpkin, sugar, cinnamon and ginger. In a small bowl, using an electric mixer, beat the cream until it forms stiff peaks.

2 Using a wire whisk or rubber spatula, fold the whipped cream into the pumpkin mixture until well mixed. Fold in 1 tablespoon of the chopped crystallized ginger.

3 Spoon the pumpkin mousse into four wine glasses or dessert bowls. Sprinkle the top of each serving with the remaining tablespoon of chopped ginger and serve.

DESSERTS

CARAMEL GINGER PUDDING *Serves 4*

8 gingernut biscuits
2 tablespoons brandy
1 cup whipping cream
1 tin (397g) caramelized condensed milk
¼ cup chopped preserved ginger

 Preparation time
15 minutes

 Cooking/chilling time
30 minutes

1. Break the gingernut biscuits into small pieces and place them in a small bowl. Pour the brandy over the biscuits and set them to one side to soak.

2. In a second bowl, whip the cream until it forms soft peaks that hold their shape.

3. Beat the caramelized condensed milk until smooth and creamy, then fold in the whipped cream, the brandy-soaked biscuits and the chopped preserved ginger, stirring gently until the mixture is well blended.

4. Spoon the pudding into individual dessert bowls or decorative wine glasses and cool in the refrigerator for at least 30 minutes until ready to serve.

CHERRY CREAM PUDDING *Serves 4*

1 package (227g) cream cheese, softened
¼ cup icing sugar
¾ cup thick cream
1 teaspoon vanilla essence
300g cherries, halved and stoned
4 cherries with stems (optional)

 Preparation time
20 minutes

 Cooking time
0 minutes

1. In a small bowl, using an electric mixer, beat the cream cheese and the icing sugar together until the mixture is smooth and fluffy. Slowly beat in the cream and vanilla essence until the mixture forms soft peaks.

2. Using a rubber spatula, fold the prepared cherries into the cream mixture. Spoon the pudding into four wine glasses or individual glass bowls. Top each serving with a stemmed cherry, if desired, and serve immediately.

GRANOLA PARFAIT *Serves 4*

1 cup granola cereal
¼ cup (45g) chopped dates
¼ cup (30g) chopped macadamia nuts
4 cups thick plain Greek-style yoghurt
Honey for topping

 Preparation time
11 minutes

 Cooking time
0 minutes

1. In a small bowl, combine the granola, dates and nuts. In each of four parfait glasses, layer ⅓ cup of the yoghurt, followed by 2 tablespoons of the granola mixture, repeating twice and ending with a layer of granola.

2. Serve the yoghurt parfaits immediately or cover with plastic wrap and refrigerate until ready to serve. Drizzle with a little honey before serving.

PAPAYA CREAM

PAPAYA CREAM *Serves 4*

1 envelope (10g) unflavoured gelatin

½ cup water

2 tablespoons sugar

1 tablespoon lemon or lime juice

1 large papaya

2 cups vanilla ice cream, cut into chunks

Thin lime slices (optional)

Preparation time
6 minutes

Cooking/chilling time
34 minutes

SERVING SUGGESTION *The creamy, refreshing texture of this fruit cream contrasts well with vanilla wafers or the almond macaroons known in Italy as amaretti.*

1. In a small saucepan, sprinkle the gelatin evenly over the water and leave it to stand for 1 minute to soften slightly. Cook over moderately low heat until the gelatin dissolves completely Remove from the heat and stir in the sugar and lemon juice. Refrigerate for about 10 minutes while preparing the fruit.

2. Cut the papaya in half along its length. Using a spoon, scoop out the seeds and discard. Scoop the papaya pulp into the container of an electric blender or food processor and process with the gelatin mixture until smooth.

3. While the blender or processor is running, add the ice cream to the papaya mixture and continue processing until the mixture is just blended. Spoon the papaya cream into individual glass dessert bowls. Refrigerate for about 20 minutes until set, or until ready to serve. Garnish each with a twisted lime slice, if desired.

PIES AND TARTS

These beautifully presented pies and tarts, some filled with fruit and others with exquisitely creamy concoctions, make perfect desserts and coffee-time snacks.

NECTARINE CHEESE TART Serves 6

1 package ready-rolled sweetened shortcrust pastry

A little melted butter

1 container (227g) cream cheese, softened

2 tablespoons icing sugar

4 medium nectarines

3 tablespoons orange marmalade

 Preparation time 28 minutes

 Cooking time 12 minutes

COOK'S TIP *Overlapping the fruit slices carefully will result in a dessert that is pleasing to the eye and ready to grace the table of a formal dinner.*

1. Preheat the oven to 220°C. Roll the pastry out lightly. Grease a 23cm loose-bottomed flan tin with the butter. Line the tin with the pastry, trimming the edges and turning them over neatly. Using a fork, pierce the pastry case all over. Place it in the oven and bake for 10 to 12 minutes until golden brown.

2. Meanwhile, in a medium-sized bowl, mix the cream cheese and icing sugar until well-blended. Halve the nectarines, remove the pips and cut the flesh into thin slices. Melt the marmalade in a small saucepan over low heat, or in a microwave-safe cup in the microwave oven.

3. Remove the flan tin from the oven and place it on a wire rack to cool slightly. Remove the pastry shell from the tin and transfer it to a decorative serving plate. Spread the cream-cheese mixture evenly over the base of the shell and arrange the nectarine slices in concentric circles, overlapping them to fit, over the cheese. Brush with the melted marmalade and serve.

Ready-prepared phyllo pastry forms the perfect base for these pineapple tarts.

PINEAPPLE TARTS

Preheat the oven to 230°C. Cut *two sheets of phyllo pastry* into eight squares and sandwich the squares with *melted butter*. Brush melted butter on both sides of each sandwiched square. Fit the pastry into eight ramekins or large cups of a muffin tin. Spread the base of each with *one teaspoon soft unsalted butter* and sprinkle with *one tablespoon brown sugar*. Drain *one 225g tin pineapple slices*. Place one slice in each ramekin. Bake for 10 minutes until the pastry is crisp and golden. Remove from the tin carefully and serve while still warm with *Greek-style yoghurt*. Serves 4

Almond sponge tart

Almond Sponge Tart *Serves 8*

1 package ready-rolled sweetened shortcrust pastry

Melted butter for greasing

¼ cup black cherry jam

1 cup milk

4 tablespoons (60g) butter

4 to 5 cups (300g) sponge cake crumbs

1 tablespoon grated lemon peel

1 teaspoon almond essence

2 large eggs

¼ cup (30g) sliced almonds

Sweetened whipped cream (optional)

 Preparation time
15 minutes

 Cooking time
25 minutes

Cook's tip Made with sponge-cake crumbs, this tart has a wonderfully soft texture. Strawberry jam may be used in place of the cherry jam.

1. Preheat the oven to 220°C. Roll the pastry out lightly. Grease a 23cm loose-bottomed flan tin with the melted butter. Line the tin with the pastry, trimming the edges and turning them over neatly. Spread the jam over the pastry.

2. In a medium-sized saucepan, heat the milk and remaining butter until melted. Add the cake crumbs, lemon peel and almond essence and stir well. Remove from the heat and set aside.

3. Using an electric mixer, beat the eggs into the cake-crumb mixture. Spoon the mixture over the layer of jam, flattening it with a spoon. Sprinkle with the sliced almonds. Bake for about 25 minutes until the filling is firm and the crust is golden. Serve the tart warm with whipped cream, if desired.

DESSERTS

FRESH STRAWBERRY TART *Serves 8*

½ cup plus 1 tablespoon sugar

¼ cup cornflour

1⅓ cups water

1 package (80g) strawberry jelly powder

4 cups (about 700g) fresh strawberries, well chilled

1 prepared 23cm crumb crust (see page 28)

½ cup thick cream

 Preparation time 10 minutes

 Cooking/chilling time 24 minutes

FOOD NOTE Fresh strawberries and cream make a delicious filling for this summery dessert. Serve with extra whipped cream, if desired.

1. In a small saucepan, combine ½ cup of the sugar and the cornflour. Add the water, stir until smooth and bring to the boil over moderate heat, stirring constantly. Continue boiling and stirring for 1 minute. Remove the saucepan from the heat. Stir the jelly powder into the mixture until it dissolves.

2. Fill a large bowl with ice cubes and set the saucepan of jelly in the ice. Stir the mixture for 2 to 3 minutes until it cools and thickens slightly (do not allow to set). Remove the saucepan from the bowl of ice.

3. Rinse and hull the strawberries and pat them dry on a paper towel. Arrange the strawberries in the pie crust and pour the jelly mixture over them. Refrigerate for at least 20 minutes.

4. Just before serving, prepare the whipped cream: In a small bowl, using an electric mixer, beat the cream with the remaining 1 tablespoon of sugar until the mixture forms stiff peaks. Spoon the cream around the edge of the tart and serve.

EASY COCONUT TART *Serves 8*

4 tablespoons (60g) butter

2 cups milk

1½ teaspoons vanilla essence

4 large eggs, at room temperature

1 cup (80g) desiccated coconut

¾ cup sugar

2 tablespoons flour

 Preparation time 7 minutes

 Cooking time 38 minutes

COOK'S TIP Although this can be served straight from the oven, it's even better chilled, allowing you to make this dessert in advance.

1. Preheat the oven to 200°C. Grease a 23cm pie plate. In a small saucepan, melt the butter over moderate heat. Add the milk and heat for a few minutes until bubbles appear around the side of the saucepan.

2. Remove the milk mixture from the heat and stir in the vanilla essence. Using an electric blender or food processor, process the eggs, coconut, sugar and flour until combined. Add the milk mixture to the egg mixture and process until well blended.

3. Pour the mixture into the prepared pie plate and bake for 30 to 35 minutes until a knife inserted halfway between the centre and edge comes out clean. Leave the pie to stand for 5 minutes before slicing. Serve warm or refrigerate to serve chilled later.

DESSERTS

BLUEBERRY SHORTCAKES *Serves 4*

- ¾ cup flour
- ¼ cup yellow maize (mealie) meal
- 1 tablespoon sugar
- 1 teaspoon bicarbonate of soda
- ½ teaspoon baking powder
- ¼ teaspoon salt
- 3 tablespoons (45g) butter, cut into tiny pieces
- 6 tablespoons plain low-fat yoghurt
- 2 cups (about 500g) fresh blueberries
- 2 tablespoons honey
- ½ cup sweetened whipped cream

 Preparation time 8 minutes

 Cooking time 20 minutes

FOOD NOTE This American favourite is traditionally prepared using fresh strawberries. Here the shortcakes are flavoured with tangy blueberries and a sweetening of honey.

1. Preheat the oven to 220°C. In a medium-sized bowl, combine the flour, maize meal, sugar, bicarbonate of soda, baking powder and salt. Using a pastry blender or two knives held like a pair of scissors, cut in the butter until the mixture resembles coarse crumbs. Using a fork, stir in the yoghurt to form a soft dough. Knead the dough lightly for a few seconds.

2. On a lightly floured surface, pat or roll the dough to a thickness of 1cm. With a floured 7,5cm cookie cutter, cut out four circles. Place them on an ungreased baking sheet and bake for 18 to 20 minutes until the shortcakes are golden brown.

3. Meanwhile, rinse and sort the blueberries. In a medium-sized bowl, combine the blueberries with the honey, crushing about one-quarter of the berries. Refrigerate the mixture until the shortcakes are ready to serve.

4. To serve, halve the warm shortcakes. Place the bottom halves on serving plates. Top with half of the berries, the top halves of the shortcakes, a dollop of the whipped cream and the remaining berries. Serve immediately.

APPLE CRISP *Serves 4*

- 4 large Granny Smith apples
- ⅓ cup white sugar
- 2 tablespoons lemon juice
- 1 teaspoon ground cinnamon
- ½ cup firmly packed light brown sugar
- ½ cup flour
- ½ cup quick-cooking oats
- 4 tablespoons (60g) butter or margarine, cut into tiny pieces

 Preparation time 15 minutes

 Cooking time 30 minutes

1. Preheat the oven to 180°C. Peel, core and slice the apples and place them in a large bowl. Sprinkle the apples with the white sugar, lemon juice and cinnamon, tossing to coat them evenly. Transfer to a 23cm square baking dish.

2. In a small bowl, combine the brown sugar, flour and oats. Using a pastry blender or two knives held like a pair of scissors, cut the butter into the flour mixture until it resembles coarse crumbs. Sprinkle the crumb topping over the apple mixture.

3. Place in the oven and bake for about 30 minutes until the crumb topping is crisp and lightly browned. Spoon the warm apple crisp into small bowls and serve immediately or leave it to cool and serve at room temperature.

START WITH A CRUMB CRUST

A pie crust created with biscuit crumbs is the perfect container for a variety of scrumptious yet simple fillings. All of these tempting desserts can be whipped up in minutes, then placed in the refrigerator to finish setting while you enjoy dinner.

Start with a crumb crust (see page 28 for recipe), then choose one of the appealing fillings given below or, if you can't make up your mind, make two and offer your guests a choice. Each pie serves eight.

◄ **Creamy strawberry tart** Rinse, dry, hull and slice *2 cups strawberries*. In a small bowl, combine the strawberries with *2 tablespoons sugar*. Refrigerate. Meanwhile, in a small bowl, beat *1 cup cream* with *1 teaspoon vanilla essence* until the mixture forms stiff peaks. In another bowl, prepare *one 90g package vanilla instant pudding* with *1 cup milk*. Spoon half of the strawberries into *one 23cm plain crumb crust*. Fold the whipped cream into the pudding and spoon the mixture over the strawberries. Top with the remaining strawberries. Refrigerate for at least 15 minutes.

► **Chocolate pudding tart** Melt *60g dark chocolate* and set aside. Using an electric mixer, beat *1 cup cream* with *1 teaspoon vanilla essence* until the mixture forms stiff peaks. In another bowl, prepare *one 90g package vanilla instant pudding* with *1 cup milk*. Fold the whipped cream into the pudding mixture and spoon ½ cup of the mixture into the cooled melted chocolate. Spread the chocolate mixture over the base of *one 23cm crumb crust*. Pour the remaining pudding over it. Refrigerate the tart for at least 20 minutes. Garnish with chocolate curls before serving.

▶ **Coconut cream tart** In a frying pan, toast *1⅓ cups (100g) desiccated coconut* over moderate heat. Beat *1 cup cream, 2 tablespoons icing sugar* and *1 teaspoon vanilla essence* until soft peaks form. Reserve *½ cup (40g)* of the coconut. Fold remaining coconut into the cream and spread into *one 23cm crumb crust*. Sprinkle with the remaining coconut. Refrigerate for 15 minutes.

◀ **Banana split pie** Peel and slice *2 medium bananas* into *one 23cm chocolate biscuit crumb crust*. Scoop *1 litre vanilla ice cream* over the bananas. Drizzle *½ cup ready-made chocolate topping* over the ice cream and sprinkle with *½ cup (65g) chopped, toasted almonds*. Freeze for at least 15 minutes.

▶ **Coffee-chocolate tart** In a double boiler, melt *100g dark chocolate* and spread it over the base of a *23cm chocolate biscuit crumb crust*. Place in the freezer. Meanwhile, mix *2 tablespoons strong coffee* with *1 tablespoon coffee liqueur*. Beat *375g cream cheese* with *½ cup icing sugar*, and add to the coffee mixture. Beat *1 cup whipping cream* with *1 teaspoon vanilla essence* until stiff peaks form. Fold into the cream cheese mixture and spoon into the crust. Sprinkle with *grated dark chocolate*. Refrigerate until needed.

▶ **Lime tart** Whisk *one 397g tin sweetened condensed milk* with *½ cup fresh lime* or *lemon juice* and *2 large egg yolks* until thickened. Pour into a *23cm crumb crust*. Freeze for 15 minutes. Top with *2 cups whipped cream* and sprinkle with *grated lime* or *lemon peel*.

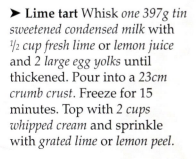

DESSERTS

KIWI AND GRAPE PASTRIES *Serves 6*

3 kiwi fruits

1 cup seedless red grapes

1 package (90g) vanilla instant pudding

2 cups milk

¼ cup cream

6 ready-baked large vol-au-vent shells (can be ordered from your local bakery if not readily available)

1 egg (beaten)

Additional kiwi fruit and grapes (optional)

 Preparation time
20 minutes

 Cooking time
10 minutes

FOOD NOTE The kiwi fruits and grapes, arranged invitingly in a vol-au-vent or 'puff of wind' shell, make a cool and elegant finale to a dinner party. You may wish to serve them with a scoop of rich vanilla ice cream, garnished with a sprig of fresh mint.

1. Preheat the oven to 180°C. Peel the kiwi fruits, trim the ends and slice the flesh thinly. Cut the slices into small pieces and transfer them to a medium-sized bowl. Cut the grapes into quarters and add them to the kiwi fruits.

2. In a second medium-sized bowl, whisk the instant pudding powder with the milk according to the directions on the package. Whisk the cream lightly and fold it into the prepared pudding. Combine half of the mixture with the chopped fruit.

3. Brush the vol-au-vent shells with some of the beaten egg and place them in the oven for approximately 10 minutes or until they are lightly crisped. Remove from the oven and place on a wire rack to cool.

4. Spread the remaining instant pudding over the centre of six dessert plates. Place a vol-au-vent shell in the centre of each plate. Scoop the pudding-fruit mixture into the shells.

5. Decorate with additional kiwi fruit and grapes, if desired. Serve immediately or refrigerate (for a short while only) until needed.

RAISIN BREAD PUDDING *Serves 6*

2 cups milk

¼ cup firmly packed light brown sugar

4 tablespoons (60g) butter or margarine, melted

4 or 5x2,5cm-thick slices raisin bread

2 large eggs

 Preparation time
15 minutes

 Cooking time
30 minutes

1. Preheat the oven to 180°C. Grease a 1-litre casserole dish. In a small saucepan, heat the milk, sugar and butter over moderate heat, stirring continuously until the sugar is dissolved. Remove the saucepan and set aside.

2. Cut the bread into 2,5cm cubes and place them in the prepared casserole dish. Beat the eggs in a medium-sized bowl. Pour the milk mixture over the eggs and mix well. Pour the egg mixture over the bread cubes.

3. Bake the pudding for 30 minutes or until a knife inserted 2,5cm from the side of the casserole dish comes out clean (the centre may still be slightly soft). Serve the pudding warm.

PECAN TARTLETS

PECAN TARTLETS *Serves 6*

2 tablespoons (30g) butter or margarine

²/₃ cup golden syrup

¹/₄ cup sugar

1 teaspoon vanilla essence

2 large eggs, lightly beaten

6 prepared individual biscuit-crumb tart shells (made in individual foil liners)

³/₄ cup (90g) pecan nuts, coarsely chopped

 Preparation time
7 minutes

 Cooking time
30 minutes

COOK'S TIP These wickedly sweet treats – a perfect fusion of butter and nuts – will be such a hit you'll want to make them again and again.

1. Preheat the oven to 180°C. Melt the butter in a small saucepan. Remove the saucepan from the heat and stir in the syrup, sugar and vanilla essence. Gradually beat in the eggs.

2. Place the tartlet shells on a small baking sheet. Pour an equal amount of the syrup mixture into each tart shell and sprinkle with the pecan nuts. Bake for 25 to 30 minutes until the filling is set. Remove from the oven and place on a wire rack to cool slightly. Serve warm.

DESSERTS

CREAMY BANANA TARTLETS Serves 6

1¼ cups milk

1 package (90g) vanilla instant pudding

1 cup cream

2 medium bananas

6 prepared individual biscuit-crumb tart shells (made in individual foil liners)

 Preparation time
15 minutes

 Cooking time
0 minutes

FOOD NOTE The flavour of bananas, rich in fibre and potassium, is highlighted by the creamy sweetness of the vanilla pudding.

1. In a medium-sized bowl, combine the milk with the instant pudding and whisk for about 45 seconds to blend thoroughly. Cover the bowl and refrigerate until ready to use.

2. Meanwhile, in a small bowl, using an electric mixer, beat the cream until the mixture forms stiff peaks. Set aside ½ cup of the whipped cream. Using a rubber spatula, gently fold the remaining whipped cream into the pudding until well mixed.

3. Peel and slice the bananas. If desired, reserve six slices for garnishing. Place four slices of banana on the bottom of each tart shell and top with half of the pudding mixture. Add a layer of bananas to each tart. Cover the bananas with the remaining pudding. Top each with a dollop of whipped cream and a slice of banana and serve.

CHOCOLATE ALMOND CREAM TART Serves 8

2 tablespoons (30g) butter or margarine, softened

2½ cups (200g) desiccated coconut

1 package (90g) chocolate instant pudding

1¼ cups milk

1 cup cream

½ teaspoon almond essence

2 tablespoons sliced almonds

 Preparation time
25 minutes

 Cooking time
20 minutes

COOK'S TIP The exotic, easy-to-make, coconut crust used in this dessert is a versatile base for many fruit-flavoured fillings. If you have no coconut, substitute a crumb crust made with Tennis biscuits.

1. Preheat the oven to 160°C. Spread the butter evenly over the bottom and sides of a 20cm pie plate, covering it to the outer rim. Pat the coconut into the butter, place in the oven and bake for about 20 minutes until golden. Place on a wire rack to cool.

2. Meanwhile, in a medium-sized bowl, combine the instant pudding with the milk and mix according to the directions on the package. Place in the refrigerator.

3. In a small bowl, using an electric mixer, beat the cream until stiff peaks form. Using a rubber spatula, gently fold half of the whipped cream and the almond essence into the chocolate pudding until it is well mixed.

4. Spoon the pudding mixture into the cooled coconut crust. Top with the remaining whipped cream and sprinkle with the almonds. Refrigerate until ready to serve.

PEACH BERRY CRUMBLE

PEACH BERRY CRUMBLE *Serves 4*

4 or 5 large (about 650g) firm peaches

1 cup (about 170g) fresh berries (eg raspberries, blueberries or loganberries)

1 cup flour

½ cup sugar

¼ teaspoon ground nutmeg

⅓ cup (80g) unsalted butter, cut into tiny pieces

Sour cream or plain low-fat yoghurt (optional)

 Preparation time 15 minutes

 Cooking time 25 minutes

Serving suggestion For those with a yen for extra sweetness, serve this wonderful dessert with a scoop of vanilla ice cream.

1. Preheat the oven to 190°C. Halve the peaches, remove the pips and slice the flesh. Place the peach slices in a 25cm x 15cm baking dish. Sprinkle the berries over the peaches.

2. In a medium-sized bowl, combine the flour, sugar and nutmeg. Using your fingertips, work the butter into the flour mixture until it resembles fine crumbs. Sprinkle over the fruit.

3. Bake for about 25 minutes until the crumb topping is golden brown and the peaches are soft. Serve warm with sour cream, or yoghurt, if desired.

Index

The index is arranged word-by-word. Page numbers in italics indicate illustrations that are not on the same page as the recipe.

A

Acorn squash, ham-stuffed 288
Alaskas, baked 338
Alaskas, mini white 369
Almond(s)
   and chocolate cream tart 388
   and coconut macaroons 345
   sponge tart 380
   toasted 369
   with angelfish 104
Alternative ingredients 14-15
Amaretti chocolate ice cream 364
Angel-hair pasta with baby marrows 215
Angelfish, foil-wrapped 104
Angelfish, pecan fried 103
Angelfish with almonds 104
Antipasto, salad bowl 312
Antipasto, vegetable 50
Appetizers 36-53
   time saving tips 47
   see also Dips; Snacks
Apple(s)
   and cinnamon soufflé omelette 251
   and grape salad 308
   and raisin upside-down cake 337
   and spice biscuits 348
   bran muffins *321*, 331
   crêpes 329
   crisp 382
   parfait, hot 367
   rings with chicken 141
   stuffed and baked *356*, 357
Apricot(s)
   and ginger chicken 168
   cake, lemon-glazed 334, *335*
   spiced, and pears 350
Artichoke
   and avocado pear salad 297
   and olive sauce for pasta 224
   dip 48
Asparagus
   and mushroom salad *298*, 299
   and pork sauté 202
   and sesame chicken 163
   and smoked salmon trout salad 314
   Dijonnaise 272, *273*

Oriental filling for omelette 263
Avocado pear
   and artichoke salad 297
   and cheddar quesadillas 39
   guacamole 47
   with chicken breasts 160
   Mexican filling for omelette 263
   ripening 277

B

Baby marrow(s)
   and chicken kebabs 153
   and tomato sauce 230
   mushroom sauce 223
   savoury muffins 332
   stir-fried with water chestnuts 275
   stuffed 283
   with angel-hair pasta 215
Bacon
   and corn chowder 85
   and lettuce pita sandwich 65
   and mushroom pizza 63
   and tomato sauce, spicy 230
   and vegetables, with spaghetti 226
   crumbled 47
   egg and spinach salad 320
   microwave tip 21
Baked
   Alaska 338
   apples, stuffed *356*, 357
   baby chickens with rice pilaff 167
   cheese and sausage 270
   chicken, herbed lemon 154
   eggs Florentine *245*, 257
   eggs Provençale 256
   fish, cheese-topped 119
   fish, herbed 98, *99*
   fish, variations 108-9
   hake over rice *112*, 113
   kabeljou, crumb-topped 116
   mushrooms, stuffed *35*, 41
   potato cakes 279
   potatoes, time saving tips 286
   snoek with tomato and onion 118
   tuna with broccoli 102
Baking, time saving tips 341, 346
Banana caramel 353
Banana split pie 385
Banana tartlets, creamy 388
Barbecued chicken rolls 142

Barbecued short ribs 170, *171*
Barley, cheese-topped, with mushrooms 244
Basic recipes
   butter cake 28
   crêpes 27
   hamburger 182
   pancake and waffle mixture 29
   roast chicken 25
   scone mixture 27
   soup stocks 22-4
Basil and pine-nut sauce 224
Basil and tomato dressing 305
Basque eggs 250
Batter-fried steak with gravy 174
Bavarian burger 183
Bean(s)
   and corn salad 302
   and ham soup 94
   and vegetables with rigatoni 214
   green *see* Green beans
   kidney, and sausage 208
   Lima, soup 81
   salad with potato 294
   tostadas 68
   with chilli beef 185
Beef 170-89
   broccoli-ginger 173
   chilli, pizza 63
   chilli, with beans 185
   corned, hash with eggs 253
   fajitas 176, *177*
   in red-wine sauce 175
   kebabs, gingered 174
   mince, rolls 70
   noodle salad 318
   patties, Russian-style 185
   rib steaks, herbed 178
   roast, canapés 43
   roast, rolls 69
   sandwich 170
   sirloin, with artichokes 180
   steak, Cajun style *169*, 172
   steak, curried with honey 179
   stir-fried, and green beans 180
   stock 23
   stroganoff 172
   vegetable soup 91
   see also Hamburger; Steak
Beetroot, and carrot salad 300
Beetroot, quick borscht 76
Berries, and peach crumble 389
Berries, quick ice cream 362
Berries, with liqueur 350

Biscuits 342-8
    apple-spice 348
    baking techniques 345
    chocolate-nut 348
    cinnamon-sugar 342, *343*
    oat-raisin 348
Bisque, crab and mushroom 78
Bite-sized cheese and red pepper quiches 36
Bittersweet chocolate soufflés *374*, 375
Blackened fish 102
Blonde brownies 344
Blue cheese dip 47
Blueberry
    pancakes 330
    sauce, and strawberries 353
    shortcakes 382, *383*
Bockwurst and lentils 209
Boerewors, roasted, and sweet potato 210
Borscht, quick 76
Braai *see* Barbecued
Braised
    baby chickens with vegetables 166
    chicken with vegetables 148
    Italian-style chicken 152
    turkey with waterblommetjies 168
Bran muffins, apple *321*, 331
Brandied spiced peaches 357
Bread crumbs, shortcuts 10-11
Bread pudding
    raisin 386
    savoury three-cheese 264
Bread(s) 322-6
    corn, chilli 322, *323*
    microwave heating tip 21
    Parmesan onion 326
Brie and ham sandwiches 199
Brinjal Parmigiana 292
Brinjal sandwiches, sautéed 57
Broccoli
    and baked tuna 102
    and cheese filling for omelette 263
    and lentil salad 312
    and orange salad 301
    custard, and sausage 254
    pesto sauce, for pasta 223
    sautéed, Italiano 274
    time saving tips 277
    with ginger, beef 173
    with teriyaki chicken 149
Brochettes of lamb 192
Brownies, blonde 344
Brownies, fudge 346

Brownies, marbled 346
Bruschetta 53
    serving suggestion 216
Buffalo chicken wings 130, *131*
Burgers
    spiced chicken 161
    see also Hamburger
Butter, softening 21, 344
Butter beans with tuna 310
Butter cake 12, 28, 338-9
Butternut squash, cheese-stuffed 268
Butterscotch sauce with ice cream 368

C

Cabbage
    diet note 93
    red, sweet-and-sour 277
    soup, Hungarian 93
    see also Coleslaw; Sauerkraut
Cajun style beef steak *169*, 172
Cakes 334-41
    and fruit with chocolate fondue 339
    butter 12, 28, 338-9
    chocolate, peanut brittle 338
    ginger, with lemon sauce 336
    grilled coconut 340
    spiced pecan 341
    time saving tips 341
    upside-down, apple-raisin 337
Calamari
    curried Thai-style 127
    grilled 126
    stir-fried with vegetables 126
Canapés, roast beef 43
Cape salmon, teriyaki 107
Cape seafood stew 115
Caper sauce, with sole 110
Cappuccino ice cream 366
Caramel bananas 353
Caramel ginger pudding 376
Caramel pecan nut squares 347
Carrot
    and beetroot salad 300
    soup, spicy cream of 78
Casserole
    saffron seafood 124
    Tex-Mex chilli 186, *187*
    tuna noodle 220
    vegetable, with couscous 240, 241
Cauliflower yoghurt soup 76-7
Caviar corn fritters 36, *37*
Cereal, fruity three-grain 234

Cereal-popcorn, herbed bites 54, *55*
Cheddar cheese
    fritters 41
    individual soufflés 265
    quesadillas 39
    soup 84
Cheese
    and broccoli filling for omelette 263
    and eggs 246-70
    and ham pizza 62
    and ham roulade 260, *261*
    and ham sandwich 67
    and ham soup 81
    and herb topping for baked potatoes 285
    and red pepper quiches, bite-sized 36
    and sausage, baked 270
    and spinach crêpes 328
    and vegetables on toast 289
    and walnuts with rotelle 219
    dip, easy 266
    fondue 268, *269*
    fritters 41
    goat's
        and walnut filling for omelette 263
        herbed tart 266
    grated, recipe shortcuts 10
    macaroni vegetable salad 306
    melts, Mexican 260
    pie, spinach 267
    quesadillas 39
    sauce 157
        and polenta 242
        for pasta 222
    savoury bread pudding 264
    smoked, and ham salad 318
    soufflé omelette
        with ham 251
        with vegetables 251
    soup 84
Cheese-stuffed
    butternut squash 268
    chicken rolls 165
Cheese-topped barley with mushrooms 244
Cheesecake cups 373
Cheesy-baked shells 216
Cherry cream pudding 376
Chicken 130-68
    and chutney croissants 142
    and rice casserole 158
    apricot-ginger 168
    baked herbed lemon 154
    braised Italian-style 152
    braised with vegetables 148

Chicken *continued:*
  breasts
    grilled 156
    savoury pan-fried 136
    with gremolata 160
    with guacamole 160
    with pepper sauce 144, *145*
  Buffalo wings 130, *131*
  burgers, spiced 161
  cacciatore with pasta 226
  club sandwich 64
  coleslaw 144
  creamy, with grapes 151
  curried 143
  dilled meatballs 42, *43*
  drumsticks, devilled 140
  grilled, lemon 140
  grilled, tangy 132
  Hawaiian 150
  honey-glazed, with oranges 136, *137*
  in red wine 154
  kebabs, and baby marrow 153
  marsala, herbed 165
  Milano, pan-fried 164
  mustard 146
  nuggets grilled 42
  orange-glazed *129*, 134
  Oriental 149
  oven-baked, crusty 135
  paprika 139
  parsley mustard 132
  pasta with pesto 224
  piccata 162
  Provençale 138
  quick-cooked 134
  roast 142-3
    basics 25
  rolls, barbecued 142
  rolls, cheese-stuffed 165
  rolls, crumbed Mexican-style 147
  salad, Chinese 144
  salad, layered 317
  salad, Oriental 296
  salad, pitas 60
  salad, with feta 143
  salad, with spinach 142
  satay with peanut sauce 152
  sausage, with chilli, onion and tomato 162
  schnitzels with mushrooms 158, *159*
  sherried-mushroom 168
  smoked, sandwiches 59
  soup 81
    Chinese 96
    vegetable 90
  spiced 139
  stir-fried with almonds 155
  stock 24
  tacos 133
  tarragon 150
  teriyaki, with broccoli 149
  tostadas 143
  with apple rings 141
  with mushrooms 146
  with sesame and asparagus 163
  with spicy sesame noodles 225
Chicken-filled crêpes 328
Chickens, baby
  baked, and rice pilaff 167
  braised with vegetables 166
  grilled 166
Chickpea, salad, marinated 300
Chilli
  beef, pizza 63
  beef, with beans 185
  beef, with rice 185
  casserole, Tex-Mex 186, *187*
  corn bread 322, *323*
  corn on the cob 282
  corn soup 87
  spaghetti 232
  tarragon prawns 122
  topping for baked potatoes 285
  vegetarian 290
Chinese chicken salad 144
Chinese chicken soup 96
Chinese egg fritters 252
Chips
  Parmesan pita 44, *45*
  tortilla 38
Chocolate
  almond cream tart 388
  and coffee sauce 334
  and coffee tart 385
  cake, peanut brittle 338
  chips, melting tip 347
  fondue, with fruit and cake 339
  ice cream pie 360, *361*
  melting in microwave oven 21
  melting tip 346
  mousse, rum 370, *371*
  parfaits *349*, 367
  pudding tart 384
  soufflés, bittersweet *374-5*
Chocolate-dipped strawberries 350-*1*
Chocolate-nut biscuits 348
Chopped spinach soup 80
Chowder
  bacon and corn 85
  salmon 86
Chunky salsa 48
Cider vinegar salad dressing 320
Cinnamon
  and apple soufflé omelette 251
  and sugar biscuits 342, *343*
  poached pears 359
Citrus juice, microwave tip 21
Citrus slaw, and ham 199
Clam(s)
  cook's tip 219
  sauce, for pasta 223
  sauce, with linguine 219
Club sandwich, chicken 64
Cocoa, and cream cheese-filled cookies 336
Coconut
  and almond macaroons 345
  cake, grilled 340
  cream tart 385
  snowballs 364
  tart, easy 381
Coffee-chocolate tart 385
Coleslaw, chicken 144
Coleslaw, citrus, and ham 199
Coleslaw, red and green 296
Compote, melon 355
Consommé, vegetable 79
Cookies
  cocoa, and cream cheese 336
Corn
  and bacon chowder 85
  and bean salad 302
  bread, chilli 322, *323*
  chilli soup 87
  fritters, caviar 36, *37*
  kernels, spiced 282
  on the cob, chilli 282
  soufflé-stuffed peppers 246-7
  see also Mealies
Corned beef hash with eggs 253
Cornflour, recipe shortcuts 11
Cottage cheese and pineapple salad 313
Courgettes *see* Baby marrow(s)
Couscous
  and shrimp salad 315
  in vegetable casserole *240*-1
Crab and mushroom bisque 78
Cranberry sauce, spiced 157
Cream, ready whipped 11
Cream cheese
  and smoked salmon with eggs 255
  cherry cream pudding 376
  for dips 47
  in cocoa cookies 336
  nectarine cheese tart 378-*9*
  toast, sweet 326
  topping for baked potatoes 285
  yoghurt dip 44

Creamed eggs and leeks 257
Creamy
   banana tartlets 388
   chicken and grapes 151
   clam sauce for pasta 223
   cucumber salad 300
   mustard dressing 303
   pasta salad 307
   peanut soup 82, *83*
   pesto chicken pasta 224
   potatoes and ham 199
   strawberry tart 384
Creole green beans 274
Crispy potato skins 56
Croissants
   chicken-chutney 142
   salmon-filled 60, *61*
Croque Monsieur 67
Crêpes 27, 328-9
Crêpes Suzette 329
Crumb crust 28
   fillings 384-5
Crumbed Mexican-style chicken rolls 147
Crumble, peach berry 389
Crunchy granola 234, *235*
Crust, crumb 28
   fillings 384-5
Crustless ham and tomato quiche 258
Crusty hot dogs 70
Crusty oven-baked chicken 135
Cucumber salad, creamy 300
Cucumber tea sandwiches 58
Cucumber-dill sauce 109
Cucumber-yoghurt sauce for tuna cakes 101
Cumberland sauce with pork 197
Currant scones 331
Curried
   beef steak with honey 179
   chicken 143
   prawns 125
   rice 242
   yoghurt salad dressing 305
Curry sauce 157
Custard, broccoli, and sausage 254
Custards and soufflés 370-7

D

Date muffins 332
Delicatessen-beef sandwich 170
Desserts
   chocolate-coffee topping 334
   custards and soufflés 370-7

Devilled drumsticks 140
Devilled eggs 38
Dill
   and lemon salad dressing 314
   frittata and smoked salmon 259
Dilled meatballs 42, *43*
Dips
   artichoke 48
   blue cheese 47
   cheese 266
   herbed yoghurt 44, *45*
   hot Mexican 49
   hot shrimp 50
   hot smoked snoek 49
   spicy vegetable 48
   spinach 49
   yoghurt cream-cheese 44
Dressings, salad *see* Salad dressings
Dumplings and sweetcorn soup 75

E

Easy basics 12
Easy entertaining 30-4
Egg drop soup, pork 96
Eggplant *see* Brinjal
Egg(s)
   and cheese 246-70
   bacon and spinach salad 320
   baked Florentine *245*, 257
   baked Provençale 256
   Basque 250
   Benedict 252
   creamed, and leeks 257
   devilled 38
   egg white, time saving tips 246
   fritters, Chinese 252
   Mexican 254
   scrambled
      sandwich 65
      with mixed vegetables 248
      with corned beef hash 253
      with cream cheese and smoked salmon 255
Entertaining 30-4
Equipment, time-saving 16-19

F

Fajitas, beef 176, *177*
Farfalle, lasagne-style 233
Favourite fudge brownies 346
Festive Mexican rice 237
Feta cheese and chicken salad 143

Fettuccine
   spinach, with ham 227
   with salmon 218
Fillings for omelettes 263
Fish
   and potato pie 114
   au gratin 119
   baked, cheese-topped 119
   baked, variations 108-9
   baked whole, herbed 98, *99*
   blackened 102
   fish cakes 120
   grilled marinated 116
   kebabs with orange sauce 122
   marinating, cook's tip 116
   roasted 121
   soup, Oriental-style 80
   spiced 121
   stir-fried, with vegetables 114
   time saving tips 98
   tuna cakes with cucumber-yoghurt sauce 101
   see also Seafood *and specific types of fish.*
Florentine baked eggs *245*, 257
Foil-wrapped angelfish 104
Fondue
   cheese 268, *269*
   chocolate, with cake and fruit 339
Fonduta, food note 242
Frankfurters, crusty hot dogs 70
French onion soup 84
French toast, oven-baked 327
French-style peas 272
French-toasted sandwiches 67
Fresh fruit salad 353
Fresh mealies with peppers 276
Fresh strawberry tart 381
Fried tortellini 38
Frittata
   dill, and smoked salmon 259
   Italian-style 258
Fritters, caviar corn 36, *37*
Fritters, cheddar cheese 41
Fritters, egg, Chinese 252
Fritters, potato 278
Frozen desserts 360-9
Fruit
   and cake with chocolate fondue 339
   ripening tips 358
   salad, fresh 353
   salad, minty 308
   time saving tips 358
   tropical, on skewers 354
Fruity three-grain cereal 234
Fudge brownies 346

G

Gadgets, time-saving 16-19
Garam masala 121
Garlic
   and lemon salad dressing 305, 314
   cook's tip 53
   garlic butter with mussels 128
   recipe shortcuts 10
   toast 324
Ginger
   and vanilla whip 360
   cake with lemon sauce 336
   pudding, caramel 376
Gingered
   beef kebabs 174
   peaches with yoghurt 358
   sweet potatoes 280
Glaze for poultry 130
Glazed
   lamb shoulder chops 193
   pineapple 354
   pork spareribs 196
Goat's cheese
   and walnut filling for omelette 263
   herbed tart 266
Goulash soup 94
Grains 234-44
Granola, crunchy 234, *235*
Granola parfait 376
Granola, raisin muffins 333
Grape(s)
   and apple salad 308
   and kiwi fruit pastries 386
   frozen 358
   parfait supreme 352
   with creamy chicken 151
   with salmon 105
Grated carrot and beetroot salad 300
Green beans
   and stir-fried beef 180
   Creole 274
Green pea soup 75
Green peppers *see* Peppers
Green salad, variations 304-5
Green sauce 109
Gremolata with chicken breasts 160
Grilled
   baby chickens 166
   calamari 126
   chicken, breast 156
   chicken, lemon 140
   chicken, nuggets 42
   chicken, tangy 132

coconut cake 340
fish steaks, marinated 116
lamb chops with mint 190-*1*
sole with mustard 110
Groats, nutty pilaff 241
Guacamole 47
   with chicken breasts 160

H

Hake
   baked, over rice *112*, 113
   Mexican-style 113
Ham
   and bean soup 94
   and Brie sandwiches 199
   and cheese pizza 62
   and cheese roulade 260, *261*
   and cheese sandwich 67
   and cheese soufflé omelette 251
   and cheese soup 81
   and citrus slaw 199
   and creamy potatoes 199
   and fried rice 236
   and smoked cheese salad 318
   and spanspek salad 198
   and spinach-fettuccine Alfredo 227
   and tomato quiche, crustless 258
   and wild rice salad, 198
   penne 198
   prosciutto and pear sandwiches 65
   prosciutto with melon 51
   rolls 56
   smoked 12, 198-9
Ham-stuffed acorn squash 288
Hamburger
   basic 182
   Bavarian 183
   Italian 183
   make-ahead 176
   pita 183
   spiced chicken 161
   with wine sauce 184
Hash, smoored snoek 118
Hawaiian chicken 150
Hearty soup *see* Soup, main course
Herb and cheese topping 285
Herbed
   baked whole fish 98, *99*
   beef rib steaks 178
   chicken marsala 165
   goat's-cheese tart 266
   popcorn-cereal bites 54, *55*

scones, savoury 322, *323*
veal chops 189
yoghurt dip 44, *45*
Herbs, time saving tips 121
Honey-baked pears 358
Honey-glazed chicken with oranges 136, *137*
Honey-mint salad dressing 308
Honey-mustard sauce 157
Hors d'oeuvre *see* Appetizers
Horseradish, cream salad dressing 305
Hot apple parfait 367
Hot artichoke dip 48
Hot Mexican dip 49
Hot shrimp dip 50
Hot smoked snoek dip 49
Hot dogs, crusty 70
Hungarian cabbage soup 93

I

Iberian potato soup 95
Ice cream
   amaretti chocolate 364
   baked 338
   basics 12
   berry 362
   cappuccino 366
   lemon, with raspberry sauce 365
   papaya cream 377
   pie 360, *361*
   softening in microwave oven 21
   trifle 363
   vanilla, with ginger 360
   with butterscotch sauce 368
Individual cheddar soufflés 265
Individual meat loaves 186
Ingredients
   basic 13
   substitutions 14-15
Italian burger 183
Italian-style frittata 258

J

Jambalaya 238
Juice, microwave tip 21

K

Kabeljou, baked crumb-topped 116
Kebabs
   beef, gingered 174
   chicken and baby marrow 153

fish, with sauce 122
yellowtail 117
Kidney beans and sausage 208
Kiwi fruit and grape pastries 386

L

Lamb 190-3
   brochettes 192
   chops grilled with mint 190-1
   in pasta sauce 190
   in pita 193
   shoulder chops, glazed 193
   time saving tips 190
Lasagne-style bow-tie pasta 233
Layered chicken salad 317
Leek and potato soup 74
Leeks and creamed eggs 257
Leftovers, meat 190
Lemon
   and dill salad dressing 314
   and garlic salad dressing 305, 314
   butter, pan-fried trout 100
   ice cream with raspberry sauce 365
   sauce for ginger cake 336
   sorbet with pineapple 362
   tuiles 344
Lemon-glazed apricot cake 334-5
Lentils and bockwurst 209
Lentils and broccoli salad 312
Lentils and peas with rice 289
Lima bean soup 81
Lime tart 385
Linguine
   spicy sesame, with chicken 225
   with clam sauce 219
Liver, sautéed 188
Low-fat mashed potatoes 278
Lunchbox tips 69

M

Macaroni, vegetable cheese salad 306
Macaroons, almond-coconut 345
Make-ahead recipes 22-9
Marbled brownies 346
Marinade for chicken 130
Marinated
   chickpea salad 300
   fish, cook's tip 116
   grilled fish steaks 116
   vegetables *52*, *53*

Marrows, baby *see* Baby marrow(s)
Masala 121
Mealies
   with peppers 276
   see also Corn
Measuring sticky liquids 346
Meat *see specific meats.*
Meat loaves, individual 186
Meat sauce for pasta 222
Meatball soup 75
Meatballs, dilled 42, *43*
Mediterranean salad 310, *311*
Mediterranean vegetable soup 78
Melon compote 355
Melon with prosciutto 51
Menu planning 30-4
Mexican
   avocado filling for omelette 263
   cheese melts 260
   chicken rolls, crumbed 147
   dip 49
   eggs 254
   hake 113
   rice 237
   see also Tex-Mex
Microwave oven basics 20-1
Middle Eastern tomato soup 72-3
Minestrone, tortellini 93
Mini white Alaskas 369
Mint-honey salad dressing 308
Minty fruit salad 308
Mixed vegetable
   egg scramble 248
   stew 292
Mocha pudding 370
Mousse, pumpkin 375
Mousse, rum chocolate 370, *371*
Mousse, strawberry 372
Mozzarella
   and tomato salad 299
   ramekins 265
   tomato and pesto sandwiches 58
Muffins
   apple bran *321*, 331
   date 332
   melts, with tuna 66
   microwave heating tip 21
   raisin granola 333
   savoury baby marrow 332
Mushroom(s)
   and asparagus salad *298*-9
   and bacon pizza 63
   and cheese-topped barley 244
   and crab bisque 78
   and onion pie 291
   and tomato sauce 109

baby marrow sauce 223
chicken 146
cleaning 47
sauce 157
   with pork chops 200
   with trout 100
soup, easy 72
stuffed and baked *35*, 41
with chicken schnitzel 158-9
Mussels
   Cape seafood stew 115
   food note 128
   with garlic butter 128
   with tomatoes and rice *97*, 128
Mustard
   chicken 146
   dressing, creamy 303
   onion sauce 109
   sauce with honey 157
   with grilled sole 110
Mutton *see* Lamb

N

Nectarine cheese tart 378, *379*
Nonstick cooking spray 11
Noodle(s)
   and beef salad 318
   and seafood soup 90
   and Thai pork *228*, 229
   spicy sesame, with chicken 225
   tuna casserole 220
Nuts
   and chocolate biscuits 348
   chopped, recipe shortcuts 11
   spiced 54, *55*
   toasting in microwave oven 21
Nutty groats pilaff 241

O

Oat wedges, Scottish 342, *343*
Oat-raisin biscuits 348
Oats, quick cooking, recipe shortcuts 11
Olive-artichoke sauce, for pasta 224
Olive-marinara sauce, for pasta 223
Omelette
   apple and cinnamon soufflé 251
   basic 262
   cheese and vegetable soufflé 251
   ham and cheese soufflé 251
   potato, Spanish 248

Onion
    and mushroom pie 291
    and mustard sauce 109
    bread, Parmesan 326
    pizzas, pan-fried 324
    soup, French 84
Onion-sausage salad, warm 319
Open-faced sandwiches
    cucumber 58
    smoked chicken 59
Orange-glazed chicken *129*, 134
Orange-glazed parsnips 280
Orange(s)
    and broccoli salad 301
    and pumpkin soup *71*, 87
    and rhubarb sauce with pork 204
    rice 242
    sauce with fish kebabs 122
    with honey-glazed chicken 136, *137*
    with spinach salad 294, *295*
Oriental
    asparagus filling for omelette 263
    chicken 149
    chicken salad 296
    fish soup 80
    salad 296
Orzo with garden vegetables 214
Ostrich fillet steaks, peppered 210
Oven-baked French toast 327

P

Paella 239
Pan-fried
    barbecued pork 204
    chicken Milano 164
    corned beef hash with eggs 253
    onion pizzas 324
    savoury chicken breasts 136
    trout with lemon butter 100
Pancakes, basic mixture 29
Pancakes, blueberry 330
Papaya cream 377
Paprika chicken 139
Parfait, chocolate *349*, 367
Parfait, granola 376
Parfait, grape supreme 352
Parfait, hot apple 367
Parmesan onion bread 326
Parmesan pita chips 44, *45*
Parmesan spicy puffs 325
Parsley mustard chicken 132
Parsnips, orange-glazed 280

Pasta 211-33
    and turkey salad 320
    and vegetable soup 80
    angel-hair, with baby marrows 215
    basics 12
    bow-tie, lasagne-style 233
    cheesy-baked shells 216
    creamy pesto chicken 224
    handy tips 212
    salad, creamy 307
    sauces, meatless 224
    shells with shrimp sauce 221
    verde 216, *217*
    with chicken cacciatore 226
    see also specific types of pasta.
Pastry, ready-rolled 11
Pâté, smoked salmon 46
Pâté, snoek, on sandwiches 58
Patties, beef, Russian-style 185
Pea soup 75
Peach Melba crush 364
Peach(es)
    berry crumble 389
    brandied and spiced 357
    crêpes 329
    gingered, with yoghurt 358
    torte 339
Peanut
    and sesame salad dressing 318
    creamy soup 82, *83*
Peanut brittle chocolate cake 338
Pear, avocado *see* Avocado pear
Pear(s)
    and prosciutto sandwiches 65
    and spiced apricots 350
    and watercress salad 309
    honey-baked 358
    poached with cinamon 359
Peas
    and lentils with rice 289
    French-style 272
    frozen, time saving tips 277
Pecan
    and caramel squares 347
    angelfish fillets, fried 103
    cake, spiced 341
    tartlets 387
Penne
    primavera 212, *213*
    with shrimps and peppers 232
    with smoked ham 198
Pepper sauce with chicken breasts 144, *145*
Pepper steak 181
Peppered ostrich fillet steaks 210
Peppers
    and cheese, bite-sized quiches 36

    and shrimps with penne 232
    corn soufflé-stuffed 246-7
    stuffed 290
    with mealies 276
Persillade, food note 132
Pesto
    broccoli, sauce 223
    chicken pasta 224
    in pasta verde 216, *217*
    mozzarella and tomato sandwiches 58
Pie crust, crumb 28
    fillings 384-5
Pies and tarts 378-89
    mushroom and onion pie 291
    spinach cheese pie 267
Pilaff
    nutty groats 241
    rice 236
        with baked baby chickens 167
Pine-nut and basil sauce 224
Pineapple
    and cottage cheese salad 313
    glazed 354
    salsa with pork fillet 205
    tarts 378
    with lemon sorbet 362
Pita
    bacon and lettuce 65
    burger 183
    chicken salad 60
    for pizza triangles 40
    lamb-stuffed 193
    Parmesan chips 44, *45*
Pizza
    bacon and mushroom 63
    bases 12
        prebaked 26
    chilli beef 63
    ham and cheese 62
    onion, pan-fried 324
    pita triangles 40
    polenta 243
    sausage 62
    sesame spinach 62
    tuna and tomato 63
Polenta
    pizza 243
    with Fontina cheese sauce 242
Popcorn-cereal, herbed bites 54, *55*
Popovers 324
Pork 194-205
    à l'orange 194, *195*
    and egg drop soup 96
    chops
        with apples 196
        with mushroom sauce 200

cutlets and noodles *228*, 229
escalopes Dijon 203
fillet with pineapple salsa 205
pan-fried barbecued 204
sausage stew 206
sausages 194
sautéed with asparagus 202
spareribs, glazed 196
stir-fried 200, *201*
sweet and sour 202
with Cumberland sauce 197
with rhubarb-orange sauce 204
Potato/Potatoes
and fish pie 114
and leek soup 74
and sweet potato salad 307
baby, roasted 277
baked 284-5
time saving tips 286
bean salad 294
cakes, baked 279
creamy, and ham 199
crispy skins 56
fritters 278
mashed, low-fat 278
soup, Iberian 95
Spanish omelette 248
Potatoes, sweet *see* Sweet potatoes
Poultry
time saving tips 130
see also Chicken; Turkey
Prawns
Cape seafood stew 115
chilli tarragon 122
cook's tip 122
curried 125
in tomato-wine sauce 123
Prebaked pizza bases 26
Primavera filling for omelettes 263
Prosciutto, and melon 51
Prosciutto, and pear sandwiches 65
Prosciutto, food note 51
Puffs, spicy Parmesan 325
Pumpkin and orange soup *71*, 87
Pumpkin mousse 375

Q

Quesadillas, cheddar 39
Queso, food note 39
Quiche
bite-sized, cheese and red pepper 36
crustless, tomato and ham 258

R

Raisin
and apple upside-down cake 337
and oat biscuits 348
bread pudding 386
granola muffins 333
Ramekins, mozzarella 265
Rarebit, Welsh 270
Raspberry
sauce with lemon ice cream 365
trifles 338
vinegar salad dressing 309
Ratatouille *271*, 282
crêpes 328
Recipe shortcuts 10-11
Recipes, make-ahead 22-9
Red and green coleslaw 296
Red cabbage, sweet-and-sour 277
Red peppers *see* Peppers
Red-wine sauce and beef 175
Rhubarb-orange sauce with pork 204
Rib steaks, herbed 178
Ribs, barbecued 170, *171*
Rice
and baked hake *112*, 113
and chicken casserole 158
and tomatoes with mussels *97*, 128
curried 242
festive Mexican 237
fried with ham 236
orange 242
pilaff 236
with baked baby chickens 167
salad, warm 302
time saving tips 238
wild, and ham salad 198
Rigatoni with beans and vegetables 214
Ripening
fruit 358
tomatoes and avocado pears 277
Risotto, perfect 238
Risotto, vegetable 244
Roast beef canapés 43
Roast beef rolls 69
Roast chicken 142-3
basic 25
Roasted baby potatoes 277
Roasted boerewors and sweet potato 210
Roasted fish 121
Rolls, roast beef 69
Rolls, savoury mince 70

Rotelle with cheese and walnuts 219
Roulade, ham and cheese 260-1
Rum chocolate mousse 370-1
Russian-style beef patties 185

S

Saffron seafood casserole 124
Salad 294-309
antipasto 312
apple grape 308
artichoke and avocado pear 297
beef noodle 318
broccoli and lentil 312
broccoli-orange 301
chicken, Chinese 144
chicken, layered 317
chicken, Oriental 296
chicken, pitas 60
corn and bean 302
creamy cucumber 300
creamy pasta 307
grated carrot and beetroot 300
ham and smoked cheese 318
main-course 310-20
marinated chickpea 300
Mediterranean 310, *311*
minty fruit 308
mushroom asparagus *198*, 299
Oriental 296
pineapple-cottage cheese 313
potato 307
potato bean 294
sausage-onion, warm 319
seafood *293*, 314
shrimp couscous 315
smoked salmon trout and asparagus 314
spanspek and ham 198
spinach, bacon and egg 320
spinach with oranges 294-5
Tex-Mex *316*-17
time saving tips 308
tomato and mozzarella 299
turkey pasta 320
warm rice 302
warm tabbouleh 294
warm winter 303
wild rice and ham 198
Salad dressings 305
cider vinegar 320
creamy mustard 303
dill and lemon 314
lemon-garlic 314
peanut-sesame 318
recipe shortcuts 11

Salami and vegetable topping for baked potatoes 285
Salmon
  Cape, teriyaki 107
  chowder 86
  croissants, salmon-filled 60-1
  smoked, and dill frittata 259
  smoked, pâté 46
  smoked, with cream cheese and eggs 255
  sole, salmon-stuffed *106-7*
  Véronique 105
  with fettuccine 218
Salmon trout, smoked, and asparagus salad 314
Salsa 121
  chunky 48
  pineapple, with pork fillet 205
Sandwiches
  bacon and lettuce in pita 65
  chicken 64
  cucumber 58
  delicatessen-beef 170
  freezing 60
  French-toasted 67
  ham and Brie 199
  ham and cheese 67
  mozzarella, tomato and pesto 58
  pear and prosciutto 65
  scrambled-egg 65
  smoked chicken 59
  smoked sausage and sauerkraut 69
  snoek pâté 58
  stacked loaf 66
  time saving tips 60
Satay, chicken, with peanut sauce 152
Satay, food note 152
Sauce
  baby marrow-tomato 230
  blueberry, and strawberries 353
  butterscotch, with ice cream 368
  caper, with sole 110
  cheese 157
    and polenta 242
    for pasta 222
  chocolate-coffee dessert topping 334
  clam, for pasta 223
  clam, with linguine 219
  cucumber-dill 109
  cucumber-yoghurt, for tuna cakes 101
  Cumberland, with pork 197
  curry 157
  green 109
  honey mustard 157
  lemon, for ginger cake 336
  meat, for pasta 222
  mushroom 157
    and baby-marrow 223
    with pork chops 200
    with trout 100
  mushroom-tomato 109
  mustard onion 109
  olive-marinara, for pasta 223
  orange, with fish kebabs 122
  pasta, meatless 224
  peanut, with satay chicken 152
  pepper, with chicken breasts 144, *145*
  pine-nut and basil 224
  raspberry, with lemon ice cream 365
  red-wine, and beef 175
  rhubarb-orange 204
  shrimp, with pasta 221
  spiced cranberry 157
  spicy tomato 109
  tomato-wine, and prawns 123
  watercress, with steak 178
  wine, with hamburger steaks 184
Sauerkraut and smoked sausage sandwiches 69
Sausage 206-10
  and broccoli custard 254
  and cheese, baked 270
  and kidney beans 208
  and onion salad, warm 319
  and Tex-Mex rice 194
  bockwurst and lentils 209
  pizza 62
  pork 194
    stew 206
  smoked
    and sauerkraut sandwiches 69
    stew 206, *207*
    with creamy vegetables 209
  Tuscan style spaghetti 230
Sautéed brinjal sandwiches 57
Sautéed broccoli Italiano 274
Sautéed calf's liver 188
Savoury
  baby marrow muffins 332
  herbed scones 322, *323*
  mince rolls 70
  pan-fried chicken breasts 136
Schnitzels, chicken, with mushrooms 158, *159*
Scones, basic mixture 27
Scones, currant 331
Scones, savoury herbed 322-3
Scottish oat wedges 342, *343*
Scrambled-egg sandwich 65
Seafood 98-128
  casserole, saffron 124
  noodle soup 90
  paprika 124
  salad *293*, 314
  stew 115
  see also Calamari; Fish; Mussels; Prawns
Sesame
  chicken and asparagus 163
  spinach pizza 62
Sesame-peanut salad dressing 318
Shelf magic
  bockwurst and lentils 209
  butter beans with tuna 310
  chicken and rice casserole 158
  chicken portions 168
  chicken salads 144
  chocolate-coffee sauce 334
  corn recipes 282
  delicatessen-beef sandwich 170
  easy cheese dip 266
  easy salads 294
  fried tortellini 38
  fruit desserts 350
  ginger-vanilla whip 360
  meatless pasta sauces 224
  Mexican cheese melts 260
  mocha pudding 370
  pan-fried onion pizzas 324
  pasta sauces 230
  pineapple tarts 378
  soups 78, 90
  Tex-Mex rice and sausage 194
  tortilla chips 38
  with rice 242
Shells with shrimp sauce 221
Sherried-mushroom chicken 168
Short ribs, barbecued 170, *171*
Shortcake, blueberry 382, *383*
Shortcake, strawberry 339
Shrimp
  and peppers, with penne 232
  couscous salad 315
  dip, hot 50
  sauce, with pasta 221
  soup, spicy 88
Sirloin, beef and artichokes 180
Smoked ham 12, 198-9
  see also Prosciutto
Smoked salmon *see* Salmon
Smoked salmon trout, and asparagus salad 314
Smoked sausage *see* Sausage

Snacks 54-70
   see also Appetizers; Dips
Snoek
   baked, with tomato and onion 118
   pâté, on sandwiches 58
   smoked, dip 49
   smoored, hash 118
Sole
   grilled, with mustard 110
   salmon-stuffed *106*, *107*
   spinach-wrapped 111
   with caper sauce 110
Sorbet, lemon, with pineapple 362
Soufflé omelettes 251
Soufflé-stuffed peppers, with corn 246-7
Soufflés
   bittersweet chocolate *374-5*
   cheddar, individual 265
   spinach 249
Soups, first course 72-81
   carrot, spicy cream of 78
   cauliflower yoghurt 76, *77*
   chicken 81
   chopped spinach 80
   fish, Oriental-style 80
   green pea 75
   ham and cheese 81
   leek and potato 74
   Lima bean 81
   meatball 75
   Mediterranean vegetable 78
   Middle Eastern 72, *73*
   mushroom, easy 72
   sweetcorn dumpling 75
   vegetable and pasta 80
Soups, main course 82-96
   bean and ham 94
   cabbage, Hungarian 93
   Cheddar cheese 84
   chicken vegetable 90
   chilli corn 87
   Chinese 96
   creamy peanut 82, *83*
   French onion 84
   goulash 94
   pork egg drop 96
   potato, Iberian 95
   pumpkin and orange *71*, 87
   seafood noodle 90
   spicy shrimp 88
   time saving tips 82
   vegetable, hearty 88
   vegetable beef 91
Sour cream and horseradish salad dressing 305

Spaghetti
   bacon and vegetables 226
   chilli 232
   Tuscan style 230, *231*
Spaghettini alla puttanesca *211*, 220
Spanish potato omelette 248
Spanspek
   and ham salad 198
   see also Melon
Spareribs, pork, glazed 196
Spiced
   apricots and pears 350
   chicken 139
   chicken burgers 161
   corn kernels 282
   cranberry sauce 157
   fish 121
   nuts 54, *55*
   peaches, brandied 357
   pecan cake 341
Spices, time saving tips 121
Spicy
   beef sirloin and artichokes 180
   cream of carrot soup 78
   Parmesan puffs 325
   sesame noodles with chicken 225
   shrimp soup 88
   tomato sauce 109
   tomato-bacon sauce 230
   vegetable dip 48
Spinach
   and cheese crêpes 328
   bacon and egg salad 320
   cheese pie 267
   chicken salad 142
   dip 49
   fettuccine Alfredo with ham 227
   salad with oranges 294, *295*
   sesame, pizza 62
   soufflé 249
   soup 80
Spinach-filled tomatoes 281
Spinach-wrapped fillet of sole 111
Spray, nonstick cooking 11
Squash
   acorn, ham-stuffed 288
   butternut, cheese-stuffed 268
Stacked sandwich loaf 66
Steak
   batter-fried with gravy 174
   curried with honey 179
   pepper 181
   with watercress sauce 178
   see also Beef

Stew
   Cape seafood 115
   mixed vegetable 292
   pork sausage 206
   smoked sausage 206, *207*
Stir-fried
   baby marrows and water chestnuts 275
   beef and green beans 180
   broccoli-ginger beef 173
   calamari and vegetables 126
   chicken with almonds 155
   fish and vegetables 114
   pork 200, *201*
   vegetables with tofu 286-7
Stock 80, 81
   beef 12, 23
   chicken 12, 24
   vegetable 22
Strawberry/Strawberries
   chocolate-dipped 350, *351*
   in blueberry sauce 353
   mousse 372
   shortcake 339
   tart, creamy 384
   tart, fresh 381
Stroganoff, beef 172
Stuffed
   baby marrows 283
   baked apples *356*, 357
   mushrooms, baked *35*, 41
Sweet and sour
   pork 202
   red cabbage 277
Sweet cream-cheese toast 326
Sweet potatoes
   and baby potato salad 307
   and roasted boerewors 210
   gingered 280
Sweetcorn
   and dumpling soup 75
   see also Corn; Mealies
Syrup, heating in microwave oven 21

T

Tabbouleh, warm salad 294
Tacos, chicken 133
Tangy cocktail dressing 305
Tangy grilled chicken 132
Tarragon chicken 150
Tart, herbed goat's cheese 266
Tarts and pies 378-89
Teriyaki
   Cape salmon 107
   chicken with broccoli 149

Tex-Mex
  beef fajitas 176, *177*
  chilli casserole 186, *187*
  rice and sausage 194
  salad *316*, 317
  see also Mexican
Thai curried calamari 127
Thai pork and noodles *228-9*
Three-cheese savoury bread pudding 264
Three-grain fruity cereal 234
Time-saving equipment 16-19
Toast, French, oven-baked 327
Toast, garlic 324
Toast, sweet cream-cheese 326
Toast, vegetable gratin 289
Tofu with stir-fried vegetables 286, *287*
Tomato/Tomatoes
  and baby marrow sauce 230
  and bacon sauce, spicy 230
  and basil, salad dressing 305
  and ham, crustless quiche 258
  and mozzarella salad 299
  and rice with mussels *97*, 128
  and tuna pizza 63
  and wine sauce, with prawns 123
  mozzarella and pesto sandwiches 58
  recipe shortcuts 10
  ripening tips 277
  sauce, spicy 109
  soup, Middle Eastern *72*, 73
  spinach-filled 281
Toppings, for baked potatoes 285
Torte, peach 339
Tortellini, fried 38
Tortellini minestrone 93
Tortilla chips 38
Tortoni 369
Tostadas, bean 68
Tostadas, chicken 143
Trifle, ice cream 363
Trifles, raspberry 338
Tropical fruit skewers 354
Trout
  pan-fried, with lemon butter 100
  with mushroom sauce 100
Tuiles, lemon 344
Tuna
  and tomato pizza 63
  baked with broccoli 102
  cakes with cucumber-yoghurt sauce 101

muffin melts 66
noodle casserole 220
  with butter beans 310
Turkey
  braised with waterblommetjies 168
  pasta salad 320
Tutti-frutti sundae 365
Two-potato salad 307

U

Upside-down cake, apple-raisin 337

V

Vanilla ice cream with ginger 360
Veal chops, herbed 189
Veal Parmigiana 188
Vegetable(s)
  and bacon, with spaghetti 226
  and beans, with rigatoni 214
  and cheese soufflé omelette 251
  and chicken soup 90
  and pasta soup 80
  and salami, topping for baked potatoes 285
  antipasto 50
  as accompaniments 271-85
  as main course 286-92
  beef soup 91
  casserole with couscous *240*-1
  cheese and macaroni salad 306
  consommé 79
  creamy, with smoked sausage 209
  frozen, microwave tip 21
  gratin on toast 289
  marinated *52*, 53
  mixed, egg scramble 248
  mixed, stew 292
  risotto 244
  soup, hearty 88
  soup, Mediterranean 78
  spicy dip 48
  stir-fried, with tofu 286, *287*
  stir-fried with calamari 126
  stir-fried with fish 114
  stock 22
  time saving tips 277
  with braised baby chickens 166
  with braised chicken 148
  with orzo 214

Vegetarian chilli 290
Vegetarian stuffed peppers 290
Vichyssoise 74
Vinaigrette 212

W

Waffle à la mode 365
Waffles, basic mixture 29
Walnuts
  and cheese with rotelle 219
  and goat's cheese filling for omelette 263
  chopping 346
  diet note 219
  in groats pilaff 241
Warm rice salad 302
Warm sausage-onion salad 319
Warm tabbouleh salad 294
Warm winter salad 303
Water chestnuts
  broccoli-ginger beef 173
  stir-fried with baby marrows 275
Waterblommetjies, with braised turkey 168
Watercress pear salad 309
Watercress sauce with steak 178
Welsh rarebit 270
West Coast mussels with garlic butter 128
Wild rice and ham salad 198
Wine sauce with hamburger steaks 184
Winter melon *see* Melon
Winter salad, warm 303

Y

Yellowtail, kebabs 117
Yoghurt
  and cauliflower soup *76*, 77
  and cucumber sauce 101
  and gingered peaches 358
  cream-cheese dip 44
  curried salad dressing 305
  frozen, basics 12
  herbed, dip 44, *45*

Z

Zabaglione 372
Ziti al forno 229